Autobiographies of Transformation

In this ground-breaking work Janusz L. Mucha and Mike F. Keen have compiled a complete history of sociology in Central and Eastern Europe in the post-Communist era. Through the autobiographies of ten sociological witnesses from the region, they turn the sociological imagination upon itself. The result is a compelling and revealing account of the struggles, triumphs, and continuing challenges of the sociology and sociologists of Central and Eastern Europe.

The great transformation of Central and Eastern Europe (CEE) has had a significant influence upon its sociology. It has led to the emergence of new liberal and democratic foundations upon which sociology can develop and has opened up completely new areas of research for the discipline. Drawing upon the biographical tradition in sociology and the social sciences, and taking into account related contemporary developments in philosophy, literary studies, and area studies, the authors explore the transformations taking place in Central and Eastern Europe. Based on this body of work they have developed the concept of "sociological witness" with which to frame their own contributions.

The sociologists included fall into three cohorts:

- late career—accounts which provide a glimpse of the post-World War II role of the Communist parties in sociology and academia, as well as how members of that generation came to be sociologists.
- mid-career—accounts which present the experiences of sociologists who participated in a later, post-Stalinist epoch when the discipline was in the early phases of reinstitutionalization.
- early career—accounts by sociologists who came to the discipline after the collapse of the Soviet Union, the independence of the CEE countries, and the disappearance of historical materialism and scientific Communism. For these academics, sociology, though lacking adequate resources, was a fully established discipline with clearly developed and professionalized career paths, and extensive contacts with the West.

As participants, each of the sociologists included has witnessed the intersection of history and biography in Central and Eastern Europe. As sociologists, they have tried, and continue to try, to connect the two so that they and their fellow citizens may better understand their circumstances and the futures that may follow.

Mike F. Keen is Professor of Sociology and Director of the Master of Liberal Studies Program at Indiana University South Bend. His research interests cover the history of sociology, theory, and urban studies. He is author of *Stalking Sociologists: J. Edgar Hoover's FBI Surveillance of American Sociology* (Transaction Publishers, 2004). **Janusz L. Mucha** is Professor of Sociology and Chair of the Department of Sociology and Social Anthropology at the AGH University of Cracow, Poland. His research interests include the theory and history of sociology and social (cultural) anthropology, as well as minority studies.

Routledge/European Sociological Association studies in European societies

Series editors: Thomas P. Boje, Max Haller, Martin Kohli and Alison Woodward

1 **European Societies**
Fusion or fission?
Edited by Thomas P. Boje, Bart van Steebergen and Sylvia Walby

2 **The Myth of Generational Conflict**
The family and state in ageing societies
Edited by Sara Arber and Claudine Attias-Donfut

3 **The End of the Welfare State?**
Responses to state retrenchment
Edited by Peter Taylor-Gooby and Stefan Svallfors

4 **Will Europe Work?**
Integration, employment and the social order
Edited by Martin Kohli and Mojca Novak

5 **Inclusions and Exclusions in European Societies**
Edited by Martin Kohli and Alison Woodward

6 **Young Europeans, Work and Family**
Futures in transition
Edited by Julia Brannen, Suzan Lewis, Ann Nilsen and Janet Smithsen

7 **Autobiographies of Transformation**
Lives in Central and Eastern Europe
Edited by Mike F. Keen and Janusz L. Mucha

Autobiographies of Transformation

Lives in Central and Eastern Europe

Edited by Mike F. Keen and
Janusz L. Mucha

Routledge
Taylor & Francis Group
LONDON AND NEW YORK

First published 2006
by Routledge
2 Park Square, Milton Park, Abingdon, Oxfordshire OX14 4RN

Simultaneously published in the USA and Canada
by Routledge
711 Third Avenue, New York, NY 10017

Routledge is an imprint of the Taylor & Francis Group, an informa business
First issued in paperback 2014

Typeset in Goudy by Wearset Ltd, Boldon, Tyne and Wear

British Library Cataloguing in Publication Data
A catalogue record for this book is available from the British Library

Library of Congress Cataloging in Publication Data
A catalog record for this book has been requested

ISBN 978-0-415-37651-8 (hbk)

ISBN 978-0-415-75922-9 (pbk)

To Gabrielle and Maria

Contents

List of contributors ix
Preface xii

1 **Witnessing sociological lives in Central and Eastern Europe** 1
MIKE F. KEEN AND JANUSZ L. MUCHA

2 **My life as a (female) sociologist** 21
MACA JOGAN

3 **Hand in hand with sociology: my life in the social sciences** 47
WLADYSLAW KWASNIEWICZ

4 **From totality to pluralistic democracy: a sociologist and sociology in the course of social change in Slovakia** 70
LADISLAV MACHACEK

5 **Sociology in my life and times** 86
VALERY MANSUROV

6 **Touched by transformation: my life and sociology** 105
NATALIA POHORILA

7 **Challenges and disillusions: my 25-year career in sociology** 126
PETER ROBERT

8 **An accidental encounter with the world of sociology** 148
PETYA SLAVOVA

9 **Belonging to a dying species: my experiences as an East German sociologist** 161
VERA SPARSCHUH

10 **Living with discrepancies: sociological self-understanding with Communistic and ethno-nationalistic collectivisms** 174
KAREL TURZA

11 **Becoming a social researcher in transitional Estonia** 193
TRIIN VIHALEMM

12 **Autobiographies of transformation** 211
MIKE F. KEEN AND JANUSZ L. MUCHA

Bibliography 224
Index 236

Contributors

Maca Jogan is Professor Emeritus of Sociology at the Faculty of Social Sciences, University of Ljubljana (Slovenia). Her main research has been in the fields of sociological theory, history of Slovenian sociology, and gender studies. She is author of five books (in Slovenian), including *Sexism in the Everyday Life* (Ljubljana: Fakulteta za druzbene vede/Faculty of Social Sciences, 2001). Her most recent work in English is "The decomposition of sexism in the second part of the twentieth century in Slovenia," *L'Homme*, Spring 2005.

Wladyslaw Kwasniewicz was Professor Emeritus of Sociology at the Institute of Sociology, Jagiellonian University of Cracow, Poland. Retired in 1996, he continued to teach at Jagiellonian until his death in August 2004. His most recent publications are "Between a post-feudal and post-industrial model: Polish society in the 20th century," *Polish Sociological Review* 4 (2003): 387–397; and "Wspolczesne realia uniwersyteckiego ksztalcenia socjologow," in Krystyna Szafraniec and Wlodzimierz Winclawski (eds), *Socjologia w szkolach wyzszych w Polsce. Ksztalcenie socjologow I nauczanie socjologii po roku 1988* (Torun: UMK, 2003).

Mike F. Keen is Professor of Sociology and Director of the Master of Liberal Studies Program at Indiana University South Bend. He is author of *Stalking Sociologists: J. Edgar Hoover's FBI Surveillance of American Sociology* (New Brunswick, N.J.: Transaction Publishers, 2004). Professor Keen is a member of the History of Sociology section of the American Sociological Association and has served as its chairperson.

Ladislav Machacek, Professor of Social Pedagogy, is the chief research fellow at the Institute for Sociology at Slovak Academy of Sciences in Bratislava and director of the Centre for European and Regional Youth Studies at the University of St Cyril and Method in Trnava. He is the author and editor of many articles and volumes, including *Civil Participation and Youth* (1996), and *Sociological Aspects of Youth Civil Participation* (2000).

Valery Mansurov is deputy director of the Institute of Sociology of the Russian Academy of Science, and president of the Russian Society of Sociologists. His publications include *Intelligentsia and Power: The Future of the Moment*

Before (Gorizia: Institute of International Sociology of Gorizia, 1993), and *Changes in the USSR–Russia Social Structure: Social Factors and Designing Civil Society of Eastern Europe* (London: JAI Press, 1995).

Janusz L. Mucha is Professor of Sociology, The AGH University of Cracow, Poland, and Full Professor of Sociology at the Warsaw School of Social Psychology, Warsaw, Poland. Recent publications in English include *Mirrors and Windows: Essays in History of Sociology*, with Dirk Kaesler and Wlodzimierz Winclawski (Torun, Poland: Nicholas Copernicus University, 2001), and "New developments, old interpretations: Polish-Americans and Hispanics in an American town at the onset of the 21st century," in *Ethnologia Polona* 24 (2003): 75–97.

Natalia Pohorila is Director of "SOCIS," a company dedicated to social and political research. Her most recent publications include: "Natsional'na identichnist': chy varto ochikuvaty autentuchnosti?" [National Identity: Should It be Authentic?], in *Ukraina shukaje swoju identychnist*'d, edited by Tetiana Grebnieva (Kiev: All-Ukrainian Charity Foundation "Postup," 2004); and "Podzial regionalny na Ukrainie: problem kultury politycznej" [Cultural Split in Ukraine: Where Does the West End?], in *Transgranicznosc w perspektywie socjologicznej*, edited by Maria Zielinska (Zielona Gora: Lubuskie Towarzystwo Naukowe, 2003).

Peter Robert is Associate Professor in the Department of Sociology, Faculty of Social Sciences, ELTE University, Budapest, Hungary. He is also a senior researcher at the TARKI Social Research Centre. His recent publications involve two Hungarian country chapters in two comparative volumes: Richard Arum and Walter Muller, eds, *The Reemergence of Self-employment: A Comparative Study of Self-Employment Dynamics and Social Inequality* (Princeton, N.J.: Princeton University Press, 2004); and Richard Breen, ed., *Social Mobility in Europe* (Oxford: Oxford University Press, 2004).

Petya Slavova is a doctoral student at the Free University of Brussels, Belgium, and at Sofia University. Her professional interests are in the sociology of professions, sociology of architecture, and urban sociology. The topic of her doctoral thesis is "Metamorphosis of the Profession of the Architect." Her most recent articles are "La Chambre des architectes bulgares—un combat infini," in *Groupes d'intérêt en Europe Centrale et Orientale* (in press); and "Formes d'exercice du métier et segmentation du monde de la conception architecturale en Bulgarie," *Sociologie du travail* (in press).

Vera Sparschuh is Privatdozentin at the University of Kassel, and teaches at the Free University Berlin, Institute for East-European Studies. Her research interests include cultural studies, sociology of knowledge, and East-European Studies. Her most recent publication is *Generationenbeziehungen in der Wissenschaft. Karl Mannheims Konstellationen der Lagerung und die DDR-Soziologie* (Krämer Verlag Hamburg, Beiträge zur Osteuropaforschung, 2005).

Karel Turza teaches Sociology and Communications in Medicine at the School of Medicine, University of Belgrade. His most recent work includes "The main obstacles to modernity in Serbia in the 20th century—and afterwards," *Sociologija* 45, 2 (2003): 117–140; and "Da li su modernost i drustvo sinonimi?" [Are modernity and society synonyms?], *Treci program Radio Beograda*, 117–118 (2003): 163–192.

Triin Vihalemm is Associate Professor in the Department of Journalism and Communication at the University of Tartu. Her research interests include transformation and identity, intergroup communications, and consumer culture. Recent publications are "Identity dynamics of Russian-speakers of Estonia in the transition period," *Journal of Baltic Studies* 34, 1 (2003): 92–116; and "The formation of imagined borders in post-Soviet Estonia," *Journal of Borderland Studies* 30, 1 (2003): 18–39.

Preface

This book completes our trilogy on the recent history of sociology in Eastern and Central Europe. Our first book, *Eastern Europe in Transformation: The Impact on Sociology* (Westport, Conn.: Greenwood Press, 1994), chronicled the period roughly beginning with Khrushchev's thaw in 1956, and continuing until the fall of the Berlin Wall. When we completed that work we did not anticipate that we would have published a second volume less than a decade later, *Sociology in Central and Eastern Europe: Transformation at the Dawn of a New Millennium* (Westport, Conn.: Praeger, 2003). However, just as no one anticipated the tumultuous collapse of the Soviet Union, neither did anyone expect that the transition that followed would occur so quickly or completely in the decade that followed.

With this final work, we bring an end to our examination of the recent history of sociology in Central and Eastern Europe. In this endeavor we have been influenced by the contemporary autobiographical turn that has cut across many disciplines, including sociology. As a result, we feel this volume brings the recent history of sociology in Central Eastern Europe alive in personal terms and compelling fashion. In so doing, it also shows how macro processes not only grow out of individual lives but also shape them as well.

In both the United States and Western Europe there has been a resurging interest in "personal documents." It has also been recognized that autobiography can be used as a vehicle through which sociology can reflect upon itself. We believe that sociology in Central and Eastern Europe can reflect upon itself in a similar manner, and this represents our modest contribution to such an effort.

As with our previous work, this project was made possible by the support and assistance of several institutions. A Fulbright Scholar-in-Residence Grant from the Council for International Exchange of Scholars enabled Janusz to join Mike at Indiana University South Bend (IUSB) for the 2003–04 academic year. During that time we were not only able to complete our second volume but also completed the groundwork for the current one. An IUSB Faculty Research Grant supported Mike's work on the project.

During the 2003 meetings of the European Sociological Association (ESA) in Murcia, Spain, our second volume was the subject of a "Meet the Authors" session. We would like to thank panel members Margareta Bertillson and Marju

Lauristin for their perceptive comments on our work. During those meetings we were also able to present a paper outlining the rationale for this final volume at a workshop organized by ESA Research Network 3: Biographical Perspectives on European Societies. The feedback from the participants in our session on Transitions in Eastern Europe helped us to further refine our project.

Central and Eastern Europe was under Communist rule and dominated by Soviet Marxism between World War II and 1989. As we have documented in our previous work, this had a strong influence on sociology. Yet not all sociologists in the region who started their careers in the 1950s and 1960s were Marxists and members of the Communist Party (CP). However, because we wanted to demonstrate how the relations between academic sociology and Party rule operated, most of the late-career sociologists that have contributed to this volume were CP members.

One of the later-career contributors to this volume was Professor Wladyslaw Kwasniewicz. He was with us from the beginning of our investigation. He contributed to the first volume, and gave us his advice when we were working on the second one. Kwasniewicz knew everything about Polish post-World War II sociology and sociologists. He was one of the founders of the European Sociological Association. Kwasniewicz retired from his lifetime career at Jagiellonian University of Cracow in 1996, but, despite his many sicknesses, was very active and very busy in the years that followed. He finished his contribution to the present volume at the end of July 2004, just a few weeks before his last hospital visit. Sadly, he passed away on 16 August 2004.

In general, we believe that the new generation of Central and Eastern European sociologists who are beginning their careers now will be increasingly similar to their Western European and American counterparts. This does not mean that there will be no regional differences among European sociologists or between the continents. However, with the enlargement of the European Union, the many European exchange programs, and the increasing exchanges with the United States, young sociologists will have much more opportunity to learn from the experiences of others. We can already see this taking place in the accounts of our early career autobiographers.

1 Witnessing sociological lives in Central and Eastern Europe

Mike F. Keen and Janusz L. Mucha

In November of 1989, the image of workers with jackhammers perched atop the Berlin Wall, as if dancing to the beat of the rock music blaring amidst the celebrative crowds below, powerfully and poignantly broadcast to the world the independence of Central and Eastern Europe and the imminent collapse of the Soviet Union.[1] Foreshadowed by the rise of Solidarity and the revolt of the Gdansk shipyard workers in Poland almost a decade earlier, with the great transformation that followed, the climate for sociology in the region changed dramatically. Planned economies were quickly replaced by newly emerging markets, and through them increased articulation with world markets and world sociology, as well as the forces of globalization.[2]

The region was opened both politically and economically to foreign goods, services and investments, as well as to foreign ideas and institutions. In most of the newly emerging or once-again independent nations, new political parties were legalized, procedural democracy was introduced, and free national and local elections were held. Ethnic and other minorities and marginalized groups, i.e., gays and lesbians, became much more visible and active. Small enterprises mushroomed, commerce bloomed, and many new occupations, for example that of "entrepreneur," were born. At the same time, many sectors of the socialist economy collapsed, especially the large state-owned industrial enterprises.

The very structure of society changed as unemployment and poverty grew quickly, and decreases in many social services followed. At the same time new elites and concentrations of wealth also emerged, leading to whole new types of social stratification and marginalization. Western culture gained a foothold: books and magazines were translated, and music and television streamed into the region, as did email and the Internet. In other words, with the transformation, upon the ruins and in spite of the remnants of the old system, a new and free civil society and state apparatus emerged as the precondition of a free sociology, as well as its primary subject matter.

Though remarkable, particularly as presented through the vivid images of the mass media, the transformation, admittedly unanticipated by sociologists or historians on either side of the Wall, did not occur overnight. As is the case with all such transformations, it was the result of a whole series of less visible and often unrecognized changes, ferment and foment. Arguably, and in

Preface

This book completes our trilogy on the recent history of sociology in Eastern and Central Europe. Our first book, *Eastern Europe in Transformation: The Impact on Sociology* (Westport, Conn.: Greenwood Press, 1994), chronicled the period roughly beginning with Khrushchev's thaw in 1956, and continuing until the fall of the Berlin Wall. When we completed that work we did not anticipate that we would have published a second volume less than a decade later, *Sociology in Central and Eastern Europe: Transformation at the Dawn of a New Millennium* (Westport, Conn.: Praeger, 2003). However, just as no one anticipated the tumultuous collapse of the Soviet Union, neither did anyone expect that the transition that followed would occur so quickly or completely in the decade that followed.

With this final work, we bring an end to our examination of the recent history of sociology in Central and Eastern Europe. In this endeavor we have been influenced by the contemporary autobiographical turn that has cut across many disciplines, including sociology. As a result, we feel this volume brings the recent history of sociology in Central Eastern Europe alive in personal terms and compelling fashion. In so doing, it also shows how macro processes not only grow out of individual lives but also shape them as well.

In both the United States and Western Europe there has been a resurging interest in "personal documents." It has also been recognized that autobiography can be used as a vehicle through which sociology can reflect upon itself. We believe that sociology in Central and Eastern Europe can reflect upon itself in a similar manner, and this represents our modest contribution to such an effort.

As with our previous work, this project was made possible by the support and assistance of several institutions. A Fulbright Scholar-in-Residence Grant from the Council for International Exchange of Scholars enabled Janusz to join Mike at Indiana University South Bend (IUSB) for the 2003–04 academic year. During that time we were not only able to complete our second volume but also completed the groundwork for the current one. An IUSB Faculty Research Grant supported Mike's work on the project.

During the 2003 meetings of the European Sociological Association (ESA) in Murcia, Spain, our second volume was the subject of a "Meet the Authors" session. We would like to thank panel members Margareta Bertillson and Marju its Eastern bloc began to devolve into a series of newly independent countries, so too did our table of contents.

Following World War II, sociology was generally defined as a bourgeois pseudo-science throughout Central and Eastern Europe. However, the extent to which this occurred in each country varied. For all practical purposes, from 1948 to 1956, sociology as an autonomous discipline with an institutionalized structure of university positions, departments, research institutes, and a set of concomitant professional organizations and associations ceased to exist. During this period it was in conflict with, or was replaced and dominated by, officially sanctioned versions of a Marxist/Leninist historical materialism. Sociology departments were dismembered and degrees canceled, research institutes were closed and professional associations disbanded. In many countries new courses on scientific Communism appeared in sociology's place.

Sociologists in the region adopted several different strategies in response to the crackdown and purges by state and Party officials. Given the ideologically charged climate, they always found themselves challenged with the dilemma of resolving the contradictions between the desire for intellectual independence and academic legitimacy, on the one hand, and political survival on the other, especially when the results of their research contradicted official orthodoxies. One means by which the discipline continued to survive was through the "sociologization" of other disciplines as sociologists migrated to other faculties such as history, law, pedagogy, and journalism, or as these disciplines took up traditionally sociological questions and problems in sociology's absence.

With the beginning of the period of deStalinization in 1956, known as "Khrushchev's thaw," the climate for sociology also began to change and the discipline began to reemerge and rebuild, though unevenly and still firmly under the watchful eye and control of the Party and state. Throughout the 1970s and 1980s, sociology slowly regained ground in the institutional structures of the scientific and academic establishments. The political authorities recognized the potential of sociology and encouraged its continued development, but with certain topics (i.e. political structure, inequality, ethnicity and identity) off limits. With the loosening of the Marxist/Leninist monopoly, the discipline that reemerged was increasingly pluralistic, but it was also increasingly empirical and applied.

The final collapse of the Soviet Union in 1991, the replacement of the previously existing totalitarian state structures with their emerging democratic predecessors, and the dethroning of the Communist Party, led to an end to the imposition of an ideological orthodoxy and a single paradigm on the discipline. In its place, intellectual freedom blossomed, and a multi-paradigmatic sociology developed. This included the continuation of research into some subjects prevalent before the transition, youth, family, rural sociology, as well as the emergence of new or previously forbidden topics, such as stratification, political sociology, ethnic relations, gender, religion, and the environment. However, this transformation did not occur through a formal and deep decommunization involving the purge of former Communist personnel, but rather was for the most part the result of a positive reconstruction of the institutional and professional foundations of the discipline, building on a process that had already begun in some nations as early as the late 1950s.

Perhaps the most dramatic development during the 1990s was the emergence of a new commercial and proprietary sector of the discipline, dedicated primarily to public opinion and to political polling and market research. Unlike in the West, where public opinion and market research roles exist but are located outside the bounds of sociological identity, in much of Central and Eastern Europe this became the dominant institutionalized sector of the discipline. In less than a decade, this non-academic professionalization has extended the institutional foundations of sociology beyond the boundaries of the university and academic spheres within which it had previously resided, and led to the emergence of new sociological roles and identities (i.e. the sociological entrepreneur).

International support from government programs, universities, foundations and development agencies, as well as corporate interests and multinational research firms, also exerted a significant influence on the discipline. Funding and investment from these sources contributed to the rebuilding of the institutional and technological foundations of the discipline, helped to make Western literature available, and contributed to advances in methodological expertise, including the introduction and legitimation of previously suspect qualitative methodologies. The new openness to the West allowed Central and Eastern European sociologists to begin to participate fully in world sociology, but not without some reservations concerning the impact of sociological globalization.

The biggest challenge for Central and European sociology during the 1990s was the chronic and widespread shortage of adequate support for teaching and research. The transformation not only brought about economic liberalization and the emergence of new markets but also economic crises as well. This scarcity of resources resulted in inadequate support for students, low salaries for faculty members, and difficulties in building and maintaining the increasingly important technological infrastructure of teaching and research. No doubt this is one of the reasons the commercial and proprietary sector constituted the most dynamic sector of Central and Eastern European sociology during the decade. Another ramification is that many professors of sociology must maintain at least two full-time teaching jobs, sometimes in two different cities, just to survive. As a consequence, they hardly have time for creative teaching as well as for conducting research.

Nonetheless, in the face of all of the challenges and adversity, Central and Eastern European sociologists continued to investigate the most pressing problems facing their societies. They also continued to develop new courses and programs, and to introduce and excite a new generation of students about sociology. While many of the problems they struggled with in the 1990s were unique to the region, or one or another of its nations, many of the issues they have faced—for example, commercialization, declining support for the teaching of sociology and sociological research, continued suspicion or at least disregard by political and policy authorities, maintenance of national identities and disciplinary autonomy and independence in the face of globalization—are challenges that are increasingly faced by world sociology and all of its sociologists. The questions we wish to investigate in this volume is how have these challenges been perceived by Central and Eastern European sociologists themselves? How have they intersected their personal lives? We believe we can find some provocative answers to these questions in their autobiographies.

The intersection of sociology and biography

In sociology in the United States, the interest in biography and autobiography can be traced back to the early developments of the discipline during the 1920s and 1930s.[5] Pioneered by members of the Chicago School of Sociology, the use of "personal documents" was recognized early on as a means by which to reveal individuals as human agents and as participants in social life.[6] W.I. Thomas and Florian Znaniecki's classic, *The Polish Peasant in Europe and America* (1918–20), is often referred to as one of the earliest examples of the use of personal documents for sociological research.[7] However, the origins of the tradition can be traced back to Central and Eastern Europe itself, particularly to Poland where, prior to coming to the US, Znaniecki initiated the tradition of *pamietniki* (memoirs) research, based on collecting large numbers of autobiographies through public competitions.[8]

In the 1930s the Social Science Research Council sponsored a series of studies on the methodological issues associated with the use of personal documents. However, the predominant and, one might argue, somewhat defensive focus of these studies on questions of reliability, validity, truth, and objectivity reflects the scientistic and positivist turn the discipline was taking at the time. It also foreshadowed the growing hegemony of quantitative methods that would effectively eclipse humanistic and qualitative methodologies such as ethnography, autobiography, and biography for the next four decades.[9]

Following the eclipse of humanistic and qualitative methods in American sociology, there was relatively little concern with or use of biography and autobiography by its sociologists for almost half a century. However, a few notable exceptions began to reappear as early as the late 1960s and early 1970s. Irving Louis Horowitz's collection of autobiographies of 14 prominent sociologists (among them George C. Homans, William F. Whyte, Llewellyn Gross, Amitai Etzioni, Seymour M. Lipset, Robert A. Nisbet) turned out to be "as close to a methodological guidebook as anything currently extant in the social science literature."[10] Donald Fleming and Bernard Bailyn (1969) used autobiography to examine the impact the intellectual migration from Hitler's Europe had upon various scholarly disciplines in the United States.[11] The autobiographies they collected demonstrated the dramatic influence of macro-social change on individual human lives. Among other contributors were sociologists Paul F. Lazarsfeld and Theodor W. Adorno.

Only in the 1980s was there a more widespread reemergence of interest in the use of biography and autobiography in sociology and the social sciences.[12]

This was part of, or, perhaps more accurately, followed quickly on the heels of, a burgeoning concern with reflexivity or what has been variously conceptualized as the "subjective," "textual," or "linguistic" turn that had begun a bit earlier in the humanities (i.e., philosophy and literary criticism).[13] It was also no doubt further influenced and motivated by developments emerging out of the civil rights movement and the feminist movement and the theoretical and methodological development of the scholarly traditions that grew out of them.[14] We will return to these issues in due course. Let us pass to the autobiographies by social scientists themselves.

In 1986, Jeffrey C. Alexander published a review essay on the autobiography of George Caspar Homans. According to Alexander, "Autobiographies by scientists are rare. They are even more rarely written by social scientists. This is perhaps because fewer people are interested in the lives of social scientists. It is also because there are very few social scientists who write well enough to pull one off."[15] Even if Alexander is right in general, published autobiographies of sociologists do exist. In addition to that by Homans, we can mention among others those by Pitirim A. Sorokin, Robert M. MacIver, Norbert Elias, William Foote Whyte, and Paul Feyerabend.[16] There are published journals, diaries, and letters as well.[17] Some of these narratives by very famous and influential social scientists were well written and sold exceptionally well. All of them reveal not only some mysteries of the authors' lives, but also help us to understand better the research process, society and culture.[18] Some of these narratives, such as Bronislaw Malinowski's diary, have stimulated long discussions and influenced the further development of the social sciences.[19]

There have also been autobiographies and published autobiographical narrative interviews within the realm of social science in Central and Eastern Europe, before and after the transition. They are not very numerous, however. Vera Sparschuh published a biographical narrative on Robert Schulz, one of the founding fathers of East German sociology and its Marxist-Leninist orientation.[20] As a part of a larger project devoted to the history of Polish science in autobiographies, Jacek Leonski and Teresa Rzepa published autobiographies of Adam Sarapata and Kazimierz Zygulski, two Polish sociology professors of the older generation.[21] Born in 1921, Sarapata was a sociologist of professions, and Zygulski, born in 1919, a sociologist of culture and a minister in one of the Communist cabinets in the 1980s. In Estonia, a narrative interview was published with Ulo Vooglaid, a leader of the Sociological Laboratory at Tartu University, which was dismantled on political grounds in 1975.[22]

Within sociology itself, in the United States, one could argue that the revival of interest in the use of the autobiographic and biographic method was also prepared for by the critical and reflexive turn the discipline experienced in the late 1960s and early 1970s, evidenced by the large number of books and articles on the sociology of sociology that appeared at this time.[23] No doubt a reflection of the broader crises of legitimation and the critical spirit of the 1960s, sociologists increasingly began to turn the sociological imagination upon themselves and to recognize that, in the words of James McKee, "there is epistemological significance in the fact that sociology is itself involved in its own subject matter."[24] McKee further observes "that sociological consciousness has been deficient in failing to appreciate how much of what happens to sociology as it changes and develops is part and parcel of what is happening to the larger world into which we are inextricably interwoven."[25] Interestingly, to our knowledge, almost no work on the sociology of sociology has been published in Central and Eastern Europe since 1989.[26]

By the 1980s, the cacophony of calls for methodological pluralism had been heard, and interpretive, naturalistic, and humanistic methodologies were once again accepted within the social scientific community.[27] During the decade, the methodology received renewed attention under a variety of guises, including not only the life story approach but also the life history method, whole life social theory, and interpretive biography.[28] A central theme shared by all was the interplay between biography and history, social structure and human agency, uniquely available through the construction and interpretation of biographical accounts.

In order to examine the passing on of knowledge from generation to generation, Robert K. Merton and Matilda White Riley asked several sociologists to provide autobiographical accounts of their relationships with their mentors. Personal recollections were written by nine scholars, including Talcott Parsons, Robert Bierstedt, Robin M. Williams, Jr., and James Coleman.[29] Continuing in this vein, in a second volume, Riley observed: "It is a sociological truism that social structures and human lives are inextricably linked ... People's experiences and positions in these social structures influence their attitudes, behavior, physical and psychological functioning—indeed, all aspects of their lives. At the same time, social structures are shaped by people's changing lives."[30] In preparing his own contribution to this volume, Merton developed the notion of the "sociological autobiography" which "utilizes sociological perspectives, ideas, concepts, findings, and analytical procedures to construct and to interpret the narrative text that purports to tell one's own history within the context of the history of one's times."[31] In Merton's estimation, "the truly sociological autobiography combines the complementary advantages of both Insider and Outsider, while minimizing the disadvantages of each."[32] He further argued that its greatest epistemological significance is that as a constructed text it constitutes an exercise in the sociology of scientific knowledge that tells of interplay between active agent and social structure.

In 1990, Bennett M. Berger assembled the autobiographies of 20 American sociologists (among them Dennis Wrong, David Riesman, James Coleman, Andrew M. Greeley, Nathan Glazer, Gary T. Marx, Jessie Bernard, Pierre van den Berghe, Herbert J. Gans, and Reinhard Bendix) in order to capture the *habitus* of sociologists, "the experienced milieu whose more or less unreflectively internalized culture shapes the sensibility evident to a close reader in a piece of prose..."[33] By 1993, the interest in biography and autobiography in sociology had become so pervasive that a special issue of the official periodical of the British Sociological Association *Sociology* was assembled to examine it.[34] A few years later, Robert Zussman also examined the revival of autobiography in the social sciences, arguing that it be used as a vehicle through which to give attention to the social structures which occasion, trigger, and inform the stories we tell about ourselves.[35]

Autobiography as sociological witness

Obviously, previous sociological analysis and use of autobiography and biography must be taken into account for our own study of the autobiographies of social scientists in Central and Eastern Europe. However, there have been several other approaches or models in the reemergence of the interest in biography and autobiography that we cannot neglect as well. Literary criticism, for example, has tended to be primarily concerned with autobiography and biography as a genre, its subjective character, the problem of textuality and intertextuality, and its focus on the self.[36] Georges Gusdorf, along with James Olney, has garnered much of the credit for being at the forefront of the literary interest in biography and autobiography.[37] Gusdorf identifies autobiography as a late phenomenon of Western culture, born of the conscious singularity of each individual life, and finding spiritual roots in Christianity and the confession.[38] He suggests that "autobiography is a second reading of experience, and it is truer than the first because it adds to experience itself consciousness of it."[39] He also distinguishes autobiography from "objective biography" and argues that its significance should be looked for beyond the concerns of truth and falsity associated with the problems of verification. Of autobiography Gusdorf concludes: "Every man is the first *witness* [italics added] of himself; yet the *testimony* [italics added] that he thus produces constitutes no ultimate, conclusive authority—not only because objective scrutiny will always discover inaccuracies but much more because there is never an end to this dialogue of a life with itself in search of its own absolute."[40] Of the autobiographer he concludes: "He wrestles with his shadow, certain only of never laying hold of it."[41]

In our own analysis of the Central and Eastern European sociological autobiographies, we are going to take advantage of some concepts and ideas presented by Gusdorf. We fully agree that it is sometimes necessary to distinguish between autobiography on the one hand, which is, out of necessity, a subjective account of one's own life, and so-called "objective" biography on the other, a detached, as impartial as possible, scholarly analysis of the described "facts." Like Gusdorf as well, we believe that autobiography is a very important source of our understanding of the outside world. Also, we are going to use the concept of the "witness," whose testimony is very important but cannot be considered an ultimate, conclusive authority. For example, Alexander makes it quite clear how even the testimony of a very self-conscious scholar like George C. Homans, who claimed to prove continuities in his work, actually revealed profound discontinuities.[42] We will return to the issue of the "truth" of autobiography in due course.

Olney distinguishes autobiography from biography (not all scholars find this distinction crucial), and offers his own provenance and explanation for the emergence of critical interest in the latter. "I am convinced that it was something deeply embedded in the times and in the contemporary psyche, something more pervasive in the intellectual and spiritual atmosphere that caused and continues to cause a great number of investigators, thinkers, and critics to turn their attention to the subject of autobiography."[43] He also notes contemporary concerns, particularly among French critics such as Jacques Derrida, Michel Foucault, Roland Barthes, and Jacques Lacan, with the text and the act of writing.[44]

Olney also recognized the influence the development of new bodies of scholarship in Black Studies, Women's Studies and African Studies has contributed, due to what many argue to be a special quality of the genre, "autobiography—the story of a distinctive culture written in individual characters and from within—offers a privileged access to an experience . . . that no other variety of writing can offer."[45] Feminist scholars and sociologists Ann Goetting and Sarah Fenstermaker further suggest in their collection that the reemergence of biography was driven by the recognition that the "personal is political," the desire to "give voice to marginalized and oppressed populations," and the need to correct the "social production of obscurity."[46] The same issues are stressed by other authors. According to Prue Chamberlayne, Joanna Bornal and Tom Wengraf, biographic and autobiographic methods (for them the distinction is not significant) help us to recognize that "the personal account provides a means to reaching those sections of society, both in the present and the past, whose experience could not be directly tapped through documentary or formal survey sources."[47]

The autobiographies presented in our volume make it clear in what sense sociologists in Central and Eastern Europe can be considered a marginalized group within the profession, and how the "personal is political" in their particular cases. It is our intention to give them voice. Ann Goetting argues that biography offers a privileged access to this experience, and in so doing can fill in knowledge gaps by serving as a vehicle for the intersection of human interaction and social structure, and the interpretation and understanding of micro and macro levels of the social order. "From a single position in the universe at a single point in time, human 'truths' are revealed through lived experience in social structure, process, and interaction . . . Truly, biography provides privileged access to the ways of humanity."[48]

Barbara Laslett and Barrie Thorne share this sentiment, but are also cognizant of the limitations of biography or what they prefer to conceptualize as life history.[49] In particular they point to the uncertainty which plagues memory, the problem of the extent to which an author is willing to be revealing, and the problem of the presence of the self in the text. Nonetheless, they conclude, and we fundamentally agree, that "Life histories of intellectuals can provide insights into the social processes through which knowledge is created, transmitted, and changed. In so doing, life histories can demonstrate intersections of social structure and human agency in ways that are more empirically rich and theoretically nuanced than other techniques more commonly used by sociologists."[50] This observation seems to be obvious, but it is very important in the context of Central and Eastern European sociology. After the decline of the Soviet Union and the totalitarian kind of socialism, social sciences, at least in some countries of the region, have been built anew. New structures have been created, but in addition to that life histories underwent complete transformations, and new individuals emerged as significant actors.

We are not alone in turning to biography and autobiography to obtain greater understanding of the transformations in Central and Eastern Europe. For example, in the Czech Republic, Zdenek Konopasek has led a project similar to our own, which uses autobiographical accounts from sociologists to investigate the Czech social transition.[51]

While much use of autobiography has been based on its presumed privileged access to the self, we intend to use it for the access it offers to the dynamic interplay between self and social structure, biography and history.[52] Diane Bjorklund stresses the fact that as "part of our socialization, we learn *vocabularies of* self to think about and assess our experiences and behavior ... Such vocabularies of self are not strictly personal; we enter into an ongoing conversation. Shared understandings about selfhood include beliefs about the extent to which human beings are in control of their lives, the traits shared by all human beings, the role of emotions in human actions, the ability of human beings to explain their own actions, what kind of change (if any) is to be expected in one's self over a lifetime, and what qualities are admirable in human beings."[53] She adds: "Autobiographies are a bountiful source of information about vocabularies of the self, and they allow us to study changes in self-understandings over time.[54]

Bjorklund convinces us that autobiographers are trying to persuade their audiences that they are a particular kind of self, a self worthy of dignity.[55] Unlike most of the autobiographers about whom Bjorklund writes, our authors knew quite well what kind of audiences they should expect. This strengthens the significance of the fact that the authors interact with their audiences. As Bjorklund observes: "What particular merits autobiographers choose to display is dependent, in part, on the qualities valued in a particular society at that time."[56] We expect that these sociological autobiographies, as any autobiographies, would be a little different if written for a different audience, for instance for the non-sociological, or for a domestic as opposed to an international one.

Various traditions within symbolic interactionism also have influenced autobiographical studies. Norman Denzin, a classic exemplar of qualitative methodology in social sciences, defined the biographical approach "as the studied use and collection of life documents, or documents of life..., which describe turning point moments in individuals' lives. These documents will include autobiographies, biographies..., diaries, letters, obituaries, life histories, life stories, personal experience stories, oral histories, and personal histories."[57] According to Denzin, lives are shaped by key, turning-point moments which leave permanent marks on the subject. He is of the opinion that in Western thought, at least since Augustine, we find the idea that lives are turned around by significant events, which he calls *epiphanies*.

Epiphanies, says Denzin, "are interactional moments and experiences which leave marks on people's lives ... In them, personal character is manifested. They are often moments of crisis. They alter the fundamental meaning structures in a person's life. Their effects may be positive or negative."[58] Denzin distinguishes four forms of epiphany. The first is the *major event*, a major epiphany that touches every fabric of the person's life. The second is the *representative event*, a cumulative epiphany which signifies reactions to experiences which have been going on for a long period of time. The third is the *minor epiphany*, an illuminative epiphany that symbolically represents a major, problematic moment in a relationship or person's life. The fourth are those episodes whose meanings are given in the *reliving* of the experience.[59] The scholar stresses the fact that epiphanies occur within the larger historical, institutional and cultural contexts of a subject's life.[60]

Glen Elder conceptualizes biographical analysis in terms of age cohorts. This is important for us since we divided our "sample" into, roughly speaking, three cohorts: early career, mid-career and late career. Elder also stresses the drastic changes and discontinuities in the life course.[61] Among our biographers, these discontinuities occur not only in the case of the late career cohort, but also in the case of younger scholars, who had a chance, for the first time in post-World War II Central and Eastern Europe, to study abroad for extended periods. With history in fast forward, they returned sometimes to a situation radically different from what it had been just a few years earlier. This idea of discontinuities is very similar to Daniel Bertaux's concept of "broken lines" of life. According to Bertaux and Kohli, we should pay attention to the fact that "most life lines are broken, i.e. that they do not obey some inner logic but rather are determined from the outside by the historical movements of sociostructural relationships."[62]

In reference to the symbolic interactionist tradition and its potential contribution to the analysis of sociological autobiographies in Central and Eastern Europe, we must note the work of the dean of "turning points" research, Anselm Strauss, and to his collaborators, partners, followers and students.[63] The Straussian approach seems to be particularly influential in the analysis of biographies, autobiographies, and narrative interviews. Strauss was first and foremost interested in child development, in the process of chronic illness, in the dying trajectory, in the status passage. Contrary to these topics, we are interested in the way the macro-social transformations are reflected in the individual life courses. However, some of his ideas seem to be easily applicable to our theme. In particular, the events of 1989 and 1990 were "turning points" for most Central and Eastern Europeans, including social scientists.

When the economic, structural, political and cultural systems changed, everyone had to search for a new identity. According to Strauss, "Some transformations of identity and perspective are planned, or at least fostered, by institutional representatives; others happen despite, rather than because of, such regulated anticipation; and yet other transformations take place outside the orbits of the more visible social structure ... These critical incidents constitute turning points in the onward movement of personal careers."[64] What occurs at such turning points are surprise, shock, chagrin, anxiety, tension, bafflement, self-questioning, as well as the need to try out the new self.

Strauss also observes that a turning point, a significant change in our relationships with others, is often gradual, and can pass unnoticed. "Sometimes the path of development is foretold but is not believed, either because he who forecasts is distrusted or because his prophecy cannot be understood."[65] Identity transformation incidents may occur in rather subtle ways, for instance as a consequence of historic changes when one has played an unfamiliar but important social role and unexpectedly has handled it well. Another significant and ambivalent aspect of the same phenomenon occurs when one "surpasses the performance of another after whom he had patterned himself."[66] Strauss mentions also the transforming experience of betrayal—by one's personal hero or a person with whom one has closely identified, or, on the other hand, by "events in general."[67] These situations have occurred over and again throughout Central and Eastern Europe during the historic transformation since 1989.

Followers and students of Anselm Strauss have stressed some other ideas which seem to us to be adaptable and applicable to our work as well. For example, Kathy Charmaz is interested in the situations in which persons experience serious life-threatening or life-changing events but do not accept this information (for Charmaz, these typically involve issues of health and well-being).[68] As a result they enter a state of denial, or to use a Marxian concept, "false consciousness." Obviously, application of this line of analysis to the experiences of persons of the transformation in Central and Eastern Europe, and in particular sociologists, is potentially fraught with theoretical difficulty. That said, however, we would like to suggest in what sense it could be useful.

According to Charmaz and her interpretation of Strauss, persons who do not recognize life-threatening or life-changing events as a turning point, who do not recognize their long-term consequences, and who do not acknowledge them, act as if they could return to life as usual, life before the event. However, when this turns out not to be the case, they must reconstruct their identity. They do that by developing a fictional identity, i.e., an identity "based on future identity claims, past actions, and present beliefs about self, but not upon present pursuits."[69] Charmaz further observes that eventually such persons "discover that constructing a valued identity has become difficult or impossible. Until then, they may believe and perpetuate a series of fictions about who they will become."[70]

Developing or actively constructing a fictional identity can serve several functions. It minimizes the need for radical shifts in self-concept. It provides a sense of continuity with the past. It provides insulation from intrusive questions and comments. In the case of events that change or threaten a person's health or life, Charmaz concludes, "Protecting self in these ways works best when illness remains invisible or can be camouflaged, for then social and experiential mirrors provide fewer reflections of an altered self."[71]

Strauss and his followers also have developed the concept of "trajectory," albeit primarily in relations to dying. However, Gerhard Riemann and Fritz Schütze have used a generalized theoretical concept of trajectory for the analysis of suffering and disorderly social processes.[72] In their formulation, the concept of trajectory can be applied to the analysis of life courses affected by larger historic processes. Riemann and Schütze stress the notion of "being driven" by social processes, of losing control over one's life circumstances. Following Strauss and Barney Glaser, they suggest a generalized concept of trajectory as a central category denoting "disorderly social processes and processes of suffering," a category that makes it possible to identify, reconstruct, and understand phenomena that had been missed and neglected in most research.[73] They have in mind social processes structured by conditional chains of events that one cannot avoid without high costs, constant breaks of expectations, and a growing and irritating sense of loss of control over one's life circumstances.[74] They also present ways of dealing with trajectory, or escaping from it.[75] Fritz Schütze analyzes not only micro-structural cases of trajectory but also trajectories closely connected with macro-social situations.[76]

Finally, as Michael Rustin recognizes, by grounding its work upon the individual as social agent, "The essential problem for a biographical sociology is both to keep hold of an essentially sociological frame of reference and to demonstrate that original knowledge of social structure and process can be derived from the study of individual life stories."[77] So, in addition to exploring the epistemological and methodological observations already present in the literature, we also wish to put forth our own response to the methodological and epistemological problems, as well as the substantive issues associated with the sociological use of autobiography, through the notion of "sociological witness."

Though not clearly articulated, we find suggestive hints of the notion of autobiographer as witness in the previous literature. We have already mentioned in this context Gusdorf's and Alexander's analyses. Robert Merton and Matilda Riley also make reference to the testimonial character of autobiography: "In composite, these testimonies begin to provide a sense of the complexities involved in the selective transmission of sociological traditions from generation to generation"[78] Bennett Berger further argues that the testimonial character of autobiographical witness can offset the "rhetoric of academic impersonality" that makes much academic work unreadable and inaccessible: "There seems to be something about the witness-like character of the first-person singular (I was there; this is what I did; here is what happened—to me and to others) that transforms indifferent, obscure, or ethereal writers into good, or at least intelligible ones."[79] Though not making explicit reference to the witness-like character of autobiography, Ann Goetting nonetheless grasps the epistemological significance of such a characterization: "The truths of autobiography do not spring from empirical research or the logic of mathematical deduction . . . We come to understand them only through interpretation, paying careful attention to the contexts that shape their creation and to the world-views that inform them."[80]

According to Norman Denzin, "Various standards of truth in autobiographies have been proposed. These include sincerity, subjective truth, historical truth, and fictional truth."[81] By invoking the notion of witness as an epistemological characterization of autobiography, we intend to withdraw it from the positivist framework and debate over the rules of method for determining the truth and validity of scientific evidence and rather to subject it to legitimation within a legalistic framework regarding the rules of evidence; that is, the ability of the witness to perceive, the ability of the witness to recall, and the ability and willingness of the witness to communicate understandably. In doing this we follow some legal scholars, like, for instance, Jon Waltz.[82]

The notion of witness gives the autobiographical account the epistemological status of testimony which makes no claims to any sort of objective truth or the myriad of "privileged" presences or accesses often associated with autobiography. Instead, notions of witness and testimony immediately and explicitly invoke and demand recognition that the accounts provided are testimonies constructed by a reporting self living and who has lived within a particular social historical context, is subject to a variety of concrete ascriptive influences (i.e., age, race, class, gender, ethnicity, etc.), and whose self and testimony is embedded within and the product of a network of social relations and interactions.[83] Once a witness has been shown to satisfy the rules of evidence, their testimony does not carry with it any claim privileged or otherwise to objectivity, but only a legitimated claim to be taken as an evidentiary account. As such, it must be critically evaluated, taking into account the social position from which the witness offers it as well as the actual experience upon which it is based. In our case the relationship of the witness to the Communist Party would seem to be an important factor. It must also be balanced against other testimonies and information, and ultimately interpreted and judged as such.

In adding the qualifier "sociological" witness, we simply mean to indicate, as does Merton with his concept of "sociological" autobiography, that this particular set of autobiographers are in fact *expert* witnesses, professionally trained exemplars of the very sociological imagination to which they have been called upon to witness. Finally, by employing autobiography as a device for giving voice to sociologists from the region, we hope to respond to concerns about the colonization of Central and Eastern sociology by Western sociologists. We have already mentioned the issue of marginalization and "giving voice" to the minority testimonies. This also informs our response to the need for an ethical approach within autobiographical research that takes into account the interests of the autobiographical subjects themselves.[84]

Sociological witness in Central and Eastern Europe

In order to carry out our project on autobiographies of transformation in Central and Eastern Europe, we invited ten sociologists from throughout Central and Eastern Europe to each write a brief autobiographical account of their life experiences as sociologists living through the period leading up to and following transformation. To identify a pool of potential autobiographers we contacted the presidents of the various national sociological associations throughout Central and Eastern Europe, as well as contributors to our previous work, for recommendations. In selecting our autobiographers we attempted to identify a small set of sociologists which represented a cross-section of the sociological experience within the region, taking into account such considerations as size of nation and the sociological community within it, length, strength, and influence of its sociological tradition, relationship to the former Soviet Union and the Communist Party, and nature of experience with the transformation (i.e., relative economic development, democratization, etc.). We also attempted to construct a group of contributors that reflected the generational and gendered differences and experiences of sociologists in the region; that is, early career, mid-career, and late career male and female sociologists.

In our sample, the early career is represented by three scholars, all female. They work in Bulgaria, Estonia and Ukraine. The latter two represent two post-Soviet countries, with completely different pre-Soviet cultural traditions and different stages of development of social sciences. All three scholars took full advantage of the post-1989 "revolution" in Central and Eastern Europe. They traveled and studied abroad, have been involved not only in academic sociology but also in market-oriented social sciences. They have fully experienced the problems that post-Communist Central and Eastern Europeans must face.

Our mid-career stage is represented by two men and one woman. The men are a younger Hungarian and a Serbian. The Hungarian is an example of the relative openness of his country, even during the Communist period. Our Serbian sociologist was very active professionally, but only recently did he become a university professor. Prior to that he served as an editor for several journals and a publishing house, and as president of the Yugoslav Sociological Association. Our mid-career female sociologist is a German, who lived and was educated in the eastern, Communist part of the country, and then, after unification, lived through the interesting and painful "re-education process." Like our other authors, she has experienced the advantages and disadvantages of the market system in academia.

The late career is represented by four people, Russian, Polish and Slovak males, and a Slovene female. During Communist times, Russia was an economic, political and ideological center of Eastern Europe but lost this position after 1989. Russian historical materialism was a standard social science in some Central and Eastern European countries. As opposed to this, Polish sociology was, even during the Communist period, a window of Central and Eastern European sociology to Western theories, general methodology, and empirical research standards. Our Slovakian sociologist lived through the "Czechoslovakian Spring" of freedom in 1968, as well as the post-1968 totalitarian reaction of the Communist regime. His scholarly career was delayed by politics. Slovenia had been a part (the most advanced in a technological and cultural sense) of Yugoslavia. The Yugoslav Federation was a Communist country, but with a "self-governing" system of management of economic enterprises as well as other areas of societal life, and with a freedom of travel which allowed for an influx of foreign literature. Our Slovenian sociologist had the additional and unique experience of being an early "feminist" voice within Central and European sociology.

Like Irving Louis Horowitz in his collective portrait of American sociology, and Robert K. Merton and Matilda White Riley who analyzed sociological traditions from generation to generation, we asked our contributors some broad questions.[85] We were interested in their experience with sociology, beginning with how they entered social science and sociology in college, and continuing to the present. What led them to become sociologists? What was their experience with Marxism/Leninism and their relation to the Communist Party? What were the major influences on their professional and intellectual career, individual as well as social, political, and economic? How did they participate in professional associations and or any political or social activities beyond the university or academy? This list was not meant to be exclusive.

In our collection, as in that of Bennett Berger, our autobiographers represent a fairly good distribution of age, as well as gender.[86] However, we did not try to take into account ethnicity, class, or schools of thought. We were also not as interested as Horowitz and Berger in the actual scholarly achievement or reputation of our authors, though we did not neglect this altogether. Like other editors of collections of sociological autobiographies, we are interested in the "culture of sociology," or, to put it in broader terms, the "culture of academia," as it existed and exists in Central and Eastern European countries.[87] Obviously, they are somewhat different than their Western counterparts.

Notes

1 Early parts of this chapter are adapted from Mike F. Keen and Janusz Mucha, "Sociology in Central and Eastern Europe in the 1990s: A Decade of Reconstruction," *European Societies* 6, 2 (2004): 123–147.

2 For additional and much more description and analysis of the transformation, see James Brown, *The Grooves of Change: Eastern Europe at the Turn of the Millennium* (Durham, N.C.: Duke University, 2001); Hall Gardner, Elinore Schaffer, and Oleg Kobzeff, *Central and Southeastern Europe in Transition: Perspectives on Success and Failure Since 1989* (Westport, Conn.: Praeger, 2000); Christian W. Haerpfer, *Democracy and Enlargement in Post-Communist Europe: The Democratisations of the General Public in Fifteen Central and Eastern European Countries, 1991–1998* (London: Routledge, 2002); and Roger D. Petersen, *Resistance and Rebellion: Lessons from Eastern Europe* (Cambridge: Cambridge University Press, 2001).

3 Mike F. Keen and Janusz L. Mucha, eds, *Eastern Europe in Transformation: The Impact on Sociology* (Westport, Conn.: Greenwood Press, 1994); *Sociology in Central and Eastern Europe: Transformations at the Dawn of a New Millennium* (Westport, Conn.: Praeger, 2003).

4 C. Wright Mills, *The Sociological Imagination* (London and New York: Oxford University Press, 1959), 6.

5 Ken Plummer, *Documents of Life: An Introduction to the Problems and Literature of a Humanistic Method* (London: Allen & Unwin, 1983), 10.

6 For a discussion of the Chicago School and its methodological history, see, among many others, Robert E.L. Faris, *Chicago Sociology 1920–1932* (Chicago, Ill.: Univer-

sity of Chicago, 1967); and Martin Bulmer, *The Chicago School of Sociology: Institutionalization, Diversity, and the Rise of Sociological Research* (Chicago, Ill.: University of Chicago, 1984). Plummer, *Documents of Life* provides a comprehensive discussion on the variety of forms personal documents, or what he refers to as life documents, can take. For an analysis of the history of sociological research methods in the US, see Jennifer Platt, *A History of Sociological Research Methods in America 1920–1960* (Cambridge: Cambridge University Press, 1998).

7 Bulmer, *The Chicago School*, xiv.

8 Daniel Bertaux, ed., *Biography and Society: The Life History Approach in the Social Sciences* (Beverly Hills, Calif.: Sage, 1981), 2–3. Unlike the case of the United States, the use of personal documents, and in particular the biographical method, remained strong in Poland and much of Europe. In Poland, Jan Szczepański, "The Use of Autobiographies in Historical Social Psychology" and Józef Chalasiński, "The Life Records of the Young Generation of Polish Peasants as a Manifestation of Contemporary Culture," in Bertaux, *Biography and Society*, 225–234 and 119–132, are recognized as two of its most significant scholars. Both of them were students of Florian Znaniecki.

9 Louis Gottshalk, Clyde Kluckhohn, and Robert Engell, *The Uses of Personal Documents in History, Anthropology, and Sociology* (New York: Social Sciences Research Council, 1945).

10 Irving Louis Horowitz, ed., *Sociological Images: A Collective Portrait* (Beverly Hills, Calif.: Sage, 1969), 9.

11 Donald Fleming and Bernard Bailyn, *The Intellectual Migration: Europe and America, 1930–60* (Cambridge, Mass.: Belknap Press, 1969).

12 Plummer, *Documents of Life*, 1; Barbara Laslett and Barrie Thorne, eds, *Feminist Sociology: Life Histories of a Movement* (New Brunswick, N.J.: Rutgers University, 1997), 2.

13 Sally Cole, "Anthropological Lives: The Reflexive Tradition in Social Science," pp. 113–129 in *Essays in Life Writing: From Genre to Critical Perspective*, ed. Marlene Kadar (Toronto: University of Toronto, 1992); Diane Bjorklund, *Interpreting the Self: Two Hundred Years of American Autobiography* (Chicago, Ill.: University of Chicago, 1998), 3–4; Liz Stanley, "On Auto/Biography in Sociology," *Sociology* 27, 1 (1993): 46; Prue Chamberlayne, Joanna Bornat, and Tom Wengraf, eds, *The Turn to Biographical Methods in Social Sciences: Comparative Issues and Examples* (London: Routledge, 2000), 6.

14 Robert Zussman, "Autobiographical Occasions," *Contemporary Sociology* 25, 2 (March 1996): 144; Chamberlayne, Bornat and Wengraf, *The Turn to Biographical Methods*, 5.

15 Jeffrey C. Alexander, "Science, Sense, and Sensibility," *Theory and Society* 15, 3 (1986): 442; George P. Homans, *Coming to My Senses: The Autobiography of a Sociologist* (New Brunswick, N.J.: Transactions, 1984).

16 Pitirim A. Sorokin, *A Long Journey: The Autobiography of Pitirim A. Sorokin* (New Haven, Conn.: College and University Press, 1963); Robert M. MacIver, *As a Tale That is Told: The Autobiography of R.M. MacIver* (Chicago, Ill.: University of Chicago, 1968); Norbert Elias, *Reflections on a Lifetime*, translated by Edmund Jephcott (Cambridge, Mass.: Polity Press, 1994); William Foote White, *Participant Observer: An Autobiography* (Ithaca, N.Y.: ILR Press, 1994); Paul Feyerabend, *Killing Time: The Autobiography of Paul Feyerabend* (Chicago, Ill.: University of Chicago, 1995). There are, also, interesting and influential biographies of sociologists. See, for example, Barbara Laslett, "Biography as Historical Sociology: The Case of William Fielding Ogburn," *Theory and Society* 20, 4 (1991): 511–538; Winifred Raushenbush, *Robert E. Park: Biography of a Sociologist* (Durham, N.C.: Duke University, 1979); and Marianne Weber, *Max Weber: A Biography*, translated by Harry Zohn (New Brunswick, N.J.: Transaction, 1988); Irving Louis Horowitz, *C. Wright Mills, An American Utopian* (New York and London: Free Press/Collier Macmillan, 1983);

Michael W. Young, *Malinowski; Odyssey of an Anthropologist* (New Haven, Conn. and London: Yale University Press, 2004).

17 Theodore Abel, *The Columbia Circle of Scholars: Selections from the Journal (1930–1957)*, ed. Elzbieta Halas (Frankfurt/Main: Peter Lang, 2001); Bronisław Malinowski, *A Diary in the Strict Sense of the Term* (London: Routledge & Kegan Paul, 1967); Bronislaw Malinowski and Elsie Masson, *The Story of a Marriage: The Letters of Bronislaw Malinowski and Elsie Masson*, ed. Helena Wayne (London: Routledge, 1995).

18 Judith Okely and Helen Callaway, eds, *Anthropology and Autobiography* (London: Routledge, 1992), xi.

19 Malinowski, *A Diary in the Strict Sense of the Term*.

20 Vera Sparschuh, "The Biographies of Biographers: Some Remarks on the History of the Social Sciences in the GDR," pp. 303–314 in *Biographies and the Division of Europe: Experience, Action, and Change on the 'Eastern Side,'* eds Roswitha Breckner, Devorah Kalekin-Fishman, and Ingrid Miethe (Opladen: Leske + Budrich Verlag, 2000). See also Robert Shultz, "Interview mit Robert Schultz: Das war eine andere Generation . . .," pp. 35–54 in *Soziologie und Sozialismus: Die Gründereneration der DDR-Soziologie*, eds Vera Sparschuh and Ute Koch (Opladen: Leske + Budrich Verlag, 2000).

21 Jacek Leoński and Teresa Rzepa, eds, *Historia nauki polskiej w autobiografiach, tom III: Historia socjologii polskiej I nauk prawnych, część I* (Szczecin: Ośrodek Badań Biograficznych, 1996).

22 Ulo Vooglaid, "Noukogude Eesti sotsioloogia algus ja loop: intervjuu Sirje Kiinile," *Looming* 1 (1995): 115–122.

23 Robert W. Friedrichs, *A Sociology of Sociology* (New York: Free Press, 1970); Alvin Ward Gouldner, *The Coming Crisis of Western Sociology* (New York: Basic Books, 1970); Paul Halmos, *The Sociology of Sociology* (Keele: University of Keele, 1970); and Larry T. Reynolds and Janice M. Reynolds, eds, *The Sociology of Sociology: Analysis and Criticism of the Thought, Research, and Ethical Folkways of Sociology and Its Practitioners* (New York: David McKay, 1970).

24 James McKee, "Some Observations of the Self-Consciousness of Sociologists," pp. 98–113 in *The Sociology of Sociology: Analysis and Criticism of the Thought, Research, and Ethical Folkways of Sociology and Its Practitioners*, eds Larry T. Reynolds and Janice M. Reynolds (New York: David McKay, 1970), 99.

25 Ibid., 105–106. We share Daniel Bertaux and Martin Kohli's ("The Life Story Approach," *Annual Review of Sociology* 10 (1984): 215–237), recognition that the biographical turn reflected in the interest in life stories is an interesting social phenomenon that bears analysis in itself. Michael Rustin, "Reflections on the Biographical Turn in Social Sciences," pp. 34–52 in *The Turn to Biographical Methods in Social Sciences: Comparative Issues and Examples*, eds Prue Chamberlayne, Joanna Bornat, and Tom Wengraf (London: Routledge, 2000), makes some very general, but also extremely fertile observations in this direction.

26 Vojin Milic has written two books that touch upon this topic. See *Sociologija saznanja* (Sarajevo: Veselin Maslesa, 1986); and *Sociologija nauke* (Nove Sad: Novom Sadu I LDI, 1995).

27 Bertaux and Kohli, "The Life Story Approach," 216.

28 Ingeborg K. Helling, "The Life History Method: A Survey and a Discussion with Norman K. Denzin," *Studies in Symbolic Interaction* 9 (1988): 211–243; Charles C. Lemert, "Whole Life Social Theory," *Theory and Society* 15, 3 (1986): 431–442; Norman K. Denzin, *Interpretive Biography* (Newbury Park, Calif.: Sage, 1989).

29 Robert K. Merton and Matilda White Riley, eds, *Sociological Traditions from Generation to Generation: Glimpses of the American Experience* (Norwood, N.J.: Ablex, 1980).

30 Matilda White Riley, *Sociological Lives* (Newbury Park, Calif.: Sage, 1988), 11.

31 Robert K. Merton, "Some Thoughts on the Concept of Sociological Biography,"

pp. 17–21 in *Sociological Lives*, ed. Matilda White Riley (Newbury Park, Calif.: Sage, 1988), 18.
32 Ibid., 19.
33 Bennett M. Berger, ed., *Authors of Their Own Lives: Intellectual Autobiographies by Twenty American Sociologists* (Berkeley, Calif.: University of California, 1990), xvi.
34 Liz Stanley and David Morgan, eds, "Special Issue: Biography and Autobiography in Sociology, *Sociology* 27, 1 (1993).
35 Zussman, "Autobiographical Occasions," 143–148.
36 James Olney, ed., *Autobiography: Essays Theoretical and Critical* (Princeton, N.J.: Princeton University, 1980), 22–23; and Marlene Kadar, ed., *Essays on Life Writing: From Genre to Critical Practice* (Toronto: University of Toronto, 1992), 12.
37 Georges Gusdorf, "Conditions and Limits of Autobiography," pp. 28–48 in *Autobiography: Essays Theoretical and Critical*, ed. James Olney (Princeton, N.J.: Princeton University, 1980). See also, James Olney, *Metaphors of Self: The Meaning of Autobiography* (Princeton, N.J.: Princeton University, 1972).
38 Gusdorf, "Conditions and Limits," 29–34.
39 Ibid., 38.
40 Ibid., 48.
41 Ibid.
42 Alexander, "Science, Sense, and Sensibility," 445.
43 Olney, *Autobiography*, 11.
44 Ibid., 22–23.
45 Ibid., 13.
46 Ann Goetting and Sarah Fenstermaker, eds, *Individual Voices, Collective Visions: Fifty Years of Women in Sociology* (Philadelphia, Pa.: Temple University, 1995). For additional consideration of the epistemological and methodological status of biography and autobiography rooted in the feminist perspective, see Mary Evans, "Reading Lives: How the Personal Might Be Social," *Sociology* 27, 1 (1993): 5–13; and Stanley, "On Auto/Biography in Sociology."
47 Chamberlayne, Bornat, and Wengraf, *The Turn to Biographical Methods*, 3.
48 Ann Goetting, "Introduction: Fictions of the Self," pp. 3–19 in *Individual Voices, Collective Visions: Fifty Years of Women in Sociology*, eds Ann Goetting and Sarah Fenstermaker (Philadelphia, Pa.: Temple University, 1995), 7.
49 Laslett and Thorne, *Feminist Sociology*.
50 Ibid., 6.
51 Zdenek Konapasek, ed., *Our Lives as Database. Doing a Sociology of Ourselves. Czech Social Transition in Autobiographical Research Dialogues*, translated by Andrew Hawker (Praha: Karolinum, 2000). See also Roswitha Breckner, Devorah Kalekin-Fishman, and Ingrid Miethe, eds, *Biographies and the Division of Europe: Experience, Action, and the Change on the 'Eastern Side'* (Opladen: Verlag Leske & Budrich, 2000); Michael Burawoy and Katherine Verdery, *Ethnographies of Change in the Postsocialist World* (New York: Rowman & Littlefield, 1999); and Daphne Berdahl, Matti Bunzl, and Martha Lampland, *Altering States: Ethnographies of Transition in Eastern Europe and the Former Soviet Union* (Ann Arbor: University of Michigan, 2000).
52 Berger, *Authors of Their Own Lives*; Bjorklund, *Interpreting the Self*.
53 Bjorklund, *Interpreting the Self*, 7.
54 Ibid., 8.
55 Ibid., 13.
56 Ibid., 21.
57 Denzin, *Interpretive Biography*, 7.
58 Ibid., 70.
59 Ibid., 71; See also Norman K. Denzin, *Interpretive Interactionism* (Newbury Park, Calif.: Sage, 1989), 17.
60 Denzin, *Interpretive Interactionism*, 17.

61 Glen Elder, "History and the Life Course," pp. 77–118 in *Biography and Society: The Life History Approach in the Social Sciences*, ed. Daniel Bertaux (Beverly Hills: Sage, 1981), 86–87.
62 Bertaux and Kohli, "The Life Story Approach," 226.
63 Anselm L. Strauss, *Mirrors and Masks: The Search for Identity* (Glencoe, Ill.: Free Press, 1959); and Hans-Georg Soeffner, "Trajectory as Intended Fragment," pp. 359–371 in *Social Organization and Social Process: Essays in Honor of Anselm Strauss*, ed. David R. Maines (New York: Aldine de Gruyter, 1991).
64 Strauss, *Mirrors and Masks*, 92–93.
65 Ibid., 94.
66 Ibid., 96–97.
67 Ibid., 97–99.
68 Kathy Charmaz, "Turning Points and Fictional Identities," pp. 71–86 in *Social Organization and Social Process: Essays in Honor of Anselm Strauss*, ed. David R. Maines (New York: Aldine de Gruyter, 1991).
69 Ibid., 71.
70 Ibid.
71 Ibid., 76.
72 Gerhard Riemann and Fritz Schütze, "Trajectory as a Basic Theoretical Concept for Analyzing Suffering and Disorderly Social Processes," pp. 333–357 in *Social Organization and Social Process: Essays in Honor of Anselm Strauss*, ed. David R. Maines (New York: Aldine de Gruyter, 1991).
73 Anselm L. Strauss and Barney Glaser, *Anguish: The Case Study of a Dying Trajectory* (Mill Valley, Calif.: Sociology Press, 1970).
74 Riemann and Schütze, "Trajectory," 337.
75 Ibid., 351.
76 Fritz Schütze, "Pressure and Guilt: War Experiences of a Young German Soldier and Their Biographical Implications, Parts 1 & 2," *International Sociology* 7, 2 and 7, 3 (1992): 187–208, 347–367.
77 Rustin, "Reflections on the Biographical Turn, 45–46.
78 Merton and Riley, *Sociological Traditions*, xiv.
79 Berger, *Authors of Their Own Lives*, xx.
80 Goetting, "Fictions of the Self," 14.
81 Denzin, *Interpretive Biography*, 23.
82 Jon R. Waltz, *Introduction to Criminal Evidence* (Chicago, Ill.: Nelson-Hall, 1983), 295–297; Jon R. Waltz and Roger C. Park, *Evidence: Cases and Materials* (New York: Foundation Press, 2004). For a comprehensive treatment of the basic rules, principles, and issues relating to evidence, see also, John W. Strong, ed., *McCormick on Evidence*, 5th edn (St Paul, Minn.: West Group, 1999); and Graham C. Lilly, *An Introduction to the Law of Evidence*, 2nd edn (St Paul, Minn.: West Group, 1987).
83 For a discussion of the significance and influence of ascribed characteristics on autobiography, see Riley *Sociological Lives* (1988).
84 See Barbara Harrison and E. Stina Lyon, "A Note on Ethical Issues in the Use of Autobiography in Sociological Research," *Sociology* 27, 1 (1993): 101–109.
85 Horowitz, *Sociological Images*, 10; Merton and Riley, *Sociological Traditions*, xi.
86 Berger, *Authors of Their Own Lives*.
87 Ibid., xiv.

2 My life as a (female) sociologist

Maca Jogan

On September 15, 2003, I read a discussion document prepared for the Science and Society Program Committee of the European Commission's Research Directorate in Brussels, *Orientations for the Work Programme 2004*.[1] I was very glad to see that in the introduction the Committee recognized that in order to make informed choices from the range of options thrown up by scientific progress in a knowledge-based society, policy-makers and citizens must be adequately equipped by "seeking both a better integration of science in society and society in science." This was recognized to require the following three aims, "to bring research closer to society;... to promote responsible research and application of science and technology;... to step up the science/society dialogue, and address also the role of women in science."

This is exactly what I as a sociologist have always argued. It is what has determined my scientific research, and other activities based upon it such as my teaching and writing. Finally, it has put me into a double critical position, on the one hand toward the theoretical heritage of sociology, and on the other toward actual social reality. Such an orientation, which has primarily been informed by Alvin Gouldner's notion of the life "for sociology" and not "of sociology," has been the constant attitude guiding my activity.[2] Both positions are interwoven, but the critical attitude toward sociology developed temporally later. For, to acquire it, adequate university study was needed.

I cannot say that during my childhood and youth I had the aim to study sociology, as is often the case with the established professions, e.g., medicine or law. I did not decide to study sociology until the end of my gymnasium schooling, which I finished in 1960 in Maribor, with a bachelor's degree. Maribor is the second biggest city in Slovenia, and in Slovenian history is remembered as the city where in April, 1941, Hitler demanded, "make this country German again." This announcement of the genocide of the Slovenian people was, tragically, also connected to my personal life.

In accordance with the Nazis' plan for the genocide of the Slovenian nation, during the first months of the occupation the German occupiers had exiled about 80,000 Slovenians. Among those unlucky people, banished from homes with hand luggage only, were my parents. From November 1941 until the end of war they were held in a series of forced labor camps in Germany, working as slaves under only slightly better conditions than those in the concentration camps. In one of these camps, Loessnitz, in February 1943, I was born.

After the war, my parents, with four children, returned to the fatherland, which had been freed through the partisan war of national liberation. They found their home robbed and the family property destroyed. My father, a skilled shoemaker, was the wage-earner of the family, and my mother was a housewife. The very difficult living conditions during the early post-war years contributed to conflict between my parents, and eventually to their divorce. My siblings and I (by then we were six in number) lived with our mother, drawing from her enormous "emotional capital," but with very limited financial support from our father.

"To know, to know as much as possible." This was the maxim my mother employed in caring for her six children. I already had accepted this maxim in preschool, and it has allowed me to overcome the various difficulties and hindrances that usually meet those who are not starting from a high family social status. A lack of money hindered my ability to travel abroad to improve my knowledge of foreign languages, even though in the second part of the 1950s, and later on in Yugoslavia and in Slovenia while it was a republic in the federal state of Yugoslavia, there were no political restrictions for travel abroad.

During my gymnasium schooling all subjects were of interest to me, although I found philosophy to be an extremely abstract discipline and too removed from reality. I was too interested in actual life. And, as it was not too long after the end of the World War II, the issue of the amelioration of life was particularly close to my consciousness—not only the issue of material conditions but also, and especially, issues of the spiritual and moral sphere.

If I had not had a fear of dead bodies prior to my decision to study at university, I would likely have chosen medicine. Since this fear caused me to dismiss medicine, I began to direct myself into the social sciences. The choice between law and history was very quickly resolved when, in the spring of 1960, we were informed that enrolment in a new study program at the University of Ljubljana, sociology, would be possible for the coming academic year (1960/61).

When I recognized the subjects and the aims of the discipline, I decided to study sociology, and in the autumn of 1960, I enrolled in the Department of Sociology at the Faculty of Arts in Ljubljana. In Slovenia, during the period of the socialist "self-managing system," enrolment in university study programs was free, and was never restricted due to the political or social (class) background of the student.[3] The only requirement was the "Matura," the general examination before leaving secondary school/gymnasium. The possibility of getting a scholarship also partially contributed to my decision to study sociology. This was very important for me, because I had to leave my home to study in Ljubljana. Due in part to my parents' divorce, but also to war damage, my family was not wealthy enough to support me.

I began to study sociology in the academic year 1960/61, and I completed my studies in February 1965. I was an excellent student, and by my third year had already participated in teaching as an auxiliary assistant. At that time the program at the University of Ljubljana progressed in two stages, following a model which was very similar to the contemporary plans of the Bologna Declaration.[4] In the first two years, instruction was concentrated on the basic subjects of general sociology, the history of sociology, methodology, political economy, recent history, and the political system. In the last two years, in addition to a deepening of general sociology, methodology and statistics, instruction was enriched by various areas of specialization, e.g., family, work, religion, local communities, etc., as well as some supportive subjects such as social psychology, demography, and ethnography.

I found the study of methodological practice very interesting and attractive because each student had to perform (as a member of a small group) all phases of a small empirical study. The methodology was markedly up to date due to the teaching staff's specialization and training, mostly in the USA. At that time the center of the development of sociology was already outside Europe, and the English language had already become the universal means of communication in sociology.

At this point I met the first obstacle that I had to overcome. As with the majority of the students, I knew German as my first foreign language, and French as the second one. I also had a basic knowledge of Latin, and of Russian. The latter was a consequence of my wish to read Russian poetry in the original language since it was at that time no longer an obligatory language in the schools. However, during postgraduate study I had to learn English, which was not easy, particularly because of the many meanings of some words. I was used to the exactness and distinctness of the meanings of words in my maternal Slovenian, or in the German language. Later on, I often used an English–German dictionary along with the English–Slovene one to look up the correct meaning of some English words.

The university education of sociologists had some characteristics that developed under the influence of the fact that a lot of new knowledge often sprang up within the English-speaking world. In addition, the "pioneer" generation of sociologists (in the mid-twentieth century in Slovenia these were mostly psychologists and jurists) was trained in sociology at the postgraduate level in the USA, e.g. Zdravko Mlinar, Ana Barbic. The hallmark of quality, modernity and a high level of scientific rigor was the use of an English or "Anglo-Slovene" word to denote some social phenomenon or process. This was often done without any attempt to translate either theoretical or even English words into Slovenian, and/or to explain them adequately. In this way students tormented themselves with the pronunciation of the Anglo-Slovene word "*kompetitivnos*" (competitiveness), or of an original English word such as "reliability," even though the Slovenian language had its own perfectly adequate and clear terms for such concepts. This tendency has only strengthened throughout the decades since. This is not just a terminological problem, because at this point we are touching the issue of the "closeness" to (real) society. I had encountered this deep epistemological and ontological issue, as philosophically informed sociologists would say, already as an undergraduate.

Until the beginning of the institutionalization of sociology as a research discipline, with the establishment of the Institute of Sociology at the University of Ljubljana in 1959, and of the academic education of professional sociologists in the Department of Sociology of the Faculty of Arts at Ljubljana in 1960, sociology was often labeled as a "bourgeois" discipline, contrary to Marxism and its "proletarian" emancipative potential. This pejorative labeling of sociology decreased in correlation with the growing number of empirical investigations and results, as well as the increased entry of the new professional sociologists into various jobs.

The education of the first generation of sociologists at the University of Ljubljana was simultaneously the teaching of the actual knowledge of sociology as a "young scientific discipline" on the one hand, and of the Marxist theoretical explanation, rather critical, but primarily oriented toward the past capitalist society, on the other. The critical dimension of the resulting perspective decreased as it dealt with actual contemporary processes in Slovenian (and Yugoslav) society. This "decrease" did not result in the disappearance of criticism altogether. Empirically grounded criticism of contemporary processes, rooted at least partially in a limited knowledge about the real situation in Slovenian society, was developed beginning in the late 1950s. As time passed there was an increase in such criticism, sometimes connected with political orientations that were unfriendly toward the developing system of self-management and "Titoism," while simultaneously glorifying the so-called Western, or American way of life.

I must point out that not at any time during my study at university was a total dogmatism entirely excluding introspection into real processes ever practiced. No doubt this state of affairs was influenced by a broader social environment in which the first changes of the self-managing social order were already taking place.

In spite of various decrees and attempts at social control by the leading Communist party in Slovenia, the League of Communists of Yugoslavia, there developed within the society a broadly ramified model of "democracy from the bottom." With the support of a mass organization called the Socialist Alliance of the Working People, it spread to all levels and all fields of activity. This tendency strengthened in the 1970s and the 1980s.

In addition, the citizens of Yugoslavia traveled freely around the world. I am pointing out this fact because this freedom represents a very important characteristic that differentiated our society from other (real) socialist societies. I know very well from my own experience what the prohibition of contacts with people abroad means in actual practice. For example, on one occasion in 1971 I was taking the train to Moscow. During lunch in the restaurant car I initially was seated at a table with several Russian citizens. When they discovered that I understood and could speak Russian, they began to speak with me about everyday affairs. One waiter noticed this "international" communication and I had to immediately leave the table in the middle of my meal. With my half-full plate and cutlery in hand, I was forced to sit down at the foreigners-only table.

On another occasion, while visiting the University of Minsk in 1976, I recognized what such a prohibition can mean, particularly for a sociologist. The books in the Soviet Union were really very cheap, and I wished to buy a Russian translation of Robert Merton's book *Social Theory and Social Structure*. However, just in time, I observed a note under the title, "*perevedeno i pererabotano*" (translated and altered). I had no time to determine how it was altered, but I did not buy such a useless book.

Parallelism of study resources was connected with multiple dualisms in the explanation of society. On the one hand, in Marxist explanations dualism existed in the classification of the stages of modern social development between capitalism with liberal and monopoly stages, and socialism established by the revolutionary action. I have to add that in the Slovenian society, and sociology, there prevailed the recognition, often empirically verified by the citizens, of the difference between self-managing and "real socialism" (the prevailing political system of the "Eastern bloc"). On the other hand, within the sociological explanation of the same historic period, the dualism was expressed by the distinction between pre-industrial and industrial (later on post-industrial) society. Such contradictory explanations of society stimulated my doubt of their legitimacy and their adequacy for explaining social reality.

The convergence between both approaches emerged in the explanation of social inequality. Class society is abolished in socialism (through the abolition of large concentrations of private property), as it is in modern industrial society, i.e., middle-class society or *Mittelschichtgesellschaft*, the society without the top or the bottom layers that is illustrated by a ball or by a diamond. In the latter, industrial society was defined as a harmonic society resulting from the highly developed division of labor and consequent necessity of social integration. Such a model of society was proposed particularly by classical functionalism, which at that time was considered to be the best of scientific sociology and as a unique and proper substitute for the "obsolete and inadequate Marxist explanations of modern industrial society." Some eminent Slovenian sociologists were convinced that each Slovenian sociologist should improve his (her) knowledge of Talcott Parsons' sociology in the USA (as I ascertained by the investigation of the situation of Slovenian sociology as a profession at the beginning of the 1970s).

As an earthly human being I was open and sensitive, always on the "lookout" for the activity within the direct and broader social environment. Owing to this attitude I also had a lot of questions during my student years, and I wanted and attempted to get scientific answers. For example, I wanted to recognize what the situation was regarding prostitution in socialism, because a lot of signs showed that, especially in the tourist places, it actually existed as a part of the "grey economy," i.e., illegally. I asked a professor (female) of the sociology of the family about this phenomenon. By the way, I have to add that family sociology in Slovenia already included the topic of the emancipation of women and gender equality, which was quite different from the prevailing character of the books published in the "developed" world.[5] The answer I received was that

Friedrich Engels had stated that in socialism prostitution will not exist because of the economic independence of women and their own assurance of existence through employment. Women will not be pressured to offer their own bodies for sale. Therefore, prostitution does not exist in our society.

I accepted this answer as a nice case of the dogmatization of an idea about a future social order. In fact, some necessary elements of woman's emancipation actually already existed in our society, e.g. constitutionally determined equality, the equal payment act, equal opportunities for the education of women. Through the marriage of these facts with Marxist anticipation, the explanation of my professor was presented or perceived to be a general characteristic of our socialism. Nor were my doubts of the adequacy of such explanations to actual social circumstances reduced or relieved by other explanations presented as "modern scientific" knowledge, e.g., the explanation that modern society functions without conflicts because opposing classes no longer exist. All this was occurring in the autumn 1962, when I was really very afraid of the possibility of a World War III, caused by the crisis in relations between the USA and Cuba.

Again and again, doubt, as one of the key stimulations of my research work, grew stronger. My conviction of the legitimacy of that doubt was further rooted in the intensive study of the works of Marx and other classic and modern sociologists. I could never seriously rely on the study of secondary literature, so I studied original works. My doubt was also stimulated by my belief in empirical investigation. I prepared my work for the BA thesis, dealing with a special form of social mobility (intermarriage mobility) on the basis of a small empirical study of one village. Finally my doubt originated for the encounter with some epistemological and methodological rules and demands regarding the objectivity of sociological scientific investigation, i.e., the rule that one must maintain ones distance from the social reality being studied as well as that of *Wertfreiheit* (value-freedom).

These were some of the foundations of my academic career, which began under conflicting circumstances and in a very chilly climate at the place of my first employment, Visoka sola za politicne vede (College of Political Sciences). I have to speak very briefly about the background of the unpleasant beginning of my work as an assistant. Since I had participated successfully in pedagogic activities in the courses on the history of sociology and on statistics during the last three years of my study of sociology (1962–65), the head of the Department of Sociology at the Faculty of Arts promised me the assistant post in "my" department after the BA thesis. Based on this promise, I rejected an offer of an assistant post at the College of Political Sciences that was made some months before finishing my BA thesis.

I was doubtful of the possibility to teach sociology at the College, which at the time was considered to be a dogmatic institution for the higher education of politicians. However, the school had the solid financial support of the Republic budget and it could attract and employ the academic staff it required. For several years the university did not have the financial resources for the appointment of young assistants. So, when I completed my BA degree, in February

1965, appointment and employment at the university was not yet possible. Because of this, my professors, who had seriously promised me the assistant post, were in an embarrassing situation. To keep their promise, they passed me off to the College of Political Sciences, the same institution I had earlier rejected.

I quickly recognized what it meant when one's appointment is a result of a favor. My female colleague, who completed study on the same day as me, but had not rejected an earlier offer, was appointed to an assistant post at the College the following day. The procedure for my appointment lasted four months. During these long months I experienced what it means to be unemployed. When my first working day finally arrived in June 1965 I found myself not well-received or well-regarded, and very quickly recognized that I had been assigned to the role of "*Maedchen fuer Alles*" (maid of all work). Nonetheless, I persisted in my post.

From the beginning, in 1965/66, I was an assistant for general sociology and the history of sociology. Beside these duties I carried out various jobs of organization, e.g., organizer of the optional seminar on international relations in 1969/70. I was heavily burdened by pedagogic work and consequently I did not have enough time for research. I wanted to continue my study at the postgraduate level, but this wish was not to be realized until 1968 when such a program was organized at "my" institution.

In between, I gave birth to two children—a son in 1966, and a daughter in 1968. I had married in the middle of my study in 1962, at the very young age of 19, my husband having finished study at the Law Faculty at Ljubljana in 1961. From the beginning of our partnership we had planned when to have children and also how to divide the household and family duties. The leading principle of the life and interactions in our family-community has been equality and equity in the carrying out of various duties. The traditional patterns of family life have been again and again abolished or at least marginalized. After more than four decades of my marriage, I can conclude that my husband represents a prototype of the "new man" for the twenty-first century.

In addition, my family "burden" did not disturb my presence at the work place very much because I employed a domestic assistant to take care of the children and to help with the housekeeping. Fortunately, at the time my first child was born, my younger sister had finished secondary school and she was kind enough to accept my offer (and request) of this employment within the private sector. She performed her job excellently for three years and two months, entirely according to the legal order. My total net wage was transferred into the base salary for my sister, but her emotional capital was invested in my children. She left my "family enterprise" when my daughter entered kindergarten.

In truth, in my work as an assistant I could not dive deeply enough into a specialized thematic field because of the dedication of my activities over more general themes. From the very beginning of their appointments my male colleagues could direct themselves to specialized fields and thus also had more favorable conditions to publish their articles than I did. The asymmetry of the burden in the workplace was not empirically confirmed until the use of quantitative measures for assessing work engagements. In comparison to my colleagues, I was several times more burdened by pedagogic as well as organizational duties. I actually functioned within a *circulus vitiosus*. I had not enough time for research because of my enormous pedagogic (teaching) duties. Due to this fact I could not produce new knowledge, as demonstrated through various publications. And so I was seen as not productive and creative enough, and consequently suitable only for teaching.

Through a Spartan lifestyle—that is, the near absolute renunciation of free time—I continued my postgraduate study. In the meantime, due to the development of new research and teaching fields, the College of Political Sciences, which at the beginning of the 1960s had been labeled as "at Marx's Beard," was transformed first into the College of Sociology, Political Science and Journalism; then, in 1967, it was transformed into the Faculty of Sociology, Political Science and Journalism, and incorporated into the university. During the following decades this faculty was the central institution in Slovenia for scientific research focusing on empirical investigation in the broader field of the social sciences. So it is no coincidence that at the beginning of the 1990s it was renamed the Faculty of Social Sciences.

In May 1972 I defended my master's work, on the concept of social class in sociological theory at the Faculty of Sociology, Political Science, and Journalism at Ljubljana.[6] I chose the aforementioned theme for my master's work for several reasons. First, was the accumulation of empirical evidence regarding the existence of social inequality and class in the everyday life of mine and other societies. Second, was a great confusion over the designation of social class in general, and in particularly within American sociology. Third, were the "scientific" and/or ideological assertions on classless society in modern times. I wanted to state what actually happens with this phenomenon. For me it was disturbing that many sociologists confronted various theories of social class without respecting the necessary condition of comparison; namely, that theories should refer to the same object. Analyzing a variety of theories such as those of Karl Marx and his predecessors, as well as Edward Bernstein, Karl Kautsky, Max Weber, Karl Renner, James Burnham, Theodor Geiger, Helmut Schelsky, T.H. Marshall, Georges Gurvitch, C. Wright Mills, Tom B. Bottomore, and Ralf Dahrendorf, I investigated several questions. Is social class an objectively existing category or only a theoretical construct? What are the necessary and sufficient conditions for the actual existence of class? How has the expression of class inequality changed over time? What is the relation of social class to other social forms of grouping?

The deep investigation of this phenomenon led me to recognize the biases and ideological elements within the so-called "pure" scientific approaches. These recognitions stimulated my cognitive interest and informed the preparation of my doctoral dissertation. While working on my dissertation I almost entirely excluded myself from normal life. The relevant works of the most important sociologists of the two perspectives accompanied me everywhere.

Due to maternity leave for two children, for several months I was prevented from normal work. However, this absence was not taken into account in determining the amount of time I was given to complete my dissertation. As a result, the three-year limit was effectively reduced to only two years and three months. Nonetheless, I had to produce the same results as my colleagues who were able to work continuously or, if they were absent due to obligatory military service, were given an extension for the period of their absence. During debates over the university statutes at the beginning of the 1970s, I proposed that female absence caused by maternity leave be treated in the same way as male absence caused by military service. Eventually this proposal was accepted, and so one of the hindrances and expressions of injustice was abolished.

I defended my dissertation on functionalism and conflict theory at the Faculty of Arts of Ljubljana University in June 1976.[7] My supervisor, Professor Joze Goricar, was satisfied with my choice for the theme and supported my dealing with functionalism, which at the time was extremely well known. In Slovenia, as was the case in other sociological communities, the functionalist perspective was often considered as a means of the deliverance of sociology from all of her sins, which were typically justified by her "youth." In the 1960s, the myth of sociology's youth was still widespread. I often asked myself how it could be possible that after more than a century of development for this science to be still young.

I had begun to be interested in conflict theory while preparing the master's work. The title of Ralf Dahrendorf's key work, *Class and Class Conflict in Industrial Society*, was very provocative and called for a confrontation with theory that excluded conflict or, at best, tolerated it as an institutionalized phenomenon. I was interested in the question as to whether the institutionalization of conflict actually meant the abolition of the causes of conflict, as some of my colleagues were asserting in monthly meetings at the beginning of the 1970s. This was particularly the case, given that it was unquestionable that a lot of conflict existed in Yugoslav society. The Yugoslav Association of Sociologists also organized a major meeting about internal conflict in 1972. As I became more familiar with conflict theory my interest in its relation to functionalism increased.

For a deeper analysis of the functionalism, I examined the work of sociologists who had subjected some questionable points of the construction and application of the approach to critical examination. It was a genuine intellectual pleasure to discover C. Wright Mills' criticism of "grand theory" in his *The Sociological Imagination*, Alvin Gouldner's famous work *The Coming Crisis of Western Sociology*, and the work of Barbel Meurer, *Mensch und Kapitalismus bei Max Weber: Zum Verhältnis von Soziologie und Wirklichkeit* (Man and Capitalism in Max Weber). Through these studies, my conviction that I was on the right path, the demythologization of sociological theory, was strengthened. I have to mention that in the middle of the twentieth century the majority of sociologists generally accepted an image of sociology based upon some myths, particularly those of the scientific purity and *Wertfreiheit* (value-freedom) of the discipline.

The more I uncovered the lack of harmony between the official self-image of sociology and its actual cognitive capacity, along with its social function, the more I enjoyed my work. This work was founded on several assumptions. Sociological theory as a total social construction should be scientifically examined, not only in regard to its logical adequacy but also regarding its adequacy to social reality. Theory is not built and does not exist within a timeless and empty social space, but it is burdened by pre-theoretical conditions and perspectives. Sociological theory necessarily includes valuation, but this very fact does not exclude its scientific orientation. The analogy between the objects of sociology and the natural sciences are not acceptable.

In my dissertation I carried out a detailed analysis of the key predecessors, as well as the most important modern functionalist, Talcott Parsons. I also looked at the followers of conflict theory, Lewis Coser and Ralf Dahrendorf. I investigated the cognitive potential and the possible applicability of each theory, their relation to social practice, and the roots of their origin. I was struck with wonder again and again upon discovering a continuity of functionalist themes in the development of sociology from Auguste Comte, Herbert Spencer, Émile Durkheim, Max Weber, and Vilfredo Pareto to Talcott Parsons. By accepting the social facts as given, these themes, which appeared in the evolution of the explanatory model of the social system, embraced a teleological explanation of society's activity and a preference for the "to-what-purpose" and not the "why" question. As a result, they allowed for only one alternative of social development, inherent in the system's explanations. Strengthened by exclusion of any doubts about the existing social structure, they acted as a cognitive boundary, serving to naturalize or even theologize the existing system, and to obscure the functionalist approach's ahistoricism.

Functionalist explanations were directed primarily to the creation and strengthening of the value consensus of the society, without questioning the unequal consequences of the existing consensus for particular social strata or the unequal burdens and benefits of those strata. Because the consensus was "scientifically" confirmed as the only existing possibility, every attempt to judge relative pluses and minuses among the social actors was seen as a pathological phenomenon, or even as a revolt that should be eradicated from the beginning. The emphasis on consensus abrogated all such judgments by assuming that the explanation reflected reality in itself since no totality exists without the integration of its parts and their collaboration.

In my opinion, the key questions that originated in studying consensual explanations concerned the conditions of social inequality. Who primarily benefits by such explanations? It did not require a lot of effort to find an answer to this question. In fact, the answer seemed so very obvious that I wondered how it was possible to defend a maxim of pure and value-free science and at the same time to defend a singular political/ideological attitude. For example, take the statement of Herbert Spencer as to how much more worthy is a worker who is diligent, calm and honest though he can not read compared to the educated worker who interrupts his employment, is a drinker, and neglects his family.[8]

Already, then, I stated that functionalistic explanations served primarily to legitimize the status quo and to strengthen the bearers of powerful social positions.

Owing to the secularization of the nineteenth and twentieth centuries, religious legitimization had lost its power, and as science became more and more the prevalent force of progress, the existing social order needed more and more scientific justification. Since, in practice, the existing social order is not justified *an sich* (in-itself), it needs to reject, through the adequate scientific mode, those explanations which question it. In such a manner, I came close to the issue of why the sociology produced by founding fathers was said to be science, while the Marxist explanation of industrial society was labelled an ideology, only a mixture of prophetic ideas.

This autobiography would be too long if I were to present more findings from my dissertation, which I published, somewhat transformed and completed, in 1978.[9] However, I cannot overlook some events that followed my critique of the prevailing sociological perspective within the Slovenian sociological community. Some colleagues were critical of me, and asserted that I was inserting ideology into the scientific recognitions of the classical authors, and that I was too critically oriented. I let these comments pass as I had carried out the difficult study of the original works and I had not written my work on the basis of common sense or preconceived opposition. If anybody could have provided me with persuasive proof, for example, that Parsons' theoretical explanation of social stratification or of the family, and its accompanying implication of the unique correctness of the "American way of life," was value-free, and not one-dimensional, I would have accepted it.

In 1977 I became a doctor of sociological science and was appointed to the post of assistant professor of the history of sociological theory, an associate professor in 1982, and full professor in 1987. With the students, I attempted to develop a sense and capacity for a critical understanding of various theoretical explanations. Among students of sociology (male and female), there always prevailed a serious interest in the subject in spite of its difficulty and complexity. My lecture room was never empty and often my lecture was transformed into the kind of bilateral communication typical of the seminar. At the very beginning of the year, I encouraged the students to raise questions if they could not understand some matter. Of course, I also set the rules of the game in accordance with the standards of "civil attention." I would write these two words from Erving Goffman on the blackboard and explain their meaning: attentive and respectful relation to each actor. When I was speaking they would listen to me. When they wished, they should request a word and I would listen to their comments and questions, and respond to them. During my whole career as a university teacher I experienced the lecture room as a space for close intellectual contact and co-operation. To create a favorable environment for such a mode of teaching I used various video aids such as posters and transparencies. I retired just before the use of power-point became common.

In addition to the attempt to develop a critical and professional consciousness with the students, I have always attempted to place my own critical attitudes within the concrete historical context. This means that I have never glorified criticism *an sich* (in itself). I always respected its relational dimension: criticism of what/whom, why, and for what purpose. In this sense I rejected the "reckless critique of all existing," often connected with the extremely anarchist attitudes of the defender of this principle. However, through the years I became more and more convinced that proper criticism of the sociological science exists as an inherent element in the entire cognitive process.

Whether in the field of intellectual judgment or everyday circumstances and interactions in my family and work environments, as well as in the broader society, my personal experiences contributed to my critical attitudes. So, for example, I was extremely unhappy with the celebration of International Woman's Day, because in spite of his egalitarian orientation my husband continued to celebrate the holiday long after the normal ending of the working day, while I had to "celebrate" the day caring for our children. The recognition of the existence of double standards for the actors in some activities, especially for those with a privileged pedigree, as well as for males and females, led to my discomfort. As a woman I discovered relatively early on that in spite of the declared gender and class equality, different gender rules existed. In my faculty, I was more than once witness to differential treatment of male and female colleagues, especially regarding promotion. For one male colleague, the son of a high political functionary of the Republic, the deadline to complete his doctor's degree (Ph.D.) was extended again and again, despite very clear legal rules to the contrary. In the case of another male colleague, a similar extension, based on the powerful position of his director, was granted, and so on. However, for women in similar posts such an option was entirely unthinkable.

Step by step I extended already established recognitions of general social inequality by acknowledging new axes of differentiation. Thus, gender inequality became more and more an interesting aspect of my reflection on social order and development. From this point of view, and similar to Engels in his analysis of the English working class, i.e., based on *eigener Anschaung und authentichen Quellen* (my own observation and authentic sources), nearly every part of social reality called for a critical judgment of the taken-for-granted cultural and institutional order. However, the majority of the relevant, valid, and reliable data, ignoring the "official" statistical data that was always available, was attainable only through empirical investigation.

I have always wished to be "down to earth," and to avoid *Soziologie ohne Gesellschaft* (sociology without society). I was able to realize this wish only in small increments. This was due to the impact of various circumstances. On the one hand, I was highly burdened by pedagogic work and the demand for keeping up with new knowledge in the development of sociological theory, which was very dynamic in the post-functionalist period of the 1970s and the 1980s. On the other hand, my interest in gender inequality was not generally accepted, given the prevailing spirit of the times, due to the largely male-dominated science. Finally, I did not possess any informal power and I was not included in any old-boy networks. As is very well known, these are all very important prerequisites for gaining financial resources for research.

When, in spite of these facts, I had the opportunity, I gladly engaged in empirical investigation. In 1969 and 1981 I participated in the first and the second major investigations, using a representative sample, of the religiosity of middle-school pupils in Slovenia. The project, *The Characteristics of the Beliefs of Slovenian Secondary School Youth*, was carried out by the Research Institute of the Faculty of Sociology, Political Science and Journalism. In the first investigation, and especially in the second one, I oriented my interest and concentrated the analysis on two institutionally very important agents of the transmission of religiosity: the family and the Church. Dealing deeply with these two phenomena, I also discovered gender inequality, especially with the recognition that women are the key transmitters of religiosity inside the family, and are also the major bearers of religiously determined patterns of behavior. Some questions which originated included why and with what purpose were women the major actors? What was their special role in the shaping of the personal identity of youth? Is a greater religiosity among women a "natural" characteristic? Are women really "closer to God," as official Catholic doctrine claimed in its justification of the special role of women to be mothers? The findings of these two investigations led me to a serious examination of these issues.[10]

My interest in religion and the Church as two historically lasting determinants of the earthly order in general, and especially important for the establishment and reproduction of gender hierarchy, continued in two directions. On the one hand, I analyzed important documents of the Catholic Church written by Pope John Paul II, particularly his *Apostolic Letter on Dignity of Woman: Mulieris Dignitatem*.[11] My aim was to explain modern statements in regard to the women's issue, and to determine the origin of the so-called "proper" role of women in contemporary society. On the other hand, I exposed the clearly sexist explanations by Catholic sociologists of the "proper" female nature (femininity) and of woman's role in society. This sociological orientation was prevalent in the history of Slovenian sociology until World War II.

The relatively strong interest of Catholic sociologists in women was stimulated by the emergence of "social evil," as they unequivocally designated the woman's movement demanding economic, political and social emancipation at the end of the nineteenth century and at the beginning of the twentieth. Investigating the explanations of four Slovenian Catholic sociologists I recognized more and more how complex and sophisticated the spiritual means of the construction of the "proper" woman's role, often equated with "natural" or "objective" reality, have been through the centuries. Discovering the androcentric essence of these explanations, I came to agree more and more with Georg Simmel who, already in 1911, had identified such a reality with the formula "objective = male."[12]

Gradually, I exposed the destructive practical potential of these sociological explanations that respected "God's law" as the highest frame of reference. They defined women as second-class, subordinate beings at men's disposal, created "by nature" for the family and home (as demanded by God's will), full of love (the bearers of "concentrated emotionality"), altruistic and obedient. Men as the bearers of the authority over women were only performers, also servants of God's will. To ameliorate this marginal position of women and to soften their factual powerlessness, these explanations glorified women, and gave them excellent titles, such as "the queens of the home," and so on. And the realization of the very burning, earthly, desire for gender equality was transferred into the transcendental sphere where everyone was said to be "equal in the face of God."

Studying such explanations, I always thought of the many women in lower strata who in difficult real-life conditions had put this "equality" to the test in the past and the present. Even as a child I had heard various stories of women who had suffered different modes of violence and injustice inside "holy" matrimony, and within the public sphere, all in the name of God's will. Among these stories, I knew very well that of my grandmother who was not married but who had had one illegitimate child—my mother. I never wondered why my mother and my grandmother did not believe in God. They reflected on "God's will" through their own experiences and in their own minds. So, through my closest role models, I had a lot of reason to pay attention to the doctrine and to the everyday practice preached by the Church.

The explanations of Slovenian Catholic sociologists legitimized the material and moral overburdening of women permitted by the institutionalized and universally supported social order, based on their so-called "perversity" and "moral depravity."[13] As with the Catholic sociologists of the first part of the twentieth century, there was only a superficial *aggiornamento* (modernization) in women's position in society in contemporary documents of the Catholic Church. For example, in the *Apostolic Letter on Dignity of Woman*, the proper human dignity of woman is acknowledged only if she accepts the role of His assistant; thus her dependent identity is a command. But women's dependence, the role of maid or servant, is softened or hidden, for the man is, too, only a "servant." In such a way hierarchy is abolished and subordination generalized, and thus rendered unproblematic. If woman's subordination is questioned, this danger can again be neutralized by recourse to the definition of the "proper nature." In short, an individual human being, whether a man or a woman, the member of a powerless and subordinated majority, has to repress his/her subjectivity and adapt him/herself to the impersonal totality.

Recognizing that the Catholic explanations reduced the actor to an obedient and adaptable being (multiply so for female actors), I concluded that a very similar reductionism is hidden in the secular sociological explanations of the classics.[14] Through further investigation I recognized that this phenomenon was not just a matter of the past. Some of the newest sociological theories, be it the systems theory of Niklas Luhmann or symbolic interactionism, ultimately posit the adaptable individual actor as the foundation of the explanation, regardless of the explanatory frame of reference. The assumption of such an actor transforms the foundations of structurally inherent and concrete deprivations of the social order to inadequacies in his/her own emotional and moral capacities.

Thus the theological, macro-sociological positivist and micro-sociological interpretative approaches all contain a predefined conception of the "proper" individual as an unquestionable ingredient. Despite their ahistoricity, the persuasiveness of all these explanations is based on selective anchoring in reality. This occurs by first reducing the basis for empirical verification through the exclusion of those activities which are connected with deprivation and suffering, even though they remain necessary for existence. This is followed by the inclusion of positive, pleasant characteristics and activities, attainable especially by the bearers of privileged positions. As a typical example of such a procedure we can take the conceptions of the family as a group with love-ties predominant, as a space of freedom and recreation, and as a subsystem without acknowledgment of the power relations. Until recently, explanations of this kind, really a kind of fairy tale, existed as the normal theoretical fare, and were transmitted to the students uncritically.

These reductive explanations fall apart without any particularly rigorous scrutiny if we recognize the simple fact that real individuals exist as male or female beings. This is an intersubjective and empirically verifiable fact. In such a way, I introduced the "gender difference" into my lectures. This contributed to a unique conception of many phenomena when compared to those interpretations created by the elimination of the experiences of the "second sex" in accordance with the imperatives of the "proper" scientific method, which acknowledged the experiences of only one (male) gender. I want to add that this assessment does not express some kind of hostility toward men; but, the fact is that the male gaze has been predominant in the observation and the description of social phenomena, whether at the macro- or at the micro-level. In this vein, I remember one of my colleagues asking at the beginning of International Women's Year (1975): "But when will we, men, get our year?" I quietly answered: "You have had the millennia, not just a year."

Let me be clear, the way to this (engendered) knowledge was not easy! Within the academic environment of the 1970s, and to a lesser extent afterwards, a discourse about the special position of women was understood as a matter that had no place in a scientific field. A science existed or it did not exist, asserted my colleagues. Of course I principally agreed with this statement, but I had always in mind the question: What kind of science? When, at the end of the 1970s, I wished to make a systematic investigation of the changes in the position of women, one of my colleagues, an eminent professor, said to me: "You are known as a really serious woman but you are entering into this very unserious field!" Nonetheless, I entered the field, though I was often very lonely.

At that time, the notion that science, and of course also sociology, is gender neutral was at that time so firm and self-evident that nobody doubted it. Since I had already confirmed my doubt about the *Wertfreiheit* of the science, I did not swear on gender neutrality. Studying several very serious and complex sociological works, often designated as "Marxist," as well as those from the broader social sciences, a realization slowly began to form in my mind. I remember the occasion when it first came to me clearly:

> In early morning hours of one of many working nights, when in my consciousness floated numerous data on the position of women in different contemporary societies, I suddenly wished to survey how and how much the problem of "the other," or "weaker" or even "worse" part of humankind is present in a neutral work . . . I turned over the pages of the book from the beginning to the end and in reverse direction, and I repeated this approach, in order not to overlook any important information. I was surprised that all the different data and generalizations referred to a gender homogenous or one gendered population. Though oppressed, exploited, and manipulated, the human being is a generalized worker, thus of male gender. Only in one-half of a page appears also a female worker who appertains to the sphere of social policy, who renders more difficult normal family life and at the same time also economic life, as this being is disturbing.[15]

Because of the generally existing conviction of the unimportance of the gender dimension, the intolerance to special attention to gender inequality in research and instruction and, finally, because of the relatively low critical mass of female researchers, this dimension could only be smuggled into closely related subjects that were unproblematic. So, it became evident that family research, whether within general sociology and/or especially within the sociology of family as a generally recognized field, was the most suitable frame for the pursuit of the gender theme. It was mostly connected with the issues of the division of labor inside and outside the family, the disintegration of marriage and family through divorce, migration, and widowhood. It also was a result of the changes of women's social position, their activity in the economy, their increased participation in higher education, and in politics.

In the 1970s, and continuing into the 1980s, the climate outside academic institutions was relatively more favorable because of repeated attention to the "humanization of gender relations." This was reflected in a set of activities contributing to the consciousness-raising of the whole population regarding the existing forms of discrimination against women and the appreciation of the alternative possibilities for the regulation of mutual relations. Among these activities was the inclusion of the topic of gender equality in sociology textbooks for the secondary and high schools, and of ethics in the textbooks for the elementary schools. It was included in manuals for marriage and family counseling, which were given to partners as a present at the civil wedding ceremony. Gender equality was also present in television and radio broadcasts as well as in the print media, though sometimes in sensational fashion. Actually, simply said, practice beyond the academy was a step ahead of the research. In part this was due to the equality of rights of gender in Slovenia. It was also due to the globalization of the efforts to abolish the discrimination against women, particularly supported by the United Nations, during the Decade for Women from 1976 until 1985.

As has been the case with many sociologists in the past, the temptation of contributing to changes in the broader social circumstances attracted me as well. I undertook this activity in various ways[16]—for example, through postgraduate lectures for specialists preparing for family counseling, physicians specializing in pediatrics or gynaecology, and middle school professors. I also authored educational broadcasts on radio programs, including three years as an external editor, and a participant in debates on TV, and as a co-author of schoolbooks for elementary, middle school, and university students. In every instance, based on available data, I disseminated a sociological knowledge regarding the gender inequality of the past and present, at home and abroad.

In the early 1980s I organized and chaired some seminars within the continuing education program in the social sciences at my faculty. These focused on the changing position of women in Slovenian society. I published popular articles in women's magazines such as *Jana* and *Nasa zen* (Our Woman), and professional articles in some anthologies and books. I delivered some lectures for teachers of home economics and I was interviewed by a variety of journalists. Often, I had to provide the questions as well as the answers for these interviews, because of the very low degree of knowledge on the theme. A lot of people were influenced by my statements. Sometimes, when someone met me personally for the first time, the greeting was accompanied by the surprised reaction: "Oh, you are that feminist, I imagined you as a strong, big woman!" My answer has always been the same: "I am the sociologist dealing with gender inequality, and, as you can see, not so big or so strong, given my body's dimensions."

In the second half of the 1970s, the need for a better understanding of Slovenian society, past and present, stimulated me to work with a group of scientists from various disciplines (medicine, law, psychology, demography, pedagogy, and the economy) to conduct a multidisciplinary research project on the changes in the family and woman's position. In the preliminary review, at the Marxist Center of the Central Committee of the League of Communists of Slovenia, the project did not get support for financial resources. It was condemned as "anti-socialistic" and rejected. At the time I was the chairperson of the section on theoretical issues of the socio-economic situation of women at the Center. Immediately after the destructive critique and the rejection of the project's proposal, I resigned as chairperson of this section.

Nonetheless, in a more limited manner, I still dealt with this theme, using empirical evidence based on investigations of Slovenian public opinion. In 1982 I investigated statements on women's employment, and I persuasively rejected the stereotypical assertions that women naturally wish to stay at home and not to be employed and economically independent. An additional impulse that drove me to disclose the inaccuracies of these assertions came from the (male) writers of the projections for the development of Slovenian society until the year 2000, which treated women primarily as housewives who "could be also employed." Of course, I immediately responded through the mass media to such a sexist exclusion of women from the public sphere.

On several other occasions I continued to use the data from the Slovenian Public Opinion (SPO) investigations to elucidate a variety of themes. Whenever I could "beg" some money for research, I included special issues in questionnaires for the investigation of public opinion. I am grateful to the director of the Center for the Research of Public Opinion, Niko Tos, for these opportunities. When the Center began to participate in the International Social Survey Program (ISSP), its general questionnaire was extended to include a set of questions catching the gender dimension.

For example, I incorporated data regarding maternity leave into a multidisciplinary research project "The Maternity Leave as an Element of Biosocial Reproduction."[17] The results of this project served as a basis for political efforts, in 1985, to prolong maternity leave to one year. In 2000 I investigated sexual harassment in the workplace, uncovering tendencies in Slovenia similar to those that exist in other contemporary societies.

In the 1990s I often used the data from many of the investigations of the SPO in dealing with the characteristics of the transition in Slovenia. During this period sexist public discourse on gender reappeared, accompanied by various practical proposals for provisions that would contribute to the re-domestication of women. This tendency was, at least partially, connected with the drive for re-Catholicization.

Because of serious health troubles in the mid-1980s, I had to limit my research ambitions.[18] So a new obstacle joined with the relatively unfavourable organizational climate I had to face. In the second part of the 1980s, in the field of gender sociology, I investigated the strikes in some of the feminized industries in Slovenia. These strikes already had been an object of general sociological investigation in Yugoslavia, but I directed the focus more specifically to the situation of the "second sex."

In 1988 and 1989 I coordinated an international research project on the role of the mass media in the abolition of gender discrimination, "The Media and the Nairobi Forward Looking Strategies for the Advancement of Women." The study was carried out in Italy, Austria, and Slovenia and was financially supported by UNESCO. In August 1990 I presented the results at the 17th World Conference of the International Association for Mass Communication Research, held in Bled, Slovenia. The investigation unequivocally showed that at the time no country, regardless of its political system, had a positive plan for the realization of equal opportunities within the media, or for the abolition of the hostile orientation of media towards women. This included the substance of media production as well as its organizational culture and practice.

At the beginning of the 1990s, through several years of continuing research, I exposed the historical roots of contemporary sexism. I was concerned especially with the contents of those contributions, of various kinds, in mass print, that were addressed to women. Sometimes the encounter with these statements of the "proper" moral order sent shivers through my body—for example, statements stigmatizing women fighting for the right to enter the university to study, labeling them as immoral and disobedient and equating them with "horizontal artisans," a characterization used to refer to prostitutes. I was not particularly aghast or surprised by such statements, because in my mind was an already relatively well-formed recognition of the immensity of the misogynist attitudes of the majority of the greatest scholars, including G.W. Friedrich Hegel and Auguste Comte. Such misogyny was expressed through the flouting, insulting, and mockery of women, particularly those women who wished to be wise, rational, and educated. From this research I made only one firm conclusion: it is really necessary to disperse the knowledge of the real intellectual character of the "malestream" explanations which contributed to the "scientific" justification of the discrimination against women. I remain entirely devoted to this objective.

It was not surprising that again and again I was struck by the sentiment that, by and large, it is not necessary to read modern crime stories, since the mass of literature, including prayer books, for the moral education of women represents a proper first-class crime story in its own right. I would suggest to the students attending my lectures on the sociology of gender where they could find such excellent crime stories. When the students investigated the print media of the past, they were taken aback by the written messages they encountered; but they were also just as often taken aback investigating contemporary media representations of women!

In the second part of the 1990s, with the support of the Office of the Slovenian National Commission of UNESCO, I investigated the situation of women scientists. Focusing on the career patterns of female assistant and associate professors, I confirmed the results of an earlier investigation that had been performed on full professors. Through it, I exposed several facts that I had experienced myself, e.g., the deficit of the support in the organization, a chilly organizational climate, subtle forms of discrimination against women, the low level of women's consciousness about their own situation and about the possibilities of empowerment, etc. As a practical consequence of this investigation, in 2001, I was made a member of the Equal Opportunities Committee of the Ministry of Education, Science and Sport of the Republic of Slovenia. Later, in 2002, I was given the post of president of this committee, and membership in the Helsinki Group Women in Science with the EU.[19]

During my pedagogic work, especially in the last two decades before my retirement in 1999, I continuously attempted to strengthen the students' sensibilities to gender inequality. This aim was achievable, particularly in the elective subjects that were often chosen to be taken by non-sociology majors, i.e., by the students of journalism. Gradually, I developed the complex subject of the sociology of gender in a manner that was very attractive, not only for female but also for male students. Within this subject, students produced a lot of interesting diploma works based on empirical mini-investigations. Step by step I thus engendered the undergraduate study of sociology through an "integrative model." At the beginning of the 1990s I also prepared a postgraduate study program, "Sexism as a Contemporary Tradition," which was offered for several years.

I have to make a point that my pedagogic practice followed the objective to make visible the synergic influence of gender and social stratification. Sometimes, it was also integrated with other types of differentiation associated with the concrete historical situation, i.e., with race, ethnicity, religion. Such an approach permitted me to explain some phenomena that sometimes appeared to the students to be incomprehensible. For example, why didn't the women's movement exist as a homogeneous activity, or how to recognize the hidden androcentric character in texts seemingly directed to emancipation? Through my research and pedagogic work, I gradually recognized the narrowness of the term "patriarchy" (and "patriarchal") because it does not catch the totality of regulative mechanisms that include and reproduce gender hierarchy. I was more comfortable with the term, "androcentrism," and, more broadly, the term "sexism." Androcentrism encompasses the entire category of the male population, which has been superior through the centuries, as well as in contemporary conditions, despite recent developments towards gender equality. I therefore entitled my last book *Sexism in Everyday Life*.[20]

To this description of my research and pedagogic activity, I must add some information on other roles connected with my "sociological identity." I have been active in the Slovenian Sociological Association (SSA) since its founding in 1965, including serving as a member of the Executive Committee and as chair of the Board of Ethics of the SSA. My efforts have been oriented towards the strengthening of the professional identity of sociologists and of their promotion within the public sphere. I also prepared a code of professional ethics that, since 1992, every student has received at the completion of his or her study. At the beginning of the 1980s, as president of the Committee for Professional Issues, I was active in the Yugoslav Association of Sociologists. At the same time, I was a member of the editorial board of the journal *Sociologija*, published in Belgrade, Serbia. I was also a member of the editorial board and an author of articles for the unique Yugoslav journal of theoretical issues of women, *Zena* (Woman), published in Zagreb, Croatia. Through the decades, I was a member of the editorial board of the Slovenian scientific journal *Teorija in praksa* (Theory and Practice), and, in the last decade, of two other journals, *Druzboslovne razprave* (Journal of Social Sciences) and *Anthropos*.

During the World Congress of Sociology in Madrid in 1990 I participated in the first preparatory meeting for the creation of the European Sociological Association (ESA). Afterwards, as a member of a steering committee, I collaborated with other European sociologists until the official establishment of the ESA, and later served as a member of the Executive Committee from 1995 until 1997. I also served as a member of the Program Committee for the preparation of the first and second conferences of the European Sociological Association. (Vienna in 1992, Budapest in 1995).

As an active participant and/or as a coordinator, I have participated at various international scientific meetings, conferences and workshops all around Europe, e.g., at the regional conference of ISA in Krakow in 1996 ("Building Open Society and Perspectives of Sociology in East-Central Europe"), and the conference of the ISA's Research Committee on the History of Sociology in Amsterdam in May 1996. As a member of an international program committee, I participated in the preparation of the second and the third European Conference of Feminist Research (Graz, Austria, in 1994; Coimbra, Portugal, in 1997), and also in two world conferences of the International Society for the Study of European Ideas, the fourth at Graz (1994) and the fifth at Utrecht, the Netherlands (1996). At the latter conference I chaired the workshop "Gendered Construction of Limited Collective Memory."

In the second part of the 1980s, and in the 1990s, I had many contacts with German-speaking sociologists, either through scientific meetings or as an author of articles published in several monographs. I collaborated with other European sociologists, in the preparation of some monographs on the social changes in Central and Eastern Europe.

Since my retirement I have traveled abroad as a tourist, but not very often and not very far. My bodily travel is more oriented towards Europe, but my mind travels all around the world. A silent partner all of my life has been the principle "think globally and act locally." Recently, I have come to respect also another principle, "*festina lente*" (you must speed slowly). Following this principle I still hope to do something in the future. I have a lot of plans, more than just one lifetime's worth.

Before I finish this small mosaic of my life, I want to add two fragments concerning the big changes in my broader social environment. I have been a witness to the brutal decomposition of the Socialist Federal Republic of Yugoslavia. At the same time, I have been witness to the establishment of the independent state of Slovenia and the transformation of the political system in Slovenia at the beginning of the 1990s. I had the opportunity—or better, I was thrown into the opportunity—to observe these big changes from inside, not only as a sociologist but also as an ordinary citizen.

Already in my childhood I was able to put to the test personally what the slogan "brotherhood and uniformity," along with the declared and constitutionally guaranteed "equality of rights of all nations in Yugoslavia," meant in practice. My family lived close to the border between the Republic of Slovenia and the Republic of Croatia. In elementary school, I had to learn the "Serbo-Croatian" language, while the pupils from the neighboring village in Croatia did not have the obligation to learn Slovenian. This experience, later on complemented by different cases of national inequality and actual discrimination, contributed to the shaping and strengthening of my attitudes regarding a more equitable solution to the problem of different nationalities in a common state.

As a member of a quantitatively small Slovenian nation, and a citizen of the Socialist Federal Republic of Yugoslavia, I often felt humiliated. As a young citizen, I took an active part in efforts aiming at the genuine realization of the attractive slogan. In the middle of the 1960s, in addition to my obligation as an assistant professor, I delivered some lectures for secondary-school students about the national question. My objective was to stimulate their sensitivity on this topic, which, at the time, was not a politically popular theme due to the fear of "nationalism." Later on, in the middle of the 1980s, I wrote about and suggested the necessity of the equality of languages in the Yugoslav army. During the public debate at this time concerning changes in the federal constitution, I also proposed and defended the creation of a special article determining the possibility and the procedure for the division of the Republic from the federal state. Of course, this proposal was considered too dangerous, and it was practically unthinkable that it could be adopted by the federal political bodies. But, after the death of President Josip Broz Tito in 1980, the disintegrative tendencies were more and more obvious.

The main, sometimes subtle, source was the politics of the pursuit of a greater Serbia, which did not occur just at the beginning of the 1990s but was kept alive through the decades after World War II. The attempt to create a greater Serbia out of the Yugoslavian state intensified in the 1980s, and it was not just limited to the sphere of politics—it spread to all fields of activity and life. So, during the professional meetings of the Yugoslav Association of Sociology in Portoroz in 1983, an outbreak of politicization by the (primarily Serbian) sociologists occurred. I was surprised, because in my mind there still lived a small hope that sociologists, scientists, would not allow themselves to be the servants of the aggressive politics of a greater Serbia being conducted by the later well-known leader, Slobodan Milosevic. I was able to see the true attitudes of some of those who had earlier been the greatest defenders of "humanism." It is surely no coincidence that the majority of Serbian sociologists openly supported Milosevic's bloody politics during the war from 1991 until 1995. Only a very few sociologists distanced themselves from his politics.

A very important role in the legitimization of the later military interventions was played by the mass media in Serbia, particularly the print media. I will never forget the day of March 20, 1989, when I had to wait a whole day for the plane to Ljubljana while traveling from Athens, where I had participated at an international scientific conference on the Social History of European Women. Because my husband was employed in Belgrade at the time, I went to his office and read the most important Serbian dailies. When I finished reading, I was really frightened. What an accumulation of lies about Slovenia and Slovenians, and partially Croatia! This finding was all the more alarming because I already knew the results of an analysis which confirmed the gradual Serbization of the leading positions within the Yugoslav army. In the same year I had many occasions to recognize the politics of a greater Serbia, and in my mind even more strongly formed the conviction that in essence this was a politics very similar to that of the Fascists or Nazis. The first military intervention of the Yugoslav army in Kosovo, some weeks later, confirmed my anxieties. I expressed this idea and my condemnation of the war (which was already "in the air") in the poem which begins, "On tanks is driving the peace..."

In 1990, and in the first part of 1991, the militant procedures against Slovenia escalated and reached their apex in the military intervention during the attack of the Yugoslav army against Slovenia after the declaration of Slovenian independence on June 25, 1991. Fortunately, due to the strong resistance of the Slovenian territorial defense forces, the war in Slovenia was not long, even though it continued in other republics of Yugoslavia.

During the 1990s, when I represented myself at international scientific meetings, I always introduced myself as from the former Yugoslavia. Once, in August of 1995, at Warsaw, during the 5th World Congress for Central and Eastern European Studies, my representation was historically even more detailed. I mentioned first, that I am from Slovenia, through the centuries a part of the former Austria–Habsburg monarchy, then later, through seven decades in the twentieth century, a part of the former Yugoslavia. I can now say that both these empires became "former" due to the suppression of all other national communities. I only hope that the multinational EU will not follow these models of social/national integration. However, all around the world many such models still exist, and thus the issue of national autonomy will be a burning topic on the agenda of future political activities.

As a nationally sensitive Slovenian (female) citizen, I was glad when Slovenia became an independent and internationally recognized state at the beginning of the 1990s. But my enthusiasm has been limited by various facts emerging simultaneously with the processes leading to independence and inherently connected with the transformation of the political system. The self-managing socialist system, which contributed to the specific situation of Slovenia in comparison with other former Socialist states, was abolished and replaced by a multiparty democracy and a market economy. In the 1970s and the 1980s, Slovenia had been relatively prosperous, with a fairly developed welfare system and a network of social services shaped practically free of the oversight of the state. I naively expected that these processes, including already developed elements of grass-roots democracy and some features of a market economy, would continue. But the reality was contrary to these expectations.

Soon after the beginning of the transition into a modern democratic society, both faces of modernization became visible. Due to the enormous increase in unemployment and the threat to social security, etc., the promised nice and human-friendly face of modernization was in a very short time seen as a sad, and to the majority of people, hostile face. This was especially true for the majority of women for whom the transformation of the social order did not mean improvement in their living conditions. To the contrary, the transition meant an increase in the sexism expressed by the tendency toward the re-domestication of women and their nearly entire exclusion from political decision-making. This aim has been supported by re-Catholicization, with the aim to return women to the home and the family, and thus to their "proper" natural role.

This process has been a part of the general critique of past socialism. In Slovenia, this criticism has occurred in a special way with several characteristics. The previous Slovenian socialist society, equivocated with "real socialist society," has been defined as "totalitarian." The developed Western democratic societies have been conceptualized as attractive societies, purged of any structurally produced negative effects and offering positive and equal opportunities for women and men. Sometimes, the discourse was reminiscent of that from the end of the nineteenth century.

My disagreement with the tendency toward re-patriarchalization stimulated my activity inside and outside the sociological community. As author and editor, I prepared a special issue of *Druzboslovne razprave*, the journal of the

Slovenian Sociological Association, titled *Transition and the Gender Inequality*. I dealt with this issue in papers prepared for some international scientific meetings, as well as within the domestic Slovenian scene. Toward the consciousness-raising of the broader public I contributed essays published in popular magazines and also through satires and humorous sketches in dailies.

In a similar manner, I also responded to the numerous attempts, which since the middle of the 1980s have occurred on a regular basis, to glorify the collaboration of top Slovenian politicians and officials of the Catholic Church with the German and Italian occupiers during World War II. This glorification has been justified through association with the early struggle against Communism and connected with the criminalization of the partisan national liberation war of 1941 to 1945. Frankly speaking, such attempts to justify the collaboration with Fascist and/or Nazi military force, which would be unthinkable in those European countries that suffered under the occupation, i.e., Norway, the Netherlands, Great Britain, France, etc., are common practice in contemporary Slovenia. I was deeply alarmed also at the first evident expressions of this tendency, and I published a short satiric essay entitled "How Charming was Hitler!" in 1985.

In Slovenia, the contemporary defenders of the collaboration with the occupiers (special military forces bound by oath to Hitler on his birthday in April 1944) demanded reconciliation on the basis of perverse historic processes. This reality is not very well known outside Slovenia, but here at home the request for reconciliation is again and again repeated as a condition for the "moral renewal" of Slovenian society. In addition to the prevailing historic memory of the Slovenian population, the great majority of which condemns the collaboration based on actual tragic war experiences, the defenders of the early struggle against Communism, i.e., collaboration, also entirely ignore assessments of the partisan struggle made by the representatives of the allies during World War II. In the estimation of Peter Wilkinson in his report to the British government in 1944: "Since the rebellion of the South Tyrolean Andreas Hoffer against Napoleon, Europe has not seen such magnificent rebellion against foreign occupants as I saw it in contemporary Slovenia."

Regarding this situation in Slovenia, I often remember Alvin Gouldner's warning in his "Anti-Minotaur" regarding the moral indifference of sociologists: "If we today concern ourselves exclusively with the technical proficiency of our students and reject all responsibility for their moral sense, or lack of it, then we may some day be compelled to accept responsibility for having trained a generation willing to serve in a future Auschwitz."[21] This very warning is the motto for the Code of Professional Ethics of the Slovenian Sociological Association that I prepared at the beginning of the 1990s. I believe that until the end of social inequality, the issue of the ethical orientation of sociologists will always remain alive all around the world. However, the old question "Whose side are we on?" should not simple refer to support of one party or another. In my opinion, for sociologists, it primarily concerns the very quality of the scientific approach we adopt and employ. The obscuring of some negative social effects and/or the obstruction of the production of new knowledge doubtlessly means to stand at the side of the powerful and the elite. Contrary to this alternative is an integral approach that produces knowledge usable for the support of activities aiming at more justice in society and also contributing to its sustainable development.

Notes

1 Science and Society Program Committee, *Orientations for the Work Programme 2004* (Brussels: European Commission Research Directorate, 2003).
2 Alvin W. Gouldner, *For Sociology: Renewal and Critique in Sociology Today* (Harmondsworth: Penguin Books, 1973).
3 In the basic model of the self-managing system workers and employees make the decisions about the conditions and results of their work. On this base, the entire political system was created. Direct decision-making was implemented from the workplace and local communities, to the federal state level.
4 The main objective of the Bologna Declaration of the European Ministers of Education (adopted in Bologna, Italy on June 19, 1999) was to establish an integrated system of higher education throughout Europe within the first decade of the third millennium, to promote the European system of higher education worldwide. A variety of measures were to be employed, including adoption of a system based on two main stages, undergraduate and graduate; establishment of a common system of credits; and adoption of a system of easily comparable degrees. The similarity between this system and that of the Slovenian system in the 1960s resides primarily in the division into undergraduate and graduate stages. According to the Bologna Declaration each stage should prepare students for employment and/or for the eventual continuation of study.
5 Talcott Parsons, *Family, Socialization and Interaction Process* (London: Routledge & Kegan Paul, 1956).
6 Maca Jogan, *Kategorija razreda v socioloski teoriji* (Ljubljana: FSPN, 1972).
7 Maca Jogan, Sociologija reda. Kriticen oris funkcionalizma in konfliktne teorije (Maribor: Obzorja, 1978).
8 Herbert Spencer, *The Study of Sociology* (Ann Arbor: University of Michigan, 1969), 339.
9 Jogan, *Sociologija reda.*
10 Maca Jogan, *Zenska, cerkev in druzina* (Ljubljana: Delavska enotnost, 1986).
11 Janez Pavel II, *Apostolsko pismo o dostojanstvu zene* (Ljubljana: Cerkveni dokumenti 40, 1989).
12 Simmel's formulation was too early for the spirit of his time. Due to this fact, it was forgotten until the 1980s when Lewis Coser contributed to its revival. See "Georg Simmels vernachlaessigter Beitrag zur Soziologie der Frau," pp. 80–90 in *Georg Simmel und die Moderne*, eds Heinz-Jürgen Dahme and Otthien Rammstedt (Frankfurt am Main: Suhrkamp, 1984). I have passed it on at every occasion possible.
13 "Moral depravity" was the usual designation by which these sociologists used to refer to those women who did not accept the existing and obvious discrimination against women. In my explanations I introduced two terms, "material" and "moral overburdening," because they adequately and integrally catch the actual structurally determined and strictly controlled situation of the majority of women, their powerlessness and simultaneously their great moral responsibility.
14 See Maca Jogan, "Redomestication of Women and Democratization in Postsocialist Slovenia," pp. 229–236 in *Family, Women and Employment in Central-Eastern Europe*, ed. Barbara Lobodzinska (Westport, Conn.: Greenwood Press, 1995).
15 Maca Jogan, *Druzbena konstrukcija hierarhije med spoloma* (Ljubljana: Fakulteta za sociologijo, politicne vede in novinarstvo, 1990), 10.

16 We can recall Auguste Comte and his desire to be "l'eclereur et reformateur" (enlightener and reformer), and Émile Durkheim's conviction that a sociological work was worthy only if its results were practically usable. And, of course, practical use is always connected with Howard Becker's question: "Whose side are we on?"

17 This project was financially supported by the Community for the Care of Children, a special body within the self-managing system responsible for policy in the field of child care. At the time, this field was already acknowledged as one of key spheres in the harmonization of the family and the work duties of employed people of both genders.

18 In the autumn of 1985 I had a big gynaecological operation which left me with an entirely ruined hormone equilibrium and an officially recognized disability of 60 percent. Since that time I have had trouble sleeping. I am catching my biorhythm; this means that I have to be obedient to my body and its requests. This has meant a reconciling with the reduced capacities of my body—unhappy, but necessary for survival.

19 In Helsinki, in 1999, a special group of 15 member states and 15 non-member states was formed at the EU. Its aims were to stimulate research on women's position in science, to coordinate the debate about the policy and measures regarding the promotion of women in science, and to search for statistically sensitive gender indicators.

I can add that as a sociologist I was active in various bodies dealing with the "woman's issue"—for example, on the Board for the Socio-economic Position of Women of the Republic Committee of the Socialist Alliance of the Working People, and on the coordinating board for family planning of the same body. In the 1980s I chaired the Board of the Center for the Development of the University. In short, I have never been narrowly academically oriented.

20 Maca Jogan, *Seksizem v vsakdanjem zivljenju* (Ljubljana: Fakulteta za druzbene vede, 2001).

21 Alvin W. Gouldner, "Anti-Minotaur: The Myth of a Value-Free Sociology," *Social Problems* 9 (1962): 199–213.

3 Hand in hand with sociology

My Life in the social sciences

Wladyslaw Kwasniewicz

To Tomek and Basia, so that they can learn about the curious times their grandfather lived in.

I was born on June 9, 1926, in Pszczyna, a small town of then 7,000 inhabitants, in Upper Silesia. My parents, Jan and Maria, were teachers. They both came from plebeian families from Sambor, a half-Polish, half-Ukrainian town to the southwest of Lviv, now in Ukraine, with a population of a little more than 10,000. When Poland was invaded by Nazi Germany on September 1, 1939, my father had to flee from Upper Silesia. We moved to Cracow, where we lived in abject poverty. There, in the spring of 1941, I joined the resistance movement, the Union for Armed Struggle (ZWZ), which, in early 1942, became the Home Army (AK). Incidentally, I had to lie about age, as volunteers had to be at least 16 years old.

In 1944, Poland, along with other countries of Central and Eastern Europe, ended up under Soviet domination. There is no denying that liberation from the Nazis did not come from the direction we had expected. And yet, it *was* liberation and a chance to do things other than underground struggle—for example, to obtain an education. In February 1945 I enrolled in a secondary school program for adults. In September 1945 I began to have problems with the military secret service (colloquially known as the *informacja*), which quite persistently tried to track me down.[1] Taking refuge with my relatives and friends in Cracow, I managed to pass the secondary school final exams (*matura*) as an external student (a student who did not attend classes but took the exams at the end of each semester) in Cracow, in February 1946. With the graduation certificate in my pocket, I fled to Lodz, where I remained in hiding until December of that year. I stayed with my father's relatives and made a living as a clerk. I even began to study sociology at the newly established University of Lodz, where some excellent sociologists, including Jozef Chalasinski, Stanislaw Ossowski, and Maria Ossowska, were lecturers.

In early 1947, a so-called "amnesty" was announced. Having turned myself in to the Provincial Public Security Authority (known as the *bezpieka*) in Cracow, I moved back to my parents and resumed sociological studies, this time at Jagiellonian University (JU). I graduated in June 1950. At the time I received my MA diploma I was working for Cepelia, the state-run folk art agency that traded in art objects and utensils commissioned from village craftsmen.

On September 1 of that year I was employed at the Chair of General Ethnography and Sociology at JU. On December 31, 1952, I received a second MA diploma, this time in ethnography. I took quite long to get subsequent degrees. It was only in December 1960 that I obtained a doctorate. My habilitation came seven years later, in December 1967, but I was not appointed a *docent* until the autumn of 1968.[2]

On April 1, 1971, I was appointed head of the Sociology Department, newly established at Jagiellonian University, a post in which I stayed until 1978. Let me add at this point that I never sought any other offices at the University, like those of a dean or rector. In my opinion, they did not allow one as many relatively unrestrained opportunities to act as the position of a department head. In May 1976, the State Council conferred upon me the title of professor *extraordinarius*. I became a professor *ordinarius*, not without some hassle, just before my retirement on October 1, 1996.

Despite repeated efforts, I was long unable to obtain a scholarship for a research stay abroad. That became possible only in August 1972, when the International Research and Exchange Board (IREX) granted to me a nine-month internship with the Bureau of Applied Social Research at Columbia University in New York. My academic adviser was Allen Barton. Both he and his secretary, Phylis Sheridan, went to great lengths to make my stay there a success. I had rich and fruitful academic contacts with Paul Lazarsfeld and Robert K. Merton. Afterwards, I was twice granted a research stay at the Institut für Hohere Studien in Vienna (for a total of five months in 1987 and 1989). While there, I established valuable academic relations with Austrian sociologists Robert Reichardt from the University of Vienna and Max Haller from the University of Graz.

My teaching activities were concentrated at Jagiellonian University. I have also occasionally taught part-time at other Polish universities. In addition, between 1978 and 1980, I spent two spring semesters as a visiting professor in the USA at Alliance College, in Cambridge Springs, Pennsylvania. In the spring of 1984, I was a visiting professor at the University of Hamburg.

During my career I have participated in the proceedings of many academic bodies. Among the domestic ones, I should mention, especially, the Polish Sociological Association and the Committee on Sociology of the Polish Academy of Sciences (PAN). Internationally, I am especially proud to have taken active part in the Steering Committee of the European Sociological Association from 1988 to 1990.

I do not discuss my family life here. Let me just mention the persons closest to me, my son Krzysztof, a graduate in English studies and a professional translator, his wife Kasia, and my two grandchildren, six-year-old Tomasz and four-year-old Barbara.

Why I decided to study sociology

In the spring of 1945 I renewed my membership in the Polish Scouting Association (ZHP). I also joint the Polish YMCA, which had just resumed its activities in the new, post-war political reality of Poland. To this latter association I owed my first holidays after the war. In July and August of 1945 I served as an instructor for two successive groups of schoolboys at the Polish YMCA summertime camp. It was located some 50 kilometers south of Cracow, on the slope of Mount Lubogoszcz, above the village of Kasinka Mala in the Beskid Wyspowy Mountains.

I remember a bonfire we held one August evening. It was customary on such occasions that one of the participants would give a talk. This time our speaker was the father of one of the boys (unfortunately, I do not remember his name), an activist of the subsequently disbanded *Stronnictwo Pracy* (Labor Movement). He referred to sociology on several occasions and expressed the view that building the foundations of a democratic system (he was clearly an opponent of the prewar *Sanacja* regime) required the use of the findings of this discipline.[3] I then realized that sociology encompassed the kind of problems that I had taken a special interest for some time, despite my young age of merely 19. I also recalled that my father had always mentioned with great respect the sociology lectures by Leon Petrazycki, at the University of Warsaw. Thanks to my father, during the war I had met Kazimierz Dobrowolski, the sociology and ethnology professor at Jagiellonian University.[4] Thus as I returned from the Polish YMCA camp, I knew I wanted to study sociology. This came as a surprise to me. During the war we did not think about our future at all.

Back home from the holidays, I communicated my intention to my parents. It came as a bitter disappointment to my mother, who had always hoped I would become a physician or a lawyer. My father, on the other hand, welcomed my decision and, to show his approval, gave me a couple of sociological books from his library. He also arranged an appointment for me with Dobrowolski.

As I look back on my choice of a study major, two conclusions inevitably suggest themselves. First, I chose sociology mainly for intellectual reasons; I did not think about what I was going to do and how I was going to make a living as a sociologist. Second, nobody, neither the students (which is not surprising) nor the professors, expected that the new political regime in Poland would turn out to be so nasty, in particular, for the social sciences.

My fellow sociology students at Jagiellonian

After the war, students of sociology at Jagiellonian University came from various parts of Poland. Men still predominated in this field of studies, although an increasing proportion of female students were already becoming apparent. The age differences among students were considerable. The oldest of us, mainly teachers who took advantage of the opportunity to study without having to pay tuition, were in their forties or even fifties. Because so many sociology students were killed during the war, those who were resuming interrupted studies made up only a small group. The majority of students were around 25 years old. There were only a few of the age typical of beginner students, i.e., about 20. Most of the students were mature, or perhaps more accurately mature beyond their years. Many of them had had wartime experiences as soldiers of the underground Home Army, as death camp prisoners, or prisoners of war.

Immediately following the war, some 150 students enrolled in Dobrowolski's seminars. Of this number, about a third had chosen sociology as their major. For the others it was an elective subject. Dobrowolski had a knack for guiding students. Many of his students, from the oldest to the youngest, went on to attain national and even international renown. They included, among the older generation, Anna Kutrzeba-Pojnarowa, Danuta Dobrowolska, Krzysztof Kwasniewski, Aleksander Matejko, Adam Podgorecki, Roman Reinfuss, and Adam Sarapata. In the younger generation, Danuta Markowska, Hieronim Kubiak, Lucjan Kocik and, especially, Piotr Sztompka must be mentioned.

Looking back on my student years today, I have no doubt that it was a very special period. Many of us were overjoyed to have survived the war. Therefore, we partied a lot. At the same time, most of us had to struggle hard to get by. Since the curriculum was not particularly rigorous, students had a relatively large amount of free time. The greater part of society lived in strained circumstances, so most of the students had to earn a living on their own. Therefore, they usually sought employment, often as manual workers. To put it bluntly, some of us lived in poverty. Economic reasons compelled many students to try to obtain a diploma and to find a permanent job as soon as possible.

The dearth of textbooks and other required reading was a real nightmare. We tried to compensate for the deficiencies of the university libraries by publishing books on our own, using a duplicating machine called a hectograph. One of these, published at the end of May or in early June 1947, in just 400 rough-looking copies, was my translation of the famous history of sociology by Pitirim Sorokin.[5] I must add that this book played an important role in my intellectual development, as it demonstrated to me with great clarity that there is room for various points of view in social science. I thus drew the conclusion that one should avoid monistic accounts and prefer pluralist approaches.

The Sorokin translation sold out immediately, which I took as a kind of personal success. However, it also nearly brought disaster upon the Chair of Ethnology and Sociology, where we studied. In the autumn of the same year, the *Kuznica* weekly of Lodz, closely associated with the leadership of the Polish Workers' Party (PPR), ran a brief but devastating review of the book by an undisclosed author signed only as "rkm."[6] The Chair was in danger of being dissolved, which would have signified the end of sociological studies at Jagiellonian. This threat did not materialize, as we complied with the conditions imposed on us in late 1947, or early 1948, and organized a cell of the Academic Association of Fighting Youth (AZWM), a satellite organization of the Polish Workers' Party.[7] Incidentally, it turned out that our Chair was the only one at the Faculty of Humanities which still lacked an AZWM cell by that time.

Following the controversy, the sociological circles at the Jagiellonian University ceased to be an enclave where students were more or less left alone and could develop their scientific, philosophical, and political outlook on their own. We paid a heavy price for saving the Chair and maintaining an opportunity to study. Let me add that when a certain research assistant from our university, a historian and a former friend of mine from the vocational school we had attended during the war and now a fierce champion of Marxist-Leninist orthodoxy, tried to return to the matter of the Sorokin textbook in the *Po prostu* journal at the end of 1947, the political authorities turned a blind eye.

Political controversies

Our most animated discussions and debates, partly in Dobrowolski's seminars, but mainly conducted in private, concerned politics. Our circles did not sympathize with Jozef Pilsudski and his political heirs in the *sanacja* regime, whom we held responsible for Poland's defeat in 1939. There were also heated disputes about the Warsaw Uprising. I was among those who believed it had made little sense, either militarily or politically.[8]

An especially momentous and divisive issue for us was our attitude towards the new political reality in post-war Poland. We saw it as a totally alien system, imposed by the Soviet Union, a country which we viewed in a purely negative light. We also bore a grudge against Great Britain and, particularly, the United States since we viewed the Yalta Agreement simply as a betrayal of Poland by its closest allies.[9] Many of us scorned France for its lack of preparedness in the war with Germany, and its performance during that war in 1940, although we did sympathize with General Charles de Gaulle. We did not have any confidence in the new regime in Poland and saw PPR members predominantly as Soviet agents and traitors to the Polish nation.

Dobrowolski was well aware of our views, which he tried to moderate. In particular, he made frequent comments about current affairs in his seminars and classes. As I try to recall his standpoint after so many years, it appears to me he emphasized four issues. First, he pointed out Poland's isolation on the international scene. He believed that if Poland wanted to continue to exist, it had to, willy-nilly, put its relationships with the Soviet Union on a constructive footing. Second, he mentioned the advantages of the new territorial boundaries of Poland after the war. Third, he stressed that pre-war Poland, revived in 1918, had failed to undertake a land reform, which was only carried out by the Polish *Sejm* under the auspices of the PPR after World War II. He also welcomed the nationalization of the economy and the plans for industrialization. Fourth, Dobrowolski forcefully stressed that an effective policy left no room for sentiment, and should only be based on uncompromisingly objective and rational decisions. He shared the view of painter Kazimierz Pochwalski, who claimed that the greatness of a society is revealed at critical moments when, facing seemingly insurmountable difficulties, it nevertheless strives to find a way out.

I was among those convinced by Dobrowolski's arguments, but I do not have the slightest doubt that the vast majority of his students stuck by their views and did not share his political diagnoses and forecasts.

Sociology, Stalinism, and my early career

In my student days, sociology enjoyed neither great prestige at Jagiellonian University, nor much popularity in broader social circles, including the opinion-making groups. For this reason, the unfavourable attitude of the PZPR (Polish United Workers' Party) toward sociology, although stemming from different motives, might have appeared natural among some intellectual circles. Nonetheless, many of us were prepared to struggle to enhance the rank of sociology.

The views of Dobrowolski were one source of inspiration for us. He was a staunch advocate of sociology as a discipline that furnishes an intellectual basis for action in both the design and the implementation phases of various initiatives, i.e. the economy. We willingly engaged in fieldwork which demonstrated the practical utility of sociology. For instance, I participated in a study, carried out by Dobrowolski in 1950, on the effectiveness of the campaign to fight illiteracy, the sad legacy of feudalism, among the builders of Nowa Huta.[10] Being confirmed optimists, we shared the conviction that our future professional activities would enhance the academic reputation of sociology. Our prediction came true in the end, but we did not know at the time what a formidable obstacle Stalinism would present.

My first personal encounter with Stalinism came in the summer of 1949. I was then sent to Warsaw to attend the First All-Polish School of Marxism-Leninism, organized by the ZAMP (Academic Association of Polish Youth). The participants were subjected to discipline of a double kind: a military-like drill, complete with reveille and a morning workout, combined with strict political rigor, based on the principles of Marxism-Leninism. Any view, even on trivial matters, that did not conform to the official doctrine met with fierce attacks. Not even the greatest minds in Poland, among them some Marxists, treated as apostates from the Marxist-Leninist orthodoxy, were spared. Brainwashing was common practice at the School, as was the indoctrination of participants about the Party as the collective bearer of supreme truth. It was there and then that I first asked myself how a system that ignored rational solutions and incessantly subjected people to cognitive dissonance could survive. I returned to Cracow, feeling intense relief that the nightmare of the School was over.

More permanent contact with Stalinism began for me a year later when I was appointed, on September 1, 1950, as a senior research assistant at Jagiellonian University. One could hardly have embarked on an academic career in sociology at a more inopportune moment. Suffice it to say that sociology had just been struck from the list of university disciplines in Poland, and sociological studies had been abolished. The compound name of Dobrowolski's Chair at

Jagiellonian, combining sociology with ethnology, allowed it to avoid the fate of other chairs of sociology in Poland and to survive. But sociology was removed from its research scope, which was restricted to "general ethnography," the term used in the Soviet Union. This name was also intended to emphasize the theoretical aspirations of the Chair.

In these complex circumstances, I decided to obtain a master's degree in ethnography, which I managed to accomplish by the end of 1952. The diploma in ethnography largely determined the further course of my academic career. Despite the dim prospects, I managed to stay on at JU. I tried to pursue a double career in sociology and ethnography until the mid-1960s, when I decided to stick with the former field.

I was hoping that my university appointment would leave me with more time for research and learning foreign languages, but I was soon disillusioned. There were several reasons for this. The first was the immense teaching load imposed on research assistants. The performance of our duties and the results of our teaching were controlled not so much by the professors as by the Party and its youth organization, the Polish Youth Association (ZMP). Stalinism allowed the youth at many universities to bully the staff, a phenomenon known as paedocracy. Second, was the lack of funds to employ auxiliary staff, which usually forced research assistants at our Chair to double as librarians and clerical workers. Third, was that in my specific case I was burdened with the onerous duties of serving as Dobrowolski's secretary. This function, however, was not part of my job description, but a private arrangement between the two of us.

My life thus was not easy, especially during the first decade of my assistantship. I even considered moving to a provincial ethnology museum. But I must have been recognized by the governing bodies of the university as a valuable employee, because they not only turned down my resignation but also appointed me as assistant professor in the Chair of General Ethnography and Sociology at Jagiellonian.

The death of Stalin, on March 5, 1953 (oddly enough I am writing these very words exactly on its 51st anniversary), left a deep imprint on my memory. It was obvious to every thinking person that under the new circumstances an opportunity for political change had opened up in the Soviet Union and its satellite countries. This allowed us to hope that the political decision-makers would also change their attitude toward the social sciences, including sociology, which was so close to my heart. And this is what actually happened. The change in the style of government in Poland took the spectacular form of an upheaval, popularly referred to as October '56, and gave rise to numerous spontaneous grass-root movements.

Because of health problems I did not immediately participate in these initiatives and only joined in toward the end of 1956, or at the beginning of 1957. At that time, the sociological circles in Warsaw and other towns were still in turmoil. But, within a couple of months, sociology was restored as an academic discipline in Poland, this time for good. The teaching of sociology at universities was resumed. At Jagiellonian University, the program in sociology was reinstated in the academic year 1957/58. At the same time important institutional changes took place. Dobrowolski's unit returned to its old name as the Chair of General Ethnography and Sociology. Simultaneously, Pawel Rybicki took the newly established Chair of Sociology and Demography. The renewal of Polish sociology reached all the major academic centers and ushered in the best period in the post-war history of our discipline.

My changing sociological interests

As I have mentioned, my university debut took place under Stalinism. At a time when sociology had ceased to function as a science, the only chance for me to do research was to do it under the guise of ethnography. In Dobrowolski's view, although he would not overtly declare it in those years for obvious reasons, even in the Stalinist period, the scope of the latter discipline bordered on sociology. Among the research subjects Dobrowolski suggested to his students and collaborators were such issues as the socio-cultural functions of the serfdom tradition in the local populations in the countryside, or the socio-economic and cultural aspects of the modernization of the farming methods used by peasants.[11]

During my 12-month stint at Cepelia, my interests had become focused on the village of Swiatniki Gorne, near Cracow. Its inhabitants were craftsmen and had nothing to do with agriculture. Their livelihood was based on the production of padlocks (still of a very primitive type in those days) in their home workshops. It was the padlock makers who formed the core of the local community at Swiatniki. They were not, however, the dominant social class. That role belonged to a dozen or so merchant families who not only organized the manufacturing of padlocks in the cottage industry system but also sold these products on the domestic and in several foreign markets.[12] A monograph of this nationally unique rural craftsman population became the foundation of my doctoral dissertation, defended in 1960 and subsequently published in 1970.[13] Thus, during the first stage of my academic career I was an ethnographer, a rural sociologist, and a cultural sociologist, all wrapped up in one.

In the early 1960s I was invited by Professor Celina Bobinska, the editor of a series devoted to the history of Jagiellonian University students from the fifteenth century to the twentieth, to write a volume devoted to the history of Jagiellonian students from 1945 to 1964.[14] This study was set in the framework of sociological generation theory. At the time, I was so engrossed in the sociology of higher education and university students, and, in time, also younger learners, that for a while the sociology of youth became my principal research interest.

In the course of my research stay at Columbia University, by chance, I got hold of the then popular book by Peter M. Blau and Otis D. Duncan on occupational structure. At that time I began to study the problems of occupational classes and groups. It seems to me that the most valuable contribution I made to this research area consists of my studies on the intelligentsia as a component of class structure.[15]

However, that was not the end of the evolution of my interests as a sociologist. In the 1970s and 1980s I did research, *inter alia*, in urban sociology, the sociology of medicine, and even the sociology of sports. Since the 1970s I have developed a lasting research and theoretical interest in applied sociology, and in social change, especially under the conditions of systemic transformation.[16] A theoretical context for the latter is furnished, in part, by the relationship between the processes deliberately initiated in society; that is, planned actions, and their unintended effects—in other words, spontaneous processes.[17]

A separate, important element of my output consists of studies, published over many years, on the development of sociology in Cracow since the turn of the nineteenth century and in post-1945 Poland.[18] I have also taken a keen interest in the teaching of sociology at universities, and the formation of the social models of the occupational role of sociologists in Poland. Surprisingly, even to myself, in the 1990s I became the editor of the first Polish sociological macropaedia. It has been clear to me that for many years my sociological interests have been not only broad but also too dispersed. This, however, may explain why I have never felt bored as a sociologist.

My vision of sociology as a social science

I have never succumbed to the temptation to work out my own theoretical vision of sociology. I have been happy with Dobrowolski's conception, unfinished though it is. Even after October '56, Polish sociologists seldom discussed the specificity of sociology as a science, and its relationship to historical materialism. In this way they avoided confrontation with dogmatic Marxist-Leninists, most of whom, incidentally, were philosophers.

Dobrowolski accentuated, in the first place, the need to apply a historical approach in sociology.[19] Following Ludwik Krzywicki, he was opposed to reducing sociological studies only to the analysis of the contemporary state of affairs. He advocated diachronic studies in which modern times were viewed as a phase in the broader context of processes of social change. Dobrowolski was an outspoken opponent of ahistorical approaches like those proposed by the German formalists.

Under the influence of Bronislaw Malinowski, Dobrowolski, being one of his few Polish students, postulated combining historicism with an interpretation of the current social reality from the perspective of the functions of intentional and unintentional consequences of human actions in society. He advocated social analysis consciously based on a combination of various kinds of existing sources, those inherited from the past as well as those deliberately elicited by the researcher. He saw the sociological potential of the interpretation of such sources for reconstructing the objective states of social reality, as well as the ways of thinking about this reality. He thus disagreed with Florian Znaniecki about the privileged role played in sociology by so-called "personal life documents." Nor did he endorse the view that the main task of sociology boils down to individual reactions to, and perceptions of, collective life.

While recognizing the importance of theoretical thinking in social science, Dobrowolski was clearly opposed to all monolithic approaches. As an economic historian by education, he appreciated the role of Marxism in disseminating economic interpretations of social reality in the social sciences. On the other hand, he did not share the view that sociological analysis can be reduced to such interpretations. As in the case of research methods, he advocated pluralism in theoretical approaches.

Dobrowolski was well aware of the inevitable tendency of sociology towards specialization and its resultant divisions into ever-narrower subdisciplines. He realized that investigating narrow sections of reality often missed their links with the broader social context, which posed the threat of viewing them as isolated entities. To counteract this detrimental effect, Dobrowolski constructed a system of epistemological postulates which he called the *genetic-integral method*, mandating that the researcher grasp the phenomena under study in their social contexts and explain them from a variety of viewpoints. At the same time he believed that this required theoretical constructs which, far from being eclectic or, worse still, syncretistic in character, should constitute logical units that offered one a holistic view of social reality, relevant to the problem at hand.

Dobrowolski also was convinced that dividing sociology into two contrasting components, theoretical reflection and empirical research, resulted in an internal split within the discipline. He was an ardent supporter of the reintegration of the various strands of sociology on the one hand, and of sociology with other disciplines, not only from the domain of social science, on the other. This was yet another aspect of the genetic-integral model. Alas, he never gave it a finished theoretical formulation.

Finally, Dobrowolski believed that every discipline, of natural and social science alike, faces a double mission, comprising both the study of reality (which can be seen as an autotelic value) and the practical implementation of the findings in real life (a utilitarian value). He was convinced that sociology, ever advancing our knowledge of society and culture, had a highly constructive role in the post-war reconstruction of the collective life of the Poles. It was a problem which always occupied a prominent position in his reflection on sociology.

I have relied on Dobrowolski's theoretical framework on many occasions in the course of my university teaching, and especially in my introduction to sociology courses. I refer to this framework even now, as I teach students who only take classes on the weekend every other week. However, I don't share all of Dobrowolski's ideas. In particular, I have long ceased to subscribe to the view that studying society inevitably brings us ever closer to an understanding of its workings.

Party members and non-members

My position at Jagiellonian as an educator was gradually strengthened, and I was being assigned an ever-greater number of functions both within the university as well as outside it. It was becoming increasingly clear to me that I would have to face the problem of my hitherto status as a non-member of the Party. Generally speaking, until World War II, the university professorate in Poland was predominantly politically autonomous and indifferent. If some dominant elements were visible, they were mostly connected with the Christian Democratic orientation. This was probably the main reason why the modern social sciences made their appearance at the Jagiellonian so late, and with such difficulty. For instance, pedagogy only appeared in 1921, ethnology in 1926, and sociology in 1930.[20] Psychology acquired the status of a separate field of instruction even later, having branched off from pedagogy only in 1954. And to this day, Jagiellonian offers no program in economics. Proponents of the political left were a rarity in those days, restricted to a small group of professors, including Dobrowolski. As a sympathizer of the Polish Socialist Party (PPS) already before the war, he lectured at its affiliated Workers' University Society (TUR).

The custom had been that political parties did not create satellite organizations at universities, except among the students, who needed permission from the university to get politically organized. Things changed after 1945. The PPR and then the PZPR followed a policy of deliberately penetrating various kinds of institutions by organizing its own structures made up by its members within such institutions.

Jagiellonian University was no exception. The first party cell was established there in 1945, although I have no idea who its members were. It operated clandestinely, probably so as to protect its members from exclusion from the various informal circles at the university. The university community was soon shocked to learn that several professors had joined the ranks of the PPR. But it was still controlled by non-partisan professors, elected in accordance with pre-war regulations, which, to the best of my knowledge, were changed for the first time only during the Stalinist period. At that time the post of the rector was held, for two terms of office, by a professor who was a Party member. After October '56, the legislation that allowed the professors to choose the rector was restored. Until 1971, the rectors were once again non-partisan. In the 1970s, as the faculty's right to choose the rector was abolished again, this function was held by two card-carrying professors in succession, followed again by a series of non-partisan ones, until 1989.[21]

During the 45 years of Soviet-imposed socialism in Poland, there were 12 non-partisan rectors and only three partisan ones. The former were in power for a total of 39 years, the latter just for 15 years. However, the situation at Jagiellonian University should not be taken to be representative of the academic community, either in Cracow or as a whole. Some universities largely toed the Party line, gaining the well-deserved appellation of the "most socialist" of the Cracow schools.

The extent to which universities were dependent on local party committees varied, even after October '56. For instance, Cracow always enjoyed the reputation of a more liberal place than neighbouring Katowice, Kielce, or Rzeszow. And, an important role was played by the personality of the local decision-makers. For many years, public sentiment among the JU faculty reflected a ranking of the First Secretaries of the Cracow Committee of the Party, based on their perceived merits/demerits for the academic milieu. For instance, Lucjan Motyka, who contributed substantially to the organization of the 600th anniversary of the JU, gained a quite good reputation.

Yet another perspective in which the academic (or any other) community can be viewed concerns the access of its members to power. The distinction between *Party members* and *non-members* was a stereotype which evolved spontaneously both in the Party and in Polish society at large. It was a manifestation of an oversimplified, so to speak Manichaean vision of the positioning of various social groups in terms of power relations. Thus, for instance, it was an utterly erroneous view that Party members displayed monolithic ideological attitudes.

From the moment I started to look at these matters more closely—that is, from the early 1950s—three general categories of Party members could be distinguished: passive participants in political life, more or less dedicated supporters of the party leadership, and people who adopted a fairly non-conformist approach to the party elite and intended to bring democratic innovations into the party. The relative size of these three categories varied. I have no doubts that the second of these was rather weakly represented among sociologists in the Party ranks, in contrast with, say, philosophers or political scientists. On the other hand, the third category was always quite prominent and often very active. The relatively low level of Party membership among academic sociologists (I would guess roughly 60 percent nationwide compared with some 80 percent among philosophers) gave rise to the widespread notion among the Party apparatus that sociology was particularly heavily affected by the pestilence of revisionism.

It was likewise a mistaken belief that joining the PZPR allowed one automatically to join the ranks of political decision-makers. People usually fail to take note of the elementary fact that the Party was a highly formalized organization with decision-making processes that were not transparent even for its members. In Party governance, the *divide et impera* (divide and conquer) maxim was often invoked, as was well reflected within the body of sociologists among the membership. Like other disciplines of social science, sociology had its representation with twenty-odd members, affiliated with the Science and Education Department of the Central Committee. Known as the "Party group," it was apparently a non-statutory body. Until early 1981, sociologists formed a joint Party group with the philosophers, who played a leading role enforcing ideological orthodoxy among its members, sociologists included.

In this context, it should be mentioned that not all non-members were of impeccable moral standing, just as not all Party members should be regarded in a purely negative light. Of course, I do not intend to leave an impression of viewing the two groups, Party members and non-members, as symmetrical with respect to the proportions of, say, idealistic versus cynical or respectable versus not respectable individuals. Far from it. Like any ruling party, the PPR, and afterwards the PZPR, attracted careerists, people of questionable morals who kept a watchful eye on all its members and insisted on adherence to the ideological essentials.

At the same time I wish to add a word of caution against a vision of society divided into two worlds separated by a wall, those of Party members and non-members. As usual, social reality was much more complex than its stereotypical perception. It is no longer possible to quantify it with precision, but contacts between Party members and non-members were not restricted to professional matters. They also occurred on a private footing and were generally amicable. This may account for the relatively high degree of independence from the Party enjoyed by certain organizations, such as the Polish Sociological Association, in which existed comparatively harmonious relationships between the Party members and non-members within its ranks. Throughout the years of the "People's Poland" there were people in the Association, Party members and non-members alike, who were determined to promote the common interests of their milieu, showing tolerance combined with considerable persuasion, mediation, and negotiation skills. It seems to me that this state of affairs has largely endured in the sociological community beyond 1980.

I should mention here the fact, now oft-forgotten, that it was in the Stalinist period that the term "non-partisan Bolshevists" made its appearance in Poland. It denoted persons who, despite their lack of formal association with the Party, were heavily subservient to it. Without any exaggeration, it can be argued that the influence of the Party in specific circles depended on the number and position of non-partisan Bolshevists available therein. I do not hesitate to say that in the sociological milieu, compared with other social sciences, their number was relatively limited.

Why I joined the Party

When writing memoirs, one often has to ask whether one's remembrance of some events is not merely a confabulation. Such was my reflection as I was setting down to writing this section. How did my views evolve to cause me—a person so critical of the new social reality in Poland, refusing to accept Marxism-Leninism as a scientific theory, disillusioned about the new Poland by the horrors of Stalinism—finally decide to join the PZPR? Let me add at the very outset that it was a conscious decision of mine, which I only took in my thirty-eighth year.

I would like to emphasize that this decision was preceded by a long series of events and deliberations. I was a second-generation member of the intelligentsia, brought up, especially by my father, to respect common people who earned their living with their hands. I am still convinced that the "People's Poland," especially after October '56, fostered more egalitarian social relationships and intergenerational advancement than its predecessor.[22] I was also influenced by Dobrowolski's views, and especially, his vision of politics as a sphere where emotions take second place, as well as his conviction that political decisions should be based on scientific analyses and forecasts.

I recognized that the Soviet Union had become a world power after World War II, and shared his conviction that it was in Poland's best national interest to maintain friendly relations with that country. De-Stalinization in the Soviet Union, and the democratization of public life in Poland after 1956, opened up prospects of increasing the scope of Poland's independence from the Soviet Union. With the demise of Stalinism, the pressure for adherence to Marxist-Leninist orthodoxy was eased. Under one guise or another, various theoretical and methodological innovations of Western sociology became introduced, even if mainly through the back door. I supported this tendency.

At the same time it was indisputable to me that in Poland any attempts to remove the Soviet presence from public life by force made no sense. On the other hand, I believed that smoothing out difficulties was a hard but feasible task. I believed that socialism in Poland would grow increasingly democratic. I was convinced that although the world of that era was divided between the United States and the Soviet Union, convergence processes eventually would encompass not only the sphere of science and technology but also that of politics. I was also influenced by the initiation of the processes of industrialization and urbanization, which led Polish society to move away from a post-feudal model in the 1950s and 1960s, to acquire the features of an industrial society.[23]

In Poland, I felt at home and never had any intention to leave my country for good. I felt I was needed here and associated my future with my country. In the year of the 600th anniversary of Jagiellonian University, I realized that my involvement at the university would have been far more effective had I been a Party member.[24] That settled it, and when the anniversary celebration came to a successful end in May 1964 I made the final decision to join the Party.

In the autumn of 1965, Dobrowolski was to retire. Not a Party member himself, he was nevertheless quite an influential figure, both in Cracow and in Warsaw. His retirement signified the loss of the effective protection our Chair had enjoyed thus far. At the same time there were rumours that some professors of our Faculty had their own candidates to take up the post to be vacated by Dobrowolski. Although most of the Faculty saw me as his successor, my appointment was practically out of the question as I did not yet have my *habilitation*. Party membership offered me some slight chance to influence the decisions affecting our Chair and, indirectly, myself.

My accession to the Party in the autumn of 1964 drew some comments from those around me. However, I did not experience a boycott, banishment, or any other social sanctions. My wife was clearly displeased by my decision. In time, this became one of the reasons for our break-up. It was the highest price I had to pay for joining the Party.

An unexpected backlash did come nine years later, during my first visit to the United States. An American political scientist, whom I had not met personally before, asked me to meet him, for reasons then unknown to me. As it turned out, he had just come back from Poland and wanted to share with me his reflections about some politicians he had met in Warsaw (probably in the hope that his words would be reported to the intended audience in Poland). I was going to end our meeting at that moment, but my host insisted I stay longer. He then asked me whether I was aware that by joining the Party I had broken the oath given to the Union for Armed Struggle. I wondered how he knew about my participation in the resistance movement and membership in the PZPR. And I was truly astounded by his linking of the two facts, one which took place in 1941 and the other 23 years later. The essence of my views, which I presented in the ensuing long discussion, was that had the Allies not handed Poland over to the Soviet Union during the conference at Yalta, there would have been no need at all to join the Party. My interlocutor, however, seemed to discount the issue of Yalta.

It is a view frequently expressed in debates on the social consequences of the systemic change in post-war Poland that the new system precluded the emergence of any grass-root initiatives, whether individual or collective. Supposedly, room was left only for top-down initiatives, taken by various Party structures and the governing institutions they trusted. It was further claimed that this situation killed all resourcefulness in large sectors of society, which, moreover, tended to shift all responsibility for the existing state of affairs to the authorities.

Such conclusions are catchy and fairly widespread, but I do not endorse them fully. In my opinion, one should not overlook the many facts which demonstrate unequivocally that the Poles did exceedingly well in many different situations, taking effective and momentous actions of their own accord despite the difficult conditions of an autocratic state. After all, they created the only society among the satellites of the Soviet Union that de-Stalinized the political system on its own (1956), forced the party leadership to soften its course (the protests of 1970, 1976, and 1980) and, in the end, brought down the system (1989), which led to a complete reorientation of Poland's political alliances in the 1990s.

For obvious reasons, I do not offer a more profound analysis of these problems as I reflect upon my own life. I would like, however, to make a point about the effectiveness of the work of sociologists in Poland after the demise of Stalinism. It was precisely at that time that Polish sociology gained a relatively high standing in world sociology, becoming something of a show window of the entire Soviet system for the eyes of the international sociological community.

Lust for action

Joining the PZPR led to a period of intense public activity for me. Although I was affiliated with a provincial university, I contributed in some measure to energizing Polish sociology at large, especially in the 1970s and 1980s. I fondly recall my involvement in the Executive Board of the Polish Sociological Association following my return from the research stay in the United States. I also recollect the years on the editorial board of *Studia Socjologiczne*, with Wladyslaw Markiewicz as editor-in-chief from 1968 to 1982, as highly productive.

But my principal focus was the establishment of a sociology department at Jagiellonian University.

This initiative originated neither from the sociological circles at the university, nor from its statutory bodies. It can be seen as a typical decision taken by the central-level political autocrats. In 1968, the leadership of the PZPR retaliated against university professors as a form of punishment for the support many of them had shown to the students' protests that came to be known as March 1968. One such restriction was the abolition of university chairs and the organization of the research staff within a broader department structure. Persons who did not support the regime were thus deprived of power.

Obviously, such a revolutionary change provoked generally negative reactions among the professors, as it turned the existing system upside down. However, for sociologists at Jagiellonian University, where there were just two chairs of sociology with a combined staff of 14 persons, the prospect of establishing a department was, without exaggeration, the chance of a lifetime. We made good use of it and in just one decade transformed the Sociology Department into a dynamic research and teaching unit with numerous domestic and international contacts.

This required, of course, overcoming many obstacles, some of which seemed insurmountable at the time. One of our problems was the extreme dearth of office and classroom space. However, after a year of efforts on our part, we were given a new location, 15 times larger in area, and located in one of the most attractive streets in the medieval section of Cracow.

A far more difficult problem to solve was that of the vision for the Department. Few of my younger colleagues remember today that as late as the early 1970s no one would mention Cracow as one of the leading sociological centers in Poland. As Cracovians, we were, of course, proud that such great men of sociology as Ludwik Gumplowicz, Florian Znaniecki and Bronislaw Malinowski had studied at Jagiellonian University. But, in post-war Polish sociology, Cracow did not rank high and there were few signs to indicate that this situation was going to change any time in the near future. And yet it did change, mainly due to two factors.

The first of these was a vision of the Department as a research unit.[25] We specialized in rapid preparation of expert reports for various non-academic institutions. For instance, we did fieldwork for many years for Hydroprojekt, a state-owned enterprise which specialized in designing and building dams. Usually, such projects involved relocation of the local population and Hydroprojekt was on the lookout for a partner who would undertake numerous diagnostic studies to minimize the individual and collective costs of resettlement. We became that partner for many years, gaining experience in our work as experts, and supplementing our meager wages with additional income.

The second crucial factor was providing sufficient intellectual potential for the Department. Many talented young people took up sociological studies in those years, and finding candidates for academic sociologists among them turned out to be less of a problem than one might have expected. Soon the

Department staff exceeded 50 scholars, mainly JU sociology graduates, most of whom we managed to place at some point in domestic or foreign research internships. It was an incredibly gifted generation. Some of those young scholars soon found their place in Polish sociology and attained a position of significant rank and reputation in Poland and abroad.[26] While I do not claim any major impact on their intellectual evolution, I do take pride in protecting many of them from the nightmarish bureaucratic obstacles that often stand in the way of reaching the successive stages of one's academic career.

I was head of the Department until 1978, when I stepped down with a sense of duty well performed. But I felt extremely tired and, moreover, was affected by alcoholism and suffered the breakdown of my second marriage. I dreamed of relaxing and concentrating on my research work. But the opportunity to do so did not last long.

Why I did not quit the Party after martial law

The emergence of Solidarity, after the upheaval of August 1980, radically altered the situation in Poland. The sense of a mounting crisis of the political and economic system in Poland pervaded all sectors of society. The sociological circles talked about this crisis on various occasions from the mid-1970s onwards. Many sociologists were frustrated by the lack of any vision of a way out, as well as the inability to pursue such a vision.

From August 1980 on, events started to unfold with the speed of an avalanche, taking practically everyone by surprise. It was especially the establishment of Solidarity that not only surprised but also excited people. It became a social movement which won massive support among city dwellers and industrial workers, as well as the rural sectors of the population. As a sociologist, I was particularly impressed by two phenomena. One concerned the mass-scale influx of the intelligentsia, including intellectuals, into a movement with a clearly working-class pedigree. This was all the more baffling as the working class and the intelligentsia had viewed each other with mutual aversion, if not hostility, since the turn of the nineteenth century.

The other had to do with the earlier reluctance of the farming population, still very numerous in those days, to join workers' Solidarity. Diverse segments of the village-dwelling population, differing in their class composition, were eager to establish their own organizational structures under various names. Nevertheless, all of them contained the word "solidarity."

In the preceding years, defections from the Party had been relatively rare. They became more noticeable after August 1980, especially among the working class and the intellectuals. A true eruption of this phenomenon occurred after the declaration of martial law on December 13, 1981. I do not know the exact number, but is seems to me that Party membership at Jagiellonian dwindled by two-thirds.

It was clear to me that Solidarity, as a rapidly expanding social movement, was unable to work out a well-defined political and socio-economic program.

At the same time I shared the views of those who believed that the policy of the Party towards Solidarity, which for obvious reasons provoked militant attitudes, should refrain from using force and coercion. I supported dialogue and a political solution to the controversy, a view which I expressed in a brief newspaper comment.[27] I realized, however, how little room for manoeuvre General Wojciech Jaruzelski and his people had in the existing internal and international situation.[28]

I was alarmed by the increasingly radical attitudes of Solidarity's working-class rank and file, as well as its governing bodies at various levels, which would necessitate drastic moves on the part of the government and the Party apparatus. I was deeply convinced of an impending armed Soviet intervention, a prospect that I viewed with horror. I likewise believed in the likelihood of a *coup d'état* in Poland and a takeover, as had happened in Czechoslovakia in 1968, by pro-Soviet Party diehards. In my opinion, mass-scale defections of intellectuals, academics, and artists weakened the democratic elements in the Party, and allowed the Party hardliners to take even more extreme positions. Moreover, I did not want to leave the impression that I had followed the herd instinct to quit the Party. Upon prolonged and deep deliberation, I decided to stay.

As its activities at all levels came to a standstill, the new and baffling situation after martial law threw the Party leadership into confusion. By late spring 1982, it became clear to Party leaders that the days of autocratic rule were over and that it was high time to start a dialogue with the remaining members. This necessitated, in particular, gradual replacement of some segments of the Party apparatus and revival of the Party groups affiliated with the Science and Education Department of the Central Committee. Sociologists finally managed to cut the umbilical cord connecting them to the philosophers, some of whom were pushing at that time for "breaking the bones" of all those who had left the Party. They started a Party group of their own, of which I was appointed a member.

Quite unexpectedly, I held the position of chairman of this group from autumn 1982 until spring 1986. I still take pride in the fact that I never met with rejection by the sociological circles as I acted in this capacity. I followed the precept that political interference with the world of science, which I had so often experienced, should be avoided at all costs. Since several other persons on the group's executive committee shared a similar way of thinking, I managed to enlist their decisive help in pushing some decisions, favorable to the sociological community, through the Science and Education Department of the Central Committee. Vital assistance in this respect was provided by the then head of the Department, the late Professor Boguslaw Kedzia, a physical chemist. These decisions concerned a broad spectrum of affairs, including the lifting of the ban on professorial nomination for several colleagues of ours, eminent scholars who had been punished for their open support for Solidarity; approval for the opening of habilitation proceedings by several promising sociologists who had been active Solidarity members; acceptance for the launching of sociological studies in Wroclaw and Torun, two university centers until then deprived of this possibility; and, finally, permission from the Science and Education Department to hold a Sociological Congress in Wroclaw, in 1986.

Ironically, the idea of the Sociological Congress was opposed both by apparatchiks from the Science and Education Department as well as by some members of the Polish Sociological Association. Among the supporters of the idea of the Congress were the Association's president, Janusz Ziolkowski, and an influential executive board member, Andrzej Tymowski. They took it upon themselves to convince the Board of the Association, and I was to persuade the Science and Education Department. Through our joint efforts, the Congress came to pass.

In mid-1986 the term of office of the governing bodies of the Polish Academy of Sciences (PAN) expired. In accordance with the usual procedure, the Academy's committees and their executive bodies were to be appointed, upon informal consultations with the Science and Education Department of the Central Committee, by the PAN Presidium. The Sociologists' Party Group faced the task of negotiating the makeup of the PAN Committee for Sociological Sciences (today's PAN Committee on Sociology) that would satisfy all of the important circles in Polish sociology, including the Warsaw milieu, composed of highly varied strands. I was then offered the position of chairman of this committee, which I readily accepted, as it allowed me to withdraw from political activity, of which I was becoming increasingly tired. However, I announced my decision only upon the acceptance of the position of deputy chairman by Professor Jerzy Szacki. I viewed his appointment as legitimizing my presence on the Committee, which I felt was needed, having been designated to my post by the Party.

My activities on the Committee for Sociological Sciences were demanding, yet free from significant political overtones. Incidentally, the only Party-organized forum in which I participated after the summer of 1987 was the Committee on the Modernization of the Political and Economic System, affiliated with the Secretariat of the Central Committee of the PZPR and chaired by the secretary of the Central Committee, Kazimierz Cypryniak. This was one of the most interesting bodies within the Party structures in which I ever took part.

As chairman of the PAN Committee for Sociological Sciences, I had to deal with the essential task of finding a formula to integrate the Committee, whose composition was quite diverse. I then hit upon the idea of compiling, under the auspices of the Committee, the first Polish sociological macropaedia. After debate, both within the Committee and within the Polish sociological community at large, and along with the participation of some of our colleagues working abroad, the idea met with support. However, my proposal to appoint Jerzy Szacki or Piotr Sztompka as head of the *Encyclopedia of Sociology* editorial board was turned down by both candidates. Instead, they put forward my name as a candidate for this function and I ended up taking charge, in 1992, of the editorial board of the Encyclopaedia. Four volumes have appeared in print to date.[29]

The Round Table talks in spring 1989 (their 15th anniversary this year was given low-key media coverage), and the resulting partially free election of June 4, 1989, were a fascinating experience for me.[30] I had never believed that leaving the Soviet sphere of influence and hence the departure from socialism would take place without bloodshed.

The autumn of life

After June 1989 I totally backed away from politics, devoting my time to research. On October 1, 1996, I retired and was presented on that occasion with an impressive *Festschrift* by my friends and collaborators. As it happened, however, retirement did not prove a turning point in my life. I still teach, if only in programs for external students, and hold a full-time post at the Faculty of Social Science and Pedagogy in Katowice, which is affiliated with the TWP Teachers' Training College in Warsaw. I also work under a part-time contract at the Sociology Department at Jagiellonian. Thus, I do not have to scratch a living on my pension alone.

I still take active part in academic life, although exclusively in its domestic dimension. Work on the last volumes of the *Encyclopaedia of Sociology*, the supplement and the indices, has just come to an end. There is no denying that the ability to continue, at least to some extent, my hitherto teaching and research activities is a source of real pleasure for me. This is not to say I am free from the feelings of sadness and sometimes profound concern. I am especially worried about some consequences of the scientific and technological revolution, the progressive fall in demand for human labor and the dissolution of many social bonds which sociological theory has hitherto viewed as inalienable. Add to this the international conflicts, whose scope and scale is beyond me, and the outlook for the twenty-first century appears very interesting, but also highly menacing.

To make matters worse, the future is becoming ever harder to predict. Sociology's inability to create visions of even the nearest future is, in my opinion, the surest sign of its epistemological crisis. I agree with those who say that changes in the social environment, on both the domestic and international scale, have gathered such a great momentum that the social sciences fail to grasp and to explain them. In this sense they are becoming anachronistic and lose importance as a foundation for social diagnoses and forecasts. This greatly affects the utilitarian value of sociological knowledge. It also seems to me that sociology has been increasingly losing its charm and does not attract as much talent as before.[31]

Notes

1 Most of the members of this AK (Home Army), which was anti-Communist, were tracked down by the secret service.

2 *Docent* is the equivalent of an associate professor in the American university system.

The habilitation procedure opens the way to the degree of habilitated doctor, ranking higher than the doctorate. It is a prerequisite for all those who seek a professor's title. In socialist Poland, a person with a *habilitation* was typically automatically granted the title of *docent*, allowing the holder to seek a professorship.

3 *Sanacja* was the popular name given to the largely autocratic political system in pre-1939 Poland, introduced by Jozef Pilsudski and his political heirs after the coup of 1926.

4 For more information, see Wieslaw Bienkowski and Wladyslaw Kwasniewicz, eds, *Kazimierz Dobrowolski czlowiek i uczony: Praca zbiorowa w stulecie urodzin* (Krakow: Jagiellonian Press, 1994).

5 Pitirim Sorokin, *Teorie socjologiczne XIX i XX w*, translated by Wladyslaw Kwasniewicz (Krakow: Kolo Socjologiczne i Etnologiczne Studentow UJ, 1947). The translation was from an abridged German edition of the work.

6 In December 1948, in the course of the consolidation of the youth movement in Poland, the PPR merged with the Polish Socialist Party (PPS), forming the Polish United Workers' Party (PZPR). Reportedly, the initials "rkm" were used by the then editor-in-chief of *Kuznica*, Stefan Zolkiewski.

7 In the summer of 1948, the AZWM was transformed, in the course of the "consolidation of the youth movement in Poland," into a new organization, the Academic Association of Polish Youth (ZAMP).

8 The Uprising, fought under the command of the headquarters of the underground Home Army (AK), broke out on August 1, 1944, and held out until October 2, 1944. Intended as a manifestation of the sovereignty of Poland in the face of the approaching Soviet Army, it remains to this day one of the most fervently discussed issues in Poland's modern history.

9 The Yalta Conference, attended by the leaders of the United States of America, Great Britain and the Soviet Union, was held from February 4–11, 1945. One of the items on its agenda was the decision to assign Poland to the Soviet sphere of influence.

10 Nowa Huta, an economic and industrial development project undertaken to the east of Cracow in 1949, was one of the largest in the history of the Polish steel industry. Its builders were primarily from the rural areas.

11 It should be borne in mind that back in the 1950s serfdom was still a living tradition, especially in the parts of Poland formerly occupied by Russia, where serfdom was only abolished in 1864.

12 As late as the third quarter of the nineteenth century the merchants of Swiatniki would carry their wares as far as Austria, Hungary, the Balkans, and even the Near East, on horse-drawn wagons. The development of railways put an end to this kind of itinerant trade, which was typical of the feudal period.

13 Wladyslaw Kwasniewicz, *Wiejska spolecznosc rzemieslnicza w procesie przemian: Studium socjologiczne wsi Swiatniki Gorne pow. Krakowskiego* (Warsawa i Krakow: Prace Komisji Socjologicznej Oddzialu PAN w Krakowie, 1970).

14 Wladyslaw Kwasniewicz, *Przemiany spoleczne mlodziezy akademickiej Uniwersytetu Jagiellonskiego w dwudziestoleciu Polski Ludowej* (Krakow: Zeszyty Naukowe UJ, Prace Historyczne, 1968).

15 Wladyslaw Kwasniewicz, "Sociological Dilemmas of the Intelligentsia: The Case of Poland," *The Polish Sociological Bulletin* 3 (1991): 169–193.

16 Wladyslaw Kwasniewicz, "Makrostrukturalne aspekty kryzysu lat osiemdziesiatych," *Studia Socjologiczne* 4 (1983): 31–51, and "Problems of Polish Applied Sociology," *The Polish Sociological Bulletin* 1–4 (1985): 59–72.

17 Wladyslaw Kwasniewicz, "Procesy zywiolowe," pp. 209–215 in *Encyklopedia socjologii*, Vol. 3 (Warszawa: Oficyna Naukowa, 2000).

18 Wladyslaw Kwasniewicz, "Between the Universal and the Native: The Case of Polish Sociology," pp. 165–187 in *Sociology in Europe: In Search of Identity*, eds Brigitta

Nedelmann and Piotr Sztompka (New York: de Gruyter, 1993, and "Dialectics of Systemic Constraint and Academic Freedom: Polish Sociology under Socialist Regime," pp. 24–38 in *Eastern Europe in Transformation: The Impact on Sociology*, edited by Mike F. Keen and Janusz L. Mucha (Westport, Conn.: Greenwood, 1994).

19 This presentation of Dobrowolski's approach to sociology is based on a compilation of his published statements and his views expressed in seminars and classes. Though an eclectic construct, it was not without some original elements.

20 To be sure, students and younger staff members made efforts to change that state of affairs, but without success. One of the episodes of the history of Jagiellonian in the twentieth century was the so-called *Zimmermanniade*, a vehement and massive protest by the student community toward the end of 1910. The protest was against Dr Kazimierz Zimmermann, a priest from Poznan, newly appointed to the Chair of Christian Sociology, contrary to the expectations of the students. The scale of the protest was attested to by the fact that the police were summoned to intervene at the university, and some 200 students were fired afterwards.

21 The issue of the autonomy of the rectors calls for a detailed analysis. Some non-partisan rectors quit their posts in protest against the interference of the authorities with the university's affairs. Others managed to get along with the authorities, working out compromises acceptable to the academic community.

22 The term "People's Poland" was frequently used as an abbreviated form of the formal name the "People's Republic of Poland," which was introduced by the new constitution that was adopted in 1952.

23 See Wladyslaw Kwasniewicz, "Between a Post-feudal and Post-industrial Model: Polish Society in the 20th Century," *Polish Sociological Review* 4, 144 (2003): 387–397.

24 I was a member of the 600th Anniversary Committee as a representative of research assistants. Within the Committee, I was assigned to its publicity section. I was surprised that the governing bodies of the University took notice of me and entrusted me with such important responsibilities, although I was only a junior faculty member.

25 I would like to stress at this point the frequently overlooked fact that the organization of science in post-war Poland did not simply replicate the Soviet model. The universities retained, in addition to their teaching role, the research functions they had performed before 1939. This facilitated the training of academic staff oriented towards both teaching and research. Unlike in the Soviet Union, Polish universities had eminent scholars on the staff. In many disciplines it was the universities, as opposed to specialized state institutions, such as the Polish Academy of Sciences, which did the bulk of empirical research in many areas.

26 Among the Department's members, mention is due at least to the following: Grzegorz Babinski, Andrzej Flis, Mariola Flis, Krzysztof Frysztacki, Tomasz Goban-Klas, Krzysztof Gorlach, Jan Jerschina, Lucjan Kocik, Hieronim Kubiak, Janusz Mucha, Marian Niezgoda, Andrzej K. Paluch, Grazyna Skąpska, Krystyna Slany, Jerzy B. Sobczak, the prematurely deceased Jacek Szmatka, Piotr Sztompka, and Jacek Wasilewski.

27 Wladyslaw Kwasniewicz, "Moim zdaniem," *Zycie Warszawy*, No. 281 (1988): 3–4 grudnia 1.

28 Jaruzelski was the head of the military group that declared martial law. Formally, he served as the first secretary of the Communist Party (PZPR), minister of defense, prime minister, and president of the State Council.

29 Wladyslaw Kwasniewicz *et al.* eds, *Encyklopedia socjologii* Vol. 1, 1996; Vol. 2, 1999; Vol. 3, 2000; Vol. 4, 2003; in print: Vol. 5 (Supplement); Vol. 6 (Indices) (Warszawa: Oficyna Naukowa).

30 The Round Table talks were official talks between the governing bodies of the Communist Party on the one hand, and the opposition leaders of the then illegal *Solidarity*. The talks ended with the decision to run the first semi-free parliamentary

elections in Poland after World War II. They were semi-free in the sense that the entire senate, a new institution in the Polish post-war political system, was to be elected completely freely. Only one third of the *Sejm*, which is the other chamber and has most of the real authority, was to be elected freely. The result was that 99 out of 100 seats in the senate and all the freely elected seats in the *Sejm* went to *Solidarity*, and the first non-Communist cabinet took over.

31 This chapter was completed on July 15, 2004. Sadly, Professor Kwasniewicz died on August 16 of that year.

4 From totality to pluralistic democracy

A sociologist and sociology in the course of social change in Slovakia

Ladislav Machacek

Discovering sociology

If I want to talk about my life course over the last 60 years, I must first go back 60 years before my birth. Only now do I realize how deeply my present is engrained in the past, of my parents, and even of my grandparents. Everything started in Austro-Hungary, continued in Czechoslovakia (1918–39), then the Slovak Republic (1939–45), the once-again cobbled together Czechoslovakia (1945–93), and finally the current Slovak Republic, which was incorporated into the European Union in 2004.

I was born in 1942 in the small town of Nove Mesto nad Vahom. My older brother, Miroslav, was born in 1939. My father Jakub (1912–66), met my mother Hermina (born in 1918) during his military service in my hometown. My grandfather, Rudolf Kasík (1889–1946), was born a Czech. His town, Plzen, was in the Czech part of the then Austria-Hungarian Empire. As an official expert, he came to Slovakia in 1914. He was a foreman in a factory making rakes and shovels. My brother and I were born in the Slovak Republic, which was created as a result of the division of Czechoslovakia when Hitler's Germany occupied the Czech territory.

This situation had two important implications. First, as a Czech who had moved in before the creation of Czechoslovakia in 1918, my grandfather did not have to leave with other Czechs in 1939 to the German protectorate Bohmen und Mahren (Czech and Moravian Lands). The Slovak Republic had a clergy-fascist-national government with a Roman Catholic priest, Jozef Tiso, as president. There was a strict nationalistic politics with a rude slogan "Cesi pesi do Prahy" (Czechs, walk to Prague).

Second, my father, who worked during these times for the military arsenal and supply depot of the Slovak army, participated with my mother in the anti-Nazi resistance, mainly during the years of 1944 and 1945. After the war was over, they both entered the Communist Party and both experienced significant professional advancement. My father went to college, and from being a mechanic became a technician for work safety. My mother, initially a tailor, finished a pedagogical college course and became a teacher at an elementary school. My brother continued in my grandfather's footsteps, as a mechanic, and even worked with my father in a factory in our hometown making soap and Palma vegetable oil. After the Communists took over in 1948, these were typical careers for young people from working-class families that did not have intellectual traditions. I finished a gymnasium (the best secondary school), and successfully applied to the university.

I pursued my university studies from 1959 to 1964 in the Faculty of Arts at Commenius University (FFUK) in Bratislava. While there, I majored in philosophy and history. The times were socially determined by the beginning of the revival forces of the reformist Communists and their cultural and political struggle to overcome the "personality cult" of the Stalinist period. Public life was literally overwhelmed by a number of sensitive questions from the recent past, and experts were making the best efforts they could to find answers to them.

The social climate for young people who were entering the world of work was welcoming and friendly. I am not hesitant to say that people were living fuller and happier lives. Many taboos of lifestyle were being broken. Boys' haircuts and the width of their trousers were changing, there were newly popular fashions such as blue jeans, music such as traditional jazz and the Beatles, and waves of drama such as micro theater. These new elements in the lifestyle of the younger generation were gradually developing into a form of spontaneous generation-based protest against the excessively tight and controlled social life with its mass forms for "manifesting the joy of life" of the working people.[1]

A large number of my university teachers, for example Igor Hrusovsky, Miroslav Kusy, Jiri Suchy, Milan Zigo, Frantisek Vartík, Vojtech Filkorn, Jaroslav Martinka, Jan Bodnar, Theodor Munz, Herta Tkadleckova, Matus Kucera, Viliam Pezlar, and Rudolf Sima, also started to play an important role in Slovak political life. In the realm of culture and ideology, they were starting their political careers on both sides of the Communist barricade, the dogmatic and the reformist.

In the same manner, university life was beginning to pick up new momentum. This especially produced results in the sphere of philosophy. In my graduation year, there were only three graduates, Jan Sefranek, Josef Vicenik, and myself. In 1964, the year I graduated, there were only about 120 graduates from the Faculty of Arts at Commenius University. Nonetheless, reunions, which are regularly held every decade, with the most recent in 2004, show that it was a real community in the sociological sense. It was shaped through joint experiences with university voluntary work assignments, and among young males also by the military training done together. The students of philosophy had, in addition, their own peculiar forms of student life, a subculture that strengthened their professional integrity and the solidarity important for future professional life.[2]

During our studies, we were able to influence our school and after-school life by bringing about a change in the internal structure of the Faculty's official youth organization Zvaz mladeze (Youth Union).[3] We managed to change the original structure of grass-roots organizational units from class-based, which incorporated all the students of a given class regardless of their varied study, to a structure which was based on study fields. As a result, in our case, it incorporated the students of philosophy from all five classes. Thanks to this change, we obtained a club room for our seminars. The club, in which we studied on an informal basis, allowed us to establish a tradition of continuity from one generation of students to the next. It also made contacts with Department of Philosophy teachers easier.

For me, the years of the post-1956 social revival process were also the years of my academic discovery of sociology, first in my seminar papers, then in my own empirical research conducted for the purpose of our diploma theses. Roman Hambalek, as the youngest junior instructor, was giving us guidance on selection of our diploma thesis topics. He advised me that it would be possible to "smuggle" something sociological in if I took a philosophical topic close to the social sciences, and to the so-called historical materialism. It was a great discovery and inspiration for me. I chose to study the ideals of university students. I had already obtained an initial understanding of the methodology of empirical research from consultations with my future colleagues (mainly Martin Katriak) when I was working as a research assistant in the Department of Social Research of the Institute of Philosophy of the Slovak Academy of Sciences (SAS). Persons who decided to tie their scientific and personal careers to this fashionable, yet undoubtedly risky issue (i.e. sociology or sociological research), were gradually entering my world and were influencing my professional and career orientation.

While still a student, through a review of the first publication of an influential group working within the Department of Social Research, I took the first step toward my future profession as a sociologist. Its focus was on the issue of the socialist work brigades and entitled *I tak sad a* (People and Problems).[4] The review was published, in 1964, in a renowned platform of the intelligentsia, *Kulturny zivot* (Cultural Life), a weekly journal for cultural and social life. In this review, I expressed my anger about the fact that almost no attention was being paid by the broader professional public to the first fruits of post-1956 Slovak sociology.

I defended of my diploma thesis, "Idealy vysokoskolskej mladeze" (The Ideals of University Youth) in July of 1964. The best parts of it were published in *Kulturny zivot*, under the journalistically attractive title, "Student Dreams in the Mirror of Statistics." The title was coined by the editor, Viera Mullerova, who became the wife of the president of Czechoslovakia, Gustav Husak, a few years later.

Since the law on assignment was still in place—i.e. mandatory assignment of a university graduate to his/her first workplace (students today cannot even imagine this at all)—my work posed a small problem for the planning authorities. They had to give me a good research job. With this entrance ticket I started my obligatory assignment in 1964, in the emerging sociological department of the Slovak Academy of Sciences where I have been employed until this day. I was the first doctoral student who worked as a scientific research assistant in the Institute. And, in 1968, I became the first postgraduate student in sociology in Slovakia to be awarded the title C.Sc. (Candidate of Sciences), which in contemporary nomenclature would the equivalent of a Ph.D., by the Academy of Sciences.

Institutionalization of sociology

In the late 1960s, the establishment of the new Institute for Sociology of the Slovak Academy of Sciences, and of other sociological institutions, made it possible for students to specialize in this, for us, new field of science. We were able to become authorities in a particular area of sociological theory. It is no exaggeration to say that we could become the founders of Slovak sociology of family, urban sociology, rural sociology, and suchlike. It was simply a miraculous pioneering period.[5] It was the sociology of youth that became my area of interest, and I have remained faithful to this area up to this day.

From the beginning of my study I was also interested in investigating the history of sociological ideas and concepts in the works of older colleagues. To a certain extent, these pioneering times of our sociology are still not, and probably will never be fully supported by memoir sources, and perhaps for this reason they will never be, fully documented. In 1969 I observed that we had had several important scholars, who had raised issues associated with the sociology of youth, i.e., children's health, education, and lifestyles of the youth in Slovakia, who had been active in the period between World War I and World War II, as well as in the post-World War II period.[6]

One of these early scholars, Professor Alojz Chura, was a doctor–pediatrician and the author of a multi-volume research publication *Slovensko bez dorastu* (Slovakia Without Juniors). He was famous for the slogan "medicine without sociology is just a corpse," which he presented on various occasions at scientific conferences. The second scholar of this kind was Professor Juraj Cecetka, a pedagogue-sociologist and author of two works on interpersonal relations, peer groups, and pedagogy.[7] Professor Cecetka was not only a great expert in the field of pedagogical sociology but also an active advocate of a new concept of state youth policy, and one of many candidates for the position of chairman of the State Committee for Youth.

Both of these professors streaked into my field of vision like comets from some remote and unknown solar system. And, to my surprise, they were still living in Slovakia. Although retired, they were writing essays and analyses, only to be placed in the drawers of their writing desks. They were just hoping someone would remember them and invite them to a meeting with students, to a seminar, or ask them for a contribution to a journal or to a collection of articles.

I was lucky enough to meet Professor Chura and to prepare his most recent reflections on the sexuality of youth for publication.[8] I also gave a paper at a conference on the problems of youth in his research pediatric institute in Trencin. Finally, in November 1999, as chairman of the National Slovak

Sociological Society (SSS), which is a member of the International Sociological Association (ISA), I gratefully accepted an invitation by the organizers of a seminar dedicated to the 100th birthday anniversary of Chura to present some recollections of our get-togethers.

In the case of Professor Cecetka, in December 1989, I, along with Professor Josef Psenak, a pedagogue, organized a seminar on Cecetka's legacy for pedagogy and sociology. Subsequently, the Slovak Sociological Society's section on youth established the Juraj Cecetka Award, to be given for the best diploma thesis of the graduates of sociology and pedagogy dealing with the issue of youth. Submissions came from students from several pedagogical and sociological institutes and departments in Presov, Trnava, Bratislava, and Banska Bystrica.[9]

It was only later that I found out that besides myself, other colleagues as well had had some professional or careers problems in the post-1968 period of "normalization" for involvement between 1959 and 1969 with figures such as Chura and Cecetka. Both, for a variety of reasons, had been marginalized and literally erased from the memory of the nation, since they were unacceptable to the Communist regime.

A large number of students from my generation were not so lucky as to have been taught that once there had been sociology or sociography in Slovakia, and that there was a scientific journal named *Sociologicky zbornik* (Sociological Booklet) published regularly. That there is a well-deserved place in Slovak sociology for such personalities as Anton Stefanek, Julius Lajciak, Peter Gula, Ignac Gasparec, etc. It was only later that I learned that a sociological seminar had existed at the Commenius Faculty of Arts in the past. For both personal as well as professional reasons, some of our professors and associate professors concealed their sociological backgrounds, either the fact that they had studied sociology or had worked as assistants in the sociological seminars of Professor Stefanek.

The sociology of the youth was only established as a real and recognized field in the 1960s, along with the general institutionalization of sociology in Slovakia between the years 1964 and 1969.[10] In this period, the Sociological Institute of SAS, the Slovak Sociological Society at SAS, the Department of Sociology at the Faculty of Arts at Commenius University in Bratislava, and the scholarly journal *Sociologia: Slovak Sociological Review*, were all established. Within this framework, research on youth was developed, conferences were held, and the first sociological findings on youth were published.

At that time, the analysis of many areas of social life was the domain of other scientific disciplines, and their already established scholars. Younger as well as older "home-grown" sociologists, entering the scientific path in the area of sociology, had to contend with scholars from other scientific fields, and with their scientific writings.[11] In some cases, sociologists did not encounter a welcoming and supportive approach from influential scholars in well-established scientific fields, especially from those who belonged to the system of Marxism-Leninism and the specific field designated as scientific Communism.

This lack of support was stronger in the pedagogical, psychological, and legal sciences than in the realm of issues regarding the sociology of youth and education. Our relations with other scholars concerned with youth, such as Ondrej Balaz, Josef Kosco, Damian Kovac, Vladislav Kacani, Ondrej Pavlik, Ernest Sykora, and Ladislav Schubert can be characterized as supportive or even friendly. This was a result of the fact that the nature of these sciences was ideologically less affected by the age differences, and also from the fact that our older colleagues, who had more real-life experiences, better understood the risks we were taking without our fully being aware of the danger.

It is necessary to mention that the renaissance of sociology also reintroduced the issue of interdisciplinary co-operation in the research on youth. Basically, there were two issues involved. On the one hand, there was a worry about succumbing to a vaguely defined "pan-sociologism." This reflected a concern not to reduce the explanation of the life expressions of the young solely to social factors. Professor Cecetka accepted the fact that the sociology of youth not only overlapped with the sociology of education but also concerned the full breadth of the life of the young. In his estimation, the tasks of the research on children and the young required a variety of disciplinary perspectives.

On the other hand, there were positive consequences from publishing new empirical findings of sociological research. It is necessary to admit that the opinions and attitudes of pupils, students, citizens, and the representatives of various professions acting in the area of the education of the younger generation had a remarkable, liberating influence on the rigid, dogmatic understanding of the social reality, as well as on the appreciation of interdisciplinary co-operation. This was reflected as well in many monographs by psychologists and lawyers that were published in the same period.[12]

It was not possible to isolate the sociology of youth from the public discourse on the younger generation, which was initiated by writers Peter Karvas, Pavel Buncak, Michal Chorvath, and Rudolf Olsinsky. Joined by sociology-bound philosophers Miroslav Kusy and Jiri Suchy, these writers presented their observations on the pages of Slovak journals and newspapers, i.e., *Kulturny zivot*, *Slovenske pohl'ady* (Slovakian Outlook), *Mlade leta* (Young Years), and *Pravda* (Truth). In the period of the 1960s, the presence of writers as "the bearers of the nation's conscience" was a considerable factor in the development of public opinion. Today, many of them have difficulty coping with the fact that their place has been taken by pop stars and athletes, and particularly in Slovakia by ice-hockey players.

Public disquiet over the non-traditional displays and subculture of youth led to the execution of several empirical research surveys. Today we can look back and recognize that the public suffered from the naive idea that empirical research was a tool that could produce clearly true, final answers—not only to the complicated questions of the relations between the younger and the older generations but also for the development of the whole society.

Contributions to the discourse on youth included publications by foreign authors such as Ernest Fischer, Andreas Flitner, Helmut Schelsky, Samuel N. Eisenstadt, and Gerhardt Wurzbacher, on generational problems, socialization, and personality, some of which some were translated into Slovak or Czech. It is necessary to recognize here our predominant orientation towards Polish sociology. Numerous examples of loyal or even friendly relations were established between the sociologists of Poland and Slovakia in the process of the institutionalization of sociology in Slovakia. The first official scientific meeting of Polish and Czechoslovak sociologists took place in Slovakia, at the House of Scientific Workers of the Slovak Academy of Sciences, in April 1967. The main lecture was given by Professor Jan Szczepanski. The first review of the leading Polish sociological quarterly, *Studia socjologiczne*, was published by Jan Pasiak in *Sociologia: Slovak Sociological Review* in 1970, its second year.

In 1967, as a young C.Sc. candidate at the Sociological Institute of SAS in Bratislava, I had the opportunity to complete a long-term study stay in Warsaw. Professor Jan Szczepanski was not only the director of our partner institute, the Institute of Philosophy and Sociology of the Polish Academy of Sciences (IFiS PAN), but he was also the head of the section on higher education research. Thus, I spent my stay with a group of his collaborators, including Zygmunt and Jadwiga Komorowski, and Miroslawa Jastrab. The results of my work in Poland were subsequently presented in my first scholarly study published in *Sociologia.*[13] In this article I quoted Szczepanski's book *Socjologiczne zagadnienia wyzszego wyksztalcenia* (Sociological Aspects of Higher Education, Warszawa 1963), which also influenced me while looking for topics for my dissertation thesis, "Mladez a skola: tranzicie zo strednej na vysoku skolu" (Youth and School: Youth Transitions to the University), which I completed in 1968.

In an interview with Jan Szczepanski, I encountered some of his characteristically sensitive analysis of the crisis of youth in capitalist and socialist countries, analysis that is applicable even today.[14] At the ISA conference in Madrid in 1990 I was elected to be a board member of the Research Committee on the Sociology of Youth (RC 34), and an editor of the *Informational Bulletin for Youth Research.* It was only then, 20 years after the ISA congress in Varna, Bulgaria in 1970, that I got the chance to contribute to the co-ordination of research in the area, which Szczepanski had called for in his interview. Today, as the discussions of RC 34 at the World Congress in Brisbane in 2002 evidenced, sociological research on youth, and its reflections on the participation of youth in global citizens' movements, are an integral part of the efforts of sociologists to support world democratic governance.

As we know, August 1968 was an important month for the young people of Europe, including Slovakia. The invasion of the allied armies of the Warsaw Pact, and the consequent "normalization" after April 1969, hindered the modernization process for the next 20 years, not only in Slovakia but in all the countries of Central and Eastern Europe. This included development in the areas of youth life, youth organizations, and of state youth policy.

For me, the invasion came as a psychological shock. At the time I was visiting my parents in Nove Mesto nad Vahom, only 150–200 kilometers from the Hungarian border. At first, the radio announcement of the military invasion seemed like Orson Welles' infamous broadcast announcing the invasion of earth by aliens from Mars. I came to accept the reality only later, when I saw the first tanks of the Warsaw Pact, in our case the Hungarian army, blocking the entrance to the military barracks in Nove Mesto nad Vahom. A bunch of town inhabitants taunted the Hungarians and started to throw stones at the tanks. The head of the military school solved this problem when he allowed the tanks into the enclosed area of barracks only through the back gate, and not through the front ceremonial entrance. In so doing he achieved a small victory over the occupiers, though it was a typical "*Svejk*" type of victory.[15]

With the occupation, a large number of sociologists in Slovakia were prosecuted and marginalized. In my case, it started with Communist Party evaluations that were unexpectedly altered to my disadvantage by interventions from higher Party levels. Never had I achieved such a high rating just before I was to fall so low. It continued with criticism on the pages of the official youth daily *Smena*, without giving me any opportunity for publishing a response. In black and white, *Smena* wrote that "Ladislav Machacek is a prominent Slovak sociologist exerting a destructive impact on the youth movement and the youth." However, there were also supportive statements from within the youth movement, intended for the Party evaluation commission, asking for mercy when announcing the final verdict about my professional future.

Finally, a decision was delivered on my punishment. My name was deleted from the list of Party members. This had an impact on various areas of my career, and it involved intermittent waves of loosening and tightening the grip over it during various periods between 1970 and 1989. For example, my articles were denied publication because I was on the list of prohibited authors. An invitation to give lectures at the Faculty of Arts at Commenius University was cancelled by the relevant Party cell. Trips to foreign countries were not allowed. My first trip abroad was not made until 1980, to the Sociological Institute of the Soviet Academy of Sciences in Moscow.

Due to my age in 1968, 26, and the solidarity and support of my colleagues at the Institute, I was allowed to retain my job there. Personally, I have never felt excommunicated from the team of the Institute. There was always friendliness, togetherness, and support throughout the important events of my personal life, as well as in my career. This included when my two daughters, Petra in 1971, and Pavla in 1975, were born, as well as when I was given a pay raise. However, my job contracts were initially only for three-month periods, then for six months, and only after 1985 for the usual period of four years.

The contemporary forms of employment at universities, and particularly at the Slovak Academy of Sciences, served as efficient tools for the CP apparatchiks to keep their political opponents at bay. In a memo, dated July 9, 1971, placed in my personnel records that were kept in the Institute's archive, there was a note that "he started with an extraordinary relentlessness (in the preparation for his Ph.D. in 1968) to plan, organize and execute a demanding research, which, due to an absolute lack of staff assistance at the Institute he had to perform practically on his own, taking all his energy, and subsequently reflected in his decreased public-political activity . . . since the comrade at issue is young and without experience, he has potential, on the condition he will be correctly guided and instructed to become a good professional as well as a useful member of the Party."

I did not have to leave my first mother institute, which took over a certain amount of responsibility for my activities. At the same time, I could not leave that place because I had no other place to go. Nevertheless, due to my status as an "unreliable" worker, I did not have any internal institutional assignments or positions. However, I was gradually given certain important extra-institutional activities with an appropriate "tutor" who had an excellent Party reputation and was trusted by the higher-ranking Party leaders. In 1972 I was appointed the head of the section on youth within the Slovak Sociological Society, and the executive editor of the journal *Sociologia*. At the time, the editor-in-charge was Jozef Hrabina.

Founded in 1969, *Sociologia* originated as the fourth of the institutional pillars of the developing sociological science, after the Department of Sociology at Commenius University, the Sociological Institute of the Academy, and the Slovak Sociological Society. Prior to its creation, and after 1964, it had been possible for Slovak sociologists to publish in the Czechoslovak *Sociologicky casopis*. The first editor-in-charge of *Sociologia* was Andrej Siracky, and he remained in that position until 1973. In 1970, the executive editor was Karol Minarik, Teodor Ollik in 1972, and then I was given the post and held it until 1995. In 1973, Harbina was made editor-in-charge, followed by Vlastislav Bauch in 1978. When Robert Rosko became the deputy editor-in-charge for sociological issues in 1978, there was a fundamental reversal in the theoretical perspective of the Board of Editors and its approach to new social topics and young authors. This reversal reflected the process of emancipation of sociology from "scientific Communism."

Though at the time no one could know exactly what was to occur in the years following 1989, there was a clear anticipation of things to come in the twentieth volume of *Sociologia*. In it is an outline for the reconstruction of sociology, elaborated under the leadership of Rosko. It is also noted that on June 14, 1989, the Board of Editors had approved a recommendation to the publisher, the Institute for Philosophy and Sociology of the Slovak Academy of Sciences, that the journal should be more clearly shaped as a vehicle for the theory, history and methodology of sociology. The editors also published a Declaration of the Chairman's Committee of the Slovak Sociological Society, dated November 26, 1989, which unequivocally welcomed the breaking events in the development of Czecho-Slovak society. In 1991, Jan Pasiak became the editor-in-charge, and I picked up the baton from him in 1995, after 25 years as its executive editor. In 1995 our efforts in the transformation of *Sociologia*, as reflected in our new statement of purpose published in Volume 3 of that year, were completed and recognized with the successful registration as one of the journals covered by the Philadelphia-based Institute for Scientific Information.

Since its creation, the Slovak Sociological Society, which is now a member of the International Sociological Association, has played an important role in the development of the institutional structure for research of Slovak sociology.

This was particularly important because of its relatively small size and few major institutions. With the exception of one department of sociology at the University of Commenius in Bratislava, and one institute of sociology, the Institute for Sociology of the SAS in Bratislava, almost all other research was carried out in small subdepartments of sociology or by individual sociologists working in non-sociological research units. The sociological association served the very important function of bringing together all of these individuals and small groups, and also allowed them to use its name and logo for their activities.

In the tumultuous years of 1988 to 1990, this professional association of sociologists played a role as a real agent of social change in Slovakia. The top-ranking authorities of the then Communist establishment were considering, after having obtained confidential information on our preparations in the year 1989, the possibility of banning the Second Congress of Slovak sociologists. Along with Rosko, who was the thematic designer of the sociological congress, I was an experienced organizer who was very well aware of what was at issue in Czechoslovak society and in the sociological community. Approximately 12 months before, in November 1989, there was a successful struggle underway within the sociological community to establish an internal democratic process, to rehabilitate those scholars who had led the revival process in 1968 and 1969, and for liberation from the oppression of Party regulation of everything. Similar struggles over political power and against the weakening Communist political structures were occurring throughout the broader society.

The meeting in 1989, at Matica Slovenska in the city of Martin, was an indicator that the position of sociology and its new opportunities within a pluralistic democracy would be much different from those of the past. The political plurality, and even the plurality within the Party, was differentiating the sociological community to such an extent that it was no longer possible to establish a consensus even in purely methodological professional issues.

In a report for the General Assembly of the Slovak Sociological Society, and as its chairman from 1998 to 1999, I reminded the audience that it was no accident that since its beginning the Slovak Sociological Society had been performing the role of a defense mechanism against the undermining of the discipline brought about by a variety of amateurish sociological surveys. I also suggested there were newly arising threats connected with a tendency to privatize sociology by various privately owned agencies. In this period, characterized in 2002 by the General Assembly of the ISA in Brisbane as a situation of general emergency for national sociological associations, we managed to organize several events that showed that sociological societies can play an important role, not only for their own community, but also for a broader professional public.[16]

Not only were scientific society and the scientific journal changing, but so was my workplace at the Sociological Institute. After 1989 there were collapses and important changes occurring among the research programs of the sociological research organizations. For the Sociological Institute of SAS, this meant the end of the traditional research on social and class structure, and re-orientation or, more accurately, a discovery of the issues of citizenship, civil society, and citizens' movements and initiatives, along with the creation of a new research program for them in the Institute. Many colleagues took this challenge as an opportunity to search for a new framework for sociological research. There were fierce discussions conducted within the Institute and throughout the entire sociological community.

At the meetings of the Second Sociological Congress in Martin, in 1989, Slovak sociologists predicted that the realm of civil society would be an important area of transformation of Slovak society, and this became the framework for our research group at the Institute. More intensive contacts with young sociologists, such as Claire Wallace, who had a classical sociological education and detailed knowledge of T.H. Marshall's theory, only confirmed us in this strategy. For a couple of years they were supporting us in person. The person appointed head of our research group was Jan Stena. After a brief hesitation, Ol'ga Plavkova, Monika Cambalikova, L'udovit Turcan, Bohus Buzik, Jan Sopoci and myself were joined by Robert Rosko, as he originally wanted to continue to concentrate on his traditional topic of social structure. It turned out that the concepts of civil society and citizenship were inventive and progressive. Our project established itself in sociology as one of the strategic research projects important for understanding the modernization of Slovakia, for explaining the troubles of the development of Slovak society after 1989, and for explaining the role of non-Party subjects of the civil society in its democratic development after 1993.

For me personally it was especially a problem of how to incorporate the issues of youth into a broader, socially relevant sociological framework. All of the sociological research on youth in the years 1964 to 1989 had been conducted within the framework of social structure. It reflected the idea that the young constituted a specific social demographic group, was made up of a clearly delineated age group (15 to 26 years), and reproduced the social structure in terms of the given social system. The conceptual framework of civil society was drawing the attention of research on the young only to that part of the younger generation that was able to present itself as an attractive component participating in various social, charitable, and aggressive ecological or anti-globalist citizens' movements and initiatives. That was also the reason that the most intensive attention was given to the issue of citizens' associations of youth, to the varied forms of citizens' participation among the young, and to the issue of its formal and non-formal education towards European citizenship.[17]

Even though the research team was gradually weakened by departures of internal and external collaborators, it was the most important research program in Slovak sociology until the year 2002. My task, as the head of research grants for two grant periods, was to inspire the team members to perform more integrated research on the topics so that we could not only present our findings through separate studies and collections of works but also through solid monographs. This was achieved especially in Rosko's work *Slovensko na konci tisicrocia* (Slovakia at the End of the Millennium).[18]

Today, the Sociological Institute of the SAS is not the most important sociological enterprise in Slovakia, but just one of many. This is a result of the fact that its scientific prestige was deeply shattered by the loss of independent accreditation for doctoral studies. This loss cannot be explained solely by the competition between SAS and the universities in Slovakia. Currently, there are many gifted graduates, from sociology, political science, social geography, demography, journalism, etc., who are in "the market" for doctoral studies and who are looking for opportunities to complete their education within a Ph.D. program in sociology. It is a great opportunity for members of the young generation of experts to obtain the specific expert profile of a sociologist, available only in a scientific academy such as the SAS.

The prestige of the Institute of Sociology of the SAS also declined as a result of not having a specific sociological publication that could serve as its representative in Slovakia. If you ask an expert from other fields of science within the Academy, or would like to recommend to students a truly sociological publication that would reflect the specific nature of this scientific discipline, you will find out that only fragmented works are available for this purpose, monographs and studies that are getting lost in the chaos of information. As a scholar who was there when the Sociological Institute of the SAS was first emerging in 1964, I have been interested in the best possible development of the Institute. I have demonstrated this interest by twice submitting my application, in 1998 and 2002, for the position of director of the Institute. Even though I failed to get the post, it was an opportunity for me to present to my coworkers my generation's message, as well as my vision for the future of a sociological institute specializing in basic research.

A sociologist's career as a pedagogue

At present, in addition to being employed by the Academy and being the editor-in-chief of *Sociologia*, I am a professor in the Faculty of Arts at the University of St Cyrillus and Methodius (FF UCM) in Trnava. It is one of the small public universities that have been established in the regional centers of Slovakia since 1989. As an expert in the field of the sociology of youth, and of the theory of education towards European citizenship, I was habilitated as an associate professor in 1997, and then received the state title of full professor from the president of Slovakia in 2002.[19]

In 1998 I became a teacher in the Department of Politology (Political Sciences), and later on in the Department of Pedagogy at FF UCM. In 2001 I established an MA program for teachers' education at the Faculty of Arts of FF UCM in Trnava. This change of my career direction toward the pedagogical sciences was due to the fact that sociologists from various universities and research institutes were not allowed, even after 1989, to get a habilitation and to receive a professorship in sociology without the permission of their home department of sociology, in my case Commenius University. However, Commenius had issued a decree that it was only possible to get the habilitation, and thereby receive approval for the application for the title of professor, for their own employees. It should also be mentioned that within this system, the

Academy's institutes, being research and not teaching institutions, could grant the Ph.D., but not the more advanced university degrees and titles. This decree was unprecedented. Because it had an impact across the disciplines, it received criticism from across the entire professional public. And, because of its past, sociology was hardest hit. For many years, under the influence of the Communist Party, there was a complete ban on sociology courses at Commenius University. And, because of the competition between old and new universities, after 1993, entire cohorts of sociology graduates from FF UK encountered career obstacles when trying to get the habilitation and the professorial title. As a result, the sociological sciences are literally fading. There is only one full professor, Juraj Schenk, and a few associate professors (docents) of sociology who are employed with a single university, i.e., Commenius University in Bratislava.

As I have mentioned above, being a graduate of philosophy and history from FF UK, and a C.Sc. from the Sociological Institute of SAS, I started my pedagogical career in the Department of Politology and at the Department of Pedagogy in FF UCM in Trnava in 2002. I give lectures in demography and the sociology of youth for the students of political science, and in the sociology of youth, state policy and youth in the EU, issues of civil society in Slovakia, and the theory of education and methodology of empirical research for future secondary school teachers. In 2001, I founded the Center for European and Regional Youth Studies, a research institution in which international research projects of the European Commission (on the political participation of youth, and the youth and European identity), as well as inter-regional projects on the youth of Slovakia, the Czech Republic, and Austria are being carried out.

I made the move to teaching in Trnava because, as an associate professor, after 1997, I did not have the opportunity in my research institute at the Academy to share my special knowledge and qualification. I took advantage of the offer to give lectures on the sociology of youth and education for citizenship to students of political science at UCM in Trnava. Finally, after 30 years of research work, and being restricted from teaching in the universities since 1970, I had the possibility to communicate with university students. At my age what is the most important is not to produce my own research reports but to direct students and to teach them to work in a scholarly way.

Of course, it also has meant a second source of income. Average salaries in Slovakia for the years 2000 to 2004 were 250 euros a month. They are the lowest among post-Communist countries such as Poland, Czechia and Hungary. An associate professor can earn approximately 400 euros, and a full professor approximately 500 euros. Since I live in Bratislava I have to travel to Trnava every week, which is about 40 kilometers away. It takes a toll on my finances, my time, and my health. With good health, I can continue these two professional activities until I am 65. I will reach this age in 2007. In Slovakia, 65 is the official retirement age for all professors and docents in BA or MA programs at the universities. Once I reach this age, my responsibility to the students of history and philosophy, Slovak, English, German, French and Russian language and literature, who are preparing for teaching jobs and wish to receive MA degrees, will end.

Conclusion

My life's course and professional career have been largely determined by factors beyond my own control. I was forced to do a lot of things because the situation demanded it. In the process I have learned that, even so, it did not have a catastrophic impact on me. Sometimes it was just the opposite. On the other hand, one of the most disappointing and devastating impacts came from being banned from teaching after the year 1970, in order that I would not "corrupt the youth." I sorely missed the contact with new students of sociology that the position of teacher offered. After 1989 and the Velvet Revolution, I finally earned this opportunity. Now a professor for several years, I have once again had the opportunity to meet with members of the younger generation that must cope with the challenges of globalization, information technology, and the development of a legislative state, parliamentary democracy, and political pluralism in our country. Before them lies the challenge and responsibility for the problems of their own lives.

My instructional activities at the university also have been related to my duties as president of the academic senate. Four of the 11 members of the senate are students. In carrying out these duties, I have found that the best students are primarily concerned with making their own careers, and do not have much interest in political or civil participation. I remember what kind of power we used to exert, when we managed at our Faculty in the years 1961 to 1964 to change the structure of our youth organization. It has inspired me nowadays to help students to overcome not only the psychological barriers of communication with university functionaries but also to show them how it is possible to articulate and legitimize the social and cultural interests of all students of the university before the academic senate.[20] Young people, whom I related to for about 40 years only as the objects of research, have become for me living personalities with their own individual faces and temperaments.

Notes

1 These included mass parades in public places on occasions such as May Day, and May 9, the date of liberation of the country from Fascism, as well as ritual celebrations in workplaces on occasions such as International Women's Day, March 8.

2 Activities contributing to this special sense of community among the philosophy students included lively inaugurations of freshmen, informal club sessions with the class tutor Jaroslav Martinka, and peripatetic lectures with the doyen of philosophy, Igor Hrusovsky, in the municipal park on the bank of the Danube River.

3 In Czechoslovakia, after the 1948 "unification" was completed, a large number of civil, social, and political associations of youth—i.e., scouts, ecologists, political organizations, young people living in villages or the countryside—were brought together in one super association, under the umbrella of the Zvaz mladeze, later renamed the "Socialist Youth Union." It was organizationally and ideologically

similar to the Communist Party of Slovakia. It was under the Party's control and functioned as a reservoir of future members of the Party. This process of unification followed the model of the Soviet Union, where such a function was played by the Komsomol, "Kom" standing for *Komunisticeskij* (Communist), "so" for *sojuz* (union), and "mol" for *molodez* (youth).

4 The brigades were teams of workers in the factories or enterprises during the socialist period. They were quite successful in completing their work plans and there were friendly relationships among the individuals of the teams. In the best case, members had the opportunity to receive a Socialist Work Brigade Diploma.

5 See Jan Pasiak and Ladislav Machacek, "Sociology in Slovakia: Fiction or Reality," pp. 89–99 in *Eastern Europe in Transformation: The Impact on Sociology*, eds Mike F. Keen and Janusz L. Mucha (Westport, Conn.: Greenwood Press, 1994).

6 See Ladislav Machacek, "Situacia sociologie mladeze a vychovy na Slovensku," pp. 7–10 in *Sociologia mladeze '69: Situacia sociologie mladeze a vychovy na Slovensku* (Bratislava: Smena, 1969).

7 See Juraj Cecetka, *Medzil'udske vzt'ahy a rovesnicke skupiny* (Bratislava: SPN, 1965); and *Sociologia v pedagogike* (Bratislava: SPN, 1965).

8 Alojz Chura, "Sexualita mladeze," pp. 39–52 in *Sociologia mladeze '70* (Bratislava: Smena, 1970).

9 Unfortunately, there was a shattering discovery that none of Cecetka's work, particularly those published in the years 1960 to 1970, were quoted by any of the candidates for the award. Of course, this was not the only instance of such an occurrence. At present, students generally work with the literature published after 1989. This indicates a need to update the professional legacy of these and other such authors. Only recently, I compiled such anthology of Jiri Suchy's work in the sociology of youth and education. See Juraj Suchy, *Generacny problem ako spolocny problem generacii* (Bratislava: Slovak Sociological Association Youth Section, 2003).

10 See Marcel Sloboda, "Niektore aspekty delikvencie ako spolocenskeho problemu," pp. 91–99 in *Sociologia mladeze '69* (Bratislava: Smena, 1969).

11 By "home grown" I am referring to the reality that the new role and identity of the sociologist was initially taken up by scholars who had been originally educated and worked as lawyers, economists, demographers, and statisticians and who became sociologists through on-the-job training at sociological institutions where they obtained positions.

12 For example, Anton Jurovsky, *Kulturny vyvin mladeze* (Bratislava: SPN, 1965); and Ladislav Schubert, *Problemy s kriminalitou mladeze* (Bratislava: SAV, 1967).

13 Ladislav Machacek, "K funkcii skoly v akulturacnom procese," *Sociologia* 2–3 (1969): 182–195.

14 Ladislav Machacek, "Rozhovor s profesorom Janom Szczepanskim," in *Sociologia mladeze '70* (Bratislava: Smena, 1970).

15 Czech author Jaroslav Hasek's stories of the good soldier Svejk in World War I are well known in Europe. They show the humor which arises from the confrontation between the insignificant soldier and the overwhelming repressive system and hidden policies of the Austrian-Hungarian Empire. Its message is that people living in authoritarian and totalitarian regimes should act in such a way in order to survive, yet with some measure of resistance to power. Our casern commander had to let the tanks into their military objective. The "*Svejk*" victory is that he didn't let them march victoriously through the front ceremonial gate, allowing entry by the back gate only.

16 In 1999, with the support of the Friedrich Ebert Stiftung, a German foundation operating in Bratislava, I organized the first international meeting of Slovak and Czech sociologists to occur after the split of Czechoslovakia. In 1998, we had also organized a press conference, in the House of Journalists, on election surveys and the course and results of parliamentary elections in that year.

17 This is confirmed by my work *Obcianska participacia a mladez* (Bratislava: Sociologicky ustav SAV, 1996); and *Kapitoly zo sociologie mladeze* (Trnava: UCM, 2002), as well as several articles published between 1992 and 2002 in *Sociologia*.

18 Robert Rosko, *Slovensko na konci tisicrocia* (Bratislava: Veda, 2000).

19 According to the law of the Slovak Republic, the rectors of the universities have authority over the appointments to the rank of lecturer, and assistant and associate professor. However, only the president of the Republic can confer promotion to the rank of professor. Unlike the case of the USA, the president of Slovakia is not the chief executive officer of the government, but rather the ceremonial first citizen of the Slovak Republic, with some small rights and responsibilities. Once a year, the president makes invitations and presides over the inauguration of new professors.

20 Ladislav Machacek, *Participacia, obcianstvo, demokracia* (Trnava: UCM, 2003).

5 Sociology in my life and times

Valery Mansurov

Before sociology

I was born on August 26, 1937, in Kirov, a regional capital that was also a small scientific and cultural center. There were two higher educational institutions: Kirov State Teacher's Training Institute and Kirov Agricultural Institute. After graduating from the gymnasium, I chose to enter the Faculty of Foreign Languages at the State Teacher's Training Institute. The choice of the career of a teacher was largely determined by the fact that both my parents and my sister had been teachers. At the Training Institute I took an active part in public life and organized cultural activities among the students.

In every year of my studies, I was selected for the bureau of the faculty of the Leninist Young Communist League of the Soviet Union (LYCLSU or Komsomol). The LYCLSU was a young Communist organization under the leadership of the CPSU. It organized about 24 million young people from all over the Soviet Union. The cells of the Komsomol acted in collective farms, plants, institutes, universities, etc. During the last two years I organized seminars for young workers at a printing office and a sewing shop, where I informed them about the most important events that were taking place in other countries. It was an interesting experience for me, since I was fond of the social sciences, and especially philosophy. Moreover, I was sure that the experience of working with people and public speaking would be important in my future career.

A year before my graduating from the Training Institute, in 1959, I got married to a fellow student and was given permission to study part-time. At the time, I began to work in a rural school, which lacked teachers, not far from Kirov. Besides English, I taught drawing, painting, physical training, and music. When the director of the school was away on business, I substituted for him. I thought about connecting my future life with this school, as there were real career opportunities there.

In 1960 I was elected as a member of the Communist Party of the Soviet Union (CPSU). It was a rare and honorable reward at the time, since priority for election into the CPSU was typically given to young factory workers and collective farmers. In this same year, I qualified as a teacher of English and German, and continued working at the school. In October, however, I was invited to join the Regional Committee of the LYCLSU as an instructor of the Department of Agitation and Propaganda. I was responsible for work with young people. The work involved constant business trips all around the Kirov region. I met with many young people and participated directly in solving the problems of their day-to-day life, their studies, and their leisure activities. I also tried to improve the communication between collective farm officials and young people.

After one year of work, I was chosen to attend the courses for Komsomol leaders offered in Moscow. These courses had a serious impact on my future career as a sociologist, as they were taught by leading professors of Moscow higher educational institutions. Their lectures were far more objective and critical of the current reality than similar lectures of the past. It was the time of the political "thaw" connected with the revelation and criticism of the cult of the personality of Stalin, and we, young Komsomol organization men, expected great changes in the life of the country. It was a time of pointed political discussions about the future of socialism, about the role of young people in the development of the country, and particularly of the role of the LYCLSU. It was the time when I first heard about sociology as a science, which offered the opportunity to obtain objective information with the help of scientific methodology.

After the courses in Moscow, I became the head of the Department of Agitation and Propaganda. This extended the scope of my responsibilities and demanded increased knowledge of the social sciences, as well as practical work with young people. Looking back, I can say that we used some sociological methods at the time, though we did not realize that it was sociology. For example, we had meetings of the regional leaders of the LYCLSU, where we discussed the most important issues that dealt with the work of young people. Before these meetings, we had constructed questionnaires that were addressed to CPSU leaders (experts) and young people (grass-roots respondents). We analyzed the answers to these questionnaires during the subsequent meetings of the regional leaders.

Due to my work, I knew well the problems of young people. I often gave lectures to them and to the people who worked with them, such as teachers, journalists, administrative workers, and others. This work required a lot of reading, and I was subscribed to many periodicals. Searching for the information on the problems of young people, I found scientific publications on the issues of leisure time and young people, as well as studies of "time budgets." From my own work experience, I knew that not everything depended on money. I knew of some collective farms where the heads were interested in attracting young people, and could always find money for the construction of sports centers and clubs. These heads of collective farms could find financial resources for different cultural events, for employment of various teachers who held literary circles, organized choruses, etc. At the same time, some of the richer collective farms did not allocate money for the leisure activities of young people, as their heads were convinced that young people would never leave a rich collective farm, no matter what.

After working for a few years as a Komsomol organization man, I had to choose my future career path. I could go into the leading bodies of the CPSU, or I could get involved in scientific work. I chose the latter. I went to work in the Kirov Polytechnic Institute. At first, I combined lecturing with administrative work. Then, I worked as a lecturer of Philosophy and English, until I made the final decision to go into social sciences. Before I left Kirov, I organized a group among leading Komsomol members that did quasi-sociological research.

Sociological beginner

The earliest sociological research I actually conducted was while working in the Regional Committee of the LYCLSU. It was related to the issues of young people. My first two research experiences were connected with studies of the leisure activities of young people from the collective farm *Put k Komunizmu* (Way to Communism) in the Sanchursk Province of the Kirov region, and with young people from the Omutninsk metallurgical plant. I undertook this research independently from the beginning up to the end. The results of the research were published in a regional newspaper, *Komsomolskoe Plemya* (Komsomol Generation), and were presented at the All-Union Scientific-Theoretical Conference, "Young People and Socialism," held in 1967 in Moscow.

The next research I conducted had to do with studies of the readers of the *Komsomolskoe Plemya*, which I conducted with the help of a questionnaire from my counterparts from Voroneg, the capital of one of the regions in the centre of Russia. The questionnaire was adapted to Kirov's specific situation and the results were also published in the newspaper.

At the time, throughout the country, there was a rather wide network of sociological groups and laboratories in regional Komsomol committees, which were supervised by the Central Committee of the LYCLSU. With the help of the workers of that group, especially Artem Kulagin, Vladimir Chuprov, and Aram Abgaryan, I got to know my counterparts from different cities and regions of the Soviet Union. I also went to Moscow to work in the libraries, and received important information about scientific conferences and research. Two works by Professor Galina Andreeva of Moscow State University had an important impact on me. From her books, *American Bourgeois Empirical Sociology* and *Bourgeois Sociology in the Search for Theory*, I learned the main principles of Western empirical sociology, as well as information about the main tendencies and problems within Marxist and bourgeois sociology.[1]

When I learned that the Soviet Sociological Association had been formed in the country, I did not think that I knew enough of sociology to become one of its members. During one of my business trips to Moscow I got acquainted with a famous sociologist, Boris Grushin, and with his colleagues, Yakov Kapelush and Svetlana Bykova, who all worked at the Institute of Public Opinion, which was affiliated to the newspaper *Komsomolskaya Pravda*. They agreed to involve me in their empirical work. One such research project had to do with the issue of whether managers of different levels in the plants should be appointed by the

Party, or elected by the rank-and-file workers. At the time, it was a rather brave and untypical investigation, as managers normally were appointed by the local Party committees and common people did not participate in the process.

In January 1967 I received 100 questionnaires, made up of 12 questions that focused on an article from *Komsomolskaya Pravda* reporting on an example of the election, instead of the appointment, of a manager of a building organization in Krasnoyarsk. I administered half of the questionnaires to the workers at two plants. The remaining questionnaires were administered among plant managers of different levels, leaders of the trade unions, and Komsomol leaders. I could only do this work due to my personal contacts in the Kirov Regional Komsomol Committee, because many managers were suspicious toward sociological research. The project encountered many other difficulties as well. The results were published in a book edited by Yakov Kapelush, from the Institute of Public opinion. However, it was criticized, and withdrawn from circulation.

That period of my life was very important for my development as a sociologist. I had conducted and participated in a few social research projects, and taken part in the development and piloting of a questionnaire used in the first All-Union sociological research survey. The first All-Union sociological survey was conducted in 1966, by the LYCLSU, prior to the 15th Congress of the Komsomol. The sample included 10,000 young people from across the USSR. I had also taken part in the first All-Union scientific conference," Youth and Socialism," held in Moscow in 1967. I participated in studies of the problems of young people in the project "*Taganrog-1*," undertaken by a large number of scientists from different places throughout the country.

At that time I became a member of the Soviet Sociological Association. My registration number was 183. By then, I had read all the sociological literature to which I could get access in the biggest libraries in the country, and had got to know famous sociologists, as well as researchers, from the regional sociological centers affiliated with the regional Komsomol organizations, the majority of whom went on to become well-known scholars and professors themselves.

In the Soviet Union of that time there were debates about the future of sociology, about its subject matter, and about its interrelations with other social scientific disciplines, especially with philosophy, historical materialism, and scientific Communism. Many representatives of the social sciences did not consider sociology to be an independent science. Some philosophers, for example, saw no sense in sociological research and disregarded it as a superficial and ideologically detrimental knowledge. At the same time, a growth in empirical sociological research was occurring that was taken as an important phenomenon by many regional Komsomol and Party leaders. This gave a green light to the development of empirical sociology, since it did not contradict Marxism and helped to adapt some of the theoretical concepts to the modern reality.

Doctoral studies at Moscow State University

It did not take me long to realize that there were serious issues, connected with the establishment of an empirical and theoretical sociology, which I could not deal with unless I received a systematic professional training in the field. In the summer of 1967 I met with Andreeva, whose books on American empirical sociology had prompted my interest in sociology and my professional choice of careers. At the time, she was a senior lecturer in the Department of Historical Materialism of the Faculty of Philosophy at Moscow State University. I told her about my interest in sociological research and indicated that I would like to do a Ph.D. in the sphere of youth studies, particularly to estimate the scope of influence of the mass media on youth. She appreciated my knowledge of English, and suggested that I write a paper on the sociology of mass communication, drawing on American sociological literature. It was decided that I would have the whole summer to prepare the paper, and then she would read it. If the paper lived up to her expectations, I would be allowed to take the exams to enter the postgraduate department of Moscow State University, and she would become my supervisor.

Twice during that summer I traveled to Moscow to work in the State Library named after Vladimir Lenin. I aimed at understanding what Western sociology of mass communication was all about, its problems, its history, its research methods, and the results of American sociologists' research. I tried to understand it within a broad sociological and socio-psychological context. Certainly, at that time I approached the literature from a Marxist stance, and my interpretation of American sociology was overly critical. However, in the process of analysis, I understood how much valuable information I could pick up from the works of Western social scientific writers regarding the issues of mass communication. I especially understand that now, when the processes that are taking place in the Russian mass media remind me of everything that I was reading about during my preparation for entry into the postgraduate department at Moscow State University in 1967.

Andreeva found the paper that I wrote to be satisfactory. And, after passing exams in historical materialism, scientific Communism, and foreign language, I was enrolled in the postgraduate department. Today, I look back on my efforts to enter the postgraduate department at Moscow State University as a type of adventurism. While the competition to enter the department was very stiff, I did not have a systematic philosophical knowledge, had graduated from a provincial teacher's training institute, and did not have any personal connections in Moscow. Today, it hardly seems possible. However, I did have the Komsomol and life experience on my side, some empirical sociological experience, the teaching of philosophy at the Polytechnic Institute, and a knowledge of foreign languages which I owed to my father. It was he who had originally suggested I enter the faculty of foreign languages instead of the faculty of history.

At that time, only a few sociologists had any deep experience in sociology, and we knew them all: Andreeva, Grushin, Andrey Zdravomyslov, Igor Kon,

Lev Kogan, Vladimir Kudravtsev, Nikolay Lapin, Gennadii Osipov, Mihail Rutkevich, Tamara Samsonova, Ivan Slepenkov, Zahar Fainburg, Anatoly Harchev, Vladimir Shubkin, and Vladimir Yadov. All of them, except the lawyer, Kudravtsev, came from philosophy. And most of them had studied sociology, especially empirical sociology, drawing upon American social scientific literature. This fact was often used by Soviet opponents of sociology, who criticized the development of sociology in the Soviet Union for its bourgeois origins.

When I began my Ph.D. studies, there was no specialization in sociology at the higher educational institutions. At Moscow State University, Andreeva and Grushin gave lectures in sociology at the Faculty of Philosophy and at the Faculty of Journalism. However, later on, as I continued my studies, one group of students in their third year got the right to specialize in sociology. In 1969, due to the efforts of Andreeva, the Department of the Methods of Empirical Sociological Research was opened at the Faculty of Philosophy. Despite a lot of hard work, we also managed to participate in major scientific events.

Andreeva helped me a lot in this process. She was very popular in the sociological community, and was always invited to participate in various scientific events. She took her Ph.D. students with her to these events, or sent them on their own. As a result, I developed good relations with the group of sociological researchers of the Central Committee of LYCLSU, which was headed by Gennady T. Guravlev, now a Ph.D. and professor. On behalf of this group, I went on business trips to work with young people from different social layers. In Leningrad, I worked with young seamen; in Tomsk, with students and scientific youth; in Dushanbe, with young leaders responsible for international relations.

It was a time of serious debates about the role and place of sociology in the modern society. I remember how, following the publication of his book, Yury Levada was openly criticized in a huge hall at the Academy of Social Sciences by the academician Fedor Konstantinov, and some other philosophers, for the promotion of bourgeois social theories and the underestimation of the Marxist paradigm.[2] The discussion went on for several hours. Grushin supported Levada, and accused Levada's opponents of dogmatism and outdated positions. Nonetheless, Levada had to leave the Institute for Sociological Research of the Academy of Sciences of the Soviet Union.

I read Levada's lectures, and did not find anything that would have justified such a sharp criticism. It was a rather objective account of the essence of sociology and its main spheres of research. However, he observed that sociology, like any other science, had its own theory. Probably, this position was understood as being critical of historical materialism, which, according to Levada's opponents, played the role of a general sociological theory while all the others had no right to exist.

At the Department of Philosophy of Moscow State University we had every opportunity for excellent study. Our professors were exacting and friendly. We could work in all the Moscow libraries, participate in scientific events, write and publish our articles in different collections or journals. My friends and I actively took part in the preparation and publication of articles. All Ph.D. students participated in the annual Lomonosov conferences, which included the publications of articles. With the help of our colleagues, Ph.D. students from the Institute of Philosophy of the Academy of Sciences of the Soviet Union, we wrote reviews of new books, including foreign social scientific literature, for the journal *Voprosi Filosophii* (Problems of Philosophy). This also helped us to earn some income, as the reviews were paid for fairly. The only thing I am sorry about is that they were published anonymously. Nonetheless, by the end of our Ph.D. studies we had accumulated quite a few publications.

Most Ph.D. work entailed time in the library, and I constantly came across new sources of information. Besides the Lenin State Library, I ordered books from the Library of Foreign Literature, and from the Maxim Gorky Library. My friends and I would leave the student hostel as early as possible to go to the center of Moscow in order to have enough time to order books and to study. This hard work brought results. My friends, Klara Barbakova, now professor, Ph.D., and rector of the Tumen State Institute of Economics, Law and Management, and Ludmila Pahar, now also Ph.D., professor and head of the Department of Philosophy at Orel Technical University, prepared our theses and defended them in June 1970, a few months ahead of schedule.

In August 1970, I returned to my work at the Kirov Polytechnic Institute as a lecturer of philosophy. In one year, I became a senior lecturer of the Department of Marxism-Leninism. At that time, there were only three Ph.D.s in Kirov, and we gave lecturers not just in our own higher educational institutions but also in other educational institutions. We also participated in conferences and seminars and held night classes at the University of Marxism-Leninism, which was affiliated with the City Committee of the CPSU. The University of Marxism-Leninism was created for the leaders of enterprises and organizations of the city. There, I taught a course in sociology for the first time in my life. I also taught social psychology courses which dealt with the issues of management and the education of youth.

In 1970, I also participated, with a group of Komsomol members, in the World Sociological Congresses in Varna (Bulgaria), where I became a member of the International Sociological Association and of its Research Committee on the Sociology of Youth. In addition, I had a chance to participate in a ten-month trip to the United States, which would have given me a valuable experience. Unfortunately, I had to leave Moscow for Kirov and did not have enough time to collect all the necessary papers for that trip. However, during the three subsequent years of my work in Kirov, I gave lectures and seminars in Tumen, Sverdlovsk, Gorky, and Perm. I also organized two scientific conferences on the issues of the education of youth, and was a leader of a fund affiliated with the Kirov regional CPSU committee, which supported sociological research.

Looking back, I think that I was lucky to participate in the development of the sociology of public opinion in Russia. I traveled the road from an amateurish local survey of youth to professional research on a regional and national basis.

Despite the fact that there was a large demand for my lectures in Kirov, I realized that the qualification that I had received at the MSU opened up more opportunities than there were in Kirov. So I was very glad to receive a telephone call from the Institute of Social Research of the Academy of Sciences of the Soviet Union, which invited me for an interview in Moscow. I had a talk with the deputy director and head of the Department of Sociological Problems, Nikolav Blinov, and the head of the laboratory of the social activities of youth, Vladimir Chuprov, who suggested I be employed as a researcher. The position was in accordance with my scientific interests. I never would have dreamed that I could work in the then only institute of social research in the Soviet Academy of Sciences. Naturally I agreed, moved to Moscow, and on June 3, 1973, started my work there.

The Institute of Sociology

For the next 12 years I worked in the Department of Sociological Problems at the Institute of Social Research of the Academy of Sciences of the Soviet Union. Due to good relations with the Central Committee of the LYCLSU, and their interest in our research, we did a lot of work all over the country. In August 1973 we began research on Komsomol leaders of higher educational institutions.

I conducted a survey of the Komsomol leaders of higher educational institutions in Moscow, and then went to Kiev. There, because the questionnaire included a lot of sensitive questions about the attitude of students toward the social sciences and programs accessible from Western radio, I was only able to conduct the research thanks to the help of the secretary of the Kiev Regional Committee of the Communist Party of Ukraine, Alexandr Kapto. Then, back in Moscow, our research was stopped by the head of science of the Moscow Committee of the CPSU as dangerous and provocative. Chuprov and I were invited for a talk with CPSU higher ups, where we had to prove that it was no more than a scientific investigation aimed at the perfection of the work with students. With the help of the Department of Propagation and Agitation of the Moscow Committee, we still managed to finish the research.

Later on I often found myself in similar situations, where various departments of the Central Committee of the CPSU had different attitudes toward research we had undertaken. As a rule, the ideological Department of Propagation and Agitation supported our research, while the other departments were less benevolent. They accused us of having the wrong ideological approach and wanted to impose penalties on us. Sometimes they were successful and managed to stop some research initiatives.

Nonetheless, we still tried to determine the attitudes of young people toward Western radio programs and their influence on social attitudes. Despite difficulties, our department conducted 10–12 surveys each year. We worked a lot with our nearest neighbors, Western Ukraine, Byelorussia, the three Baltic republics, and the Murmansk region. When Chuprov left his post, I became the head of the department and tried to incorporate my knowledge of American research on the mass media. Thus, when I conducted research in Estonia, where people could watch Finnish TV programs, I drew from the research on TV watchers versus non-TV watchers; namely, those who could watch TV programs and those who could not, since their TV sets could not pick up a signal from Finland. The responses of these two groups were different, which allowed me to prove the influence of the Finnish TV program.

We also had a lot of open-ended information about the values and social attitudes of young people, and this gave us an opportunity to take part in scientific seminars and publish scientific articles. I often participated in scientific conferences in Kaunas, Lithuania, that were devoted to the problems of students, and took part in all scientific conferences held by the central and regional committees of Komsomol.

For the first two years in Moscow, I was asked to read evening lectures at the University of Marxism-Leninism, affiliated with the Moscow CPSU Committee. Then, I was asked to be the head of the Chair of Social Psychology and Sociological Research at that university. There, I participated in the publication of a few methodological textbooks and a reader in sociology. I also gave lectures at the Higher Komsomol School for Soviet and foreign listeners, and I gave a special course on the Sociology of the Intelligentsia at Moscow State University. For the last six years, at the Department of Sociological Problems of Propaganda, we studied young people not as a homogeneous group but rather studied different layers among the youth. We started with students, and then moved on to study young workers, and later on young members of the intelligentsia.

In 1977, as a member of the Institute of Sociology of the Academy of Sciences of the Soviet Union, I took part in a conference of experts, sponsored by the United Nations Educational, Scientific and Cultural Organization (UNESCO) in Ottawa, Canada, on the problems of the ethics of communication. In 1980, I was a participant in a working group of sociologists which took part at a symposium devoted to the problems of mass communication in Tampere, Finland. At that time I edited a few collections of articles devoted to the critical analysis of the conceptions of the intelligentsia in Western sociology.

During that period of my work I remember one more episode. In 1980 there was a fire in the Hotel Russia. As acting head of the Department, I decided to do an immediate investigation on what people knew about the fire, its origin and victims, using survey methods. I wanted to investigate in what form and in what ways rumors were passed among the people. I gathered the workers of the Department, instructed them about the content of the research and the questionnaire. Three days later, I wrote a short analytical report about the results. Two days after that, I was summoned by Timon Ryabushkin, the director of the Institute, and a corresponding member of the Academy of Sciences. Ryabushkin issued me a reprimand for the research done without his permission. As it turned out, someone from my department had informed him about the research. The director decided to consult with the Department of Science of the Central Committee of the CPSU, and they advised him to reprimand me. It is quite interesting that at the same time I got a call from the Department of Ideology and Propagation of the Central Committee of the CPSU, who thanked me for an interesting and timely report. Three months later, the reprimand was revoked.

Although I was busy with constant empirical research and business trips all over the country, I tried to find time for writing articles and books. In 1981 I wrote a book with Barbakova on the young intelligentsia in the developed socialist society.[3] In 1982, I defended my doctoral thesis, "Problems and Social Mechanisms of the Formation of Personality." Two years later I was awarded a habilitation degree. In 1982 I also participated in the XII World Congress of Sociology, in Delhi, India.

Sociology of public opinion from the 1960s to the 1980s

I was connected with public opinion polls during this time, and as a result have my own views on the development of this branch of sociology in the USSR and then Russia. Only at the end of the 1950s, when Nikita Khrushchev came to power, was there a general liberalization of the situation in the country that allowed for the growth of interest in sociology and its methods. In 1958, the Soviet Sociological Association was founded. This was followed by the creation of a sociological research infrastructure, such as laboratories, centers, and small groups all over the country. Eventually, in 1968, the Institute of Social Research of the Soviet Academy of Sciences was founded.

As a result, quite a broad spectrum of social problems became the subject of the research of social scientists as they acquired new methods of research and information analysis. Almost all political and administrative structures throughout the Soviet Union became interested in using the opportunities that sociological research offered. The renaissance of the use of surveys of public opinion began.

In 1960, the Institute of Public Opinion was opened under the directorship of Boris Grushin. Affiliated with the newspaper *Komsomolskaya Pravda*, during the first two years of its existence, the Institute carried out eight national surveys that used different sampling procedures and methods for the collection of information. This particular institute paved the way for the creation of social research groups all over the country.

In 1964, the Central Committee of the LYCLSU assembled a group of scientists, under the leadership of Artem Kulagin, to conduct social research. This was followed by the creation of similar structures in 40 regional Komsomol committees. They conducted surveys on youth public opinion on a whole series of different issues. In May 1967, the results of this research were discussed at the All-Union conference "Youth and Socialism," organized by the Soviet Sociological Association and the Central Committee of the LYCLSU.

Research on the opinions and social attitudes of the Soviet people was also done within the frameworks of the Sociology of Work, Sociology of Leisure-time, Sociology of the Mass Media, etc. Surveys were most popular in the areas of research aimed at the understanding of leisure activities, hobby groups, and plans for life. The research on these subjects was conducted regularly, providing an opportunity to compare the results, and to perfect methodological tools. This prompted the development of research methods in Russia.

However, it was almost a tradition that all surveys were conducted at the behest of, and for the information of, a limited group of recipients. Sociologists worked for the social order. They studied communicative behavior, the mechanisms of the formation of public opinion, the scope of social inclusion of people into the systems of mass media and propagation, and the socio-political attitudes and values of the youth. And, quite often, those who ordered the research, i.e., representatives of the press and political bodies, did not feel like sharing it with the wider public. Ironically, the results of social research on public opinion that were not shared were denied to the very target of that research in the first place. And, as a result, it was not an explicit factor in the formation of public opinion, except to the extent that it increased the efficiency of official agitation and propagation.

In general, in the mass surveys of the 1960s, Soviet sociologists dealt with methodological and organizational problems. Investigations using questionnaires and formal interviews became widespread in the practice of empirical research. During the surveys of readers of the central newspapers, interviews were usually conducted in respondents' residences or at work. In addition, interviews with representatives of small professional groups (for example, writers, heads of the enterprises, etc.) were often specially organized as they seldom appear in sufficient numbers among the respondents in randomized samples.

Postal surveys were also widespread. Social researchers managed to increase the response rate for postal surveys by using repeated personal references to the respondent, reminders in the mass media, especially on local radio and local TV, and repeated delivery of questionnaires. Due to such efforts, in some areas of Russia, return of the postal questionnaires reached about 20 percent.

Toward the end of the 1960s, and throughout the 1970s, two issues dominated the field. First was the exploration of mechanisms of the formation of public opinion, using local mass surveys. Second, and at the same time, was the development of methods for the creation of national probability samples and the means by which to carry them out.

In 1968, the Institute of Social Research began the Taganrog Project. In it, sociologists were joined by demographers, economists, and ethnographers. The founders of the project identified two primary goals. One was to improve the efficiency of the ideological work of the Party and the state, with the help of the mass media such as the press, radio, and TV, as well as various forms of oral propagation. The other was to expand and perfect the mechanisms of participation of workers in the management of social processes under the conditions of the advanced socialist society. Taganrog was chosen as a typical city in which the researchers could study economic and socio-political conditions, as well as ideological atmosphere. Naturally, since the research was supported by the Central Committee of the CPSU, it was expected to give information that would help to increase the efficiency of socio-economic planning and management, as well as Party propagation.

Within the framework of the Taganrog Public Opinion Project, Grushin created a so-called Methodological Laboratory for the Research of Public Opinion. There, detailed methodological tools for mass surveys, the content-analysis of the press, observing procedures at the meetings of work collectives, and interviewing heads of Party and state bodies were developed. These methodological developments of the Taganrog Project were published under the title *47 Piatnits*, referring to Grushin's weekly Friday seminars, which served as a methodological manual for Soviet sociologists.

The Taganrog Project used a stratified random sample to collect information from the population. The model for the stratification was constructed on the basis of a census of adult inhabitants of the city who had taken part in local elections in the spring of 1967. Four parameters were chosen as the basis for the stratification: a social status (i.e., factory workers, technical officers, the intelligentsia, service workers, technical workers, military men, students, pensioners, housewives); gender (male, female); age (18–24 years, 25–29 years, 30–39 years, 40–49 years, 50–59 years, 60 years and over); and education (up to four grades, 4–6 grades, 7–9 grades, 9–10 grades, incomplete higher education, higher education).

It is necessary to draw attention to another method of gathering of information in the Taganrog Project, namely diary records. For three months, daily diary entries were completed by administrative and Party leaders. Every day, different managers filled them in. This rotating schedule for the completion and collection of diaries allowed for the participation of a large number of leading managers. By the end, all political and administrative leaders in the city had participated in the research, while the common people were involved via an open-ended survey. Overall, 16,159 respondents participated in the open-ended surveys, 10,762 respondents gave personal interviews, and 8,882 diaries were filled in.

Mass surveys under the control of the Party

All mass surveys from the 1960s to the 1980s were carried out with the help of non-professional interviewees who worked for free. Many researchers, especially at regional sociological centers, conducted their surveys in the workplace or where students were studying. During this stage of its development, Soviet sociology of public opinion managed to solve many organizational, methodological, and theoretical issues. In 1966, under the initiative of Central Committee of LYCLSU, the first All-Union network of social research centers was established. Through the network, mass surveys of youth were organized. Among the most popular was the survey conducted before the Fifteenth Congress of the LYCLSU, in 1966.

As a result of the Taganrog Project, a complex program which drew on the experience of the representatives of various social science researchers was developed in the Institute of Social Research. The project helped to create original designs for sampling and to work out the most effective methods of gathering sociological information.

Through a co-operative effort between the Leningrad Branch of the Institute of Social Research and Leningrad State University, a well-grounded sociological collective was formed, which carried out a whole range of investigations, including studies of the audiences of the mass media by Boris Firsov, studies of the formation of social attitudes and values by Vladimir Yadov, and studies of methodology by Andrey Zdravomyslov, Yadov, and Galina Saganenko.

In Novosibirsk, under the auspices of the Soviet Academy of Sciences, various models of sampling were created, along with methods for increasing the response rate of postal questionnaires, which helped to increase the reliability of sociological information and to increase the efficiency of the use of quantitative methods in sociology.

There were also increasingly mature professional collectives of sociologists in Estonia at Tartu University, in Latvia at Riga State University, and in Ukraine at Kiev and Kharkov. During those same years, if it did not correspond to the ideological canons or, especially, if it directly contradicted them, the information received through polls of public opinion often was not published. The range and scope of questions that could be asked was also restricted. For example, we could ask respondents about the activity of the Party or Komsomol organizations at a certain enterprise or in an area. However, we could not ask about their opinions of the CPSU leaders, about the political system in the USSR, about the foreign policy in the country, or about their satisfaction with the internal policy of the state.

Even the numerous articles in the press, based on surveys, seemed to be threatening to those people who were responsible for censorship. This was because these surveys showed that there was no unanimity in the position of the respondents, including their political views. In addition, the new political leaders, which came to power in the late 1960s, did not want to be subject to public opinion. In the 1960s, this led to the reduction of liberal sensibilities and a more austere approach to sociology. The scope of social research in the country was reduced and a system of Party control over it, especially mass surveys, was created.

To begin with, in 1968, the Department of Science of the Central Committee of the CPSU took the Institute of Social Research of the Soviet Academy of Sciences under tight control. Sociological research was confined to the Department of Applied and Social Research, and this department was allowed to conduct surveys only under the direct supervision of the Central Committee of the CPSU. Almost no data from the results of mass surveys was published. Then, in all regions and Soviet Union republics, special Party committees were created to supervise regional social research. Without their direction and control, no one could conduct or share the results of even a small-scale survey of public opinion.

Between 1973 and 1984, the Department of Applied and Social Research, where I worked, carried out about 10–12 mass surveys annually. Most attention was given to the public opinion and social attitudes of various groups of the young, i.e. workers, students, the scientific and technical intelligentsia, the population of some cities and regions, such as Murmansk, Odessa, Lvov, Ivano-Frankovsk, Brest, Tallinn, Riga, Vilnius, and Kishinev. Under my direction, three waves of investigation of the public opinion of the inhabitants of Orsk were conducted in 1976, 1980, and 1986. Other projects at the Institute, led by Ivan Levykin and Andrey Vozimitel, involved two All-Union mass surveys on issues of the mode of life of the readers of the newspaper *Pravda*. The sector of public opinion, headed by Valery Korobejnikov, worked with the newspaper *Izvestia*.

Sociology in the period of glasnost and perestroika

In the beginning of the 1980s, after the Plenum of the Central Committee of the CPSU in June 1983, the situation in sociology was once more liberalized as political leaders again showed renewed interest in studying public opinion. At the Institute of Social Research of the Soviet Academy of Sciences, the Center for the Study of Public Opinion was created. However, survey research continued to have a local character. For example, in Moscow, surveys on the most important local issues were carried out on a regular basis.

The Institute started to develop contacts with similar centers which studied public opinion abroad. Surveys started to include questions about the issues of Soviet international relations. For example, international investigations, which studied the stereotypes different countries had about one another, were conducted with Finland by me, and with Japan by Korobejnikov.

A Soviet–French investigation that I supervised in October of 1987 became an important step in the direction of increased publicity of the results of public opinion surveys. For the first time, citizens of the USSR answered questions about their attitudes toward Andrey Sakharov, about the war in Afghanistan, and about their thoughts on anti-alcoholic policy. They also made judgments about the changes that were taking place in the country under the initiative of Mikhail Gorbachev, which came to be popularly known as "perestroika."

Within the research project the World Barometer, Korobejnikov conducted a few international polls with foreign colleagues, and headed some all-European projects. Since the end of 1980s, the conduct of mass surveys with foreign social research and commercial centers has become commonplace. The path to such wide international co-operation was opened by the democratic reforms and increased publicity. Finally, in 1988, the Central Committee of the CPSU made the decision that it was necessary to develop sociology in the USSR. The All-Union Center for the Study of Public Opinion was formed and headed by Tatyana Zaslavskaya, with Grushin and Yury Levada as deputy directors. Later on, Levada became the director of the Center. Many professional sociologists from the academic institutes and other research organizations came to work at the Center.

At that time, in the 1980s, new groups of interviewers were formed with the co-operation of regional research organizations and regional Party schools connected with the Academy of Social Sciences of the Central Committee of the CPSU. Groups of interviewers that had been formed earlier were also employed in the research. The Institute of Social Research had its own group of interviewers, which conducted mass surveys on radio and TV programs in co-operation with regional political organizations. The Ministry of Higher Education also had its own group of interviewers, headed by Alexandr Ovchinikov, which regularly conducted surveys of the public opinion of students.

Organization of the All-Union, and later of the all-Russian mass surveys encountered a lot of methodological difficulties, including the creation of representative samples. Some principles of the design of such samples had been worked out by then. However, they had to be improved, particularly taking into consideration that not all regions had all the requisite statistical information. In some regions there were no groups of interviewers, and remote regions were difficult to access. These organizational and methodological difficulties were solved by surveys during the 1990s.

In the 1990s, the interview stage for the first All-Union mass surveys lasted for 2–3 months. Samples in these surveys were not random, though in the final stages of the studies some attempts were made to do random sampling. The intermediate steps of the surveys, as a rule, were done on the basis of quota sampling. Not all regions could participate in mass surveys, as not all of them had sociologists, and sociologists normally could conduct research only in those regions where they worked. As a result, in the beginning, there were more territories of the Soviet Union where we were unable to conduct research than where we could.

Only in the 1990s were professional sociological centers—which participated in national mass surveys on the demand of Moscow and/or in co-operation with foreign countries—established in each of the geographic and economic regions of Russia. In addition, by the end of the 1990s, many regional services were offered by the All-Union Center for the Study of Public Opinion. These regional establishments made it possible for other all-Russian centers to conduct national surveys, i.e., the Fund for Public Opinion, headed by Alexandr Oslon and Elena Petrenko; Vox Populi, headed by Grushin; as well as my own Monitoring of the Public Opinion at the Institute of Social Research.

The co-operation of the regional centers with Moscow's highly professional centers specializing in the studies of public opinion led to the improvement of the professional skills of the regional sociologists, and prompted the growth of their professionalism. The leading sociological center in the study of public opinion, the Institute of Sociology of the former Soviet Academy of Sciences, renamed the Russian Academy of Sciences in 1994, regularly carried out training of regional and Moscow interviewers, using modern technologies such as videorecording and the analysis of interviews.

A bright page in the history of sociology in the Soviet Union was an original mass survey undertaken, in May 1989, under the leadership of Professor Yadov, then the director of the Institute of Sociology of the Academy of Sciences. The survey was conducted in co-operation with the All-Union Center for the Study of Public Opinion during the First Congress of Deputies of the USSR. On the eve and during the two weeks of the Congress, two research collectives, the Congress group of the Institute of Sociology under my leadership, and a similar group of the All-Union Center for the Study of Public Opinion, headed by Alexandr Levinson, carried out daily polls of public opinion of the citizens of the USSR. They were asked what they thought about the events that took place during the Congress.

For the first time, sociological methods were used to enable the general public to judge the work of the supreme body of representative authority, and deputies had an opportunity to compare their position with the positions of the people who had voted for them. Results of the mass survey were quickly analyzed and published as special releases for participants of the Congress, as well as in the dailies *Izvestia* and *Vechernaya Moskva*. They were also reported on television in the evening news broadcasts.

The Institute of Sociology conducted seven waves of interviews during the Congress, using telephone surveys in Moscow, Leningrad, Kiev, Tallinn, Tbilisi, and Alma-Ata. In each city, 250–300 people were interviewed, using telephone numbers that were selected randomly. The All-Union Center for the Study of Public Opinion used face-to-face interviews. Interviewers of the regional branches of the Center interviewed people in the workplace, in the street, and in their houses. Their sample reflected the population of the region and the interviews were conducted in Alma-Ata, Vilnius, Gorky, Dnepropetrovsk, Yerevan, Kiev, Krasnoyarsk, Leningrad, Lvov, Moscow, Novosibirsk, Perm, Riga, and Tallinn.

Due to the co-operation of the two leading research centers, the unique historical situation was captured and analyzed through attitudes, opinions and estimations of the population of the country.

Unfortunately, only half a year later, during the Second Congress of Deputies of the USSR, such teamwork failed. Only the Institute of Sociology studied the opinions of the population about the Second Congress, and thus the frequency of surveys decreased. Nonetheless, they still were carried out not only in big cities but also in the countryside, and even more regions were included in the sample. During the next congresses, the attention of sociologists moved to the interviewing of the deputies themselves.

In 1985, Professor Vilen Ivanov was appointed director of the Institute of Sociology. He had been a head of the department where I previously worked, and he nominated me for election to become his deputy for scientific work. After my candidacy was discussed by the Academic Council and the Political Bureau, I was elected deputy director. I was the first deputy director to be elected rather than appointed. I was entrusted with the supervision of a few departments, international collaboration, the work of the methodology council, the scientific library, and of the organization of scientific events.

At that time, many things were being done for the first time. In 1987, I became a head of Soviet–French research on the issues of television. For the first time, the Soviet people answered questions on what they thought about Andrey Sakharov, and the war in Afghanistan. They also expressed their attitudes toward the first Soviet co-operative, on immigrants, and about French–Russian interrelations. In addition, the Institute started to do comparative research within the framework of the international World Barometer Project. The first collaborations with Japanese and German sociologists also took place.

Soviet–Finnish collaboration was very strong. It was organized under the auspices of the Soviet–Finnish working group, of which I was a co-chairman until the demise of the Soviet Union. This collaboration helped us a lot, as it became a window on Western sociology. My colleagues and I got a chance to work in the libraries of Finnish universities, which held the latest books of foreign social researchers that were not available in the Soviet Union. Some of these works came to the Soviet Union later, and some were kept in special depositories to which researchers only had a limited access. Each year we held joint scientific conferences, the results of which were published in Russian and in Finnish.

In 1991, under my supervision, the Institute conducted a research project in the Soviet Union within the framework of the international Class Structure and Class Consciousness Project. Prior to beginning, we did some serious methodological work to co-ordinate and integrate different approaches. The leader of the project, Eric Olin Wright, and his colleagues from the University of Berkeley, came to Moscow. I traveled to Berkeley, where I worked on the final version of the questionnaire for ten days. As a result of this research, I learned many new things about the organization of such wide international investigations, as well as the theoretical concepts of social stratification that had existed in Soviet sociology only as an object of criticism. We also had a more pragmatic stake in the project. I returned to the Institute with two modern computers, which began the computerization of our Institute.

Technologically, our Institute was ahead of many of the humanities institutes of the Soviet Academy of Sciences. In the 1970s, we already had our first computer, the Minsk-22, and by the 1990s we had about 130 computers. Not taking into consideration technical institutes, ours was the first to establish a local network, and, in 1995, established Internet connection with other countries. After 1992, the Institute was in a difficult position, due to the steep decrease in state support for science. As a result, we were constantly plagued with overdue back wages.

The method for providing finance also changed as money began to be paid only for the work that was actually completed. Many sociologists applied for grants, and we had to earn money by taking orders for social research from different organizations and private persons. In response, the Center for Express and Applied Research was organized at the Institute, and as deputy director I became its head. While we did a lot of research, I would like to pay special attention to the first national social research project, Mirror of Opinions, which began in 1992. Unfortunately, in 1995, since we were a self-supporting unit and finances were scarce, we had to discontinue this project. Although our methodology is often used by other sociological firms, some of them do not give us credit in their own research.

After 1992, the Institute also had to cut back its publishing activities. Before that we had published around 30–35 collections of articles and 10–12 monographs through the publishing house *Nauka*, as well as others. After 1992, the rare publication was done with money that came from grants and from foreign colleagues.

My section and I managed to do research on the problems of the intelligentsia. We received a grant from the Ministry of Science for research on the problems of the social adaptation of engineers from defense plants during the transition period. We also got a grant from the Russian Fund of Humanitarian Sciences and International Association for the Promotion of Co-operation with Scientists from the New Independent States of the former Soviet Union (INTAS) which was headquartered in Brussels, for a project studying the social attitudes and social standing of Russian doctors. My section and I have participated in the XII, XIII, XIV, XV World Congresses of Sociology, and in all six ESA conferences.

Because of the demise of the Soviet Union, our sociological association has not been active for several years. In 1992, at the last meeting of the Board of the Presidium of the Soviet Sociological Association, its authorities were passed on to the Russian Society of Sociologists. I was the vice-president since its foundation. In 1997, with the support of my colleagues from the Institute of Sociology and from different Russian regions, I was elected the president of the Russian Society of Sociologists. The Society has grown stronger, increased its numbers, and it regularly publishes a bulletin. Sociological research committees under its auspices are actively at work. The Society has taken part in two all-Russia sociological congresses, and the numbers of Russian sociologists in the ISA and ESA have increased.

For more than ten years I have been the head of the Dissertation Council of the Institute of Sociology. During this time, more than a hundred Ph.D. theses have been defended. Now, I continue to lecture at the Institute of Sociology and in other higher educational institutions, and I supervise a few Ph.D. students.

To conclude, I want to say that sociology has been a part of my life. It has made my life one full of events, allowing me to meet with interesting people and to participate in activities important for the country, science, and myself. Without a doubt I can say that, due to sociology, I have seen the world in all its diversity. I have learned to understand other people, to be tolerant toward different attitudes and actions, and to reveal the hidden motives and essence of the behavior of people.

My life has intersected with the process of the development and growth of sociology as an independent science in our country. Before my eyes and through my personal participation, sociology became institutionalized. It grew from a single department at the Institute of Philosophy of the Soviet Academy of Sciences and a single Institute of Social Research, to hundreds of research centers and departments throughout the country. It has grown from a few tens of enthusiasts interested in social research, but who had no sociological education, to thousands of sociologists working in the country today. I hope future generations of social researchers will further elevate the status of sociology in the country through the sociological education of wider masses of people, especially of people who make important administrative decisions on various levels of management.

Notes

1 Galina Andreeva, *Sovremennaya Amerikanskay Burguaznaya Empiricheskaya Sotsiologia* (Moscow: Misl, 1965); and *Burguaznaya Sotsiologia v Poiskah Teorii* (Moscow: Znanie, 1966).
2 Yury Levada, *Lektsii po Sotsiologii* (Moscow: Institute Sotsiologicheskih issledovani AN SSSR, 1969).
3 Klara Barbakova and Valery Mansurov, *Molodaya Inteligentsia v Razvitom Sotsialisticheskom Obshestve* (Moscow: Nauka, 1981).

6 Touched by transformation

My life and sociology

Natalia Pohorila

In 1985, in the city of Kryvy Rig, in the Dnepropetrovsk region of Ukraine, I finished high school with straight "A" grades. Even though both my parents had only received a secondary education, they thought higher education important, and there were always lot of books in our home. Our parents did not encourage me or my brother to enter university, nor did they discourage us. They left it up to our discretion. However, the general atmosphere at home was of the kind that it was very probable that we would go to university. By the time I finished high school, my older brother had already graduated from Dnepropetrovsk University, the second largest university in Ukraine. He was my first English teacher.

In the autumn of 1987 I entered the Philosophy Faculty at Kiev State University (KSU), now known as Shevchenko National University. There were four specialties at this faculty: sociology, psychology, philosophy, and scientific Communism. My choice to study in the department of sociology was a rather haphazard matter. Instead of having no idea where to study, I had too many ideas. Among others, I had been thinking about the philosophy department. I eventually chose sociology for several reasons. Competition was relatively low, only four candidates for every place. And, there was no need for a recommendation from the regional Party Committee, which was a requirement for application to the philosophy department.

I was also concerned about having good prospects for the future. Though I knew little about sociology, I was told that is was an occupation with a future. This was to be only the second cohort of students recruited in sociology in the Soviet Ukraine since the early 1920s. The other had had been done the year before in Kiev and Kharkiv State Universities. At Kharkiv, the program was actually housed at the Faculty of Biology. Prior to this, i.e., 1985, sociology had been absent from the universities and research institutes for decades. Historical materialism, the Stalinist version of Marxism, was the only version of social science permitted in the Soviet Union.

At the beginning of my study we still had an intensive introduction to the history of the Communist Party and historical materialism, and English lessons were heavily focused on a review of political news. We were taught sociology with the text *Rabochaya kniga sotsiologa* (Work Book for Sociologists). It was the only textbook we had, and it contained a mixed set of selections. Some were obscure, while others fairly good, though the latter had been stolen and translated from Western sociology without reference or even acknowledgment of its existence. Classical sociologists were prohibited or not yet translated into Ukrainian. The only classical work available in the library was a pre-Revolution edition of Émile Durkheim's *Suicide*.

The first computers in the department only appeared in 1991/92, during the final year of my study. None of those who taught at the Faculty had any formal sociological background. The opportunity to use the Central Scientific Library, the biggest in Kiev, was reserved for fifth-year students. Only the smartest students managed to get in earlier. I was among them.

The atmosphere at the Faculty was slightly disappointing for me. The students majoring in philosophy, psychology, and even in scientific Communism, were deeply engaged in the intellectual processes of study. They had an established teaching staff, and a set of scientific traditions. They were obsessed with their theories and testing them on other students. There was nothing like this in the sociology department, and I was envious. There were only pragmatic "goody girls" (at sociological departments in the post-Soviet countries female students prevailed), who were primarily concerned with getting good grades in all subjects. I was particularly good in math, an advantage that I only recognized many years later. But, at that time, it was not enough for me. Sociology, and sociologists, had not yet established an independent intellectual identity at the university or in the country.

This does not mean that studying at the Faculty of Philosophy was not fascinating. Charismatic lecturers were teaching courses for us on philosophy and psychology. And, comparing my experience with that of today's students of sociology in Ukraine, I can say that we were given a much more universal knowledge. We studied logic, social psychology, math, and political economy in much greater depth. In the third and fourth years we had excellent courses on social structure and the analysis of documents, the history of modern sociological thought, and sampling methods.

The best lecturers also worked at the Institute of Sociology that had been newly created by the Ukrainian Academy of Science. Unfortunately, many of these people do not teach now, because they cannot teach in the Ukrainian language. During Soviet times, and in the early 1990s, they taught in Russian. This is no longer allowed in the main Ukrainian universities.

Published works in sociology were so rare that we literally bought every single new book that was published in our subject. I remember when the first translations of Max Weber and Durkheim appeared, as well as the texts of Pitirim Sorokin.[1] Most of these very first editions were published in Moscow, as was our first "professional" textbook, written by Vladimir Yadov.[2]

Following on the heels of Gorbachev's famous Plenum of the Communist Party of the Soviet Union in 1985, which put an end to ideological domination of the Party, the late 1980s was a time of enthusiasm. It was popular to speak about misunderstanding of Lenin's ideas on socialism because Stalin had distorted them. Plays by Michail Shatrov about the "true" Lenin, hard-working but surrounded by enemies, were popular. My friends from the Department of Scientific Communism, who were intelligent and passionate people, used to organize small meetings, in somebody's room in the dormitory, after the lectures to discuss the destiny of a socialist utopia in the modern life and the new challenges facing it. In parks and other gathering places around Kiev, groups of people would gather together to talk about politics. We eagerly defended privatization. We watched every remarkable foreign movie that came to Ukrainian cinemas, such as *The Narayama Legend*. Festivals of film from different countries were shown at the Kinopanorama, situated close to the Red Building, the main building of Shevchenko State University, where I studied.

It was a time of euphoria in the aftermath of ideological liberation. We knew that we were enjoying much more freedom than our predecessors. Only a few years earlier, five students had been dismissed from their last year of the study at the Faculty of Philosophy because they were meeting together to talk about some mistakes in the interpretation of Marx's theory made by Lenin and Stalin, even though they never questioned the general correctness of the socialist theory at issue. They were denounced by the KGB, and were forced to quit the university. Then, they were dispersed throughout the Soviet Union, and struggled to defend their diplomas and to obtain degrees at different universities. Sadly, one guy committed suicide. A few months after this tragic event, Mikhail Gorbachev himself was denouncing the ideological despotism of the Communist Party, and its distortions of socialist theory—in other words, broadcasting the same criticisms to the entire country. But, for my colleague, the freedom came too late.

How quickly times have changed. By the late 1980s we had learned that Lenin was not just misled by his followers, but he himself was much mistaken, and, my goodness, that he had had syphilis! On the eve of the 1990s, popular disappointment with the collapsing economy had increased. Student strikes and a movement for national independence began. I regret to say that I somehow missed the significance of the moment. At the time I was sick and tired of missing lectures that had been cancelled because of strikes. I remember one day when I was walking through the Red Building and a huge gray cat came out from behind a column in one of its corridors. Its loud "Meow" echoed through the absolutely deserted halls of what should have been a crowded midday.

Everyone suddenly began to speak Ukrainian and began to impose a "language control" on colleagues. Ukrainian became fashionable among student youth, even though just a few years earlier only a few people actually spoke it. For the most part, they had been recent arrivals from the countryside. All others considered Ukrainian to be a "rural" language, as opposed to the much more "urban" Russian. Many things and places have had their names changed (i.e., cities, streets, money, and institutions). My own Faculty of Philosophy became a Faculty of Sociology and Psychology. Scientific Communists, who remained with philosophers in the Philosophy Department, were desperately searching for how to exchange their outdated and discredited credentials for some more relevant to the political moment.

I lost interest in politics. Free love became widespread. No male student approached a girl without citing Sigmund Freud. Plays by Roman Viktiuk, with their constant reference to sexual and personal freedom, became popular. It was a time of chaos after the liberation. In the early 1990s, times continued to change. Now it was Marx that was determined to be thoroughly wrong.

In 1991, independent Ukraine started to recreate its history from the very beginning. The first private research institute, the Kiev International Institute of Sociology (KIIS), was established to conduct surveys. In the student canteen I was approached by the director of KIIS and offered a job. At the time there were only about 50 professional sociologists in the capital of the country! Unfortunately, I did not recognize the importance of this opportunity and responded that I was not good enough in quantitative methods to participate in survey research.

Good for nothing it seemed, or so I thought. While still a student, I worked as a secretary for a private company. This was a typical solution for university graduates then, particularly since the private sector of the economy was rapidly developing. In the meantime, I was spending a lot of time in the libraries. I especially liked libraries located in older buildings—for example, the Central Scientific Library and the Library of History at KSU.

I had a hard time figuring out what my specialization of interest would be. I was fascinated by qualitative critics of quantitative methods, and was naively looking for the new methodology that I figured must have been already developed to replace that of surveys. Since professional literature in Ukrainian on the subject was rare, I was reading English-written journals. These were mostly American journals such as the *American Sociological Review* and *American Journal of Sociology*, but also the *British Journal of Sociology*, and the *Polish Sociological Review*. I also read the Polish periodical *Przeglad Socjologiczny*, and, incidentally, learned to understand Polish. There were some Polish books in the Central Library, such as Stanislaw Ossowski's *Dziela* (Work), and Wlodzimierz Wesolowski and Kazimierz M. Slomczynski's book on stratification and mobility.[3] These books helped me to advance my knowledge of methodology as well as of Polish academic language.

Seventy percent of the work I did for my diploma was based on what I learned from Alexander Vinogradov, the brilliant statistician and social psychologist, who introduced me to quantitative analysis. After graduating from KSU, with the diploma (equivalent to a BA degree) of sociologist, I worked for three years as a teacher and research assistant at the Department of Sociology. My duties were to teach sociology to the students of law, and to write articles for sociological journals. I published two articles in Ukrainian, one on research methods for studying social structure, and the other on the problems of bureaucracy as a sociological concept.[4]

At the same time, I was working at KIIS carrying out simple tasks connected with data coding and input. The most challenging task I was given was the development of the Ukrainian classification of occupations. It was to be done through the adaptation of Polish and the International Classification of Occupations (ISCO) to Ukrainian conditions. Ironically, at the same time, I could not find satisfying occupation for myself, and became more and more uneasy about my future. Life in the country was far from stable.

During the early 1990s, referred to as the "time of chaos," there were shortages of goods, a symbolic transformation of the currency from *roubles* into *kupons*, and the introduction of a rationing system. "*Kupon*" was the name given to the temporary currency that was used after Soviet *roubles* had been banned, but before the new Ukrainian currency, *hryvna*, was introduced. It was a time of huge inflation, as *kupons* of increasing denominations quickly succeeded one another. Because of inflation, consumer goods were in short supply, and that is why the *kartochki* (rationing) system was introduced. Instead of money, everyone was given a certain number of cards that allowed them to buy a limited amount of sugar, butter and other kinds of scare goods.

I saw no opportunities to support myself in Kiev, and I did not want to return to my native town, Kryvy Rig. Instead, I came up with the idea to study at the Central European University (CEU) in Warsaw, Poland. The Central European University was the first Western institution to offer generous stipends for Eastern Europeans and instruction in the English language, of which we became aware. In the early 1990s, this information was virtually top secret. In addition, obtaining a passport and traveling abroad was still a rare and problematic affair, kind of a scarce good in its own right. I was told about the CEU by a friend who had read an online announcement in a Kiev newspaper. I applied to enter CEU twice. The first time was in 1994, when the Department of Sociology was located in Prague. The TOEFL English language exam was quite difficult, and I was not well prepared for the interview and was not accepted. In 1995 I succeeded, and was enrolled in the one-year MA program, "Society and Politics," which was located in Warsaw. Ever since then my life has been divided into two parts: B.P. (before Poland), and A.P. (after Poland).

Life in Poland

I arrived in Warsaw in September 1995 ready and eager to take advantage of my opportunity to study in a country with strong sociological traditions and good library facilities. I still remember that the first book, which I had on the reading list I carried with me when I arrived in "civilization," was Theodor Adorno *et al.*'s *The Authoritarian Personality*.[5] The first impression I had of Poland called to mind exactly the term "civilized." This was how I perceived the center of Warsaw, Krakowskie Przedmiescie street, where CEU was located in Staszic Palace. This was also the location of the Polish Academy of Science, in which the Institute of Philosophy and Sociology was situated. CEU rented apartments for the students, two to four students per apartment, each in a different region of Warsaw. The conditions were really favorable.

The five and a half years I spent in Poland made an enormous impact on my attitude toward sociology and my place within it. Passionate lecturers and scholars taught me through their own experience how sociology could be not only a means for making money and writing boring books but also a fascinating adventure and investigation. Before Poland, this is how I had perceived psychology and philosophy. While I studied at CEU I met international scholars such as Ernest Gellner, Lord Ralf Dahrendorf, and Seymour M. Lipset who delivered addresses at Staszic Palace. Zygmunt Bauman, Alfred Stepan, and Leszek Balcerowicz taught courses there. Through summer school and conferences, I met John Goldthorpe, Christopher Whelan, Paul Robert Magochi, and Shmuel Eisenstadt. Among my teachers and colleagues were Kazimierz M. Slomczynski and Krzysztof Zagorski. Poland gave me the chance to meet and to work with prominent scholars, while my Soviet background made me think that they lived at an unattainable height.

I have a mixed impression of the impact that the CEU program itself exerted on my professional growth. To my chagrin, I had little chance to read anything other than Adorno, since the schedule was quite tight with about nine papers a semester, as well as extended essay and diploma work, all to be written in just one year. I had problems with written English, and discovered that good reading skills and good writing skills were not the same thing. The necessity to use two foreign languages at once, English in classes and Polish in the city, made my life very stressful. I believe I was amongst the slowest speakers and writers in our group of 25 students. Nevertheless, I received "A" for the extended essay, which I devoted to the changing fashions in the study of elites, as well as for my MA diploma work. I finally managed to get the MA diploma, with distinction, mostly due to the high grade I got for my diploma work. It was devoted to the structural reasons for the growth and decrease of individual incomes in Ukraine from 1992 to 1996.

Thanks to CEU, I acquired academic writing skills. However, besides a course on post-modernism, taught by Zygmunt Bauman, and elegant studies of migration made by Claire Wallace from Vienna's Institute of Advanced Studies, I can hardly recall any others that left a lasting impression.

The supervisor of my work was Professor Henryk Domanski, who is known in the Polish Academy of Science for his love of quantitative methods as well as for the rigorous style of his tutorship. I only understood the reasons for his style of work much later, when I was teaching myself. Due to the work with him, I continued to develop my skills to do quantitative analysis that I had begun with Vinogradov.

The year also brought me into contact with the research team headed by Kazimierz M. Slomczynski. Slomczynski led the research group that worked on social inequality in Warsaw, at the Institute of Philosophy and Sociology of the Polish Academy of Science (IFiS PAN). He had also taught at Ohio State University. He and Bogdan Mach gave me master classes in statistics, and helped me a lot with the work on my MA diploma thesis. I believe that sometime in this period Slomczynski told me: "But, please, don't think that being occupied with non-quantitative case studies is a good idea for you. Just don't do it!" This strengthened my decision about the choice of the mode of sociological analysis that I would pursue.

In the autumn of 1996, after I had graduated from the CEU program, I was enrolled in the four-year Ph.D. program at the Graduate School for Social Research (GSSR) in Warsaw. This was another school funded by George Soros that worked in close collaboration with the Institute of Philosophy and Sociology of the Polish Academy of Sciences. CEU graduates enjoyed the favor of the GSSR staff, largely because we were fluent in English and already familiar to some of them who were teaching at both institutions; so it was not difficult for me to get admitted there. Foreign students got good stipends, but we were on our own to find housing. Normally students would rent a room and live with a landlady in a single flat, but some managed to share two- or three-room apartments. I tried both, changing housing every year of the four-year term.

Intellectually, the students at GSSR were much more heterogeneous than those at CEU. Philosophers, anthropologists, historians, linguists, psychologists, and sociologists were all doing their Ph.D. work there. However, ethnically, there was more homogeneity. Poles formed the majority, while Russians, Lithuanians and Ukrainians made up a solid minority. I liked the atmosphere much more than at CEU. We had more free time, especially the CEU graduates who were fast in writing essays in English and preparing presentations. At last I made friends and had time for the libraries. After Kiev, Warsaw seemed to me a true library's paradise. The library of the Institute of Philosophy and Sociology was rich in sociological journals, and the new building of the Warsaw University's library seemed like some utopian academic town to me.

There were several noteworthy courses taught. For instance, while one cannot say that Jadwiga Koralewicz's course on cultural values was well organized, the readings she gave us have remained among the most important texts of my scientific life. She was the only lecturer who put an effort into editing a book made up of the works of some of the participants in her seminars. My article, a comparison of attitudes toward inequality, unemployment, justice, and other aspects of the market society in the Netherlands, Great Britain, and Poland was included.[6] To a large extent it was inspired by the classical analysis of civic culture made by Gabriel Almond and Sidney Verba, and was devoted to the controversy over cultural versus structural explanations of the variation in values.

The course taught by Hanna Malewska-Peyre, on identity and inter-group relations, was attended by many people who brought a surprising variety of approaches to the identity problem. Among presentations on this seminar we heard statistical reports, studies of children's psychology, dancing clubs, and the identity of artists. Mira Marody's course on social identity was also very interesting in some parts. Edmund Wnuk-Lipinski was astonishing in his ability to interpret the topics of student's presentations in such a way that they seemed to make a new contribution to the topic of his seminar on radical social change. Admittedly, these contributions often surprised the speakers themselves. However, I would give the highest grade to two courses on comparative studies, both of them taught by Krzysztof Zagorski. Just back from Australia, Zagorski was a natural-born teacher. He exhibited a talent for the comprehensive explanation of statistical methods, an ability to present brilliant empirical examples, and to present sociological study not merely as an occupation but as an exciting adventure.

Besides regular coursework, I was involved in carrying out statistical analysis on Polish and Ukrainian data, with the intention to include the results in my Ph.D. thesis. This time, all of the groups—of Slomczynski, as well as Krystyna Janicka and Wojtek Zaborowski—helped me a lot. This was on data from Melvin Kohn's study on social structure and personality, collected in 1993 in Poland, and in 1992 and 1996 in Ukraine. I had been in the Ukrainian team that worked on this in 1993, and had based my MA thesis on this data. Actually, this is how I originally met Slomczynski and his team. This time I concentrated on the Polish–Ukrainian data. I became convinced that international surveys are the most advanced modern mode of sociological analysis. Slomczynski was a brilliant tutor, very patient and demanding. He never left an explanation of an issue unless he saw the light of understanding in my eyes, even when I was too shy or lacking in confidence to say for the second or the third time that I did not get the point.

When looking for a topic for my Ph.D. dissertation, I turned my attention to the topic of marginality. For some mysterious reason, this topic attracts the attention of many sociologists in Ukraine and Russia. After a series of readings and consultations, I understood that nobody in Europe or the Americas used it as post-Soviet sociologists did; i.e., in Robert Park's or the Simmelian sense of "marginal man" as a cultural hybrid, someone located on the border of two cultures. Instead, it is associated with poverty or deprivation. Next, I started looking for empirical operationalization of the concept of marginality in the psychological sphere. My intention was to compare whether or not the objective situation of marginalization coincides with psychological feelings of marginalization. Since serious comparable data on this topic were lacking, I tried to adjust my interests to the available data—i.e., those of Kohn's study. These data fit my purpose well, since they contained a large number of psychological variables. Slomczynski helped me in the formulation of the problem enormously.

International and conference life

I will turn to my dissertation later, since, before even starting it, I experienced many interesting events. I have been to five summer seminars. In my opinion, since it is impossible to provide a sequence of six to ten topics that would be permanently interesting to 30–80 participants with different backgrounds and professional interests, the practical academic value of summer seminars is limited. However, contacts with colleagues and peers, and a greater experience of the life of the broader world, is very important for the broadening of a young scientist's outlook. The first summer seminar I attended, was held in Ohrid, Macedonia, in June 1998. Its topic, the Balkans between East and West, with a focus on teaching history teachers how to write textbooks on the history of the

Balkan people, didn't contribute much to my knowledge. However, in the library there I found a book, *Europe at the Margins*, which gave me information that I had sorely lacked in my professional life. Concerned with the side effects of European integration, one of its authors, Kevin Robins from the UK, was one of the lecturers in the seminar.

I also met Paul Robert Magocsi, half-Ruthenian, half-Hungarian, born in Canada.[7] Magocsi delivered two lectures, one on Ukrainian nationalism and the other on Ruthenian sovereignty. He inspired me to read his history of the Ukraine, which happened to be the first book on Ukrainian history to replace the school textbooks on USSR history.[8] He spoke Ukrainian to me in an idiosyncratic manner, which in combination with my Ukrainian, strongly affected by Polish, must have been perceived by native Ukrainians as an extremely funny dialogue. And, of course, I will forever remember the special warmth and hospitality of the Balkan people, Bulgarians and Macedonians, whom I met there.

I attended another seminar later that summer, in August 1998, in Oslo. It was focused on comparative social studies and sticks in my memory mostly due to a massive compendium of 400 pages, which, following the instructions of the organizers, I read carefully. It included articles written by defenders of case studies and qualitative methods, and those who took a qualitative approach to comparative analysis. The compendium and the course were prepared by Charles Ragin from the USA.

A scientific seminar held in March of 1999, in Cologne, at the Zentralarchiv fur Empirische Sozialforschung, impressed me mostly for the mastery of the Germans in dealing with panel data, which they used in their national socioeconomic panel. The German people I met surprised me by their warmth and openness, and put an end to any stereotypes I might have held of Germans as reserved and obsessively rational people.

The summer seminar in Oxford, at Nuffield College in September 2000, was, maybe, the one from which I benefited the most. In addition to that living legend of sociology, John Goldthorpe, I also met a scholar there whose scientific style I found to be an appealing one. This was Chris Whelan, from the Economic and Social Research Institute in Dublin, who happened to be a modest and helpful person. His approach to the study of poverty showed his high competence in statistical methods, as well as his loyalty to "non-statistical" theories of marginality and the underclass. This can be seen in his numerous attempts to integrate both things in one study. John Goldthorpe won kudos by taking us for a Sunday trip around Oxford, exhibiting something of the medieval university's tradition of a kind of intimacy between students and the tutor. This was something that I couldn't imagine being done by Soviet professors.

Summer seminars were regularly organized by the GSSR, in late September each year, at the Wierzba resort on the Mazurian lakes in Poland. I attended two of these in 1998 and 1999. Meetings were scheduled mainly before noon, and participants were somewhat reluctant to do anything afterwards. I remember a good portion of the discussions we had on collective memory, and the acquaintance with new colleagues from Germany, Hungary, and Poland. The fresh air of the northern forests, rowing across the lakes, perfect hotels and cuisine, were delightful. This was really a place for starting friendships and collecting memories during the golden Polish autumn.

From the point of view of pure professional growth, I found scientific conferences to be much more useful than summer schools. Also, conferences are equally as fruitful as summer seminars for making ties in academic circles. The two most important conferences I participated in were the regular meetings of the Research Committee on Social Stratification (RC 28), of the International Sociological Association held in Warsaw in 1999, and in Mannheim in 2001. During these two meetings, Americans, Dutch, and Israelis made up the majority of participants overall, while Hungarians and Poles were the most numerous participants from Eastern Europe. Brilliant presentations by American participants, and the leadership style of Mike Hout from Berkeley, caused me to think of the USA as a Mecca for sociologists. Presentations by Gary Marks from Australia, John Goldthorpe from the UK, Hary Ganzeboom from the Netherlands, Thomas DiPrete from the USA, and Yossi Shavit from Israel were intellectually challenging and provoked many discussions. Some participants based their argumentation a bit too much on statistically sophisticated analysis that often was difficult to follow. Nonetheless, they gave me examples of the truly scientific research that serves as the model for me now.

Sometimes I also felt left out of the discourse due to the problems that were discussed by Western scientists. The decreasing role of education in the status attainment process, increasing inequality, the effects of the welfare state, were too far from the current context in Ukraine. It is difficult to imagine that the role of education, which just has started to grow in Ukraine, will decrease in the near future because of a deindustrialization that has not yet even begun. So, besides the reports on poverty and on transitional societies, I was hardly able to add to my understanding of the situation in contemporary Ukraine. Sometimes it felt like social stratification was no longer a fashionable topic within the international community itself. The question asked by Seymour M. Lipset and Terry N. Clark, whether or not the classes have died, although not answered positively by all sociologists, seems to signal the decline of the interest in this topic and a shifting of it to areas such as globalization, poverty, and ethnic inequality.

Thanks to my ISA membership, I once witnessed a desperate fight between the adherents of qualitative and quantitative approaches to mobility studies via the members of the ISA mailserve list. It started with a request by Robert Miller, from Belfast, Northern Ireland, to help him with literature on qualitative studies of social mobility. Immediately it turned into a hot discussion between the "quals" and the "quants," including John Goldthorpe, Daniel Bertaux, Gary Marks, and others. It was truly exciting to observe the best sociological minds fighting without any pseudo-tolerance.

Another very important conference for me was the one held by the International Institute of Sociology in Krakow in July of 2001. It was quite long and covered a variety of topics concerning various moral issues in contemporary society. My interest in the problem of trust was born in Krakow, and inspired by the speeches of Shmuel Eisenstadt, Piotr Sztompka, and many others. During my stay in Krakow I met marvelous people such as Martin Krygier, from Australia, whom I am proud to call a friend. I also had a chance to communicate closer with Melvin Kohn, the classic analyst of social structure.

Two other conferences in which I participated took place in Poland, i.e., the All-Polish Congress of Sociologists in Rzeszow, in July 2000, and the conference of the World Association of Public Opinion Researchers (WAPOR) in Warsaw, in November 2001. In November 2002 I also participated in a conference on the problems of border zones organized by the University of Zielona Gora. These conferences, together with the many round tables, lectures, and seminars that I attended while studying at GSSR, convinced me that Poland is a very sociological nation with a special love for thoughtful, scientific insight into sociological and philosophical questions.

Two other conferences remain memorable for me because they represent the first times that I made presentations based on my own analysis, without having a supervisor who would define the topic or the mode of the analysis. The first presentation, made in Warsaw in November 2001, was devoted to the nostalgia for socialist times in Ukraine, based on an analysis of the data that belonged to the Institute of Sociology of the Ukrainian Academy of Sciences. A strange thing had occurred within the statistical data from the year 1998. The proportion of people who no longer saw changes for the worse in the material situation, their health, opportunities for recreation, the rearing of children and the like, dropped significantly. The same happened with the feeling of control of one's fate, level of self-confidence, and the perceived social standing of respondents' families. I was puzzled as to whether the social mood in Ukraine followed some cyclical pattern, where periods of relative enthusiasm are followed by "tiredness," caused by reforms, as Krzysztof Zagorski observed in Poland.[9] Or, rather, was it due to the painful events of 1998, like financial crisis in Russia, that hurt millions.

In November 1982, in Lagow Lubuski, a Polish town where the University of Zielona Gora held its conference, I presented a paper on the regional aspects of political culture in Ukraine. Using statistics collected by KIIS, I was contesting the view that in Ukraine political culture could be understood as falling along a linear continuum from apathy to participation. I tried to illustrate the uniqueness of the political culture of the central regions of Ukraine, whose "in the middle" position is often interpreted as an explanatory factor for the intensity of political moods and behaviors that characterize it.[10]

Back to Warsaw

Among the seminars offered for professors, which I attended when studying in Warsaw, was one on poverty organized by Elzbieta Tarkowska during the 1999/2000 academic year. It was led off by Zygmunt Bauman, and his disciple,

Maria Hirszowicz, who impressed me by her ability to answer the numerous questions from the audience in a way that composed a coherent narrative. These seminars were noteworthy for the wide variety of approaches and problems concerned with poverty that they presented, e.g., poverty among women and children, statistical indicators of minimal survival, the effects of welfare, urban and rural poverty, and subjective deprivation. My interest in this topic was substantially reinforced by the participants of the seminar.

The representation of institutions outside of Warsaw was quite strong, especially by sociologists from Lodz and Katowice. The seminar culminated in a small conference that was held in April 2000 in Wisla, a small town in the south of Poland. That conference was a clear example of the enthusiasm and energy of Polish scholars. They participated in the sessions from 9 a.m. to 9 p.m., and afterwards some still were discussing hot issues. No one even thought about taking time out for a stroll across the Beskidy Hills.

Thanks to the organizer of the conference, Elzbieta Tarkowska, I took part in a field study for the first time. This was a study of poverty, headed by her and Katarzyna Korzeniewska, conducted in one northern province of Poland in the summer of 2000. Part of Ivan Szelenyi's project on the underclass in Eastern European countries, the Tarkowska team was conducting in-depth interviews with the inhabitants of two Polish villages. One was largely made up of individual farmers, and the other of former collective farmers. A variety of hypotheses were tested about the history of poverty in the villages, future planning, survival strategies, new patron–client relationships, and the efficiency of social assistance. I am not an admirer of case studies. Nevertheless, the experience of immediate contact with the people who are the subject of one's analysis has provided me with plenty of material to think about. Observing young Polish sociologists in the field, I was once more astonished by their keenness and devotion to their subject.

Another seminar was devoted to the problems of aggression, and was held at IFiS PAN. This was a doctoral seminar and only a few GSSR students were usually invited. The topic of this seminar was not directly connected to my academic interests, but I was glad to have a chance to witness once more the work of some of the world's most productive "sociological brains." Not all of the participants were sociologists. Jerzy Jedlicki was a historian, Stefan Amsterdamski a philosopher. Biologists, psychologists, and journalists were also present to bring intellectual breadth to the discussions. The lunches that were served afterwards added a special dimensions to these meetings.

My stipend at the GSSR was quite big, the equivalent of $200 per month. It was more than enough to pay for a room in an apartment. Usually students rented rooms from a landlady's apartment, or shared a room or an apartment with other students. Quite a few of us lived in dormitories, since housing is scare in Warsaw. During the five years that I lived in Warsaw I tried out all the options. I lived alone, shared an apartment with a landlady, shared one with roommates, and stayed in a small student dormitory within one of Warsaw's monasteries. While studying at GSSR we had enough time for social life, and I met some very nice friends in Poland. I spent many hours in Warsaw's cinemas. My favorite was the Illusion, where old movies could be seen. The Warsaw Cameral Opera was my favorite concert hall. With my friends, I visited almost every prominent exhibition that was brought to Warsaw. We also visited some Polish cities—for example, Lodz, Sopot on the Baltic seashore, the Tatry Hills, the Silesian town of Glubczyce, and small towns in Mazury-Warmia Voevodship. Poland fascinated me just as much as did other European nations. My finest memories are of the atmosphere in Warsaw and other Polish cities during Christmas and Easter. Never were they celebrated with even half the enthusiasm in central Ukraine where I was born and studied.

Since our schedule allowed us to have some extra time besides that for our studies at GSSR, I took some contract jobs. I have to mention three projects in which I participated. The first was connected with a project on migration from the former USSR to the Eastern European buffer zone. It was contracted by the Austrian Bank in 1995/96. We conducted interviews with Ukrainian cross-border traders or immigrants for Claire Wallace, who worked then in Vienna's Institute for Advanced Studies. I did three interviews with cross-border traders, one with a student, and one with an emigrant. This encounter with empirical data provided me with professional experience and pride. Based on this project, Gennadi Korzhov, my colleague from Donetsk, Ukraine, and I wrote an article on the identity strategies of cross-border traders, which, depending on the motivation of their activity, could be characterized as either of a survival or a professionalization mode. We did not manage to publish it at the time in Poland, but did so much later in Ukraine.[11] Prior to that study, I had also gained similar experience interviewing for a representative survey conducted by KIIS on the basis of place of residence.

The second job, which I got in Warsaw in 1997, was for a Polish–American company that was investigating the establishment of a Ukrainian retail network. This was my first experience with a marketing study. From the very beginning the study was not designed to study market segmentation—but rather, to study customers. Turnover and the structure of the market were what American clients were interested in. Later, however, the question as to whether and where people buy high-volume consumer goods was asked in a representative survey.

My task was to describe the buyers of various types of good in the shops, kiosks, and bazaars. I have mixed feeling connected with this study. From the very beginning I liked the independence associated with managing the project, and the money I was able to earn. I thought that this kind of work might be a more appropriate fit for me than an academic career. However, later I discovered the specific character of businesspeople as customers of market research. They are only interested in extremely brief presentations of information that is of practical use to them. The summary of the scientific information for the sake of "practical use" was not a challenging task for me. However, the lack of experience and awareness of what marketing research was all about were my weak points. I returned to academic activity with pleasure.

For the fall of 1999, and the winter of 2000, I edited two issues of the *International Journal of Sociology*, under the title "Social Problems in Post-Communist Ukraine." I was given the invitation by Tadeusz Krauze, the periodical's chief editor. I believe that we put together a well-balanced collection of papers. They covered a variety of issues which reflected the most pressing problems challenging Ukraine, i.e., poverty, crime, personal income, the elites, and attitudes toward transformation and ethnic issues. Statistical articles on incomes and attitudes were counterbalanced by theoretical articles on ethnic policy. Well-known sociologists such as Evgeny Golovakha and Vladimir Paniotto appeared next to younger sociologists of my generation such as Nataliya Kharchenko, Gennadi Korzhov, and Andriy Bova. The authors were from different institutions in Kiev, with the exception of one author who was from Donetsk. I co-authored an article with Slomczynski on income gains and losses, and provided an editorial introduction.[12] Generally I liked the editorial job. I worked on my editing for half a year, but it looked much better after the proofreading that was done for me by Joshua Humphreys, a young, willing, and hard-working political scientist from the USA.

After carrying out all of these tasks, as well as my regular presentations at GSSR, I only had one year to complete the text of my Ph.D. dissertation. Finally, my topic was specified as depression and fatalism in Ukraine and Poland in 1992 and 1993. Although the reviews were quite satisfying, I can say that writing such a large monograph was not my favorite kind of work. Maybe this is partially explained by the fact that Melvin Kohn's data were not designed especially for my task, and had already been heavily analyzed by Kohn himself, and the Polish and Ukrainian teams. I published a small article from my dissertation in a Ukrainian academic journal, but so far I have no plans of publishing a book.[13] However, experience of a large study on one topic was important for me, because at least I now know how not to write academic texts.

I received my Ph.D. in sociology (*Doktor nauk humanistycznych* in Polish) on November 28, 2001, from the Institute of Philosophy and Sociology of the Polish Academy of Sciences. The enthusiasm with which my Polish senior colleagues, peers and friends greeted my defense showed me how important this achievement was in their eyes. Unfortunately, I cannot say the same about my soon-to-be Ukrainian colleagues.

Back to Ukraine

A few words should be said about my decision to return to Ukraine. I was very uncertain about my post-Ph.D. future. During the final, fifth year of my stay in Poland, and despite my fluent Polish and friendly and professional ties in Poland, I was feeling fatigued because of the culturally different environment. I also felt an alien in Polish science because my knowledge of Polish reality was not very deep. On the other hand, because of my absence for more than five years, my familiarity with Ukrainian reality had also lessened. I thought that work in Ukraine might upgrade my knowledge and provide me with some sense of practical utility. I hoped that my qualifications would be in demand in research institutions and universities as I was planning a research and academic career.

I got back to Kiev in January of 2001, shortly after I had defended my Ph.D. dissertation. I had obtained a job at a university in Kiev, and on just the second day of my arrival I had to deliver my first lecture to a group of 21 students. For the first time in my life, I was given the most miserable pay one can imagine, 25 *hryvnas* per month, about five US dollars. It soon increased tenfold, but that was still only $50 per month. I was living off the money that I brought from Poland and had received from Western colleagues who ordered various types of works from me. After three months staying at my friend's place I bought a small apartment in Kiev. That was only possible due to my work for a Polish–American marketing project. For quite some time I was working to pay off the debt that I still had after buying the flat.

My non-monetary expectations were only partially met. For the first year I was teaching a group of very good and passionate students, and my dream about my value in Ukraine became reality. Later, they would become my best friends.

At the university, I taught three courses at once. One was devoted to systemic transformation in Eastern Europe. I based it on theories that I had read about in the libraries and learned from Edmund Mokrzycki, Andrzej Rychard, and Edmund Wnuk-Lipinski, as well as empirical data that I had brought from the Centrum Badania Opinii Spolecznej (CBOS), a major survey center in Warsaw. I based the second—on comparative international research—on empirical quantitative and qualitative studies that had been conducted since the 1950s in the Western world. The third course, for my MA students, about poverty, the underclass, and marginalization, entailed a short review based on theoretical and empirical developments in poverty theory. I was also recruited to give an introduction to sociology courses to the students of economics and law.

From the very beginning, my enthusiasm was maintained by the eager response of the students. Despite the low pay, I got a great deal of satisfaction from the feeling of being understood, respected, and needed. I found that BA programs were overloaded with courses that do not demand any analytical skills of the students at all. They spent years doing abstracts of the readings they were given by a lecturer. Even though they had been taught a significant amount of statistics, they were hardly able to formulate a problem and figure out a hypothesis that they were going to test. In other words, the program was designed in such a way that theoretical knowledge never met with practical use. The novelty of my courses was having the students carry out their own analysis, starting with the formulation of hypotheses, testing then, and presenting the results in the form of a short course paper. I thought I could be useful in helping students to avoid two pitfalls: either becoming a cabinet scientist of the Soviet type (i.e. an armchair scientist who is concerned only with abstract theorizing), or an unthinking empiricist.

From the beginning my students understood my intentions entirely, and I enjoyed working with them during seminars, and on their semester papers and diploma theses. I had an extremely positive opinion of my students. Starved for knowledge, fast and flexible, they were studying in difficult conditions. A lack of literature, a lack of computers, and miserable stipends, which forced them to work after seminars, were just a few of the difficulties that they had to overcome. Nonetheless, they were better prepared for life and work than my generation. And though they were fond of science, research for its own sake, they were able to earn money in the early stages of their adult life, while we used to start careers only after graduation. Due to the computerization and quantification of the program, many of them were already better prepared in statistical methods than I was myself, to say nothing of their understanding of contemporary Ukrainian politics. I will be always proud that among my students were Andrij Kosetsky, Evgeniy Bolshov, Sergij Khrulev, and many others.

Because of my meager income at the university I had hoped to supplement my salary by working for a small private commercial research company. The company I chose had a small staff of about thirty people, and also one of the highest turnover rates in Ukraine, particularly among those in the area of political studies. However, the situation there was not nearly so promising as my experience at the university. I could not get a full-time job in the institute since the position of project manager, which corresponded to my qualifications, was already occupied.

I cannot say that I was very attracted to project managing. I felt that analytical work would be better for me. However, I soon came to realize that even the most advanced private research institutes in Ukraine were not at all used to paying for the preparation of scientific publication, since they typically only prepared technical reports for their clients. Thus I failed to convince the administration of the institute that grant-seeking and application activity was a highly qualified job and must be paid for even if unsuccessful. Nor did I succeed in getting a computer with access to the Internet for grant-seeking or any of the work I did for the institute. I earned money by translating statistical reports from Ukrainian to English, since they paid twice as much for this as actually writing the reports in the first place. At first, I did not pay much attention to these problems. I was full of enthusiasm and regarded the quickly changing tasks as the most appropriate type of challenge for my temperament.

During my first year back in Ukraine I had some projects to finish with Polish colleagues. First, I was writing an article on the history of sociology in Ukraine for a book on Eastern and Central European sociology in the 1990s, edited by Mike Keen and Janusz Mucha. I took a quick trip to Torun, Poland, to meet them and the other authors, and was happy to learn once more that my work was worthy of being acclaimed. In Ukraine, my contribution to the project was positively appraised by Evgeniy Golovakha, vice-director of the Institute of Sociology.[14] She indicated to me, "All Ukrainian sociology should thank you for its popularization."

Second was for a project by Kazimierz Slomczynski and Elizabeth Osborn, from the USA, on political elites. They were collecting data on candidates in democratic elections to national parliaments. In Ukraine, their interest embraced four democratic elections to the Verkhovna Rada (the Ukrainian parliament), held in 1990, 1994, 1998, and 2002. I enjoyed this work very much, although it was not very creative. Since the candidates from 1990 had not been filed in a computer, like detectives we had to sift through stacks and stacks of Soviet newspapers. Also, I was working with Slomczynski on a book on comparative Polish–Ukrainian analyses, that has yet to be published.

In November 2001, the director of the commercial research institute offered me the position of his personal assistant. This was a semi-autonomous job. If needed, I had to give him help in preparing for publications or presentations, most of which were devoted to the upcoming parliamentary elections in 2002. Otherwise, I was free to choose the topic, as long as it was within the framework of institutional interest, and to publish an article on it. My most important texts were on the reasons why people abstained from voting (2002), political culture (2002), and institutional trust (2003).[15] So for the first half of 2002 I was occupied with electorate analysis. It looked like I was finally making a career.

Simultaneously, I continued to teach at the university. I am immensely grateful to my colleagues from the West for sending me free textbooks and materials for my students. Tadeusz Krauze sent me several parcels with textbooks and monographs from New York. Claire Wallace sent a lot of materials from Vienna. I also received books and articles from Wolf Teckenberg (Heidelberg, Germany), Ted Gerbner (USA), Peter Robert and Matild Sagi from TARKI in Hungary, Joerg Blasius from Cologne, Germany, and from Elzbieta Tarkowska and Krystyna Janicka from Warsaw. And, whomever I asked to send me their presentations at conferences did so. On one occasion, during a short stay in Warsaw, I went to IFiS PAN Press, the publishing house of the Institute for Philosophy and Sociology at the Polish Academy of Sciences, to look for books. I do not know how, but rumor that I was buying books for my students spread through IFiS. Almost immediately, Jolanta Glebocka, the scientific secretary of the Institute, entered the room and told me that the director was allowing me take as many books as I needed—for free!

Due to the efforts of Krzysztof Zagorski, I was given two grants that made it possible for me to travel to Mannheim to attend the conference of the International Sociological Association in April of 2001, and to participate in the sessions of the World Association of Public Opinion Research in November of 2001.

My eventual disenchantment with teaching and research in Ukraine did not initially come from the low pay. I had several different projects and was satisfied with my work. It came from my observation that, just as in the past during my student days, administrators hated having talented people around them, admired power, and only wanted loyalty, not merit, from their subordinates. I soon discovered that none of the rules approved by the university about deadlines and requirements for students' papers were followed by the Faculty. Sanctions were applied only if needed to persecute some daring students who happened to be more intelligent than their teachers.

I was embarrassed to discover these characteristics in "democratic progressive" professors, one of whom was just few years older than me. None of them showed any interested in my innovations in teaching, but if they learned that I had a different opinion about some practices used at the university they quickly turned into my most ardent critics. The worst thing was that this was occurring at a university that was known for its invention of strong democratic traditions in teaching and student self-government, and for taking no bribes.

I was further discouraged by the fact that the Ukrainian higher education system did not recognize my Ph.D. diploma, despite the fact that Poland recognizes the Ukrainian Ph.D., based on a mutual agreement on doctoral and lower degrees that had been signed in 1977 with the then Soviet Ukraine. The Vyscha atestatsijna komisia (Higher Certifying Commission) informed me that I must complete a long list of bureaucratic formalities in order to defend my Ph.D. again, or the miserable pay of lecturer would become even smaller, only $50/month.

Another discouraging factor was a decline in the quality of the students. The groups that followed my first set were not nearly as good. Not surprisingly, most of the students were not enthusiastic, they were pragmatic. I do not mean to claim that these were the worst students in the world or in Kiev. However, in the absence of the established traditions of respect to human dignity and the rule of law, they needed proper administration. I have noticed that the 18- to 20-year-old students only show respect to the older professors and the chairs of their departments. They believe only in force, and are ready to obtain their credits by threat and through lies, exactly in the way that their supervisors used to.

In October 2002, not too long after I had said some words in defense of my students who were being illegally persecuted, I was dismissed from the commercial private institute at which I had been working. Since the chair of department in which I was teaching and the director of the Institute were closely connected, I think this was done as a "warning" for me. After that I had severe difficulties finding another job, particularly since I was teaching at the university at least twice a week and had no time for a second full-time job. Because it was the beginning of the semester, even though I was quite capable of it, I considered it dishonorable to quit the university to get a full-time position in some marketing research institute. As a result, I missed many job opportunities. And, to make matters worse, I ended up quitting the university after all because of a lack of support from the administration.

At the time, I was quite confident about finding a new, well-paid position, say, in a marketing research company. I could not believe that no one needed a specialist like me. So, in June, when it was offered, I turned down positions at the Institute of Sociology of the Academy of Science, and the Ukrainian Institute for Social Research (UISR), a private research company that works mostly on social projects with children, youth, and families. Work in both institutions was attractive for me, but they offered miserable pay, less than that for a shop assistant at the bazaar. However, my applications to two leading marketing companies were rejected—one because no positions were available, the other because I was found to be overqualified for writing marketing reports.

For a while I did write reports for UISR on a contractual basis. That turned out to be more profitable than project managing on a full-time basis. UISR worked on a variety of topics, including the human rights of minorities, women, and children, the sexual behavior of youth, and the teaching of life skills to school pupils.[16]

I was also writing articles for an Internet analysis agency, Dialogs, that was purported to be on a mission to evoke a public discussion on the future of Ukraine and Ukrainians. I wrote articles on ethnic identification, poverty, the middle class, elites in Ukraine, and the Russian–Ukrainian relationship (2003).[17] Finally, I had got an opportunity to use my knowledge of statistics and theory, and to present them in a short and intelligible form. I really appreciated this work. However, much to my chagrin, I was not hired for a full-time position since the chief editor perceived me as an "academician," i.e., too much of a specialist to be a journalist.

Still, I do not believe that this streak of bad luck came because of my mis-education or over-education, and I hope that things will take a turn for the better. However, sometimes I think that my return to Ukraine was a bad mistake. The desire to stay in Poland, or to go West, is considered by many immigrants from Ukraine to Poland to be a completely justifiable decision. I think that most Polish professors also view the immigration of "brains" from the East with empathy. Zagorski once joked about me, after I returned to Ukraine: "She has not chosen freedom." This was not exactly the case. I wanted to live in a Ukraine with a merit system of pay, free from the rule of the "strong hand" of corruption, and open to the civilized world. As it happened, Poland corresponded much better to this dream than Ukraine. But I felt that I lacked a real life there; everything I observed was done somehow without me.

In this sense, my return to Ukraine was not a mistake. Of course, I obtained the first-hand knowledge and real-life experience that I had wanted. And I found here my young friends, the best people on earth, who reopened the culture of the new Ukraine for me. Yet, quite often, I recall a conversation with Nils Christie, a sociologist from Norway, who said to me: "I am envious. You live in such interesting times and in such an interesting place! As a sociologist you can learn everything from reality. We have such a boring time. Everything has happened already, and we don't know what to want."

I was so astonished by his total lack of awareness about the matter of which he was talking that I could not reply. Then Martin Krygier did it for me instead. He said: "Yes, you're right. But, you know, people in that part of the world acquire a certain tiredness because they have to fight for the usual, small, taken-for-granted things, everyday."

In 2004, things did get better for me. I found a job as the director of an eminent private company for social research in Kiev, and it fit me just right. I had to carry out a variety of tasks: managing the company, negotiating with clients, applying for grants, preparing analytical reports on political and social topics, participating in press conferences, and so on. The work was interesting since its content differs from day to day, and it gave me a chance to feel needed and respected.

Nonetheless, after working at it for six months I started to get tired of the routine nature of the work. Although my situation had become a hundred times better compared to not having a job, or having a poorly paid job, there are still too many obstacles in Ukraine that make normal work nearly impossible. Meritocratic considerations are not popular, and position in the power hierarchy is much more important. The rule of force displaces the rule of law and no one is interested in the long-term perspective in science. This is not intended to be a comment on my colleagues, who have been nice, hard-working people. However, they continue to follow the same habits without any interest in changing anything. That is why, in my estimation, the conditions for scientists in Ukraine are poor. Working in Ukrainian sociology, despite having exciting experiences and meeting interesting people, has left me with the uneasy feeling that I will never get what I desire and deserve as scientist and person—that is, respect and the conditions that would allow for creative work.

Now I have found my own answer to Christie: "It is good to observe transformation when it is not happening to you but only touches someone else."

Notes

1 Max Weber, *Izbrannye proizviedienia*, ed. Yu Davydov (Moscow: Progress, 1990); Émile Durkheim, *O razdelenii truda. Metod sotsiologii* (Moscow: Nauka, 1991); Pitirim Sorokin, *Chelovek. Cyvilizacia. Obschestvo* (Moscow: Politizdat, 1992).

2 Vladimir Yadov, *Sotsiologicheskie issledovania: metodologia, programma, metody* (Moscow: Nauka, 1987).

3 Stanislaw Ossowski, *Dziela*, Vol. II: *Wiez spoleczna i dziedzictwo krwi* (Warszawa: Panstwowe Wydawnictwo Naukowe, 1966); Kazimierz M. Slomczynski and Wlodzimierz Wesolowski, *Struktura i ruchliwosc spoleczna* (Wroclaw: Ossolineum, 1973).

4 Natalia Pohorila and Volodymyr Volovych, "Sotsiologichni problemy vyvchennia sotsial'noi stratyfikatsii," *Buleten natsionalnoho Universytetu imeni T.H. Shevchenka* 1 (1995): 14–19; and Natalia Pohorila and Olexandr Shtokvish, "Filosofs' ta sotsiologichni problemy burikratii," *Politologichna dumka* 1 (1995): 53–59.

5 Theodor Adorno, Else Frenklel-Brunswik, Daniel J. Levinson, and R. Nevitt Sanford, *The Authoritarian Personality* (New York: Harper & Row, 1950).

6 Natalia Pohorila, "Structure or Culture?: Cross-National Analysis of Market Values' Determination in Europe," pp. 45–62 in *European Value Systems*, ed. Jadwiga Koralewicz (Warsaw: Collegium Civitas and ISP PAN, 1999).

7 Ruthenians are a small ethnic group that used to live on Ukrainian, Slovak, and Hungarian parts of the Carpathians. They have their own language and sometimes pretend to national sovereignty.

8 Paul R. Magocsi, *The History of Ukraine* (Toronto: University of Toronto, 1996).

9 Krzysztof Zagorski, "Wstep: Opinia publiczna w okresie przemian ustrojowych," pp. 7–24 in *Nowa rzeczywistosc: Oceny i opinii 1988–1998*, ed. Michal Strzeszewski (Warszawa: Centrum Badania Opinii Spolecznej, 2000).

10 Natalia Pohorila, "Podzial regionalny na Ukrainie: problem kultury politycznej," pp. 527–548 in *Transgranicznosc w perspektywie socjologicznej*, ed. Maria Zielinska (Zielona Gora: Lubuskie Towarzystwo Naukowe, 2003).

11 Natalia Pohorila and Gennadi Korzhov, "Social Identification in the Society of Crisis: A Case of Cross-Border Traders in Ukraine," *Naukovi Zapysky* 19 (2001): 58–64.

12 Natalia Pohorila, "Guest Editor's Introduction," *International Journal of Sociology* 29, 3 (1999): 3–13; and Natalia Pohorila and Kazimierz Slomczynski, "Individual Income Gains and Losses in Ukraine, 1993–1996: A Test of the Human Capital and Mental Adjustment Hypothesis," *International Journal of Sociology* 29, 4 (2000): 54–76.

13 Natalia Pohorila, "Depression as Psychological Consequence of Material Status Inconsistency: The Case of Poland and Ukraine," *Naukovi Zapysky. Sotsiologichni nauky* 20 (2002): 34–39.

14 Natalia Pohorila, "Sociology in Ukraine, 1990–2000: A Decade of Firsts," pp. 175–186 in *Sociology in Central and Eastern Europe: Transformation at the Dawn of a New Millennium*, eds Mike F. Keen and Janusz L. Mucha (Westport: Praeger, 2003).

15 Natalia Pohorila, "Khto ne holosuvav na vyborach i chomu," *Politychnyi portret Ukrainy* 25 (2002): 83–93, "Regional Split in Ukraine: The Case of Political Culture," pp. 57–69 in *Magisterium: politychni studii. Vypusk desiaty*, eds Serhii Riabov and Olga Klimenko (Kiev: National University Kiev-Mohyla Academy, 2002); and "Dovira do dejakych politychnych ta publichnych instytutsi u porivnialnimu kontek-sti," *Sotsiologia: teoria, metody, marketing* 3 (2003): 144–156.

16 According to the World Health Organization, life skills refer to the ability for individuals to deal effectively with the demands and challenges of everyday life. They include the psychological and social capabilities to make informed decisions, solve problems, think creatively and critically, build healthy relationships, and manage their lives healthily and productively.

17 Natalia Pohorila, *U tini patrona* (http://dialogs.org.ua, 2003); *Ukraintsi-bidni?!* (http://dialogs.org.ua, 2003); and *Pershy raz v seredni klas* (http://dialogs.org.ua, 2003).

7 Challenges and disillusions

My 25-year career in sociology

Peter Robert

Background and motivation

If this were an autobiography to be written for the eyes of a bureaucrat sitting in the personnel department of a state-owned socialist company, and if I wanted to tell the truth in this case, I would begin by mentioning that I was born into a petty-bourgeoisie, middle-class family. My grandparents from my father's side of the family were running a shop, and died in World War II. I did not know them. My mother's father was in a managerial position in a large private company, and was dismissed when the company was nationalized after 1949. For the rest of his working life, he worked as an unskilled laborer in a state butchery.

I was born in Budapest in 1953 into a family where my grandmother was a homemaker, and both of my parents were working as office clerks. Originally, my parents only had secondary school qualifications. But, during their careers, they completed higher education. My father ended up as the head of department in a trade company, my mother carried out business transactions for a foreign trade company. My father had a good salary, and my mother had opportunities to travel abroad. Our living conditions were above average. As the only child in the family I could not complain.

I do not remember any professional ambitions from my childhood, but am sure I had no aspirations to be a sociologist. I probably did not even know about this profession. My parents wanted me to become a medical doctor, but I had no interest. In the 1960s I realized that I had better and nicer toys and clothes than my schoolmates, and that this was due to the fact that my mother could bring them from abroad. Thus, I also thought I had to find a job that would allow me to travel or to work abroad. In secondary school, between 1967 and 1971, I studied in a technical high school. While there, I participated in a special foreign trade program with an unusual curriculum: two Western languages (English and German, no Russian!), some statistics, bookkeeping, etc. After leaving this school I went to the Academy of Foreign Trade. In 1974, after three years of study, I received my BA. With this qualification I could have started my career in a foreign trade company; but, I didn't.

I was 21 years old, and my thoughts about life had changed by that time. I had written short stories for a couple of years, and had managed to publish a few of them. I thought I could become a writer. Even while studying at the Academy, I already knew that I did not want to work for a foreign trade company. I wanted a job with more freedom. All of my life I had lived in Budapest in a close-knit family atmosphere directed by such values as diligence and discipline. I wanted to learn more about other people, their lives, and other parts of the country. I wanted to collect experiences for my writing.

In the fall of 1974 I started work as an interviewer for the Institute of Mass Communication at Hungarian Radio. The job did not require any tertiary education, only a secondary school diploma. At that time, this organization was the only "public opinion research institute" in Hungary. It had been established in 1969, when the first economic reform period, the New Economic Mechanism, took place. About 20–25 persons worked there in the same position as me, and our job was to collect face-to-face sociological interviews in the homes of randomly selected individuals in Budapest and throughout the country. We were given address cards, with the name and the address of the respondents, and questionnaires. They usually started with easy questions about the frequency of listening to radio and watching television, and about the favorite programs of the respondent. But then the questions turned to actual political and economic issues in order to measure political knowledge and the attitudes of the respondents. These questions were about the economic prospects of the country and of the families, the level of knowledge of the five-year economic plan for the country, as well as information and opinions about political speeches and Communist Party meetings.

In addition to these regular topics, I recall a survey, in 1975, which targeted the joint space program, the Soyuz–Apollo program, of the USA and the USSR. It contained questions on how people felt about the political relationship of the two countries in influencing economics and politics in the world. Another survey dealt with the event in 1978, when the US gave back the Holy Crown of the early Hungarian kings, which American troops had taken with them after World War II. People were asked about the US on this occasion. Only a small group of researchers were allowed to analyze this survey data. Some reports were prepared in only two or three copies on a typewriter, and were sent directly to the Central Committee of the Communist Party. Other reports became available as working papers of the Institute and were circulated also in professional spheres.

This was an interesting way of life. All the interviewers were Budapest residents. We traveled to the countryside in the large black Volga cars of the Hungarian Radio, and carried official IDs from Hungarian Radio. Hungarian Radio had a lot of prestige at that time, and inhabitants were not afraid to be interviewed by us. We were the "official people" who came by car from the "capital," but we were not regarded as Communist "Party people." As a result, folks were open and the response rate was high—over 95 percent. The job was not difficult and we worked in a friendly atmosphere, especially in the smaller villages.

I think most of the respondents told their true opinions to us. Frequently they gave us more than we asked for in the questionnaire. Many times they believed that Hungarian Radio would be able to help when they were unhappy with Communist decisions or regulations. This feeling was stronger among less-educated people, and we met more resistance and distrust in the case of higher-educated people or Party members. They would suspiciously ask us: "Where did you get my name and address? Who told you to come and see me?" In fact, I do not think that the Party or the police exerted this kind of control in the mid-1970s in Hungary. Sometimes we also participated in the sampling procedure. We went to the local municipal office of the town or village, took the list of names and addresses of the inhabitants, and picked every tenth person on the list. These instructions were giving to us by the statisticians of the Institute, who had selected the settlements, and who were responsible for the sample.

I do not know much about the selection of the researchers, but there was no political screening for the selection of the interviewers. However, there was an entrance exam and psychological tests of concentration, decision-making, and contact-building abilities. Most of us were young people who did not know exactly what they wanted to become, who had studied something in which they were no longer interested, or who planned to study something but had failed to pass the entrance examination. In addition to the regular staff, the Institute occasionally employed additional interviewers. Many times they were people who belonged to the "civic opposition" and could not get steady employment. Instead, they made a living from irregular work such as this, or from translation.

During the time I worked for the Institute, from 1974 to 1979, my interest and readings changed again, from fiction and literature to "sociography" and sociology. I quit writing novels, but started to do small analyses with simple statistics from the Institute's surveys, mostly on media consumption. Formally, I had not yet studied sociology, but due to my past secondary and tertiary education in statistics and bookkeeping I was not afraid of the numbers. I was also able to write in a clear and structured manner.

It the meantime, I had met and married my wife Olga, who had an MA degree from the University of Economics and worked for the Institute of Sociology of the Hungarian Academy of Sciences. My interest in sociology became deeper and I decided to give up my job as an interviewer, which I did not find so interesting and exciting anymore. My attempts for a move up the internal ladder of the Institute of Mass Communication into the department of the researchers failed. They recruited young people who had studied economics or some social sciences at the university. It was clear that I would need a formal degree in the field if I wanted to be a sociologist.

With my BA degree and the promise of enrolling in the university and studying sociology, I found a job at the Psychology and Ergonomics department of the Volan Transport Company. The company employed bus drivers and ran bus lines between Budapest and towns in the countryside. Our department was made up of two psychologists, two assistants, and me as the "sociologist." This was the only time in my life that I had a job with fixed working hours, and had to sit in an office all day; it only lasted for one year between 1979 and 1980. My job was to talk to workers who had decided to leave the company, and to ask them about their reasons. I had to write a report to the management about the causes of worker's fluctuation.

During this time I wrote an article titled "Their Profession is Interviewer: Who Are They and Where Do They Come From?" It was published in the monthly journal *Valosag* (Reality), in the spring of 1980.[1] It became a success and gave me a good start. In the fall of 1980, without any problems, I was able to begin my sociological studies in an evening program for an MA at Eotvos Lorand (ELTE) University. By then I was already working for the Institute for Social Sciences of the Communist Party. At age 27 this represented the start of a new period in my professional career.

Formal and informal studies in sociology: a real "laboratory" under socialism

In 1980 Tamas Kolosi had established his Stratification Model Research Group in the Institute of the Communist Party, formally called the Institute for Social Sciences of the Hungarian Workers' Socialist Party. Earlier, he had published books on social structure and conducted empirical research on how people felt about social inequalities. He had planned a project, using a large-scale survey, on social inequalities. The study assumed that social status had various dimensions and that status inconsistency could also exist in socialist Hungary. Interestingly enough, the Party Institute could be a place for such research in Hungary in the 1980s.

Kolosi wanted to bring together a group of young people who were ready to work hard in his department. It was Olga who informed me about this possibility, as one of her colleagues at the Institute of Sociology, and Kolosi, were close friends. After a personal interview, he selected me as a junior research fellow, even though I did not have a university diploma, but with the condition that I had begun my studies in sociology at ELTE University. It was good to feel that he seemed to trust me. Later he became my mentor for the start of my professional career. I owe him a lot of thanks, as one can see from what follows.

When I started to work in the Party Institute, I was not a member of the Communist Party. But that was not a problem. In fact, I never joined the Party during the years I worked there, which was practically until the collapse of socialism, in 1990, when the Institute was reorganized. In Hungary in the 1980s, even to work in a Party Institute, it was not compulsory to be a member of the Party. The Kolosi group consisted of three senior members, including Kolosi himself. They were all members of the Party, but they were also completely liberal and open-minded persons. Of the junior members of the group, only three persons—less than half—were Party members. Of course, the majority of the faculty in the Institute were members of the Party. However, my memory is that the climate, at least in the 1980s when I worked there, was not orthodox but critical, sometimes perhaps even cynical. Still, I heard that colleagues were dismissed from the Institute, or even purged from the Party, for political reasons. But, not being a Party member, I was not in danger. I did not attend any formal political events of the Institute and I did not speak about politics there.

Working in a Party Institute was an advantage in comparison to working in an academic institute or at the university. Research conditions were better, and I tried to take advantage of these better facilities. For example, the Party Institute had a very good library where one could find many English language books and journals, including the *American Sociological Review*. In the 1980s, relevant literature was already available without political obstacles in other Hungarian libraries as well, but financial conditions for buying books or subscribing to journals were more favorable in the Party Institute. The Institute had a Department for Library and Documentation. It was their job to follow the international publications in various fields of the social sciences, to provide regular lists of new books, and to circulate the table of contents of several journals (translated into Hungarian) to the researchers on a monthly basis. If someone had language problems (this occurred especially among the older researchers), they had the opportunity to order the Hungarian translation of articles or chapters of books. Several translators worked for the Institute and many translations of this kind were available in the documentation section of the library.

Like the other academic institutes in Hungary, the Party Institute had a liberal rule on working hours. Researchers had to work at the Institute two days a week. Since office space was a problem even there, researchers were expected to work (i.e., read and write) at home. Only the head of the Department had a separate office. Older colleagues would share two to an office, the younger ones three or four. This was the case for most of the research departments, but not for our department.[2] Kolosi came to the Institute every day, and he expected the same from the young members of the group. Senior members of the department were allowed to work in line with the general rule.

Kolosi's ambition was to create an intense climate of collaboration for the young researchers. He was a hard worker and he required the same from his young co-workers. The stratification research project was scheduled for five years in accordance with a planned system regarding scientific goals and financial means. Though this did not mean a formal five-year contract, Kolosi had an impressive publication plan with a series of ten volumes to come out of the project.[3] The young researchers were also expected to write a book on their subtopic in social inequalities by the end of the period. Between 1982 and 1988, the group produced nine volumes in the Stratification Model Survey series. Four were edited collections, and five were single-author works. The Party publishing house, Kossuth Kiado, printed the tenth edited volume in 1988, which discussed the basic findings of the project. I think my 20–25 years of activity in sociology, as well as my views on social problems, were strongly influenced by being socialized in such a high-achievement climate.

The group had regular meetings. The first series of these meetings was devoted to developing a division of labor. Everybody had to choose a topic, one aspect of social inequality. Since I had just started my formal study of sociology at the university I did not have a strong preference or special interest in any subtopic within social stratification. Then, almost by accident, my name was linked to the theme of the origins of inequality. What aspects of the life-paths of individuals led people to their concrete social positions (i.e. to social mobility). Frankly speaking, at the time I did not know that this was one of the great classical research issues in empirical sociology. In 1981, I had almost the entire year just to read the literature, both the previous Hungarian studies as well as international ones. There was a lot in Hungary, mainly by Rudolf Andorka and his collaborators in the Central Statistical Office, but also by Istvan Kemeny, Zsuzsa Ferge, and Ferenc Gazso. Budapest has a special open library with a large collection of sociological books, where I found some basic readings by Pitirim Sorokin, Seymour M. Lipset, Reinhard Bendix, and David V. Glass. The Party Institute's library had some essential books in its collection as well, such as works by Peter Blau and Otis Duncan, Donald Treiman's work on social prestige, and Robert Hauser and David Featherman's work on the process of stratification. In addition, I was able to study the European research on social mobility, particularly Karl Ulrich Mayer and Walter Muller from Germany, and Krzysztof Zagorski from Poland.

We had regular meetings at the Department where we discussed our reading experiences, exchanged various drafts of the manuscripts we prepared, and developed research plans and hypotheses with regard to our subtopics. We also studied concrete empirical materials and worked on the questionnaire for the survey, which was scheduled to be carried out in 1982. According to the division of labor in the group, my task was to develop a series of questions on the origins of social inequality, with particular attention to the cultural and financial aspects of family background. In 1982, we published an edited volume discussing the conceptual framework for the research, and the basic hypotheses for the various dimensions of social inequality as well as for the whole stratification model.

The empirical survey was carried out in collaboration with the Central Statistical Office. They provided the sample, the interviewer network, and fielded our questionnaires. We had a household questionnaire as well as an individual questionnaire for every adult member of the family. We collected plenty of basic information on various aspects of social inequality from more than 15,000 individuals in Hungary. The Central Statistical Office used the same sample in 1981 and 1982 for a variety of surveys; thus a huge amount of additional information was available on the respondents. By the end 1982 we had the data in hand.

Besides the general climate of hard work and achievement orientation, the strong quantitative and methodological approach was a second important factor for my professional socialization in sociology. Between 1983 and 1985, we analyzed the empirical material by applying a statistical program package that was practically identical with the SPSS, though we could not use a legal copy of the software. At that time, there were no PCs in the Institute. A mathematician and a programming assistant worked with the group, and the Computer Science Institute of the Hungarian Academy carried out the statistical analysis. We submitted our programs to the mainframe and we received the tables the next day. Kolosi convinced the Party Institute to establish a telephone line between the two institutes as well, but this was not a big improvement because telephone technology was underdeveloped and the connection was slow and noisy. We had a few Commodore computers, and we used some special statistical programs written for them.

All of this may sound very primitive from today's perspective, but the Kolosi group was one of the few research units in Hungary that applied "Western" methodology. Other examples can also be mentioned. Rudolf Andorka led a group dealing with social mobility research in the Central Statistical Office. Elemer Hankiss had a department at the Institute of Sociology in the Academy, where changes in the value system were studied. Zsuzsa Ferge ran another department in the Academy for Social Policy Research. And Janos Timar led a department at Karl Marx University for labor market analyses. I believe that the 1980s were a very good period for Hungarian sociology, since its professional character was emerging. Young researchers like me, who could work in one of the laboratories mentioned above, received a much better education in sociology in a professional sense than what the formal teaching in sociology at the university could offer.

The possibility of getting a formal degree in sociology developed in Hungary later than actual research in sociology. The Institute of Sociology at Eotvos Lorand University was established in 1972, and it was the only place where lectures were given in the field at that time. Later, other sociology departments were established at other universities, but this institute remained the largest one. I studied there as well, but the curriculum did not impress me much. I cannot remember any political influence or socialist rhetoric during my studies, and I have the feeling that it was accidental to some degree what curriculum we had to follow. The main courses had titles such as Introduction to Sociology, Changes in Social Structure, and Social Processes. A few other classes dealt with some aspects of the history of sociology, regionalism, mass communication, the sociology of culture, and family sociology. The curriculum also contained social psychology courses, and some math and methods too. In sum, the whole program was mostly of a theoretical character and had only limited influence on my views of what (empirical) sociological research was all about. In 1984 I graduated in sociology with an MA, but I believe that the "original accumulation of intellectual capital" of my sociological knowledge took place for me in the Kolosi group. Even today I believe that empirical sociology can be learned much better by doing it in an "on-the-job" manner than in university classes.

During these intensive years of work, my private life had a regular flow. After getting married, Olga and I lived in my small room in the house of my parents. With the financial help of relatives, we managed to move to our first own apartment in downtown Budapest in 1981. My older daughter, Julia, was born there one year later. Soon, we managed to move to another, larger apartment, and my second daughter, Katalin, was born there in 1986. My wife continued to work at the Institute of Sociology of the Hungarian Academy of Sciences, though she stayed at home with the girls for some time while I concentrated more strongly on my work. Looking back, this traditional division of labor sowed the beginning of future tensions in combining work and family life.

The academic world is opening up

Working in the Party Institute had some clear advantages. And, I don't mean salaries, at least for myself, because I was paid according to my scientific rank, while my Party member colleagues at the institute were paid according to their political rank. But obviously there was more travel money and more travel opportunities in the Party Institute as compared to the academic institutes or the university departments. In the beginning of the 1980s, Hungary was open and liberal enough for money to be a more important factor influencing the chance to attend a conference abroad than was political trustfulness.[4] In fact, travel to the West was less of a political issue than attending a meeting where Russian, Bulgarian or East German sociologists were also present. The appropriate behavior or making the right points in a political sense were much more important in those meetings, where free speech was much less tolerated, than in Western conferences. Thus, in comparison to fellow sociologists of the same age—in our thirties—I had more travel opportunities, mostly to the West. I never attended any socialist conferences. Even within the Party Institute, this would not have been possible without my membership in the Kolosi group.

Kolosi was very keen on getting in touch with Western sociologists and in presenting his results to them. In 1982, he joined the ISA Research Committee 28 on Social Stratification. A very active scientific community, it had meetings twice a year, once in Europe and once in the US. Kolosi offered to organize a meeting for the RC in Budapest, and this idea was very welcome as Western sociologists were interested in visiting a country behind the Iron Curtain. Apparently, Kolosi made his proposal knowing the Party Institute was behind him. Despite of what I have said about the climate in Hungary, inviting Western sociologists, including Americans, needed both political and financial support. Kolosi was not the only Hungarian member of RC 28. Rudolf Andorka, with his mobility research in the Central Statistical Office, was already very well known and respected in the international community, but the Party Institute was a more acceptable place for hosting an international meeting than any other institution.

The conference took place in the spring of 1984. It should be noted that the Prague meeting of RC 28 only took place in 1991, and the Warsaw meeting occurred even later in the 1990s. The Hungarian meeting was a well-attended conference, with many papers. Quite a few scholars came from abroad, including Bob Hauser and David Featherman from the US, Jonathan Kelley from Australia, and a young Czech colleague, Petr Mateju.

The conference was successful both professionally and socially. One evening the Party Institute organized a trip on the Danube; the next evening there was a luxury reception at the central building of the Hungarian Academy of Sciences. Andorka and Kolosi edited a book entitled *Stratification and Inequality*, with chapters by leading Hungarian sociologists in the field, including themselves and Zsuzsa Ferge, Tibor Huszar, Ferenc Gazso, young members of the Kolosi group, and some others from the Party Institute and from the Andorka group in the Central Statistical Office.[5]

I also had a chapter in the book, and it was my first English language publication, though it was printed in Hungary.[6] In it, I went beyond the traditional approach of occupational mobility and I tried to measure the cultural and financial aspects of the inheritance of social inequality. It turned out that some young Dutch scholars who attended the conference expressed special interest in my work, and also in the Hungarian data that I had analyzed. They were also interested in testing hypotheses about cultural and material reproduction, in line with Pierre Bourdieu's theory, and socialist Hungary was an interesting case for them. Thus, the so-called Utrecht Mobility Seminar invited me to work with them for four weeks in 1985.

This was not my first official study tour in the West, to say nothing of the fact that I used all my formal opportunities for tourist trips every third year. In 1982 I was able to travel to Germany, for which I can thank Kolosi since the trip was financed by the Friedrich Ebert Stiftung, a social democratic foundation with good connections to the Party Institute. There, in Mannheim, I had the opportunity to meet briefly with Walter Muller, Karl Ulrich Mayer, and the Austrian scholar Max Haller. But Utrecht was the first time when I had a chance actually to work with foreign scholars. Though I have been able to do this quite a few times in the 20 years since then, the first time was particularly important. If I look back on my international career, Dutch friends appear at several points and they were very helpful to me. In the mid-1980s, members of the Mobility Seminar included scholars such as Wout Ultee, Harry Ganzeboom, Ruud Luijkx, and Paul de Graaf, who became very well known. I must express my acknowledgments to them.

The Western cities and windows were not completely novel to me, given my tourist trips. Beginning in the 1970s, Olga and I visited Paris, London, some German cities, and the Scandinavian countries, with friends. But I had no experiences with Western universities, institutes, working offices, or computers. Also, I had had less opportunity to see the everyday working life of other people who worked in the same way as I did—that is, doing empirical sociological research on quantitative data. I think we spoke the same language in the professional sense. Still, while sitting with these people in Utrecht and discussing what kind of analysis we wanted to do on the Hungarian data, I realized how much I had to learn in quantitative sociology. Thus a new period of accumulation of knowledge started for me, partly through the books and articles they showed me, partly by just talking about work. I remember I used up all the copy cards of my Dutch friends because I recognized how many reading materials I simply did not know or have in Hungary.

We worked hard during these four weeks on the first draft of two papers. One was about cultural reproduction in Hungary, the other was a more traditional occupational mobility paper which even incorporated historical data sources from 1930 and 1949. My impression that one can best learn about sociological research by doing it became even stronger. We presented the cultural reproduction paper one year later at the RC 28 meeting in Rome in 1986. Not counting the Budapest meeting hosted by the Party Institute in 1984, this was the first time that I had attended an RC 28 conference abroad. I traveled with Rudolf Andorka. We stayed in the same hotel room, and he introduced me as a capable young scholar from Hungary. At that time he was the president of RC 28, and John Goldthorpe was the secretary. I was glad to see and hear researchers that I knew previously only from their published work. These trips and conference experiences strongly contributed to my early professional socialization. They gave me an opportunity to become better recognized abroad and to build an international network, while still in the socialist period.

By the mid-1980s, the Kolosi group had completed the Stratification Model Survey. The research provided plenty of materials for publication. I wrote articles for *Szociológiai Szemle* (the Hungarian language Sociological Review), *Statisztikai Szemle* (Statistical Review) and also for *Valosag* (Reality), where my first article had been published.[7] This was the case for the other young members of the group as well. Kolosi strongly supported our careers, and he also wanted us to submit our work as theses for formal academic degrees. This was not a problem for those members of the group, like me, who had written monograph-length pieces from their research. In Hungary, under the conditions of the dual institutional system, one could get a doctorate degree at the university as well as a higher degree given by the Hungarian Academy of Sciences, which was called "Candidate of Science." Four young members of the Kolosi group became such candidates in the 1980s. I defended my thesis on social mobility analysis in 1986. Finally, at age 33, this made me a formally recognized and qualified scholar in Hungarian sociology.

As the Stratification Model Survey was completed, the cohesion of the group started to disappear. Though we remained employees of the Party Institute, members turned to differing individual career paths. In addition, Kolosi was not much interested in keeping the group together. He did not want to start another large empirical project; rather, he had more ambitious plans and wanted to establish a research institute. This institute was the original Social Science Informatics Center, known as TARKI in Hungarian.

Kolosi wanted to combine two models, the Zentrum für Umfragen, Methoden und Analysen (ZUMA) in Mannheim for empirical data collection and analysis, and a data archive. He did not have in mind a new state organization within the framework of the Academy of Sciences, but wanted to establish a consortium where different academic institutions, university departments, the Central Statistical Office, other state institutions, etc., were the co-operative owners of the new research center. Again he was able to persuade the leadership of the Party Institute about his idea. At the end of the 1980s this ownership model was not atypical in the Hungarian economy, but it did not exist in the field of science. With the help of the Party Institute, the initial fund raising was also successful and TARKI started to operate, in 1985, in a large apartment of a big building. Only two research fellows of the former group were invited to join this new organization; I was one of them. To begin with, all of the founders and first employees of TARKI had full-time positions elsewhere. I remained employed by the Party Institute. However, something different had begun, a new pathway opened up, even though the private sector did not yet exist in the academic world.

At the same time, my international collaboration with the Dutch colleagues continued. Harry Ganzeboom, Ruud Luijkx, and I gathered and analyzed all of the Hungarian mobility data that was available and published it in a Working Paper in the Netherlands in 1989.[8] The other paper, on cultural reproduction and co-authored with Harry Ganzeboom and Paul de Graaf, became my first publication in the US (in *Research in Social Stratification and Mobility*) in 1990.[9] I also had further opportunities to attend conferences. I was one of the three young members of the Kolosi group to give a paper at the World Congress of Sociology in New Delhi in 1988. I also participated in some international comparative research with Kolosi. An important outcome of this work was a joint publication with him and Max Haller, in 1990, where we compared the mobility processes in Austria, Hungary, and Czechoslovakia, i.e. in the area of the former Austro-Hungarian monarchy.[10] Parts of my other papers also appeared in books and conference proceedings in Germany and the Netherlands, and these publications made me better known. Kolosi learned about a research community based on an international variant of the American General Social Survey, called International Social Survey Programme (ISSP). Hungary (or, perhaps more accurately in practice, TARKI) joined the project in 1986 as the first institutional member from a socialist country. Later Kolosi introduced me to this group of scholars and working with ISSP became an important part of my international activities.

One way or another I had quite a few opportunities to build contacts with scholars from Europe and the US at international conferences. I met Ivan Szelenyi for the first time at the convention of the Austrian Sociological Association in Graz. Szelenyi was the chair of the Department of Sociology at the University of Wisconsin, Madison, at that time. My first American professional contact was with Albert Simkus, who had worked on Hungarian mobility data with Andorka in the 1980s, and spent quite a bit of time in the country. I also got acquainted with Bob Hauser from Wisconsin, and I decided to apply for a Fulbright fellowship and go there. With the support of letters from Simkus and Szelenyi, my application was accepted and I could spend one year, 1988/89, in Madison.

My first trip to the US, and spending an entire year there, was an exceptional experience and a cultural shock. Of course, I needed special permission to bring my data (on tape) with me to the US. I had to fill in several forms for the Hungarian custom officers. I also attended a meeting organized by the political police for all Fulbright scholars, even in 1988. But spending hours in the long queue of the Immigration Office at Chicago O'Hare airport was no easier.

I learned a lot in the US. It was the first time that I used e-mail or worked alone on a mainframe computer. I met outstanding scholars at the department in Madison, though unfortunately Ivan Szelenyi was no longer there. However,

I did not start any collaborative research with people there. Everybody was very friendly and helpful, but all relationships remained on the surface, and we did not share much of mutual interest. I did work together with Albert Simkus, although this resulted in a publication only several years later.[11] From this perspective, the trip could have been more successful and productive, but I still have very good memories about my stay in Madison when I think back on that part of my life.

I had my family with me in the US. Julia was six years old and completed the first grade there. Katalin was two and went to a half-day kindergarten at the university. Both girls spoke English and this was to their great advantage later, especially for Julia. I helped Olga to get a library card and a pass for the PC lab at the university. We were both sociologists, though my career developed much faster in the years that she was busy with the children. I wanted her to benefit professionally from our stay in the US as well, but this did not really happen. She felt she had to be a housewife there, just like some of our Hungarian friends in Madison. The husbands were biologists and worked in the laboratory at the university, while the wives stayed home with the children. Indeed, when I was invited to conferences in Berkeley and Los Angeles, I traveled by myself and left my family behind in Madison.

The democratic sociology emerges

I returned from the US at the end of August 1989 with masses of packages, including my first desktop PC that I had bought there and continued to use for several years at home. This was a rare and valuable item in Hungary, and I spent a long time with the customs officials. They made a long list of every item I wanted to "import," and I had the feeling that ages divided my country from freedom. Despite that, I had been following the news coming out of Hungary and I knew that massive political changes had taken place while I was in the US. In a sense I missed a significant part of the collapse of Communism during this year of absence. Indeed, my first observations upon return home focused much more on the differences between Hungary and the US than on the changes that had occurred in the country during the last year.

When I returned to the Party Institute, which was still my formal full-time employer, it was a different place. One could simply smell it in the air. Kolosi did not work there anymore. He moved to TARKI, as the full-time director of the center. My original department existed only in principle, and all research programs at the Institute were on hold. It was a time when people cared more about their personal prospects for the future than about studying the political and sociological changes in the society. The following year, in 1990, Hungary had free elections. One of the former opposition parties, the Hungarian Democratic Forum, won and a conservative government came to power.

Nobody had any doubts that the Party Institute could not continue to exist. But it was not only this institute that faced dissolution. All of the departments of Marxism-Leninism and scientific socialism that existed in every university had to face the same uncertainty. The years of 1990 and 1991 were devoted to the slow and gradual process of academic reconstruction in the country. In my judgment, this process was very peaceful and tolerant, without any political revenge. Nobody was fired for political reasons or previous activities, and it quickly became evident that the dual system of the universities and academic institutes would survive. In the Party Institute, the typical response on an individual level, at least for those employees older than 50, was to sign up for an early retirement program. They received a quite big sum in compensation. Many others not eligible for such a program decided to leave the Institute as well. About half of the employees departed in this way.

Young researchers and members of the management who decided to stay began to work on the reconstruction of the Institute. A similar strategy was common with the universities. The Party Institute was turned into the Institute of Political Science of the Academy of Sciences, just as the university departments mentioned above were turned into political science departments. Nor was there a change in the general tenure system at the universities and in the academic institutes. Everybody who continued to work in the universities and institutes after 1990 maintained the tenured positions which they had held before.

After the reconstruction, only three of us from the former stratification group remained, and it was clear that we could not continue our earlier research. While all of the other employees of the now ex-Party Institute, the Institute of Political Science, started to relabel themselves as political scientists, we made an attempt to define ourselves as sociologists. We did not formally join any new units, but were independent researchers and raised some funds for a project dealing with the newly emerging civil society in Hungary. We could sell this project as political science, but it was also sociology as we studied empirically the formation of a new middle class, and the rise of self-employment in post-socialist Hungary.

I also continued to work for TARKI, where Kolosi gave me a position immediately when I returned from the US. By that time the center was already established, well equipped with computers, and had just installed an e-mail system. It was still a small institute. Kolosi himself had hired three of his young students from a university course he had taught, and I was the senior research fellow in the Institute, which was still located in the same apartment building but by then on two levels. By that time there were several full-time employees at TARKI, and this could have been an option for me as well. But I was afraid to leave the public sector of academic research completely and join a semi-private institution. TARKI was still a consortium of a non-profit character with a budget which came from the owner institutions, from the state, and from the market, on a year-to-year basis. It seemed to me a better solution to be present in both sectors, and remain partly a state employee and partly a private employee.

Without any doubts, TARKI was a better place professionally than the former Party Institute, and the work was much closer to my interests. We started several projects. In 1992 I became the leader of a social mobility survey which we fielded. Andorka and Kolosi became the principal investigators of a household panel survey, which had six waves between 1992 and 1997, with a focus on income differentiation and labor market participation. At TARKI, I became responsible for the international comparisons within the framework of the ISSP, and we fielded one module every year. In 1991, when the Pope visited Hungary, we fielded a survey on religion. In 1992, it was a survey on the attitudes toward emerging social inequalities. Also in 1992, in a further step toward becoming an independent and professional institute, TARKI developed a separate fieldwork department with its own interviewer network. In these first years after the transformation, TARKI was a place that followed the good traditions of the "laboratory" Kolosi had developed in the Party Institute, and we did relevant sociological research on issues that strongly related to the social consequences of the transformation.

Although it was a challenge to perform empirical sociological studies in Hungary in the 1990s, and I enjoyed participating in this work, I put my greatest emphasis on my international presence in sociology. Shortly after I returned from the US I applied for another extended fellowship to the European University Institute, but I failed and was only able to spend two months there in 1990. I worked with Hans-Peter Blossfeld, who I had met before at the RC 28 conferences. I started to learn a new approach and method of empirical sociological research, somewhat related to social mobility analysis. This was the life-course approach and event-history analysis. In 1992 I was invited to the Netherlands again, and I spent six months in Tilburg working on the long-term tendencies of Hungarian social mobility processes with my old friends.

These longer trips abroad did not improve my family life. They were quite long as absences, but too short to take my family with me. In fact, this was not an option since Olga did not want any further interruptions in her work, and both of my daughters were in primary school and could not just up and leave for a few months. Olga visited me during my trips abroad, but the family ties were getting weaker and weaker.

When I returned to Hungary after this grant, I left the Institute of Political Science and moved to the Institute of Sociology at Eotvos Lorand University from where I had graduated in 1984. Frankly speaking, this change was not a result of my own initiative. In actuality, I had had very little connection to the faculty there since I had left them as a student. Nonetheless, I received a phone call about a job opening and an invitation to apply for an associate professor's position. I was hesitant because I did not have good memories about my studies there, and I had not heard about any significant changes, either institutionally or in personnel during the 1990s. However, this was the case for most Hungarian universities, with the exception of the departments with a concrete political curriculum, i.e., Marxism-Leninism and scientific socialism. The political transformation did not have much impact on the sociology curriculum in Hungary, so there was no reason to reorganize it.

For all practical purposes, I found the same structure of classes there as I had had as a student ten years earlier. Still, I decided to move to the university for three reasons. I could have managed in the Institute of Political Sciences, but I was a sociologist with different professional interests after all. I was told at the university that they wanted to build new courses. They wanted to educate research sociologists and my duties would be to take part in this program. Along with me, other colleagues were also being recruited and we had similar preferences for empirical research. So I hoped that we could change the curriculum, which was dominated by theory. In the end this turned out to be an illusion.

In 1993, at the age of 40, my work life had become firmly secured through my institutional affiliations, linking me partly to the public and partly to the private sectors of sociology in Hungary. While it might be a bit of an overstatement, I had two and one-half jobs—as I like to phrase it. One job was lecturing at the university, for which I was paid there. Another job was doing partly academic, partly applied research at TARKI, for which I also got a salary. The remaining half job, unpaid, was writing papers for international conferences and participating in international research projects.

Between 1993 and 1997 I spent about five years in Hungary without a break. During these years we experienced a huge expansion at the university. In 1993, the number of sociology students averaged below 20 in a class. By 1997 it had climbed to over 50. This development was characteristic of other institutions as well because the Ministry of Education increased the enrollment quota, for students who had passed the entrance exam, from year to year. While the number of undergraduates increased, the former Candidate of Science degree of the Academy of Sciences was abolished, and the universities started to introduce Ph.D. courses for postgraduate training, following the Anglo-Saxon examples. Another change in the system of scientific qualification was the universities' introduction of the habilitation for becoming a full professor, in line with the German system.[12]

Though the number of students increased significantly, the number of faculty remained the same. There were no job openings at the university, and the same number of staff had to deliver more undergraduate classes, as well as give lectures at the postgraduate level. In 1995 the budget at the university was seriously cut, in accordance with other financial cutbacks across the country in the public sector. This was the so-called *Bokros-package*. As a result, lecturers were being dismissed at several departments in almost all universities.

Facing this situation, the director of the Institute of Sociology came up with an alternative solution, and suggested that all employees of the Institute sign a declaration of their willingness to work for only 70 percent of their regular salary. He did this on the grounds of solidarity, in order to save everybody's jobs. Only four persons were against this idea out of 40–50 faculty members. I was one of them. In my judgment, as some of the lecturers in the Institute had no scientific degree, did not perform any research, did not publish anything, they deserved to be discharged. In the end we all signed the declaration, though I think I was the last one.

Perhaps it was a mistake that I changed my mind and followed the majority, giving up my principle of achievement for the principle of solidarity, which was stronger among the faculty. In any case, I assume that my colleagues remember that I (a newcomer to the Institute!) had taken a different stance from them and was ready to accept it if one or two of them had been fired. This was the beginning of my conflict at the university, as it became obvious that I was not a "one-of-us" or "belonging-to-us" kind of person. Moreover, I made critical observations about the level of methodological training, which I found quite weak, at least compared with my standards. These were partly based on my education in the Kolosi group, and partly on the grounds of what I had seen and experienced during my trips abroad.

Another criticism I repeatedly made in discussions at the university was about research and publication. In line with the old division of labor, in which people do teaching at the universities and research in the academic institutes, only the number of classes and students that one taught, and not participation in research programs or publishing articles, served as the basis for evaluation. Compared to most of my colleagues I was quite effective in the latter, but this was not much appreciated or taken into account. In fact, I was considered to be one of those persons who just benefits from his internationally developed networks and helps foreign researchers to exploit valuable Hungarian data in order to further his own career. This was a typical view in Hungary in the first half of the 1990s, and I was not the only one who was denounced in this way.

In addition to lecturing at the university in classes with increasing numbers of students from one cohort to the next, I attended the annual RC 28 conferences and the annual ISSP meetings. Along with several colleagues I participated in the research project "Social Stratification in Eastern Europe after 1989," led by Ivan Szelenyi and Don Treiman. I also joined another international research network, the European Consortium of Sociological Research, which was based on institutional membership and where I represented TARKI. These activities required quite a lot of research and writing papers. Formally, this work was unpaid, but the return from these investments was that I became even more internationally visible and recognized. In 1994 I became a member of the Board of RC 28, and held this position for eight years. I was proud to follow in the footsteps of Andorka and Kolosi onto this board.

My activities in the private sector also changed as TARKI faced rising competition in the market. At the beginning of the 1990s, more and more private profit-oriented public opinion research companies were being established, while TARKI remained a non-profit organization with a kind of academic profile that worked for academic institutions and the government. Nevertheless, the Institute was already quite large, and we moved from the old apartment to a building of the Academy of Sciences and rented offices there. However, compared to the private customers our for-profit competitors served, our state customers had declining budgets with which to contract our research services. Thus, we had to increase our share of market-oriented activities, and, among others, we had to end the Hungarian Household Panel survey due to financial difficulties. Slowly, my research interests in social mobility turned out to be a less-demanded topic in the center. Still, we did significant research on social inequality, though with a much stronger policy orientation. Purely academic papers written for conferences became less welcome.

In 1997 I had an opportunity to go on sabbatical. However, in Hungary, sabbaticals do not exist in the traditional sense that people can go away for some time while they still get paid. Instead, a sabbatical is an unpaid leave, so one has to apply for some grants to go on one. In 1997 social mobility became one of the core topics in the Netherlands Institute for Advanced Studies (NIAS), and I was invited and received a fellowship to join the nucleus studying social mobility for five months. Again, I could work with my Dutch colleagues and also with some famous scholars in the field, such as Don Treiman and Tom DiPrete from the US, and Walter Müller from Germany. This was a very good and productive period in which I could once again be a 100 percent academic researcher.

This long absence, however, brought an end to my family life. In fact, Olga and I were no longer "together," though we lived in the same house. The girls were no longer so young, 15 and 11 years old, and we decided to separate. Mainly as a result of my longer trips abroad, I had enough savings to buy a small apartment in Budapest. In the summer of 1997 I moved out of our family house with some furniture, my PC, my records and professional books, and my personal belongings, leaving everything else, including 20 years of marriage, behind.

The next, longer period, between 1997 and 2001, brought a particular financial advantage for me. I have received a four-year grant from the Hungarian state, a so-called *Szechenyi fellowship*. This was a special program organized by the Ministry of Education aimed to improve the financial situation of the best Hungarian scholars, with the condition that they teach at the university, do some research that would lead to publication, and remain in Hungary instead of going abroad for an extended period. As a result, I mostly stayed in Hungary during this time, and continued my teaching activity at undergraduate and postgraduate levels at the university.

The increase in the number of undergraduates persisted. We had cohorts with 70–80 students in the field of sociology, and the Ph.D. program took about 20 students. Moving from our old building to a new one was the only improvement in the general situation at the university. In addition to general education and directing diplomas, I gave classes on three particular fields of empirical sociology: educational inequalities, middle-class formation and the emergence of self-employment, and perceptions of social inequalities. These classes provided me with the only opportunity to develop some relationships with students who seemed to be more interested in empirical research, and many of them went on to the Ph.D. program.

By the end of my grant period I had put together a volume of my writings on the three topics mentioned above. Some of the papers were originally written and published in English, and were now being published in Hungarian for the first time.[13] I also edited a course book with basic texts on social mobility research translated from English.[14] Finally, I made my habilitation and became eligible for the position of full professor.

The end of the 1990s brought a further rise in the applied character of my research work at TARKI as well. In 1998, it turned from a non-profit institute to a for-profit one, a real think-tank, and kept only part of its activities in the non-profit sector. This was a move necessitated by reality. For a long time the Institute had not received any support from the state. We lived almost entirely from policy-oriented and market-oriented activities, and could no longer afford pure academic research. Nevertheless TARKI did start a Household Monitor Survey, and it became one of the four or five biggest survey houses and public opinion research institutes in Hungary. Still, we had financial problems. For example, we had to move to a cheaper office building located less centrally in the city.

In sum, it seemed to be reasonable to establish a corporation where employees could also buy shares and become the owners of the center. I bought some TARKI stock, but I was never among the biggest shareholders, as were Kolosi and the other directors of the Institute. Probably, the reason that I did not buy more stock was that I felt ambivalent about the changes in TARKI. I fully understood that these steps were necessary, but I could not put my heart into them. My research interests were of an academic kind and I wanted to keep my old-fashioned approach to science alive.

In order not to abandon my life as an academic researcher completely, I found I would have to leave the country again. But I could not formally migrate because my grant required me to stay at home. However, due to my former collaborations, and being embedded in international research networks, I was invited to participate in several projects. I started to work again with Hans-Peter Blossfeld, for his Globalife Project in Germany. I was asked to write a chapter on the trends of class mobility in Hungary for a project by Richard Breen and John Goldthorpe, and I was able to join a project on self-employment led by Walter Müller, and by Richard Arum from the US.[15] Once again it was my unpaid activities that brought the most satisfaction into my professional life, but this was hard work in addition to my two paid jobs.

I also applied for foreign fellowships, and when my Hungarian grant period was over I went on sabbatical again. From January 2002 until mid-2003 I spent three semesters abroad on the usual unpaid leave. This was less a problem with TARKI, but required more negotiation with the university. They hired someone to teach my classes for this period, but I was told that I must return to my job after this sabbatical or I would loose my tenured position at the university.

At the beginning of the sabbatical I worked at the Hanse-Wissenschafts-Kolleg in Germany. Then, I was a Jean Monnet Fellow at the European University Institute in Florence. There I worked with Jaap Dronkers on educational inequality and on public–private school effectiveness, using partly Hungarian and partly international data. All of these projects and grant periods led to several publications, articles in journals, and chapters in edited books. In fact, in the last couple of years I published more in English than in Hungarian. I simply had no time to write everything twice; that is, in both languages. In the end, this strategy did not turn out to be successful at home because foreign publications did not help me in my formal academic career at the university. They simple ignored this part of my activity. My international research was more of a disadvantage than advantage in Hungary.

While I was abroad I applied for the position of full professor, but I did not receive it. Colleagues who had spent more time at the university teaching were preferred. And, in the meantime, universities had changed their rules and decided to offer full professorships only to those who had the Doctor of Academy degree as well. Since this was the only remaining scientific degree in the hands of the Academy, in effect the universities were declaring that the Academy of Science was more selective and rigorous than they were. My insider's view, from the time I had served as secretary to the Sociological Board that vetted Academy candidates, suggests that this was not the case. During my time there, getting the Academy of Science degree in sociology became much easier, so that in the end I decided to resign from my post.

Anyway, when I returned to Hungary again in 2003 I simply continued as before, working in my two jobs. Fortunately, I did not return to this life alone. By that time I had a partner, Erzsebet, a young sociologist who worked for the Central Statistical Office. We had had a relationship since about 1996, but this became stronger when I separated from my family. We came together both personally and professionally, and all of the Hungarian chapters I have done with the various international projects in which I participated were co-authored with her.[16]

Coda: where am I now?

Just like sociology in Hungary, I have had to face challenges, and my activities as a sociologist have been influenced by the political and economic changes in Hungary. I work both in the public and the private sector of sociology. I try to maintain rigorous academic standards, which is not easy under the present conditions of the discipline in Hungary. With respect to the challenges my university in the public sector faced, I believe that it was not able to respond adequately to the generally increased demand for education. Hardly any changes have been made in the curriculum. We teach students who are not very interested in sociology, but who just want to obtain a degree. Sociology is seen as an easy field in Hungary, as well as one that opens up quite a wide range of various kinds of employment. The entrance exam is also not as difficult as in other fields. For example, a math exam is not required, and this seems to be a major point when students decide to continue their studies at the tertiary level. I share some of the blame for this since I did not do much to change anything in the university. I have generally chosen to absent myself on a fairly regular basis, and, while I have voiced my opinions, I have not been particularly loyal or actively participated in university affairs.

TARKI, in the private sector, responded better to the challenges, even if I was not always happy with them. I have been more active in TARKI probably because I have felt more "at home" there in comparison to the university. I understand and I can accept the logic of the market that drives TARKI, even if I dislike it sometimes. And it is possible to keep a certain level of academic quality for research there. I also understand, but cannot accept, the logic of state redistribution—flavored now by market directives as well—that drives my university, and I am afraid that the level of quality for teaching cannot be maintained there, either by academic or by market standards.

Nostalgic thoughts are frequent in post-socialist countries these days, and I also have some feelings of this kind for the 1980s. I did not need to work two jobs. I participated in high-level academic research in Hungary, and I could combine it with international research activities. I was able to make successful career moves in every respect. Surprisingly, combining different roles, trying to be active both in Hungary and abroad, turned out to be more difficult after the collapse of socialism. As a result, I had to make a choice and my preference was to be more recognizable internationally during these years, while my local career slowed down. Also surprisingly, my standards for hard work, achievement orientation, and the high quality that characterized the early stages of my professional career in the Kolosi group, did not become the general principle of sociology in Hungary. Belonging to a special interest group or network matters more than the quality of one's work. I do not feel that Hungarian sociology has become more meritocratic than before. In fact, "laboratories" of an academic kind similar to those we had in the 1980s do not exist anymore in Hungary. There are fewer funds for basic academic research, where outcomes can be expected only five years or even more afterwards. All research must be much more practical and utilitarian in the short run. Colleagues who decided to stay close to some of the new parties, or who appear frequently in the media, are more successful than their less-connected or exposed counterparts. These activities buy more in the local market of Hungarian sociology than does careful academic research that leads to more serious publications, even though the latter is likely more relevant over the long term.

With respect to my personal life, I continue to live with Erzsebet. We do plenty of things together, including work and leisure. My relationship to Olga is on an even keel. Julia is already 22, and studies at the university. She is interested in the arts, especially in theater. Katalin is 18 and graduated from secondary school in the spring of 2004. She is more interested in the social sciences (e.g., communication studies), and plans to continue her studies at the University of Economics. At this point it seems that neither of my daughters will follow me into sociology. However, if I think of myself, I did not want to be a sociologist at their age either. And, given what I think about sociology in Hungary these days, I would not recommend this choice to them.

My own future I can predict much easier. I turned 50 in 2003, and I can continue to work my two and one-half (or three) jobs, teaching at the university, writing policy-oriented reports for TARKI, and participating in academic projects in the international realm. But I am getting older, and I am getting tired of this workload as well. I occasionally think of migrating abroad, but this doesn't seem to be a very satisfactory solution to me. It would be better to have only one job of an academic character. But I do not see much chance for this because one job in sociology would hardly provide an adequate salary in Hungary.

Since the country has joined the European Union there are some opportunities to apply for funding for EU projects, and I have done so. If we are successful it might be possible for me to buy out part of my teaching obligations at the university, or of my report-writing duties at TARKI. Then I could participate in international projects for money, and not on the unpaid basis I have done for so long. This gives me some hopes for the future, but otherwise I do not expect much improvement or change in the short run. I will continue to work my "three jobs" until I can no longer do this, or I give up something—most likely my international activities.

Notes

1 *Valosag* was run by the Society of Public Education and was made up of non-fiction articles about society in a popular format targeted for a broad intellectual audience.

2 In addition to our department, there was one on social structure (applying a class approach), one on studying workers' parties and workers' movements in Western countries, and one on the youth problems

3 In Hungary, the research and teaching staff in the Party Institute, the academic institutes, and the universities had tenured positions.

4 One could make a private tourist trip to the West every third year, and one could travel to the West with an organized tourist office group even more frequently.

5 Rudolf Andorka and Tamas Kolosi, eds, *Stratification and Inequality: Hungarian Sociological Studies I* (Budapest: Institute of Social Sciences, 1984).

6 Peter Robert, "A Multidimensional Approach to Social Mobility," pp. 223–244 in *Stratification and Inequality: Hungarian Sociological Studies I*, eds Rudolf Andorka and Tamas Kolosi (Budapest: Institute of Social Sciences, 1984).

7 Peter Robert, "A tarsadalmi mobilitas tobbdimenzios megkozelitese," *Statisztikai Szemle* 62, 12 (1984): 1225–1240; "Tarsadalmi mobilitas-Statuszmobilitatas," *Szociologia* 14, 1–2 (1986): 111–142; and "Mobilitas es reprodukcios folyamatok a magyar tarsadalomban," *Valosag* 30, 10 (1987): 37–47.

8 Harry B.G. Ganzeboom, Ruud Luijkx, and Peter Robert, *Trends in Intergenerational Occupational Mobility in Hungary Between 1930 and 1989*, Working Paper Series 58 (Tilburg: Tilburg University Department of Sociology, 1989).

9 Harry B.G. Ganzeboom, Paul M. de Graff, and Peter Robert, "Reproduction Theory on Socialist Ground: Intergenerational Transmission of Inequalities in Hungary," pp. 79–104 in *Research in Social Stratification and Mobility*, Vol. 9, ed. Arne L. Kalleberg (Greenwich: JAI Press, 1990).

10 Max Haller, Tamas Kolosi, and Peter Robert, "Social Mobility in Austria, Czechoslovakia, and Hungary: An Investigation of the Effects of Industrialization, Socialist Revolution, and National Uniqueness," pp. 153–192 in *Class Structure in Europe: New Findings from East–West Comparisons of Social Structure and Mobility*, ed. Max Haller (Armonk: M.E. Sharpe, 1990).

11 Albert Simkus and Peter Robert, "Attitudes Toward Inequality: Cross-National Comparisons and Class Divisions in Hungary," *International Journal of Sociology* 25, 4 (1995–96): 85–102.

12 The Academy of Sciences kept only one remaining scientific degree in its hands, the title Doctor of Academy. There is a separate board for each discipline conferring the degree. It appoints a committee for the public defense through which one can obtain

this title. In the 1990s I served as the secretary of the Sociological Board of the Academy.

13 Peter Robert, *Tarsadalmi mobilitas a tenyek es velemenyek tukreben* (Budapest: ARTT-Szazadveg, 2000), 344.

14 Peter Robert, ed., *Tarsadalmi mobilitas: hagyomanyos es uj megkozelitesek. Szoveggyujtemeny* (Budapest: Uj Mandatum, 1998), 323.

15 Hans-Peter Blossfeld, Erik Klijzing, Melinda Mills, and Karin Kurz, eds, *Globalization, Uncertainty and Youth in the Society* (London: Routledge, 2005); Richard Breen, ed., *Social Mobility in Europe* (Oxford: Oxford University Press, 2004); and Richard Arum and Walter Müller, eds, *The Reemergence of Self-employment: A Comparative Study of Self-employment Dynamics and Social Inequality* (Princeton, N.J.: Princeton University, 2004).

16 Peter Robert, Erzsebet Bukodi, and Ruud Luijkx, "Employment Patterns in Hungarian Couples," pp. 307–331 in *Careers of Couples in Contemporary Society: From Male Breadwinner to Dual Earner Families*, eds Hans-Peter Blossfeld and Sonja Drobnic (Oxford: Oxford University Press, 2001); Peter Robert and Erzsebet Bukodi, "Winners or Losers?: Entry and Exit into Self-Employment in Hungary: 1980s and 1990s," pp. 245–276 in *Self-employment Dynamics in Advanced Economies*, eds Richard Arum and Walter Müller (Cambridge: Cambridge University Press, 2004); and "Changes in Intergenerational Class Mobility in Hungary: 1973–2000," pp. 287–314 in *Social Mobility in Europe*, eds Richard Breen and Ruud Luijkx (Oxford: Oxford University Press, 2004).

8 An accidental encounter with the world of sociology

Petya Slavova

The story that follows is not built upon any particular methodology. To be more precise, I have tried to apply a historical method in analyzing my own professional biography. I have aimed at identifying those factors and events that have played a significant role in my professional development so far.

The university

My encounter with sociology began in a rather random, accidental, and to a certain extent, unpleasant way. After graduating from high school in a small town in the southeastern part of Bulgaria, I decided to apply to Sofia University "Saint Kliment Ohridski." I wanted to study law. According to the rules for applying for a university back then, I had the right to take exams that would allow entry into a number of disciplines. Since I wanted to study law, it was my first choice. I chose the other disciplines more or less randomly, without giving them much thought. I had to take two entry exams. One was in Bulgarian history, the other in language and literature. My biggest wish was to receive high enough grades in both exams to become a law student. To my great regret, although I received good grades they were not high enough to get into the law school.

For better or for worse, I had made it into sociology.[1] I was disappointed I had not achieved high enough grades for law. I was also concerned that I really didn't know what sociology was, and wondered what I would do once I graduated. All of my friends and relatives congratulated me on having been admitted to university, but they seemed not to hear the name of the discipline, or if they did, just smiled and wished me good luck. At the time, the academic year of 1994/95, Sofia University was the most prestigious institution of higher education in Bulgaria, and it remains in the top three of the best Bulgarian universities. Nonetheless, I felt as if I had failed personally.

I was faced with one of the most important decisions in my life. I could accept the fact that I could study sociology and go for it, or I could stay with my parents in my home town and prepare to take the exams again the next year. With the help of my parents, I decided that there was no point staying in the small town. It had nothing to offer me anymore. The most reasonable choice for me was to go to the university and then decide what to do after having studied sociology for a year.

Already at that time my father had foreseen what was going to happen in just a few years, i.e., that prestigious fields such as law or medicine would soon be saturated. Nowadays, instead of graduating with a "prestigious" major in which one must compete with huge numbers of fellow graduates, it is better to graduate in a major that is not as prestigious as law or medicine; one that only has a class of 30–40 students each year. Because of poor legislative and academic policy, at the present moment there are hundreds of unemployed lawyers in Bulgaria. To be sure, there are also unemployed sociologists, but they do not present in any way the social and economic problem created by the large numbers of unemployed young lawyers and economists.

Thus, on October 2, 1995, I timidly stepped into Auditorium 65 at Sofia University, and afterwards walked over to the building of the Faculty of Sociology. My confusion and tension grew, when, during the warm welcome, one of our future professors informed us that it was extremely difficult to answer the question "What is sociology?"

"It's easier to list what sociology is not," he added, "and it certainly is not building bridges." The only thing that got me through that day was finding out that of 40 or 45 students in the discipline, only one had actually applied for sociology as his first choice. The rest of us were failed applicants for law. During the first months, my fellow-students and I were hoping for excellent grades in our exams so that we could try to change sociology for law at the end of the year.[2]

Though hesitant and uncertain, I regularly attended the lectures and seminars, and carefully prepared for the exams. The first year flew by. At the end of the second semester, although I had an excellent average score in the exams, I decided not to change my major and to continue with sociology. The reasons for that decision were varied and numerous, and I am not going to list all of them. However, the ultimate reason was the fact that *sociology had become interesting to me!*

To a great extent, I sensed it intuitively. During the two semesters of the first year I had lectures in general sociology, social policy, methods of statistical analysis in sociology, and the history of sociology. I also took the required course in computers, where we were taught how to operate with DOS, although in Bulgaria and at the university people already were working with Windows. Though reluctantly as first, I had accepted the "invitation to sociology."[3] I also started taking classes in French, organized by the French Cultural Institute in Sofia.

During my five years at Sophia University there were several different factors that kept my interest in sociology alive, and that eventually defined the professional path that I am still following.[4] Perhaps most important was the process of education and communication with my professors. One of the big advantages of the majors that admit smaller numbers of students is the opportunity for professors and students to establish close and friendly communication. Students that are interested in particular issues are able to consult the teachers frequently.

Initially, I just watched as some of my fellow students were getting practical advice, and materials and books that were then unavailable in Bulgaria. In my class, only five or six students were actually interested in sociology, and they were reading extra books and papers and had the ambition to achieve something more in the field than the rest of us. Those students were supported by our professors and step by step they were being introduced to academic life. I got that kind of support in my third year, and it had an extraordinary influence upon my professional interests from that moment on.

For example, in the sociology of culture we had a new teaching assistant who had obtained her Ph.D. degree from the Éole des Mines de Paris. She organized her seminars in a way that was different. Unlike other seminars that were filled with tension and unpleasant feelings, hers were a lot more dynamic and the feedback was great. Not surprisingly, the workload was also much heavier. We had to translate papers, prepare and present our own articles, and write short papers during the semester. But that teacher had the talent to work with every single student. Under her guidance, I translated my first scientific text, an article by French sociologist Bruno Latour. It was later published in a collection of translated works. Perhaps what was most remarkable about that was that at the time my French was still below average.

Influenced by my teacher, I decided to apply to a summer seminar for students from Central and Eastern Europe, in Strasbourg. It was my first visit to a Western country, and my first encounter with Western European sociology. I was impressed by the rich university library and by the convenient access to many books and papers that were completely inaccessible in Bulgaria. I was also impressed by the diversity of courses that were offered.

The papers I had to write during my two-semester study of the sociology of culture acquainted me for the first time with the subject of urban space and the street. In the years to come my interest in the subject matter would only get deeper. As a result, the topic of my Ph.D. thesis is on one of the professions that focuses on the city: architecture.

I do not exaggerate if I state outright that the mutual influence and coexistence of two elements of my life as a student determined my future professional realization and interests. On the one hand, in the third year of my studies I had already gone through the fundamental sociological subjects (such as history of sociology, economic sociology, sociology of culture, sociology of labor, sociology of economic organization, statistical methods, etc.), which gave me a greater certainty and self-confidence. On the other hand, I had had the chance to meet a teacher educated in a European manner, who I was delighted to work with. For me, she became a model in whose steps I wanted to follow.

My friends from the university years were also very important. I do not know how, but at the end of the second year and the beginning of the third I became friends with five students who were really interested in sociology. We started discussing the quality of the educational process, the papers that we were reading, and the way the seminars were going. After classes we always went to the university caféwhere we talked about what we wanted from life, what our expectations were, what we liked or disliked. We started helping each other by exchanging books and explaining terms and ideas to each other. We even used to go to the library together looking for and finding the books and articles we needed.[5] I describe all of these things because to me they are the real foundations of a very strong motivation, based on true friendship and common professional interest. Today four of us are studying for a Ph.D. degree in different countries and institutions, but we still co-operate with each other, still help each other, and we meet whenever we have the opportunity to do so.

By that time, my personal interest had already transformed into something new. From the third year on my interest in sociology was no longer by intuition. I had already chosen a role model to follow. I was starting to plan my professional life. I had already accumulated very important knowledge based on the classical sociological books from the end of the nineteenth century and the beginning of the twentieth (i.e., Durkheim, Weber, Simmel, Pareto, etc.). However, most important, the environment motivated me to read, to look for, and to orient my own interests.

The third year in question turned out to be crucial for my development because it was precisely then that I dared to take an optional course on Karl Marx's sociological ideas. I say "dared," because everybody in the faculty was talking about how difficult this course was, and how hot-tempered and strict the professor who was teaching it was. I was worried about whether or not I was prepared for the upcoming work with Marx's texts, but there was no way to find that out without having started the course.

The course was extremely demanding from the point of view of the work we had to do, as well as of the lecturer. The whole idea was for us to put aside the prejudices about Marxist theory that had been in existence in Bulgarian society after the fall of socialism and to try and follow the logic and the application of the Marxist scientific method that even today is part of many theoretical movements. We read Marx's original texts, as well as papers by scientists that had applied Marxist theory, such as Georgian philosopher Merab Mamardashvili, Georg Lukacs, etc. I have to admit that after the end of the course, throughout which I was really stressed and did not even dare to speak, I was very pleased that I had actually taken it. With time, I realized that macro-sociological theory wasn't my best interest and I started orienting myself towards Max Weber's ideas, and anthropological methods.

The path of development that my friends and I were following was absolutely different from the pragmatic one the rest of our fellow-students had chosen. The majority of them, instead of reading and analyzing sociological literature, had chosen to work in part-time jobs in several marketing agencies and thus practice sociology. As a student, the only job one could get was to take part in the conduct of surveys or code survey sheets. It had its good points, of course, not to mention the money earned. If one had a job at a marketing agency, there was hope that maybe after graduating from the university, promotion could be achieved and a start made at making a living.

Frankly speaking, the work in the academic environment did not seem very prestigious. It was poorly paid, and a future of constant reading in dusty libraries or offices was not exactly a dream come true. I cannot lie. Sometimes reading seemed pointless to me and I, like most of my colleagues, was tempted by the idea of finding a job and directing my future career toward business, not academic life. Despite the temptations, until the end of my studies my top priority remained the university work, the additional classes in sociology, and the ongoing French language course.

Eventually, I came to the final semester when I had to prepare my MA thesis. I had thought of the topic long before that moment. It was in the sphere of urban sociology.[6] While attending the summer seminar in Strasbourg I had the chance to read a few articles about the city and the street. The city I was interested in was the capital of Bulgaria, Sofia. The subject of analysis I was interested in were the old public buildings and the process of their construction. The naïve question I had asked myself so many times while walking along the streets of Sofia was: "How come these beautiful Baroque buildings, from the end of the nineteenth century and the beginning of the twentieth, not many in number but distinguishable from the others, appeared in a declined town like Sofia that has been just chosen for the new Bulgarian capital?"[7]

Keeping in mind that urban sociology was not very popular and poorly developed in Bulgaria, I could not figure out which of my professors I could ask to be my supervisor. Eventually, I turned to the most friendly and open-minded of our teachers. She was very intelligent and used to answer all our questions. She was also very interested in everything related to France and, just as I assumed, she had read books on urban sociology. It turned out that she knew personally one of the greatest French historians of the city, Bernard Lepetit. I was delighted to learn that my professor had some of his articles, along with other valuable books. After my meeting with her I went home with a bag full of books and a head full of ideas.

The final semester of my studies I spent among the archive documents in the National Library and in the State Archive of Sofia, as well as buried beneath the piles of books back in my flat. I had taken the writing of my thesis pretty seriously, and the subject I was working on was simply fascinating. In the meantime, one of my friends was also working on his thesis with archive documents in the National Library, so we helped each other or just sat down and talked over coffee when we were tired of reading.

During that period, besides my work on the thesis, there was a difficult and obtrusive question that was always on my mind and would not leave me alone: "What am I going to do and where am I going to work after I defend my thesis in a few months?" I was always trying to put it out of my mind since the writing of my thesis gave me enough troubles. I kept telling myself that if I went on like that I would neither be able to prepare my thesis, nor to find a good job. During those years I could not recognize that life is not ordered in drawers, and that whenever we want we can open one and close another drawer. I just could not picture that there could be several drawers opened at the same time and that unpleasant things could escape from some of them.

I defended my thesis and received the highest possible grade, even though I didn't think I really deserved it afterwards. Right after I had given the thesis to the reviewer, I discovered some really weak points in it. However, there was nothing I could do. Besides, the high grade was not an incentive since everybody received good grades, and they continue to do so even now. The thing that made me feel really good was the fact that for the first time I had conducted my own research on archive documents, and that I had found very interesting facts and information that I use even now in my work. In fact, just this year I have finally had the chance to rewrite my thesis and turn it into an article that is about to be published.

After the wild party I threw for my graduation, I woke up as an unemployed MA in sociology.

And now what?

I have to admit that the morning after the party the first thing that came to my mind was the thought of relief: "It's over! No more dusty archives or constant rewriting of the text! No more university classes! I am free!" Unfortunately, I was wrong.

A month before the defense of my thesis my favorite teaching assistant had returned from France. She asked me whether I had seen the news about the scholarships granted to Ph.D. candidates by the Agence Universitaire de la Francophonie. For the second year in a row, the Agence was selecting graduates from the humanities who spoke French and was giving them the opportunity to get a Ph.D. degree either from the Éole des Hautes Éudes en Sciences Sociales in Paris, or from the Ph.D. School for Graduates from Central and Eastern Europe in Bucharest. The students that would go to Bucharest would spend a year there preparing, and after that, based on the projects they wanted to do for their Ph.D. theses, they would be sent to different universities in France, Belgium, Switzerland, or Canada. I told her I already knew about the program, because for the past two years I had been regularly attending the seminars organized by the Agence, either at the university or at the French Cultural Institute.

I was still deciding whether to apply or not, but nevertheless wrote a paper and took it to that same teaching assistant. The topic was Sofia, but this time the subject of analysis was the present project for renewing and reconstructing the buildings in the center of the capital. Just as I thought, she told me that the paper did not have the structure of a project, did not have all the necessary elements, and that there were mistakes. But she liked the idea very much, as well as the arguments I had stated to support my choice. While writing my thesis I had found valuable information that helped me to write this paper. With the help of my teacher, the paper was shaped as a good project for me to apply with.

For the first time in my life I was going to present ideas in French, and in front of an international jury. The very thought of it was frightening to me. My teacher helped me out by organizing a "mock presentation" of my project.

She corrected the way I expressed myself and gave me some valuable advice on how to act and react. Thanks to all these efforts, I made a brilliant presentation. I won a scholarship for Romania, while the one for France was won by the son of one of my professors at the university. I do not recall being very disappointed, when the French professor who was the head of the jury told us that only the one scholarship for France was certain. The others for Romania were not because the school was having some financial problems. So it turned out that I had won the scholarship, but I did not know whether I was going to go or not. I also had the upcoming defense of my MA thesis to worry about. Therefore, I forgot about Romania and focused on the present moment.

I defended my thesis successfully, and during my first days as an unemployed MA in sociology I started thinking about what kind of a job I wanted and how to get it. The main thing for me by that time was to become financially independent from my parents. During the years of my study they had given me all the financial support I needed to live in Sofia, and to take language courses at the French Cultural Institute. The idea to become a doctoral student did not attract me because I knew that the grants for Ph.D. students in Bulgaria were not high enough to cover my living costs. For that reason I stopped looking for Ph.D. scholarships, abroad or in Bulgaria.

Unfortunately, one cannot find ads that offer work for sociologists in the Bulgarian newspapers. After ten days of going through the papers and consulting friends and relatives, I went looking in the yellow pages for all the marketing research agencies that I had heard of. Even though it was my first time looking for a job, and I was still very timid, I decided to call all of them. At the first agency I called I was rejected in a very pleasant way. At the second agency, after a few minutes of hesitation, they told me to bring over my CV that very day.

I could not believe my luck since it was one of the best research agencies in Sofia, and it was also a branch of a big European research agency. My first interview with the president of the agency went very well. My lack of experience, and the fact that I preferred French to English, did not help me, and he told me that he needed some time to think about it and would call me soon. The next day I got a call and was invited for a second interview with the president. You can imagine how happy I was. It turned out that he had called three of my professors at the university. They had recommended me, and on the second week after my graduation, without a day of experience in an actual sociological research project, I was starting as a researcher in the Services Department of one of the most prestigious agencies in Bulgaria. I had forgotten about Romania and the possibility that I might receive a scholarship, and that maybe I would have to go to Romania in September or October later that same year.

I loved the work at the agency. For the first time I was organizing and participating in actual surveys from the very beginning through to the final data processing. Every research, survey, or poll had its own specifics and I was learning new things every single day. It was difficult. I was taking work home with me or for the weekends, or I stayed late in the office, but the feeling of complete satisfaction made all of it worth while. The salary of a new researcher, like me, was above the average wage level for Sofia, which itself was higher than in the provinces. However, the cost of living was also higher in Sofia. Nonetheless, I immediately became financially independent.

Three months and five days later I received a letter from the Bucharest School notifying me that I had been given a scholarship and that I had to be there by November 9. That was the second time in my life that I had had to make a crucial decision for my future, following my original decision to study sociology. I was rather hesitant because I loved my job. But I was only 23 years old, and if I wanted to go on with my studies this was the perfect opportunity to do it. My friends and relatives knew all about it and were unanimous that I had to quit my job and go to Romania. In any case, it was going to be a valuable experience. So I resigned, even though my boss had offered me a permanent job, something extremely rare for the Bulgarian reality, and a raise. A few days later, in a bad mood, I got on the train to Bucharest.

The Romanian experience

My feelings about my stay in Romania are mixed. At the Ph.D. School for Social Sciences for Students from Central and Eastern Europe, every week we had a guest lecturer from one of the university partners of the School. The guest professor lectured for three days, and at the end of the third day he/she gave us a written assignment on some topic. I felt as if I was back in secondary school and not at the university. We received grades for every assignment, and, after the first month, a type of a hierarchy was established among the students. The grades were an incentive to do as well as we could, and some of my colleagues were cheating instead of trying to achieve something on their own. Presences and absences were also marked.

In fact, the general idea of the school was to prepare us for the time when we were going to study for our Ph.D. degrees at one of the Western universities. The program was based upon the judgment that we did not speak French well enough, which was true, and that we needed general knowledge in social science. Every single week we had lectures from diverse fields of study, i.e., from the history of ancient art to the origin of political parties in a changing Central and Eastern Europe.

The school required us to attend the lectures regularly, get good grades, and at the end of the program present a proposal for a Ph.D. thesis. They were going to evaluate our work and, according to the results, send us to one of the Western universities.

Personally, I did not feel comfortable in that environment for different reasons. The seminars and lectures were not well organized. The program consisted of many subjects, but nothing specific, only general studies. Due to its location, the school was more of a Romanian one and not an international school. In my class, out of 15 students, two of us were Bulgarian, one was Polish, two girls were from the Republic of Moldova, and the other ten were

Romanians. All of this made me feel bad, and during the seven months I was there I regretted the decision to quit my job and go to Bucharest. The scholarship was one and a half times lower than my salary at the agency. I was spending most of my time at the library, in front of the computer logged on to the Internet, or reading a book. I also learned how to work out a research project and how to present it in public.

For the seven months in Bucharest, one of the real bonuses for me was the access to the small but very valuable Library of Social Sciences, where I found a book by the French sociologist Florent Champy.[8] This discovery shaped my idea on my upcoming proposal. Now, this very book, along with some other articles by Champy, provides the theoretical foundation for my Ph.D. thesis. On the Net, I also found his e-mail address and decided to contact him. Since then, he often sends me articles and works of his, and has also agreed to read and review my papers. I have not yet had the opportunity and pleasure to meet him personally, but for the first time in my life I feel strongly influenced by somebody's ideas and work.

During those seven months I managed to get to know and recognize the characteristics of the different lecturers coming from different French-speaking countries and universities. The Canadians were the most pragmatically oriented ones in terms of choosing a subject of analysis, as well as in their research methods. The next in pragmatism were the Swiss lecturers. Between the Belgium and the French professors, I have to admit, I could not find considerable differences. My work in Romania was most influenced by Champy's works, and by the advice and suggestions of a Belgian professor and a Swiss professor.

Unfortunately, I did not make much progress with my French since it was only during the lectures that we actually spoke French. During the rest of the time, the ten Romanians and the two Moldavians spoke Romanian. The other Bulgarian student and I spoke Bulgarian, and only used French when speaking to our Polish and Romanian colleagues. However, since none of us spoke French very well, in the end we all spoke with broken grammar and a pronounced accent.

At the end of the academic year, the research proposal that I had prepared was reviewed and the board of the school decided to send me to the Université Libre de Bruxelles (ULB), where my supervisor was to be a professor I had already met through his lectures at the school. Jean Michel de Waele worked in the field of political sciences, and more precisely on political systems and parties and in Central and Eastern Europe.

To tell you the truth, I was very surprised by the choice of the school. A political scientist was going to be my supervisor, which meant that his field of studies was far from the studies of socio-professional groups and even less close to the sociology of architecture. The only common thing between my project and his work was the fact that he was interested in the changes in Central and Eastern Europe, and I wanted to study the post-Communist transformations of the profession of architecture in Bulgaria. The two things I wanted most at that moment were finally to leave Romania, and in the future to study a topic that I found interesting and motivating. Both of my wishes came true. After my not very pleasant stay in Romania, I was about to have an extremely difficult but also very important and interesting academic year in Belgium.

Finally a Ph.D. student in a Western university

In spite of the year I spent in the Ph.D. school in Bucharest, the following year I still had to obtain my masters degree at the Free University of Brussels in order to enroll in the Ph.D. program there. My education in Brussels was seen as a year of preparation for my Ph.D. degree, and that is why I had to earn high grades in the exams as well as to write a 60–80 page paper at the end of the year. The most important thing for me was to determine at the end of the academic year whether I was well prepared to organize and conduct a research project of my own, and whether I wanted to remain in the field of research.

Until the day I left for Brussels, my life had been going in a routine and school-like manner. In Brussels, I was to find out whether I was prepared for research activity, and, if so, to what extent. After the preparatory year in Bucharest, I went back to Bulgaria for a summer, and after that I went to Brussels. My family and friends gave me full moral support and encouraged me in the difficult choice to prepare the Ph.D. thesis in a language different from my native one.

On September 15, 2001, I landed with two suitcases at the International Airport of Brussels. My supervisor was there waiting for me. During the correspondence we had exchanged to that point, I had understood two important things. First, I could keep the subject I wanted to investigate, and second, that that teacher was an extremely dynamic and open-minded person. Moreover, my fear of the unknown that was awaiting me must have been so obvious that my supervisor put all his efforts into closing the distance between us so that I could easily overcome my stress and fear. That friendly manner, combined with a benevolent strictness, was the first factor that helped me quickly to adapt to the totally different and unfamiliar situation.

The second factor that influenced my successful integration and the achievement of good grades on the exams, as well as the writing of a relatively good paper in the shortest time ever, was the invitation that I received to become part of a research team. The Group for Socio-Political Analysis of the Countries of Central and Eastern Europe,[9] whose leader was my supervisor, consisted of Ph.D. students mostly from Central and Eastern Europe. The main topics of investigation were the political parties and the political systems of the young European democracies. At the beginning I felt out of place with my interest in the professional group of the architects in Bulgaria, but I soon found a common language with the rest of the students. That helped me to broaden my interests in all aspects and problems concerning the transformation of the countries of Eastern Europe. I "saw" that the architects were not alone on this planet, and, for instance, that the architects and the political parties in Bulgaria had a lot in common.

It was then that I stopped wondering why the board of the Bucharest School had chosen exactly that professor for my supervisor. By talking to the students in the team, I got to know what writing a Ph.D. thesis actually meant, what steps one had to go through, and what fears a Ph.D. student had to deal with. Maybe the most important thing was that I started to feel part of the team, and that meant that the integration had been successful. All of my colleagues, regardless of how busy they were, were helping me by reading the paper I was writing, correcting my mistakes, and giving me ideas and recommendations. They always found time to answer all of my questions.

The third factor that made my year in Belgium successful was the university environment in which I had the pleasure to work. I had access to an enormous library, and to the Internet and all its resources. I had the opportunity to attend a great number of seminars and conferences. All that helped me to broaden my view of life, as well as my understanding of what work in a normal academic environment meant.

The fourth factor that made my year in Belgium successful was once again the friends I made. I had the opportunity to live on the university's campus and to be surrounded by students from all over Europe (i.e., Belgium, Spain, Italy, etc.). Even though I spent most of my time at the office that the Institute of Sociology had given me, and I was rarely going to the wild parties that the students were throwing, I managed to create long-lasting friendships that I still keep up.

During the first year in Brussels I had to work hard in order to manage to continue in the program. For that reason I had no time to go sightseeing in the city or to travel around the country. Nonetheless, in Brussels I felt very good, more so than in Bucharest, probably because everybody was speaking French. Even so, I missed Sofia and Bulgaria, and my old friends and my family missed me.

At the end of July 2002 I left Brussels happy that I was going back home, but also feeling somewhat nostalgic for the friends left behind, of the team of Ph.D. students and the nice relationships with them. The thought that was comforting me was that the next year I was going to return to Brussels.[10] So I left Belgium feeling satisfied with the work I had done and the conviction to continue my research. I was certain that I wanted to obtain a Ph.D. degree at ULB.

My return to Bulgaria, however, presented me with a few problems that I had to face. I had no income that would allow me to start working on my thesis, and I was not in touch with any research or investigation institution to back me up. Again, my parents were there to help me out financially, and I started to gather archive documents and interviews, and to look for scholarships. I also decided to apply for a Ph.D. degree in Bulgaria. Meanwhile, I wrote my first real article based on the paper I had prepared in Belgium. It was published in a French journal.[11]

I took the exams for a Ph.D. program in Bulgaria because it was going to give me some income during my stay in Sofia, and I would have the support of the university. I already knew that when one prepares one's thesis the most important things are the teamwork and the people who are working in relatively similar fields that one meets. Unfortunately, that was not everything.

In September, the Bucharest School informed its students that there was no money for the two-month scholarships. That upset me very much because so far I had always played by the rules and I had fulfilled all of their requirements. In the end, everything went well and we got the money, but I made the decision to go for the Ph.D. in Bulgaria. I wanted to feel certain that I was going to be able to conduct my investigation even if I did not have the financial means to go to Belgium the following year. During all that time, one of the few people who was always there for me, backing me up, and encouraging me that everything was going to be all right, was my supervisor in Brussels. As a person with considerable experience, he was right.

I was in a very strange and ironic situation. After my graduation from the Sociology Department at Sofia University my priority had been financial independence. Two years later, my priority had become my Ph.D. thesis, whatever the costs, even if I had to starve. At the end of 2002, after a two-month preparation for the exams for the Ph.D. program at Sofia University, I won one of the grants and became a doctoral student there.[12]

Just now, I am writing my thesis under the parallel supervision of Sofia University and the ULB. The topic of my thesis is the "Metamorphosis of the Profession of Architects in Bulgaria." I firmly believe that in future the study of the city and urban professions will be primary areas of research in Central and Eastern Europe.

Before finishing my story I would like to mention a vital factor that has motivated me over the past few years in my work in sociology, as well as to thank everyone who has supported me throughout all the difficulties. That factor is love, this time not for sociology but for one of my friends, as well as for the fellow students in the MA program with whom I continue to discuss articles and exchange ideas. We share a common fate as Ph.D. students with him, and build together our personal and professional lives. I will not list the names of all the friends, teachers, and relatives who have supported me in good and bad times. I only wish to extend to them, instead of a clever conclusion, a big "Thank You!" from my heart.

Notes

1 In Bulgaria, sociology first was established as a separate university major at Sofia University in 1976. Before that, sociologists in Bulgaria first had to graduate in philosophy, and in the last year take two semesters of sociology. The Institute of Sociology that still exists within the frames of the Bulgarian Academy of Sciences was established in 1968.

2 Within the frames of the university, there still exists the possibility of changing the majors if one has a high average score from the exams during the year or from the admittance exams.

3 Peter L. Berger, *Invitation to Sociology* (New York: Anchor Books, 1963).

4 Until recently, most university programs offered only a five-year course of study, at the end of which the students obtained a Masters degree. A couple of years ago the

educational system underwent considerable change. Three degrees of higher education were introduced, Bachelors, Masters and Ph.D.

5 We were looking for two types of books and articles. The first was papers published by Bulgarian authors, mainly sociologists such as Georgi Fotev, Kolyo Koev, and Ivan Hadzijski. The second was translated works of Western sociologists such as Max Weber, Georg Simmel, Karl Marx, and Émile Durkheim.

6 Urban sociology is a discipline that had not yet been introduced in the (MA) program (in Sofia) when I was studying sociology (1995–2000). The course of urban sociology was introduced in 2001–02.

7 Sofia has been the capital of Bulgaria since 1879. Before then, it was an administrative and military center without much importance within the Ottoman Empire. Until the seventeenth century, the town was a prosperous place, but between the seventeenth and the nineteenth centuries it was devastated by natural disasters (earthquakes, floods, fires). In addition, the Ottoman Empire was generally in decline. The decision to make Sofia the new capital of Bulgaria was a political one, since during the Bulgarian Renaissance other towns had developed a lot more.

8 Florent Champy, *Les architects et la commande publique* (Paris: PUF, 1998); and *Sociologie de l'architecture* (Paris : La Decouverte, 2001).

9 See Group d'analyses des pays d'Europe Centrale et Orientale (GASPECO), www.ulb.ac.be/cevipol/gasppeco

10 The financial and academic conditions for the scholarship that I had won were a grant for a year in Bucharest. Upon graduating successfully from it I would receive a one-year grant for a Western university. If I passed the exams with high grades, and if I successfully defended my thesis, I would receive two grants for two months each that I could use for the following two academic years.

11 Petya Slavova, "L'architecture bulgare en transformations: quelques aspects organisationnels," *La nouvelle alternative* 17, 3 (2002): 39–50.

12 Those who want to become Ph.D. students in Bulgaria still have to pass a written and an oral exam in general sociology. Those who have taken both of these exams know that this is one of the most unpleasant experiences in the academic life of a student.

9 Belonging to a dying species

My experiences as an East German sociologist

Vera Sparschuh

During my school time I probably never heard about sociology and consequently could not start out to be a sociologist. In the beginning of the 1970s, when I was taking my final exams, I actually wanted to become a journalist. At the time, the education of journalists at Leipzig University was not a theoretical and classroom study, but rather an applied study through placement in a publishing house, television company, etc. After passing a demanding entrance examination at the publishing house Berliner Verlag, the next requirement was to work for one year as a trainee at a newspaper. I carried out this task at several newspapers in East Berlin, my home town. These included an evening newspaper (*BZ am Abend*), a small weekly company newspaper ("*Bremsenecho*" at *Berliner Bremsenwerk*), and a political weekly (*Horizont*).

My first actual professional encounter with the social reality of the German Democratic Republic (GDR) was fascinating. I learned a lot about life, especially the work life in which I participated at the company newspaper. It was at the company newspaper, for instance, that I completed my first night shift. The next morning, on the way home, I fell asleep leaning against the shoulder of a stranger sitting next to me on the Berlin city train. Thinking back to this time, I remember that the factory workers seemed very relaxed, apparently somehow untouched by their "socialist" environment. They had the certainty that their bosses depended on them, rather than the other way round. In contrast, I had to attend management meetings, where I observed management's fear of not reaching the production targets that had been set for them.

In some respects this was an artificial world. However, I understood that the workers were really the "leading class," although in another sense than the one I had been taught in school. Nevertheless, this experience in no way changed the open-minded and interested attitude I had about my socialist home country. On the contrary, I was eager to learn more. But when I was confronted with censorship during my work in the political weekly *Horizont*, I realized that being a journalist under socialist conditions was not congruent with that purpose.

At about the same time, by chance, I heard of an institution in the city of Halle, at the Workers and Farmers Faculty of the University of Halle, that prepared students for study in what was at the time called "socialist countries abroad." This institution was in constant need of students because, due to the strongly politicized environment and the high level of skill in the Russian language that was required, many of them used to leave during the preparatory year. Having spent five years of my childhood in Moscow while my parents worked as journalists for the GDR news agency *Allgemeiner Deutscher Nachrichtendienst*, I felt sufficiently qualified to study there. In Moscow I had attended a Russian school, and later a school for East German children at the East German embassy.

I decided it would do no harm to expand my geographic horizons by leaving the GDR for a while. So, I went to Halle, where I experienced an odd situation. The person responsible for the study abroad program offered me a wide choice of subjects. I could have studied medicine, economics—whatever I wanted. Asked for an immediate decision, I selected philosophy. That's how I came to Leningrad (now St Petersburg) in 1973.

Leningrad surpassed my expectations in every respect. Architecturally, it was beautiful. In addition, the town was steeped in history, and the museums, theaters, and concert halls were stunning. At the same time living conditions were harsh compared to my life in East Germany. I felt as if I were living in revolutionary times. I was quartered in a dormitory in Petrodvorez, more than an hour away from town. It was constantly cold. Warm water, if any, we only had once a week. We slept four to a room. My roommates were Ryskul, from Kazakhstan, Nina, from Siberia, and Marion, from a small village close to the Baltic Sea.

Zdanov University, which we attended, was located in the center of an old building full of long corridors. We would leave the dormitory at seven in the morning, be at the university from nine until five, and come back at seven in the evening when it was always dark. The libraries were well looked after and well-stocked, and it was in Leningrad that I first read Franz Kafka's *Castle*. We were not allowed to take it out on loan, but poring over its pages by the light of a green glass lamp in the reading-room was much more atmospheric anyway.

I made many contacts in Leningrad, getting to know not only Russian, Polish, and Hungarian students but Swiss and Americans as well. This kind of "contact with Westerners" was officially forbidden, but as we were only a small group of East Germans, the system of mutual surveillance did not function completely. It soon became clear to us which students in the group could be suspected of writing reports for the authorities back home. I do not think that they were Stasi agents, but they started very early to collaborate with the authorities.

It is very complicated to explain this situation from the contemporary point of view. Everyone was fully aware of the Stasi system. However, we did not speak about it except to very good friends, which in my case was my husband Jens Sparschuh. I met him on the train to Russia when he helped me to carry my heavy luggage. We decided to marry quickly, having known each other for only ten months, because this was the only way to receive a separate room in the student dormitory. He was 18 and I was 19 when we got married. We did not think this decision over too much since it was very easy to get divorced in GDR. Now we have been married for more than 30 years.

At the university, instead of being exposed to a constant stream of ideology as I had feared we might be, we were taught philosophy as a system of universal science embracing mathematics, psychology, ethnology, and anthropology. We were also treated to a detailed introduction to the history of philosophy. The classical Greek period took up a whole year, and one full semester was devoted to the work of Immanuel Kant.

Of course, we also had to listen to lectures on the history of the Russian Communist Party, and on Marxist theory. Moreover, not only was it a requirement to read every work and letter of Lenin's, but, because of the rigorous examination rules, we had to know everything by heart. This led to a more game-like attitude towards this part of the study. When did Lenin write these words or that letter? Remembering the date often made it easier to recall the content. Compared to the other subjects, this presented a trivial intellectual challenge.

In the fourth semester, I heard an introduction to sociology by Vladimir Yadov. A few lectures were enough for me to detect that this would be my special province. Yadov connected sociology with historical materialism, as this was then the only politically opportune way to present sociology at all. At the same time, he was a Mertonian. From his point of view, real sociological work could start only at the level of middle-range theories. He had co-founded the first sociological laboratory in Leningrad in 1962. When I met him he was the head of the department in the Institute of Social-Economic Problems in the Soviet Academy of Sciences.

Sociology was not taught as an independent subject at universities at that time, and I asked him if I could work by special arrangement under his supervision. He promised to make a decision on that question after having read my first scientific essay. I wrote about the relationship among the elements of Auguste Comte's methodology: observation, experience, and the comparative method. The full title of the essay was "The positive method of Comte's philosophy as a prerequisite of modern sociological positivism." Yadov liked the essay, and I started to commute between the university and his institute.

This sort of private study was not nearly as effective as a comprehensive program in sociology would have been. In any case, I learned a lot. Yadov was very strict when I did not progress with my studies. Once I tried to excuse myself and explained to him that I had to take part in the mandatory meetings of the German student group. He became very serious, it would be better for me to learn English and to engage in solid empirical research! I stress this incident because it shows that I learned to separate ideology from science under the same regime that was responsible for the ideologization of East Germany. Not until after the fall of the Iron Curtain, in 1989, did Yadov, who in the middle of the 1980s had been an adviser to Mikhail Gorbachev, tell me about the hard times he had experienced under Stalin's rule.[1]

Another unique aspect of my study was immersion in Kant's philosophy. In every aspect, intellectual, political, moral, he became the most important philosopher to me. In the GDR, Hegel was preferred, since the dialectical method allowed scientists to connect facts and events which were in fact discrete.

Although I finished my study with very good results, in June 1978, I became increasingly uncertain about using what I had learned in a professional career. Students from the USSR were often forced to start a "political career," and this was exactly the direction I wanted to avoid. Although I still felt sympathetic to the idea of socialism, I tried not to be too close to political power. This was due not only to Yadov's influence but also to that of my husband, who became increasingly critical toward the political system. He managed to finish his Ph.D., and then he left the academic system for political reasons and worked as a freelance writer.

In 1978 I managed to establish contacts with sociologists at Humboldt University, in Berlin, and got a temporary contract as a scientific assistant there. I was made responsible for the field of history and theory of sociology. I remember that the most important book for me at this time was Igor S. Kon's work on positivism in sociology, a history of sociology from the beginning of the nineteenth century that ended with a chapter on "critical sociology" in the United States.[2] My appreciation of Kon came from the work I was doing at Humboldt: a comparison of the history of the sociology of work in Russia and the Soviet Union and America, as well as from the scientific orientation of my German superior, Dieter Dohnke, who taught theory.

Given the theoretical and abstract nature of my work, and its distance from empirical research, it was probably easier for me than others to maintain a relatively independent and autonomous perspective. After having chosen my Ph.D. topic, the new French sociology, and especially the work of Alain Touraine, I felt more or less pleased with myself. At that time, a focus on Western theories implied a slightly critical orientation, a sort of competition with dogmatic theory using external sources. This helped me to overcome my insecurity concerning the question of the relevance or effect of the social sciences. Now I was able to concentrate entirely on research.

Yet, deep inside, I still was not content with my niche. I remember that at the same time there was a project about the *Lebensweise* (lifestyles) being run at Humboldt. Every member of the staff was involved in the fieldwork. I visited many flats to collect data, usually taking along our six-month-old daughter since I had not yet found a place in a nursery for her.[3] I collected very interesting material and observed interesting conditions. Regrettably, what I later read in the report did not reflect my own experiences in the field. Still, I became interested in changing my topic of research. While such a change might seem easy from a contemporary point of view, I had been hired to teach theory and my contract was scheduled only for four years. Moreover the lifestyles subfield was already occupied by other staff members who were not too interested in newcomers. I look back on this episode as a missed opportunity to leave the "ivory tower" of theory.

In 1984 I completed my doctorate (Ph.D.) on Touraine's action theory, *summa cum laude*. I was pregnant with my second child and I had already found another job. A new Department of Theory and History of Sociology, headed by Helmut Steiner, was founded at the Academy of Sciences of the GDR. The working conditions there were very comfortable, especially for a mother, since it was only required to show up at the academy once a week due to the limited amount of work space. However, I began to loose all my contacts with real life. At least in the university the students were present!

The GDR Academy was somehow far from being "real." Science was structured in accordance with the planned socialist society. Five-year plans of research activity were scheduled, and projects were designed that had to be realized within this period, regardless as to their topicality or feasibility. My first task was to prepare an encyclopedia of sociologists. In West Germany a new one had just appeared and ours was designed to rethink it from a Marxist perspective.[4]

The enterprise failed for reasons I no longer remember, but it did eventually have a fruitful outcome. The academy was forced to co-operate with the academies from other socialist countries, especially with the Academy of the USSR. At the same time, co-operation with Western partners, though unspoken, counted for more. So, everybody tried to make contacts with the West, and to become a *Reisekader*; that is, to become a part of the workforce sent abroad to the West. Co-operation with the East was an unavoidable necessity, but only a very few people were really interested. Insufficient command of the Russian language played a role in this lack of interest. For me, however, this offered a chance to travel to Russia, mainly Moscow, for about two weeks every year. And the more perestroika won ground, the more interesting these journeys became.

In the late 1980s, the Russian Academy was conducting a project on the history of Russian sociology. Biographies of Russian, and later also Soviet sociologists were collected. For the first time, Nikolai Bukharin was introduced in the history of sociology written under socialist conditions. Sociologists who worked in the 1920s and 1930s, and later suffered under Stalin's repressions, were also included. The project turned into a Russian–(East) German collaboration. I wrote the biographies about the sociologists of work. The book was printed in Russian, German, and English, but never succeeded in becoming more than "gray literature"; that is, it was published only in a special edition of the Academy of Sciences of the GDR and of the Soviet Academy.[5]

In one of the GDR Academy's five-year plans—I believe it was the one from 1985–90—a project on the history of Marxist sociological thinking in Germany was included. This meant that Helmut Steiner was to write a book on the subject. However, because of internal struggles, he left the institute before he had even begun. Such plans were regarded as "laws," so the project was handed over to me. As it happened, at that very moment I was beginning to long for a change—not so much in political terms but rather in personal and professional terms. Due to professional, political, and generational tensions, I was not able to cope with this topic.

The research group that I had to lead consisted of five people with very heterogeneous research experiences and interests. Perhaps it was a mistake on my part to agree to lead this group; but it was Steiner's wish. An older colleague felt better prepared for the job, and hence the collaboration became difficult. However, we did agree that the topic was not all that important at that moment. Nevertheless, we were unable to come up with an idea of how to move the project in another direction. The project had been designed to provide a broad view of the Marxist heritage. Unfortunately, it was a topic we were only partly interested in writing about. We started to read about the discussions on Marxism in the labor movement, and proposed to write about the impact Marxism had had on sociology in Germany. Our change in its conception was not accepted by the commission of the Sociological Research Council in charge of supervising and approving our project.

Given what I had experienced, I was very pleased to see the first signs of the end of the GDR, which appeared in 1988 and 1989. Oddly enough, in the beginning, I was more relieved professionally than politically. From my perspective, the political transformation seemed to be occurring too fast. The period of the "round tables," the start of a real political discussion, was rather short from my point of view. I soon had the feeling that political decisions were once again being made from "above." On the other hand, I was very curious. It was really a new world that we were able to experience now.

In the beginning of the 1990s I went to the USA for the first time in my life. My husband was invited to be a writer-in-residence at Grinnell College in Iowa. This journey opened a new world to the entire family, especially for our daughters who were 13 and eight at this time. Since my husband was invited on several occasions, I began to improve my English, and to get acquainted with the American education system. We even managed to travel to the West Coast and New York City.

Many colleagues of mine regarded the dispersal of the Academy of Sciences of the GDR at the end of 1990 as a tragedy. They feared, and rightfully so, that this change would cost them job security. I felt quite the opposite. For me it meant liberation from a constraining work task. However, I did not start a new topic or undertaking in 1989; rather, I supported other projects. For example, I traveled by car through the country and helped to establish a set of interviewers for a public research group that came into being at my institute. While doing this work, I observed the changes occurring in Berlin as well as in the small towns and villages across the country. I met people preparing themselves for the new life. I also took part in the political renewal of my Berlin home district. I attended the first negotiations of the politicians, and observed the first steps of political reorientation.

Very early on it became obvious to me that we East Germans were trying too hard to become West Germans, and trying to forget our past too quickly. In 1990, many of my colleagues were already quite decided on and confident about the direction of their further scientific and professional development. No doubt this was easier for those with an empirical research orientation looking forward to the "social experiment" that was expected in the near future or had already started to take place right in front of their eyes.

Surprisingly enough, I was more interested in the past than in the future. Perhaps my earlier engagement with the Marx project was one reason for my "backwardness." I had the feeling that there had remained something to be resolved. Furthermore, self-revelations from a variety of sociologists, concerning their life and work in the GDR, affected me. For example, one professor, who was a sort of "hardliner" from my point of view, confessed that he had collaborated secretly with Western institutions.

I began to wonder, what kind of science, mentality, and morality had developed in GDR sociology? How could one explain it? And, at about the same time, Jürgen Friedrichs, a professor from Cologne, asked me to assist him in collecting and documenting the Ph.D. works that had been done in sociology in the GDR. He hoped to discover critical and innovative views in the works of the younger generation. And, even though this may not have been the case, I was able to expand my knowledge concerning the history and the substance of GDR sociology significantly.[6]

In 1992, the *Wissenschaftler-Integrations-Programm* (WIP), a special program for former researchers of the academy, was developed by the government of the newly unified Germany. The aim of the program was to reintegrate gifted scientists into the scientific infrastructure of the reunited Germany. I applied with a project entitled "Socialism and Sociology," and was given an award. For the first two years my official employer was the *Koordinierungs- und Aufbauinitiative für die Forschung in den Neuen Bundesländern* (Initiative for the Coordination and Rebuilding of Research in the New Lands), which emerged as an outgrowth of the dissolution of the Academy of Sciences of the GDR.

During this time I believed that there was a real possibility for a new start in science for me. I attended conferences in Germany and in Europe, worked really hard, and had the feeling I was doing an important job. I established new contacts, for example with Dagmar Simon, a colleague from the Berlin Wissenschaftszentrum. Together, we published several articles on the history of sociology in the GDR.[7] Another important relationship developed with the Berlin branch of the Social Science Information Centre (IZ), especially with Ulrike Becker.

Upon completion of the first two years, the WIP program provided for the integration of the participants into a university, preferably in the New Lands. However, I was in no rush to find a university placement. The reason for this seems unclear to me now. One explanation might be that I had tried to avoid bringing any kind of attention to myself because I still felt unsure under the new conditions. I remember being very nervous at conferences. I did not believe that I could succeed in presenting my views and results. Perhaps I did not have faith in the goal and promise of the program either. In the end, this fear was not unfounded as only a few scientists actually received tenure positions. A final reason could have been that I really did not want to take a tenure position so soon after my previous one with the GDR Academy, but wanted to work as a freelance scientist, independent and involved in different projects. Yet even this latter explanation seems insufficient to me because in the family we often discussed the risks of freelance occupation for both wage earners.

Nonetheless, in 1994 I was assigned to work at Humboldt University in Berlin. Gerd-Joachim Glaessner, a scientist from the Free University of West Berlin and the chair of Political Science in the newly founded Institute of Social Sciences at Humboldt agreed to include me. My scientific interest in GDR history suited the profile of the chair very well. However, working as a sociologist I found myself incompatible with political scientists. I only realized very late that this arrangement was very convenient for Humboldt University, but less so for me. It turned out that the WIP program was a good opportunity for the university to acquire new resources. Furthermore, it was seen as politically correct to employ some East Germans during the time of the general reconstruction of the university.

Reconstruction meant the implementation of a new faculty and department system, even as the old structures were taken down. New professors from West Germany started their work at the university, with the support of staff mainly brought from the West as well. Only a few former East German scientists managed to gain new positions, and often these positions were for a limited time period. No one really wanted to employ WIP program members on a long-term basis. In my estimation, the university never seriously planned to integrate these people into the staff. So the contradiction between my background and the one of my chair eventually would provide a convenient excuse for the non-renewal of my contract.

On a more personal level, Glaessner addressed this issue quite openly. He "explained" to me that East German scientists should learn to live on grant writing, the way he himself used to operate. He recalled that during the demonstration on November 4, 1989, when we East Germans were in search of a new direction for our country, West Berlin scientists had already started to discuss the new job opportunities. This mentality irritated me. I knew the weakness of East German sociology very well and understood the necessity for a renewal. But this total shift to the disadvantage of the "Easterners" seemed unjust to me.

Still, I was very optimistic about the future. In general, I believed that the fall of the Wall was such an incredible historical event that much of what followed could be accepted. Nonetheless, during the next three years at Humboldt University I experienced a kind of discrimination, especially on the social level. Several East Germans worked at my chair in funded projects, but the real positions were held by Westerners—one professor and two young men. This fact alone amounted to a ranking. In contrast, the secretary was an East German woman. The atmosphere was not tense, but there was no real attempt to collaborate either. I felt as if I was regarded as not up to par, not only in scientific terms but also in terms of administration. There seemed to be an ongoing, though nebulous and never openly recognized confrontation, even if it was difficult to define where the borders were. Maybe it was due to a certain amount of awkwardness on my part, but still I had the feeling that this tension came from the other side.

Perhaps I was not used to this kind of competitiveness. Strangely enough I felt more and more that I had to be careful about what I was saying, much more so than ever in GDR times. I felt tolerated at best. I had never experienced this kind of "collaboration" before. In the GDR Academy I had encountered a lot of problems as well, but I was able to define them and the stakes of the game were not very high. Now I found myself in a fight, without visible opponents.

In contrast to the "real" collaborators, I had no office. I solved this problem by becoming the *Frauenbeauftragte* (a special position to support the interests of women) of the Department of Social Sciences. Through this position I got an office separate from Gerd-Joachim Glaessner's chair, and close to the chair of Claus Offe, who had come from Bremen to found the chair of political science and political sociology at Humboldt. With his group, I was able to establish a normal co-operative relationship.

Humboldt University was not my only place of work. Along with Bálint Balla, Anton Sterbling, Katrin Mattusch, Heinz Zipprian, and Ingrid Oswald, I took part in the foundation of the Eastern Europe Group of the German Sociological Association, in which I am still engaged. In Kassel, at the chair of Johannes Weiss, where I later received my *venia legendi*, I participated in a study concerning Russian emigrants of German origin. And last, but not least, I finished my book on GDR sociology, which was published in 1997.[8]

I continued to travel and Europe became more familiar to me. I found the work with students very exciting. The university changed during the three years of my stay. More and more students from West Germany enrolled, and the work in the seminars was stimulating. For example, I taught a class on comparative history of sociology in East and West Germany, and held seminars on the oeuvre of Karl Mannheim and on the GDR intelligentsia.

In 1996 my WIP contract ended and I was unemployed for the first time in my life. I had never been as productive as during my time with the program and thus it was a great disappointment to see it close. This was perhaps the most awkward moment of my scientific career. From time to time I had the feeling of belonging to a dying species: the East German social scientist.

In these times, support from research associations and contacts with networks of sociologists were virtually nonexistent. In particular, contact with my scientific peer group in the West was missing. The working group for East European Studies, in which I was involved, played a marginalized role in the Sociological Association. In the GDR, there had been a professional association of sociologists, Wissenschaftlicher Rat für Soziologische Forschung, which, chaired by Hansguenter Meyer, was restructured and renamed Ostdeutsche Gesellschaft für Soziologie at the beginning of the 1990s. For a while this association existed in co-operation with the West German Deutsche Gesellschaft für Soziologie. Gradually all the characteristic features of the Eastern association vanished. A newly founded journal, *Berliner Journal für Soziologie*, was taken over in 1992 by the new Department for Social Sciences at Humboldt University. A lot of the members moved into other jobs as opportunities for GDR sociologists decreased. Finally, in the 1990s, the chair declared the "self-dissolution" of the East German group, with the recommendation that they join the West German organization. Only a few people did. The main justification for the dissolution was to bring an end to the necessity of supporting two separate structures. However, from this point onward integration was no longer a collective effort, but an individual problem.[9] Opportunities to become a part of the unified German science system became more difficult, especially for independent researchers who were not already affiliated with an institution.

After my first contact with the unemployment office, I found new meaning in Helmut Schelsky's sociological and conceptual differentiation of independent versus dependent persons. During GDR times, I had had my share of dependency, so the return to that situation was terrible for me. I started to think seriously about leaving science, as the struggle was too difficult for Easterners. But even though the situation in the university intimidated me, I wanted to prove myself in scientific terms.

At the end of 1996 I applied for a *Habilitandenstipendium* (habilitation stipend) from the Deutsche Forschungsgemeinshaft (German Research Society) with the aim of obtaining my *venia legendi*. I presented a project, "Generational Interrelations in Science." After six months my project was funded. I have never been so proud of a professional accomplishment. This was my first success in a regular program, one not designed especially for "Easterners." Moreover, the scholarship was sufficiently generous that I had the chance to focus entirely on my studies. Once again I began to read as much as I had during my student days. I began to conduct my interviews and went to Great Britain for several weeks to complete my studies on Karl Mannheim. I held seminars at the University of Kassel, and attended the research workshop of Ralf Bohnsack at the Berlin Free University, where I discussed my results in a very co-operative atmosphere. There, the general atmosphere seemed to me very productive and relaxed at the same time, not as tense as that I had experienced at Humboldt University.

The results of my work became relevant to me on a personal level, something I had not at all anticipated. I made use of Karl Mannheim's work on the sociology of generations. I dealt especially with the problem of generational reciprocity. Furthermore, I tested my conclusions in an empirical study in the sociology of science, investigating the relations between teachers and their students. Since I had already studied the founding generation of GDR sociology, it made sense now to investigate the next generation. Born between 1950 and 1975, this generation (i.e., my generation) is social-historically labeled "the children of the GDR." I was able to identify three subgroups within this generation. By comparing these generations I developed an understanding of the missing *Entelechie* (spirit) of the children of the GDR in comparison to the previous generation. My professional insecurity during the GDR times now acquired a sociological explanation. Compared to the ideological rigidity of the founding generation, the children of the GDR only had the goal of ensuring scientific "objectivity." We were not able to introduce any new perspectives into either the scientific infrastructure or in terms of scientific concepts.

In December 2001 I finished my habilitation exams by delivering my test lecture, "Sorokin's Integralism: Worldview or Scientific Method?," at the University of Kassel. At the moment I am working to turn my habilitation into a book.

From 2000 to 2002 I had the chance to participate in a very interesting and extensive project dealing with the development of the social sciences in Eastern Europe during the last ten years; that is, since the transition started. For one year I managed the project at Collegium Budapest and another year at the Social Science Information Centre in Berlin. I was responsible for the application, established contact with participants, organized the conferences, and last but not least took a huge part in the edition of the final handbook.[10]

Furthermore, through this project I got the chance to discuss the transition in science with Western partners such as Max Kaase and Hans-Dieter Klingemann, and with Eastern colleagues such as Nikolai Genov, Gábor Klaniczay, Janusz Mucha, Piotr Sztompka, and Pál Tamás. The time I spent in Budapest during the project gave me the chance to observe some of the changes in Eastern Europe, especially in the scientific environment. In my observation, the general conditions of science in Hungary, compared to those of the New German Bundesländer, are much more difficult. Still, I felt the slower transformation there to be somehow more "human" than the radical change in my home country, which expelled a whole generation and has had far-reaching effects on my own as well.

Since 2003 I have become an independent *Privatdozentin*, working temporarily in projects and giving lectures. For example, currently I am at the Eastern Europe Institute of the Free University, at the chair of Nikolai Genov. All in all, my experiences after 1989 suggest to me that it would have been better to abandon science. However, nobody could have known in advance that the conditions for science would decline so dramatically.

Nonetheless, I feel it has been a big advantage to have worked as a scientist under different systems. My education in Russia provided a well-founded basis for my work. My experiences as a sociologist in GDR, except for the fundamental problems described, also provided for interesting projects and scientific results. This work enabled me to understand the scientific language of "world sociology." Most importantly, I regard my work on the history of East German sociology as a successful project of translation and interpretation between these different sciences and worlds. In certain respects, the handbook on social sciences in Eastern Europe is an attempt at a similar "translation."

My freelance occupational status has opened up a sociological perspective beyond "official academia" to me. After 1990, dismissed GDR social scientists founded new scientific institutes. Immediately after *die Wende* (the system change) more than a hundred institutes were established, though only a few of them still exist.[11] However, the ultimate result of these developments has been a diversified non-university academic landscape. This is very important for those, who like me, want and/or have to work outside the traditional institutional structures.

Currently, a critical discussion concerning the setbacks in the process of unification has emerged. The setbacks include deindustrialization, the mistaken idea that people can live on transfer money rather than on work, unemployment rates over 30 percent, and the exodus of the younger, well-educated population, to name just a few. With a former colleague from the Academy of Sciences of the GDR, I have recently joined a research group at the Thünen Institute for Regional Development (Rbel) dealing especially with the situation in the land of Mecklenburg Vorpommern.

Notes

1 See the interview with Yadov, pp. 118–127 *in Sozialismus und Soziologie. Die Gründergeneration der DDR-Soziologie. Versuch einer Konturierung*, eds Vera Sparschuh and Ute Koch (Opladen: Verlag Leske + Budrich, 1997).

2 Igor S. Kon, *Der Positivismus in der Soziologie. Geschichtlicher Abriß* (Berlin: Akademie Verlag, 1968).

3 Finding a place in a nursery or kindergarten depended on the social position and the importance of the work of the mother. Sociology was not seen to be a particularly important type of work.

4 The title of the West German encyclopedia is *Internationales Soziologenlexikon*, eds Wilhelm Bernsdorf and Horst Knospe (Stuttgart: Enke Verlag, 1980). The other model was a GDR encyclopedia of philosophers, *Philosophenlexikon* (Berlin: Dietz Verlag, 1982).

5 Alla Chernykh, Sinaida I. Golenkova, Vera Sparschuh, Helmut Steiner, Jan Wielgosh, Rose-Luise Winkler, and Sergej V. Zakharov, eds, *Portrats russischer und sowjetischer Soziologen* (Sonderheft: Akademie der Wissenschaften der DDR, 1987); and *Portraits of Russian and Soviet Sociologists* (Moscow: USSR Academy of Sciences, 1990).

6 See Jürgen Friedrichs, Vera Sparschuh, and Iris Wrede, *Sozialwissenschaftliche Dissertationen und Habilitationen in der DDR, 1951–1991: Eine Dokumentation* (Berlin: de Gruyter Verlag, 1993).

7 Dagmar Simon and Vera Sparschuh, *Der Nachlaß der DDR-Soziologie—bloßes Archivmaterial oder soziologisches Forschungsfeld?*, Discussion Paper P-92-001 (Berlin: Wissenschaftszentrum Berlin für Sozialforschung, 2001); Dagmar Simon and Vera Sparschuh, "East German Sociology: Between the Production of Weltanschauung, Ideological Adaptation, and Empirical Research," pp. 101–112 in *Eastern Europe in Transformation: The Impact of Sociology*, eds Mike F. Keen and Janusz L. Mucha (Westport: Greenwood, 1994).

8 Vera Sparschuh and Ute Koch, eds, *Sozialismus und Soziologie. Die Gründergeneration der DDR-Soziologie. Versuch einer Konturierung* (Opladen: Verlag Leske + Budrich Verlag, 1997). See also my article "The Biographies of the Biographers. Some Remarks on the History of the Social Sciences in GDR," pp. 303–314 in *Biographies and the Division of Europe: Experience, Action, and Change on the 'Eastern Side,'* eds Roswitha Breckner, Devorah Kalekin-Fishman, and Ingrid Miethe (Opladen: Leske + Budrich Verlag, 2000).

9 I would argue that the attainment of the successor to the former Communist Party (Partei des Demokratischen Sozialismus—PDS) was a result of this process of individualization, which took on a widespread basis. Those former citizens of the GDR who were left out and left behind offered fertile recruitment grounds for the "new" party.

10 Max Kaase, Vera Sparschuh, and Agnieszka Wenninger, *Three Social Science Disciplines in Central and Eastern Europe: Handbook on Economics, Political Science and Sociology, 1989–2001* (Budapest/Berlin: IZ Sozialwissenschaften, 2002).

11 Karin Lohr, Raj Kollmorgen, Dagmar Simon, and Vera Sparschuh, "Ohne Netz und doppelten Boden: Lage und Zukunftsaussichten freier sozialwissenschaftlicher Institute und Vereine in den neuen Bundesländern," pp. 165–192 in *Soziologie und Soziologen im Übergang. Beiträge zur Transformation der außeruniversitären sozialwissenschaftlichen Forschung in Ostdeutschland* (Opladen: Leske + Budrich Verlag, 1997).

10 Living with discrepancies

Sociological self-understanding within Communistic and ethno-nationalistic collectivisms

Karel Turza

Introductory dilemmas

According to Cicero's famous saying, "Historia est testis temporum, lux veritatis, vita memoriae, magistra vitae, nuntia vetustatis"; to Hegel's philosophema that wisdom—namely, philosophy—always comes retrospectively (i.e., "Minerva's owl takes off at sundown"); and finally to the so-called common-sense belief (δοξα = doxa) that the older and more experienced we are the more we know (and so on and so forth), we all should be much more clever, and smart, and wise ... afterwards.[1] In other words, as Hegel puts it, "when reality accomplishes its development and comes to an end."[2] But, is it so? The answer is, it is not so any more! Because what we ultimately can learn from both general and our own individual (life) histories nowadays, in a world of radical compression of time and space on the one hand, and congruent to that, of an incredible acceleration of (historical) time on the other, and in a world the main attributes of which are contingency, uncertainty, insecurity, ambivalence, and risk..., is almost nothing! Or, formulated in a more succinct manner, not all generations at earlier stages of human history could have learned from their general and their individual pasts.

Why? Because they belonged to "the fixed social and cultural formations of community and kinship," and to more or less "fixed traditions and established customs and habits."[3] In other words, to coercive (in the sense in which Durkheim's "*les faits sociale*" are coercive), though more often than not stable and well-known structures of (therefore) mostly predictable behavior. By contrast, we are "fated to choose, and to shape our own lives through everyday decisions about almost everything," e.g., from the color of the socks which we are trying to harmonize with our suit every morning, to the way we should negotiate at a business meeting, to those issues concerning our sexual life, our marriage and family relations, our friendships, our neighborhood.[4] As Nikolas Rose puts it: "biography and identity become (thus) self-reflexive, to be constructed, worked upon, the outcome of choices about clothes, marriage, diet etc., in which the individual himself or herself is the self-conscious center of action."[5]

In other words, we have to supply ourselves, to import ourselves into our own biographies through our own actions. And, in the words of Ulrich Beck and

Elisabeth Beck-Gernscheim, "one has to win, know how to assert oneself in the competition for limited resources—and not only once, but day after day . . . The normal biography thus becomes the 'elective biography,' the 'reflexive biography,' and the 'do-it-yourself biography.'"[6] But, and in fact the main point of this story, "the do-it-yourself biography can swiftly become the breakdown biography . . . owing to the wrong choice of career or just the wrong field, compounded by the downward spiral of private misfortune, illness, divorce, the repossessed home."[7]

Zygmunt Bauman offers another precise and heuristically fruitful view of the circumstances to which we are fated in contemporary world. "Nowadays," writes Bauman, "everything seems to conspire against lifelong projects, permanent bonds, eternal alliances, immutable identities. I cannot build for the long term on my job, my profession or even my abilities. I can bet on my job being cut, my profession changing out of all recognition, my skills being no longer in demand. Nor can a partnership or family provide a basis in the future."[8]

In short, no matter what notion/term is used in defining it; i.e., late or high modernity, second modernity, post-modernity etc., the contemporary world is a world in which social/cultural milieux (structures) exert constraint over our actions; we are indeed often driven by "outer forces" to which we can only react. We are "fated to choose," i.e. "pushed to freedom." We really are actors within the dialectics, or, as Anthony Giddens puts it, the duality of structure and action (much more, to say it again, than people were in all previous historical systems of human interdependence).[9] And, because we often do not fully understand the risky, contingent, ambivalent, and insecure nature of those outer forces or structures, what we are continually facing nowadays is an anxious, distressing, annoying, and sometimes quite depressing feeling that we are deprived of being aware of the consequences of our own choices, decisions, actions/reactions; namely, that the effects of our freedom are beyond our comprehension. Furthermore, this means that our entire knowledge about general global, regional, or national histories cannot secure us many practically useful suggestions on how to form our decisions and how to shape our actions in the right way. Nor can it provide us with the knowledge, experience, awareness, or (self)-consciousness, etc., required for a certain/undoubted recipe for a successful and happy, or, at least, predictable life.

All these insights/views/theories of living in the contemporary modern, or high/late modern, or post-modern world are, *ceteris paribus*, valuable and applicable in analyses of the *Lebenswelt* (lifeworld) in the Balkans as well.[10] This, in spite of the fact that the Balkans—or, to be more specific, Yugoslavia/Serbia and Montenegro—has always been an intrinsically *premodern* and/or *antimodern* area. What does that mean? Well, that means, as I have shown elsewhere, that the main attributes/conditions of modernity, namely (post-feudal) *private property*, *market economy/commodity production*, *individualism* and *rationality* have never been fully developed in the region.[11]

Actually, the prevailing pattern of the dialectics/duality of structure and action and thus of the *Lebenswelt* in the region, has throughout its history almost always been anti-modern! For instance, the main attributes/conditions of Communism between 1945 and, say, 1991, were simply opposite, in nature and tendency, to modernity. Instead of *private property*, state or so-called social ownership prevailed. Instead of a *market economy*, a centrally planned/commanded economy existed. *Individualism* was suppressed by Communist (proletarian) collectivism; *rationality* was replaced by ideology. Nonetheless, some (pro)modern actors/forces/tendencies have existed in the milieu over the past, say, two centuries, and have never been totally defeated. In fact, from October 2000, when the reign of Slobodan Milosevic and his entourage was finally brought to an end, the pro-modern and anti-modern rival forces have still remained at war in Serbia (and Montenegro). The outcome of that cannot be predicted.

The insights/views/theories have to be "enriched," particularly when dealing with the countries that used to be parts (former republics) of the Socialist Federal Republic of Yugoslavia. The necessity of the enrichment comes from the fact that the main characteristics of a contemporary modern, late/high modern, or post-modern world (i.e., contingency, risk, insecurity and so on) should, in that case, say, be doubled or even tripled, in both a qualitative and quantitative sense, especially regarding the period of the last 10–15 years.

Today I live in a political entity named the State Union of Serbia and Montenegro, the future of which is absolutely uncertain. Between 1992 and 2003 I lived in the Federal Republic of Yugoslavia. Before that, the state/political entity was called the Socialist Federal Republic of Yugoslavia, and before that it had been the Federal People's Republic of Yugoslavia, and so on. Quite confusing. Regarding my life, and the lives of the people I know well, the worst things have happened over the past 10–15 years. During that period, the 1990s were literally unbearable to most of us, regardless of the names of the state/political entities. I dare not say, however, that such an attitude prevails in all of Yugoslavia/Serbia and Montenegro. For, according to my insights, the thoughts and beliefs of the majority of population are still at a stage in which they cannot be calculated in terms of an elementary "sociological arithmetic." That is, many, I would add *too* many, men and women in Serbia and Montenegro still do not recognize the connection between their own misfortunes or even tragedies, and a diabolic, *Thanatos*-oriented, sociocidal, anti-modern, or simply disastrous reign of the worst possible power elite amalgam, composed of the militant ethno-nationalism and reckless kleptocracy that existed throughout the 1990s.

Owing to many factors in the period—the first being the wars that were waged between 1991 and 1999 in Slovenia, Croatia, Bosnia, and Herzegovina and, finally, in the Federal Republic of Yugoslavia (Serbia and Montenegro), which were all extremely cruel and severely destructive conflicts in every sense—even a superficial comparison between risks, contingencies, insecurities, and uncertainties that are ascribed/attributed (and that, in my opinion, really are inherent) to the contemporary modern/post-modern socio-cultural milieux, and those risks, contingencies, insecurities, uncertainties that we have been facing (especially in the 1990s) in the region, would confirm that the latter attributes are far more troublesome. Or, to put it quite precisely, in this milieu, contingencies, insecurities, uncertainties, and risks have been, and still are, too often deadly.[12]

Regarding the context of the story that I am going to tell, there is an important thing that should be added, and stressed! In the milieu where I live, Minerva's owl (Hegel's metaphor of wisdom/philosophy) has regularly taken off at the historical sundowns, which over the past two centuries at least have occurred approximately every 50 years. But, generally, the people's attention has never actually been focused on the owl (wisdom/philosophy), but rather on the sundowns! That is to say, instead of rationally analyzing and summarizing those structures and actions, by means of philosophy, and historical and social sciences, and the circumstances and processes that preceded the (historical) sundowns, they arbitrary construct their meaning. Even when those constructions are dressed in philosophical and/or scientific jargon, pretending thus that they are based on rational thought, argumentation and data, they are often nothing but dim and opaque views that at best resemble fairy tales and/or myths.

What I want to say is that we, the people that belong to the region, are some kind of chronic "sundownerholics," whose ability for rational thinking and comprehension is not, however, disturbed by alcohol (in English dictionaries the noun "sundowner" is defined as "drink, usually of something alcoholic at sundown") but by a much more dangerous addictive, mythomania. That is, by a strong propensity for an irrational and exaggerated, false, and merely wishful-thinking-based perception and reception of reality. Mythomania has, in this milieu, always significantly affected the very structure of the mental configuration of the people (i.e., their basic ideas, thoughts, perceptions, feelings, wishes, intentions, memories, recollections etc.) at both the collective/public and individual/personal levels. Every time a historical reality has been completed and brought to an end, and when the need for its illumination and comprehension has appeared, it (the mythomania) has hypertrophied and assumed quite bizarre and ridiculous features, and has brought about the same bizarre, ridiculous, and disastrous results.

As illustrations I will point out just two of the very many examples. One, when the NATO military action in FR Yugoslavia stopped in June 1999 Yugoslavia's president, Slobodan Milosevic, declared that the war was over and that we were the winners! Second, ten years before that, in June 1989, at the public meeting in Kosovo Polje that was held on the anniversary of the Battle of Kosovo, in which the Ottomans had defeated the Serbs in 1389, more than a million men and women hailed Slobodan Milosevic as a leader who would continue with the historical triumphs of the Serbs! Simple sociological arithmetic, or logic, whatever, suggests that the latter "triumph" had caused the first "triumph." The point of these examples is that Slobodan Milosevic's mythomanic and thus intrinsically irrational conceptions, narratives, and politics were, between 1987 and 1999/2000, quite in line with the thoughts and beliefs that were more or less collectively accepted by the Serbs. Frankly speaking, I suspect that if Slobodan Milosevic appeared nowadays in Serbia he would be hailed again by many—even by those who suffered very much during his period in office. It should be stressed, though, that such an absurd and self-destructive collective consciousness is not unique to the Serbs. A voluminous book could be written about similar mythomanic stupidities that other ethnic communities/nations in the Balkans cherish as their ideals, or even as their sacred values.

The diagnosis I have offered implies two things. First, that dealing with the region where I live primarily means dealing with its pathological nature. Second, that since I have lived in it I have been affected as well, as least to a certain degree, by its pathological nature, whether I like it or not. The logical and legitimate question, therefore, is who is likely to benefit from a sociological autobiography such as mine, one written by a person who belongs to a milieu in which rationality and even common sense have always been on the margins? Yes, as a sociologist, I am absolutely aware of the fact that, to use Durkheim's words again, *les faits sociale* (social facts) exercise coercive power over individuals and, what is more important, that the constraining nature of *les faits sociale* very often is not recognized by people—they usually comply with the social facts convinced that they follow their own choices and interests. But, I am not sure at all whether such sociological awareness has made me immune from mythomania, for example, as well as from other pathological social facts. So the question now—one I have been posing to myself ever since I started to think sociologically *sensu stricto*—is: do my sociological insights and views have any real scientific value or are they just a variety, a special case of the collective false consciousness?

What does encourage me though is that, more often than not, there has been, and still is, considerable discrepancy between my insights, views, comprehensions, etc., of the nature of our *Lebenswelt* and the ways it has been understood and interpreted within the prevailing collectivistic *Weltanschauung* and general belief systems or, to be more specific, within both Communist and ethno-nationalist ideologies. Yet that could be cold comfort. For, ultimately, in a world in which risk, contingency, uncertainty, insecurity, and ambivalence generally prevail globally, what I have determined as pathological patterns of collective and individual thought and behavior might some day be, for reasons beyond my comprehension, proclaimed as the most opportune options or, in other words, as solutions which are good for a purpose. To be more specific, the so-called international community, actually the international power elite, might decide some day to proclaim Slobodan Milosevic and his entourage free from all the charges that have been brought against them, and send him (them) back from the Hague international court of justice to Belgrade.

A surrealistic scenario? No! For, while he was in power between 1987 and 2000, Slobodan Milosevic was treated in diametrically opposed ways by the politicians and the media in the USA and Europe—that is, from a "butcher" to the most important factor for peace in the Balkans (and vice versa)! Thus, some day, the so-called international community—namely the politicians of the USA and the European Union—might decide that the best solution for Serbia and its surroundings would be restoration of the Milosevic reign. Why? Not for the sake of Serbia and its population, but to the advantage of the rest of Europe. Then, Serbia would be a warning, a "scarecrow" for all the Europeans who do not obey the rules of EU: "You see what living in Serbia is like? Don't make us Balkanize, 'Serbianize,' your country!" If that happened (though such an option is very unlikely, it shouldn't be dismissed entirely) all my sociological and psychological insights, views, and theories, as well as my disagreements with the milieu in which I have lived and to which I still belong, would become absurd.

In spite of all my hesitations, dilemmas, and basically agnostic views concerning general and personal histories that burden my sociological self-understanding, I have decided to tell the story of my sociological life. For, as hermeneutics suggests, the interpreter can understand a text better than its author. So readers may benefit from the story that follows.

Living in the Communist womb

Generally speaking, compared with all other former Communist regimes in Central and Eastern Europe, and particularly in comparison with living in the FR Yugoslavia from 1992 to 2003, and in Serbia and Montenegro from 2003 until now, the former (Communist) Yugoslavia was a "womb." Or, as some psychoanalytically oriented authors might say, it was a practical metaphor of paradise. This was not only due to the fact that the majority of its population enjoyed material and other benefits which they had not actually earned, but first and foremost because we all lived more or less carefree and thoughtless lives, lives free from any heavy responsibility. Almost everything, from the most abstract and general political, economic, and social issues to the ways in which groups and individuals should play their roles in everyday life, was defined by the "collective consciousness" embodied in the Communist Party (the League of Communists of Yugoslavia).

The first to question the monopoly over political, economic, social, and historical truth, during the 1960s and early 1970s, were the theorists from all over former Yugoslavia brought together in *Praxis*, a journal of philosophy published in Zagreb (Croatia) that had a strong international reputation. Although their critical thought was in-house, for they ultimately remained within the paradigm of Marxism and Communism, they were soon proscribed and denounced as dangerous to the historical interests and aims of the proletariat and its avant-garde (namely, the Party), and thus for the socialist society as such. In short, the result was that, in 1975, eight professors of philosophy and sociology at the University of Belgrade were fired from their posts at the Faculty of Philosophy.

My interest in sociology started at approximately that time, at the end of the 1960s and beginning of the 1970s. Actually, I first encountered it in grammar school (in Yugoslavia/Serbia grammar school is a kind of secondary school which concentrates on academic rather than practical/technical courses), when I came to the climax of my rather chaotic, adolescent subversiveness, usually expressed in words, "I do not exactly know what I want, but I want it now!" Philosophy, logic, and psychology were the subjects that occupied my attention, but primarily due to my professor, sociology seemed to me the most enlightening discipline—a discipline that would turn my thoughts, which were critical of everything but at sixes and sevens with one another, into an argumentative critical attitude. That led me, in 1972, to the study of sociology in the Faculty of Philosophy at the University of Belgrade.

To become a student of sociology at the University of Belgrade one had to pass some exams, write a sociological essay, and to explain/clarify it to a professor. The professor, to whom my cohort of about 200 candidates (of which some 40 were ultimately accepted) was obliged to interpret the writings and to discuss the idea of sociology, was Dr Zagorka Golubovic, a professor of Anthropology. And she was cruel. I still remember the words she used to use when a candidate did not show sufficient knowledge and/or was in her opinion narrow-minded: "You had better give up studying sociology. But do not worry, for your knowledge and the way you think will be quite sufficient for almost all other schools and faculties in this primitive society."

To us, this was an unusual treatment, and her statement that we lived in a primitive society came as a shock to us all. A few months later, as a proud student of sociology, I asked Professor Golubovic why she had been so cruel to some candidates. Her answer was: "Sometimes you have to be cruel to be kind. It would have been much worse, and even more cruel," she added, "if I had let them waste their time in studying something they would never really understand." with regard to her words "primitive society," I came to understand their full meaning quite soon.

Studying sociology gave me real pleasure. Most professors were open-minded, liberally oriented, and very learned men and women. As a teenager I was particularly impressed with their critical attitude, which, by contrast with mine, was clearly articulated and sophisticated. They were Marxists, but of the *sui generis* sort. In short, their visions of socialism/Communism were based on humanism and critiques of all kinds of alienation. That, together with their erudition, was the quality that in my opinion made their perspective intellectually and morally superior to the official, collectivist/populist, fundamentally ideological, and, in fact, "stay-in-power-oriented" version of Marxism/Communism of the then power elite.

This power elite, and the Marxists who were in its ideological orbit (namely, the Communists), proclaimed themselves "guardian-angels" and the only genuine supporters of the doctrine of Karl Marx. They were a "collective consciousness" that was exclusively qualified to determine what was and what was not the truth; what was and what was not good for the proletariat and therefore for the majority of population. I say "therefore" because they used to employ Marx and Engels' famous holistic thesis from the *Communist Manifesto* which, and I am paraphrasing, the proletariat does not represent any particular class but general human, and thus general social interest. Every single political action or endeavor was justified from that position, including the campaign against eight professors of the Faculty of Philosophy at the University of Belgrade.

Personally, by adopting a more rational and critical attitude, enriched with new knowledge, I became much more self-confident, though, sometimes, I admit, probably filled with too much pride and conceit (i.e., "wise" in my own judgment only). A benefit from that, which was very precious to me, was that I became firmly convinced that I no longer had to think, believe, feel and behave in accordance with the expectations of the majority of population, and/or according to the standards that were imposed by a "collective consciousness," whoever or whatever it was composed of. In addition, I could at any moment offer some good reasons for such an attitude. Thus my, up to that time, pretty raw and wild individualism became civilized.

At the same time as this somewhat rough process of consolidation was taking shape in my head, a real drama was occurring in my family. My father, who was one of Marshal Josip Broz Tito's partisans from the very beginning of World War II, and a Communist who occupied a relatively high position in the Yugoslav army, heard that I was going to study sociology at the Faculty of Philosophy in Belgrade. He was astonished. Sure, he was aware that I was the *enfant terrible*. My elder brothers were, by contrast, good students at "politically correct" faculties (i.e., the School of Law and the Faculty of Electric Engineering at the University of Belgrade). I was a hippie, my hair was very long, and I played the guitar. The pictures of my favourite musicians (John Lennon, Jimmy Hendrix, Jim Morrison, etc.) covered the walls of my room, and their music, more often than not too loud, was my usual way of communicating with the family.

During my summer vacations I used to put my passport in my pocket, a rucksack on my back, and disappear. Sometimes my parents did not know where I was for more than a month, or even two. At the time, Yugoslavia was an open country. One could freely come in, and one could freely go out (without visas!). That enabled me to be "on the road," and to meet many young men and women from all over the world. Those were the days when one could meet a group of people from, say, Holland, Sweden, France, Germany, Great Britain, the USA, Belgium, or Norway in Dubrovnik or Opatija (Croatia), or in Vienna, or Trieste, and to join them on their way to England, India, or Nepal, for instance. A simple phrase then was "Make love not war."

All those things were, more or less, acceptable to my father. But that I would determine or, in his words, destroy my own career and life by studying the "diabolic doctrines" of Zagorka Golubovic, Trivo Indjic, Mihailo Markovic, Dragoljub Micunovic, Nebojsa Popov, Svetozar Stojanovic, Ljubomir Tadic, and Miladin Zivotic was beyond his worst predictions and anxieties about me. Those people were the target of the political campaign against philosophers and sociologists in Serbia during the 1960s and 1970s, and they were the professors who lost their posts at the Faculty of Philosophy in 1975. Most of them, except Professor Miladin Zivotic, who died few years ago, are still more or less active in our public life.

Of course, he knew very little about philosophy and sociology. About the "diabolic doctrines" he knew literally nothing except what he read or heard in the media. And that was quite sufficient for him, as it was for the majority of population, to form "clear" and "certain" opinions about them. So we were at "war" for about nine months after I had started my studies. "Peace" was agreed when he saw that I had passed the exams with excellent marks. "OK," he said, "as you like it."

Many years later he confessed that in my obstinacy he had recognized his own stubbornness that had led him, against ordinary common sense, to become a Communist before World War II. He had sympathy with my "foolish decision," but did not want to encourage something that might have had, at least in his estimation, unpredictable consequences. "One Don Quixote," he told me then, "with lofty but entirely impractical ideas, was more than enough in the family."

"Yes, and who was our Don Quixote?" I asked.

"Me," he answered.

The only person who did support me was my mother, a genial, open-minded and highly educated woman. She spoke fluent Italian, French, and German. When World War II was over, she had returned from a Nazi concentration camp, married my father, and stayed at home, entirely devoted to her husband and sons. My father died in 1993, and my mother died five years later. I know that I cannot prove it, but I am pretty sure that they were, along with many other honorable men and women in Yugoslavia, the victims of the horrible sociocide, or, to be more precise, the killing of Yugoslavia, which was the very basis of their identities. They were not in bad health, they simply expired. I believe that they just could not swallow the (new) mythomanic narratives, the system of values, and especially the politics/practices, especially in Bosnia and Herzegovina, Croatia, and Serbia, of those who preached ethnic intolerance, many of whom had supported the Nazis during World War II and had suddenly become the so-called "good guys."

The conflict with my father, though in its "dialectical" effect quite useful to me, was tiresome and sometimes very unpleasant for the whole family. Because of it, I started to search for ways to become more independent, at least materially. Relatively soon, after a year or so, in 1975 I started to work as a journalist for *Student*, a newspaper of the students of the University of Belgrade. At the time it was prominent and popular, not only in Belgrade and Serbia but in the whole of the former Yugoslavia. When my first articles appeared, I was, naturally, very proud. I believed that journalism would be my future.

About a year later, since working in the newspaper simply ate all my time, and as I had started to neglect my studies, I quit. Frankly, I was not a journalist *sensu stricto*, because even when I had to write an ordinary story or, to be more precise, an article about some common problem, I could not help trying to enrich it with abstract and sometimes pretentious, often quite unnecessary and journalistically needless theoretical reflections and generalizations. Perhaps, due to that, soon after I had left *Student*, in the middle of the 1970s, I got a very attractive offer to become editor-in-chief of a journal for philosophy, social issues, and culture, *Vidici* (Views), a periodical that also belonged to the students of the University of Belgrade.

Working for *Vidici* was a very precious experience because I dealt with the theoretical issues in which I was interested. Furthermore, the post enabled me to meet the most important philosophers, sociologists, and social theorists of that time from the whole of the former Yugoslavia. I had enough time to perform my duties as a student. Finally, and by no means least important, it was a well-paid job.

It was during the second half of the 1970s, when I was close to the successful completion of my studies, that I decided to continue with postgraduate studies and pursue an MA degree. At the time, I had no ambitions, though there were some opportunities for me to start an academic career. For, in comparison with the jobs I had had up to then, working as an assistant seemed to me rather pedestrian, and even dull and boring. So when I graduated I continued at the postgraduate level, though a year later I gave up. The reason was that I was working with Miroslav Pecujlic, then rector of the University of Belgrade and a professor of sociology at the School of Law, to establish a publishing house. It was named *Radionica SIC* (Workshop SIC) and formally belonged to the University of Belgrade. I became its first editor-in-chief. That seemed to me a logical continuation of my previous activities, though at a somewhat higher level.

My idea was to create an oasis of liberal thought, literally a workshop producing books that would contribute to the formation of a new world-view, different from the prevailing ideology (collective consciousness) and to some extent subversive. Was it a utopian ambition? Yes, looking from today's point of view it certainly was. Actually, *Radionica SIC* was, along with *Vidici* and *SKC* (Student Cultural Center), part of a network through which liberally oriented students, mostly young academics, artists, and writers found a way to communicate their alternative world-philosophies.

Many learned, clever and talented people were engaged in the undertaking, e.g., Vladislav Bajac, Jesa Denegri, Goran Gnus, Bratislav Grubacic, Mirko Ilic, Slobodan Inic, Slobodan Jovanovic, Ljubomir Kljakic, Slobodan Kljakic, Zarko Korac, Nikola Kostandinovic, Mladen Kozomara, Slobodan Mijuskovic, Horhe Mikele, Andjelka Milic, Dusan Pajin, Dragan Papic, Miroslav Pecujlic, Milo Petrovic, Nada Popovic-Perisic, Vladan Radovanovic, Slobodan Samardzic, Misa Savic, Jadranka Vinterhalter, and Milan Vlajcic. Within only two years, some 20 really "fresh" books, on various issues from philosophy and sociology to cultural studies, and written by domestic and foreign authors such as Milorad Belancic, John Cage, Slobodan Divjak, Davor Rodin, Iring Fetscher, Susan Sontag, Miroslav Stanojevic, Lino Veljak, Slavoj Zizek were published.

We caused a real public scandal when we published Rius's *Marx for Beginners*, Richard Appignanesi and Oscar Zarate's *Lenin for Beginners*, and *The Communist Manifesto for Beginners* by Ro Marcenaro. I was criticized in the media, "Marx and Lenin in comics, a blasphemy!!!" Yet, the greatest contribution was that of

Zarana Papic, a sociologist who worked with me from the very beginning of *Radionica SIC*. She was a diligent, clever, and brave woman who, among other things, first initiated serious discussions on the status of women in Communist Yugoslavia. Her feminist works and actions brought about contempt and many sneering utterances in public, and rather serious political reactions. In spite of that she and her feminist companions persisted in their efforts, and made remarkable changes in the intellectual map of Belgrade, Serbia, and Yugoslavia.[13]

All those things happened by the end of the 1970s. At the turn of the 1980s I had to spend a year in the Yugoslav army. It was the legal obligation of every young man between 18 and 27 in the former Yugoslavia to spend a year, or even 18 months, in the army. For me it was a horrible experience of rigid collectivistic senselessness. I was 27 at the time and married to Vera, a pretty, clever, and brave woman who I still dearly love, and without whom I would not have survived the atrocities we experienced. I was the father of a beautiful and beloved baby girl, Ivana, now a pretty, clever, and very creative young woman who is close to completing her studies in the Faculty of Architecture at the University of Belgrade. I had up to then created my everyday life almost entirely according to my own individual interests and preferences.

I tried at first to treat and comprehend the whole situation as a sociologist—but in vain. What I managed to understand was nothing except that the Yugoslav army was an extract, the very essence of collectivism that permeated the whole of Yugoslav society. Collectivism brought to its pure structure and action. My higher mental activities were paralyzed. For example, I could not even read books or listen to music. I put them aside. I knew that I had to endure, and I functioned as a robot. Paradoxically, I was proclaimed as one of the best soldiers in the unit, which shortened my stay in the army by almost 20 days!

When I came back home, after some 11 months, I was dysfunctional and my brain needed several months to recover from its hibernation. And then I got a surprising—even shocking—offer. I was asked to occupy the post of secretary responsible for science in the Marxist Center of the Central Committee of the League of Communists of Serbia, and I accepted! Though I was a member of the League of Communists of Yugoslavia there were "certain problems with my ideological past." I was informed, by the brother of a girlfriend of a cousin of a good friend who was some sort of policeman, that my biography, and the biographies of my parents and probably grandparents, would be thoroughly investigated.

Incidentally (or at least I believed that it was incidentally), I met the policeman at a party. In confidence, he told me that I was under surveillance, and started to talk about what were, as far as he knew, some of my ideological/political "deadly sins"—my open sympathies for the "group of professors," my anarchic-liberal orientation, my "too close" connections with some dissidents and other "suspicious individuals." Since he was drunk, and since those remarks were too abstract and general, his story seemed ridiculous to me, the empty phrases of a boastful policeman. That was up to the point when he started to paraphrase the words I had said about Zagorka Golubovic's book, which had appeared a week or two before, and about which I had organized a public discussion. He also cited some of the titles of my works that had been published in various journals. His story suddenly turned into a serious warning. I realized that what until then had been happening to some others, in the almost incredible stories I had heard, had begun to happen to me.

Actually, the worst part of his story was when he said that "they were only 'refreshing' the information they had already had." Since when? I did not know. That made me feel really bad. Yet, from today's point of view, that whole episode, including the policeman, our James Bond, secret agent, or whatever, looks rather silly and clumsy. Possibly that is because I did not experience any serious misfortune. Most likely it is because today I still have in mind the comparison to the police and intelligence services of Milosevic's era. Their cruelty was really horrible. Deadly horrible.[14]

Anyway, I worked as a secretary for less than ten months, and then I ran away. At first I had believed that some changes could be made from inside. I was wrong! Eventually, in 1989, I quit the League of Communists when I definitively realized that the League, which I thought was the only real force that might have stopped the rise of militant ethno-nationalism, lost its internationalist orientation and became nationalistic itself.

Shortly after my stint as secretary I began to look for a new job. Soon, I found it in Treci (Third) Program Radio Beograda. Treci Program was an intellectual milieu of high renown in the former Yugoslavia. Particularly famous was its periodical (a quarterly journal) in which many original works and discussions of the most prominent Yugoslav and foreign theorists had appeared. The journal was widely used at all Yugoslav universities as an essential source of the latest information about domestic, European, and American philosophy and social sciences. I worked there for almost nineteen years, until 2003, when I started to teach medical sociology in the School of Medicine at the University of Belgrade, and where I remain a professor. It was a very fruitful period during which I completed my MA and Ph.D. studies, and published three books, and numerous articles and translations.

From today's point of view, my second (and late) engagement in MA and Ph.D. studies was nothing but an escape, a getaway from the chaos, wars, mobilizations, hyperinflation, penury, tormenting survival, and total insecurity that was under way in my country during the 1990s. By that I was trying, I think, to find a relatively stable situation where I could be at anchor, mentally at least, in an academic milieu. When I came back after some ten years to the Faculty of Philosophy in Belgrade, with my idea to formalize my knowledge with the academic degrees, I was welcomed. My colleagues and friends, Marija Bogdanovic, Mladen Lazic, Dragoljub Micunovic, Andjelka Milic, Aljosa Mimica, and Sreten Vujovic, professors at the Faculty of Philosophy, helped me very much at the time. It was symptomatic that for my MA I chose a socio-historical analysis of the origins of modernity, which led me to the Renaissance—that is, very far away from the Balkans of the 1990s.

Working professionally for Treci Program had an additional value and significance for me. During the ascendancy of Slobodan Milosevic, it was one of those rare (public) places where his ideas and politics, and, generally, every kind of ethnic nationalism and militant totalitarianism were despised. People with whom I worked there, and who were my good friends, such as philosophers Milorad Belancic, Slobodan Divjak and Rade Kalik, writer Rade Kuzmanovic, and historian Slobodan Ristic, were not only learned and wise but also tolerant and liberally oriented. Mostly owing to that, I managed to survive that horrible era.

Thinking back on my "evolution" as a sociologist in a more strict sense of the word, my first serious theoretical and methodological hesitations began in the second half of the 1970s, when I was close to my graduation; that is to say, close to the end of my studies of sociology at the Faculty of Philosophy. Being psychologically, or mentally, or temperamentally predisposed to favor an individualistic *Weltanschauung*, I could not accept most of the so-called holistic sociological conceptions, including many varieties of Marxism, which had forgotten the very idea of the individual: functionalism, which was in that sense similar to those dogmatic and totalizing versions of Marxism and moreover was obviously conservative; structuralism, in which there had been very little room for rational freedom and rational action of individuals; positivism, which had turned, as Pitirim Sorokin precisely noticed, into "quantophrenia"; and the many other connected "isms." They were all, I felt (I would be lying if I said that I had clearly known this), nothing but mere varieties of, as post-modern authors have so appropriately labeled them, "*les grands recits*" (the grand narratives) in which general/holistic/collectivistic presumptions about everything, more often than not, simply annihilated the differences. Namely, the *sui generis* character of every concrete phenomenon, event, process, action, and group or individual.

That is why, I suppose, my favorite theorists at the time were (early) Marx, Herbert Spencer, Wilhelm Dilthey, Heinrich Rickert, Wilhelm Windelbandt, Sigmund Freud, Erich Fromm, Theodor Adorno, Max Horkheimer, Herbert Marcuse, C. Wright Mills, Jean-Paul Sartre, and Jürgen Habermas. Actually, all those authors who, in my understanding, in their own original way, were the pathfinders of sociological anti-sociologism/anti-holism/anti-collectivism. That is to say, those who opposed traditionally prevailing theoretical and methodological ideas (of the so-called sociological realism versus sociological nominalism) according to which, as Ralf Dahrendorf put it in his *Homo Sociologicus*, sociology should not be concerned at all with individual(s), since concrete people, concrete men and women, should be left aside, out of the sights and interests of sociologists and sociology as such.

Therefore, my first theoretical works dealt with the issue of family. That aspect of human social life seemed to me an area that was unavoidably connected with my general conception of the sense and meaning of sociological thinking as such. For dealing with family, I thought, no matter how abstract it could be, always included some very personal/individual questions/issues.

Affected or, better, "infected" by feminist ideas that I had "discovered" due to Zarana Papic, most of my works on family life were, in fact, reckless critiques of it. And I was surprised indeed when one of those articles, originally published in *Vidici*, appeared in a textbook for the students in the School of Law at the University of Belgrade.[15]

In the years that followed, during the 1980s, my sociological attention was mainly focused on political issues. This was logical, since the crisis of the (Communist) system(s) was obvious. I did not know, I confess, what was really going on at the global level, and I could not predict what would happen. Those who say today that they knew what would happen and how—namely, that they predicted that Communism would collapse and be annihilated in Europe—lie! But I could feel that the crisis was deep, and that instead of searching for acceptable and practical solutions for overcoming it, the power elite in Yugoslavia was trying to minimize and to trivialize its nature and potential effects.[16]

Actually I found some satisfactory answers to both the abstract theoretical/methodological and practical questions later, during the 1990s when the "reality started to accomplish its development and was near its end." From the very beginning I regarded the changes that were under way in the former Yugoslavia as the worst historical scenario possible; my sociological attention was focused on Minerva's owl. I desperately tried to get plausible answers, and, at the same time, to find ways of avoiding "sundownerholism"—namely, a new mythomania that arose simultaneously with the horrible events that became the hallmark of our "transition."

Living in post-Communist chaos

It seemed totally senseless and incomprehensible to me that people who had lived together in relative harmony and well-being for many decades could almost immediately become irreconcilable enemies. Moreover, the conflicts that started in 1991, in Yugoslavia, turned into one of the cruelest wars in Europe over the past few centuries. What was at first sight obvious to me was an absolute absence of rationality, and that Communist collectivism was quickly transformed into another, ethno-nationalistic collectivism. Both phenomena were transparent, but what were their sources and/or causes? Regarding the latter, I witnessed transformations of the masses, and of the people I knew or who were even my close friends. They simply changed their systems and patterns of ideas, values, and beliefs within only a few months, significantly, or even radically and profoundly. For example, some former internationalists almost immediately became militant ethno-nationalists. Former radical atheists turned into committed believers. Most of the former Communists, even those who had declared themselves as Communist in their heart of hearts, became bizarre "amalgams" of radical militant nationalism, theism and a variety of neo-liberalism!

Trying to explain that, I was thinking in terms of Giddens' conception of structuration; namely, of duality of structure and action. Logically this brought me to the questions: What was the nature of the "structure?" And who were the "actors" in our drama? What I found out then was that the old social structures—perhaps, instead of the *Gesellschaft* of social structures, it would be more appropriate to say the *Gemeinschaft* of old community structures, since society *sensu stricto* scarcely existed in former Yugoslavia—were destroyed, but not replaced by anything reasonable and comprehensible. Therefore, we suddenly found ourselves in senseless ruins, generally and as individuals. Most of the individual transformations happened as a result of the coercive influence of collective irrationality.

Several ideas occurred to me at the time. First of all, at the end of 1991, I started to write about "sociocide" in Yugoslavia. Most people, including my sociology colleagues, argued that the notion was an exaggeration. A year or two later, in 1993/94, some of them adopted it, while others chose another term, "destruction of society." Some, however, continued to believe that everything was OK, or that Serbian society finally had come into being. Another idea that came to me was that the wars that were then under way in Croatia, and in Bosnia and Herzegovina, were ultimately nothing but a late "primitive accumulation of capital," since under the "grand ethno-nationalistic narratives" a grand robbery or, to put it another way, radical redistribution of wealth was occurring. Furthermore, I somehow figured out that the notion of modernity might be of some use in searching for respectable sociological answers.

All this led me to new fields of investigation. As a result, several articles appeared that dealt with the issues mentioned above, along with two books, *Who Needs Sociology?*, and *Modernity on a Bicycle*.[17] In the first one, I published my discussions with the most prominent Belgradian sociologists about the problem, which could be formulated in short as a "syllogism": If sociocide was under way, sociology was going to lose its very subject; namely, society. Sociology would thus become "subjectless" and therefore a senseless discipline. What was sociology supposed to do then? As I have already said, society *sensu stricto* scarcely existed in the former Yugoslavia, for it was a simulacrum of society, actually a community that proclaimed itself a society. Some significant attributes of society did appear, a relatively differentiated social structure, with, for example, a middle class that was developing recognizable features. Some social spheres, like science, culture and arts, the university, the private sphere, gained relative autonomy. That is why, in the 1990s, I wrote and talked in public about sociocide and not about communitycide. It is ridiculous indeed that we, the Yugoslav sociologists, had a quite short period when we dealt with society *sensu stricto*, after which we had to reorient our sociological style into a sad necrologic genre.

The second book was about the origins of modernity, a study in historical sociology in which I analysed the historical changes that had brought about the main attributes and conditions of modernity in the Italian cities during the period of the Renaissance. In it, as well as in some articles, I offered a new definition of modernity, significantly different from the definitions that had appeared in the works of Stephen Toulmin, Anthony Giddens, and Ulrich

Beck. Aside from the typical definition, the main attributes of modernity, as I have already noted, were new (post-feudal) forms of private property, market economy/commodity production, rationality, and individualism. I am mentioning them again because they can be used as relatively precise parameters by which one can determine whether a system of human interdependence is premodern or modern (or anti-modern!). They were useful in my reconstructions of the nature of former Yugoslav society (a premodern system), of the sociocidal period during the reign of Slobodan Milosevic (an anti-modern "system of chaos"), and are still useful nowadays for analyzing the nature of some quite concrete political decisions and actions in Serbia and Montenegro.

Suddenly, in 1995 or thereabouts, I became very, very tired of, and fed up with, all the stupidities, atrocities, destructions, misery, and penury that I had been facing, as well as with my desperate efforts to digest them in a rational way. That feeling was brought about—deepened even, I think—by my stay in Bamberg, Germany, in 1995, where I participated in an international scientific conference. It was my first journey abroad since 1991, as due to international sanctions we could not travel out of our country between 1992 and 1995.[18] When I flew to Germany (it was as if I had traveled by plane for the first time in my life!) and saw that normal life still existed on the planet, I got sick. Then, I decided, very firmly, to leave my country. But, for many reasons, my family coming first, I did not do that. However, I did get an invitation to work on my Ph.D. thesis at the University of Pennsylvania in Philadelphia, and I went there in spring 1996.

I was, as I have said, fed up with the "anatomy," "physiology," and "pathology" of a substantially deformed milieu, and I decided to focus my Ph.D. thesis on a neutral (escapist?) issue. This was similar to my MA work a few years before, through which I had escaped via a sociological time-machine into the Florence, Milan, and Venice of the fifteenth and sixteenth centuries. The topic for my Ph.D. thesis was Lewis Mumford, an interesting and almost forgotten architectural critic, urban planner, and historian. It was a refreshing change in my work, as was my stay in the USA. My mentor and tutor at the University of Pennsylvania was Professor Seymour Mandelbaum, an erudite and subtle theorist, and a patient teacher who generously helped me to complete my work, and to gain, in addition, a lot of new knowledge. He had enabled me to come to Penn after an almost year-long correspondence. It was an old-fashioned correspondence, based on handwritten letters, for I had no access to the Internet and e-mail then. In fact, I had no PC at the time.

When I came back, very refreshed, I soon received my Ph.D. from the Faculty of Philosophy of the University of Belgrade, and published my thesis.[19] My interests turned then to some cultural issues—initially to multiculturalism. In addition, I became more active in our sociological organization, and after some time was elected to be president of the Yugoslav Sociological Association (YSA). About that time, in 1999, we experienced NATO military action. The YSA organized an intensive correspondence (via e-mail) with some 800 sociologists all over the world in order to inform at least the world's sociological public about the real effects of that intervention. The correspondence was published in an issue of *Sociologija*, a journal of sociology, social psychology, and social anthropology of the YSA.

With the exception of the journal, which appeared regularly, the activity of the YSA was poor. There were many problems connected with it. One was that because of international sanctions it had been excluded from the International Sociological Association (ISA). Somehow, I managed to bring it back into the ISA. Then, since the organization was some kind of inheritor of the former greater Yugoslav sociological association, but now reduced to sociologists from Serbia and Montenegro, we were continually burdened with the issue of its identity. Unfortunately, the YSA, which is now the Sociological Association of Serbia and Montenegro, still has many problems that will, I am afraid, never be solved. In the first place, there is no real will, nor interest, among our sociologists to spend their time and energy in an organization that has an identity which is as similarly phantom as is the identity of the political and social cultural unit to which it should refer and belong.[20]

Finally, regarding my political engagement, there is nothing much more to be said. A long time ago I concluded that the closer one is to politics, the less one can think sociologically. That relation between sociology and politics has been confirmed many times in my surroundings, and, in addition, in my experience. I was quite active during the reign of Slobodan Milosevic as a participant in numerous public protests, though I confess that my wife Vera was much more engaged in them. I took part in many public discussions arguing against Milosevic and his entourage and their catastrophic politics, as well as against the whole atmosphere that existed in the milieu. But I have rejected all offers to join a political party that I have received since political pluralism appeared in Yugoslavia.

A member of a political organization, of a party, whatever—no thank you! Too individualistic an attitude? Probably. My individualistic self-understanding has, I am certain, spared me many intellectual, moral, and emotional losses, if not material ones. And it has spared my sociological ethos too. Well, that should be the point of this story, shouldn't it?

Notes

1 An approximate translation of Marcus Tullius Cicero's *sententia*, written in his *De oratore*, would be: "History is a witness of time, light of truth, life of memory, teacher of life, herald of the past." See Albin Vilhar, *Latinski citati* (Beograd: Matica srpska, 1991), p. 114.

2 Georg Wilhelm Friedrich Hegel, *Osnovne crte filozofije prava* (Sarajevo: Veselin Maslesa, 1964), p. 19. It should be stressed that the meaning of "reality" in that context implies both socio-historical and individual dimensions.

3 Nikolas Rose, "Authority and the Genealogy of Subjectivity," pp. 294–327 in *Detraditionalization*, eds Paul Heelas, Scott Lash, and Paul Morris (Cambridge: Blackwell Publishers, 1996), pp. 301–302.

4 Ibid., 302.

5 Ibid.

6 Ulrich Beck and Elisabeth Beck-Gernscheim, "Individualization and 'Precarious Freedom': Perspectives and Controversies of a Subject-oriented Sociology," pp. 23–48 in *Detraditionalization*, eds Paul Heelas, Scott Lash, and Paul Morris (Cambridge: Blackwell Publishers, 1996), pp. 25–26.

7 Ibid.

8 As cited in ibid., p. 26.

9 Anthony Giddens, *Sociology* (Cambridge, Mass.: Polity Press, 2001), p. 669.

10 For more on *Lebenswelt*, see Alfred Schutz, *On Phenomenology and Social Relations* (Chicago, Ill.: University of Chicago, 1975), pp. 72–76.

11 Karel Turza, "Da li su modernost i drustvo sinonimi?," *Treci Program Radio Beograda No. 117–118* (Beograd: Radio Beograda, 2003); and "On Modernity in General and On the Main Obstacles to Modernity in Serbia in the 20th Century—and Afterwards," Sociologija 45, 2 (2003): 117–140.

12 The assassination of Dr Zoran Djindjic, the prime minister of Serbia, on March 12, 2003, was the climax of *la danse macabre* that had been performed in the region ever since 1991. Among other things, that "performance" includes several thousands murdered and wounded; about 500,000 people who have lost their homes; hundreds of thousands of young, highly educated men and women who have escaped abroad, etc. The region in question refers to Serbia and Montenegro only. Of course, regarding the former Yugoslavia, all those quantifications should be multiplied. For instance, according to realistic estimations almost 10 percent of the population of that country—namely, about two million people—have lost their homes, or have become refugees during the 1990s!

13 Papic was 54 when she died, in 2002. Unfortunately, there is no room here to pay an adequate tribute to her. There is also no room for describing, or even mentioning, all the things that we did together at *Radionica SIC*.

14 According to some analysts, the whole period from 1945 up to now has been nothing but a history of repression and torture in Communist Yugoslavia and in Serbia and Montenegro. See Aleksandar Roknic, "Neprekinuta represija," *DANAS PRAVO plus* (September 10, 2004): 3. Absolutely wrong, I say. The victims of Tito's era (the majority of them were those who hailed Stalin in 1948, when Yugoslavia became independent of the so-called socialist community; that is to say, of the USSR), and the victims of the post-Tito period, since 1980, when Tito died, cannot be equalized. It is true that in the 1980s, in SFR Yugoslavia, some 500 people were put in prison for political reasons only. In my humble opinion, however, some of them should have stayed in prison much longer. I have in mind primarily those who were accused of preaching and spreading ethnic nationalism (i.e., Alija Izetbegovic, Vojislav Seselj, and Franjo Tudjman). I am absolutely sure that if they, and the others who shared their malign political ideas, had been kept out of political scene in the 1980s, the Yugoslav drama in the 1990s would have been less bloody.

15 Karel Turza, "Kritika gradjanskog oblika porodice," pp. 372–375 in *Marksizam i savremeno drustvo*, ed. Jovica Trkulja (Beograd: Savremena administracija, 1979).

16 Karel Turza, "Trivijalizacija krize," *Treci Program Radio Beograd No. 70* (Beograd: Radio Beograda, 1986).

17 Karel Turza, *Cemu jos sociologija?* (Beograd: Gutenbergova galksija, 1996); and *Modernost na biciklu* (Beograd: Akademia nova, 1996).

18 It was a conference on life-long learning that was held at the University of Bamberg. It was an excellent gathering at which theorists from all over the world took part (i.e., from Europe, including former Communist countries and Canada, to the USA and Japan). Professor Jost Reischmann (from the University of Bamberg) was a great host. Thanks to him the whole thing turned into a real confirmation of the best attributes and parameters that a scientific community should include. I am personally especially grateful to Michal Bron from the Nobel Institute in Uppsala, Sweden,

who, through various international activities, worked for almost a year to enable me to attend the meeting.

19 Karel Turza, *Luis Mamford, Jedna kritika modernosti* (Beograd: Zavod za udzbenike i nastavna sredstva, 1998).

20 Along with everything else, there is a chronic problem that seems totally insoluble nowadays: lack of money. From time to time, the association gets some money from the Ministry of Science. However, that is scarcely enough to cover the expenses of *Sociologija*. It cannot pay even the membership fee to the ISA, which is, as far as I know, approximately US$300. Over the past three or four years I have tried to convince my colleagues that we should leave the very idea of a classic sociological association behind, in favor of a new "post-modern" (a classic political term—"anarchic," would be more appropriate) organization. It would be non-national (that is. regional—southeast Europe), and noncollective (that is any sociologist from the region could freely become a member). It would also be without the so-called stable organizational institutions, such as presidency, assembly, numerous sections, etc. Rather, it would be a virtual sociological community, with its website, e-mail address, and no more than ten sociologists from the region who would be elected by those who participate in the undertaking no matter where they are from, in relatively permanent communication via e-mail. They would have face-to-face meetings once or twice a year. An electronic periodical, and occasionally a printed volume, would be published in English and/or in original languages. Though the idea has been accepted and supported by many prominent sociologists and social theorists from Bosnia and Herzegovina, Croatia, Macedonia, Montenegro, Serbia, and Slovenia (e.g., Dragoljub Djordjevic, Djokica Jovanovic, Franc Mali, Aljosa Mimica, Nenad Miscevic, Mojca Novak, Ljubinko Pusic, Zeljko Skuljevic, Miroslav Stanojevic, Lino Veljak, and Sreten Vujovic), it has never been under serious consideration in the YSA. Why? Frankly, I do not know. I have tried, two or three times, at our formal meetings in the YSA to raise the problem and to suggest a solution, but in vain. It was as if I had talked about, let us say, quantum theory—namely, about the hypothesis that in radiation the energy of electrons is discharged not continuously but in certain fixed amounts, or quanta. My words obviously have not had any resonance. Therefore, I have given up. I have no ambition any more to persuade anybody.

11 Becoming a social researcher in transitional Estonia

Triin Vihalemm

My motivational background

After finishing secondary education in 1986 I was admitted to the Department of Journalism at the Faculty of Philology of Tartu University. I already had decided to study journalism by my next to last year of secondary school. My father, Rein Vihalemm, a professor of the philosophy of science, and my mother, Tiiu Vihalemm, an assistant professor of biochemistry, fully supported my choice. By the time I started my studies in 1986 the Department of Journalism, which was incorporated into the Faculty of Philology, had a relatively strong tradition of social surveys and analysis. Students were offered courses on theories of mass communication, public opinion, and survey methods.

By the 1980s, sociological research was being done in virtually every university in Estonia, including the Tallinn Pedagogical Institute, the Estonian Agricultural Academy, and the Tallinn Polytechnic Institute. However, there were only about a hundred persons doing empirical research in the entire country.

Some candidates for the department admitted during their entrance interviews that their aim was to work in social research rather than in journalism. I did not have any such plans, though articles I had published in the upper forms of the secondary school were mainly analytical and based on empirical research. Although one might assume that my choice of journalism was influenced by my uncle, Peeter Vihalemm, a professor in the Department of Journalism, in reality the situation was quite the contrary. I still believe that he did not much care for the idea of his niece studying journalism. Perhaps he was worried that I would attempt to use my family connections. He also thought that I was too much of an introvert to be successful in the profession.

The Department of Journalism at Tartu was the home for many students who went on to become renowned politicians and prominent figures within the nation. Examples include Juri Luik, the Minister of Defence and of Foreign Affairs for the Republic of Estonia, and the Ambassador of the Republic of Estonia to NATO. Tiit Matsulevits was the Ambassador of the Republic of Estonia to Germany, the Vatican, Ukraine, and Russia. Katrin Saks was the Minister of Population. Compared to the stars of the department, I was rather naïve and had little charisma. Only later on did it become evident that my class represented a new generation of students. While charisma, creativity, and social consciousness dominated the sensibilities of the senior students and previous graduates, my classmates had notably more pragmatic objectives.

The social and political atmosphere in the late 1980s and early 1990s

The beginning of my studies coincided with remarkable changes in society. In 1987 the so-called "phosphate rock war" broke out. It was a mass campaign against a plan to establish phosphate mines in the northeast of Estonia. The mining of phosphate rock would have resulted in a dramatic deterioration of the ecological situation in the area, as well as a new influx of immigrant workers. A campaign in the press, led by Estonian researchers and scientists, became a mass protest activity, and the leadership of the Estonian Soviet Socialist Republic was forced to abandon the plan.

Students that had marched in the May Day parade, in 1987, replaced the conventional "Long-live-the-friendship-of-nations" banners with those reading "No to phosphate mines!" Several other students and I wrote an article about a public rally in which the issue of the phosphate mines was discussed. However, Marju Lauristin, our mentor, advised us to tone down the emotions in the text. The situation in Estonia was rather odd at that time: nobody knew exactly where the line of acceptability was drawn. Thoughts and ideas expressed in the media and at public meetings became increasingly radical. Now and then, sanctions were imposed. But these were rather unsystematic.

On one occasion I attended a meeting of activists wishing to conserve the national heritage. The blue-black-and-white flag of Estonia, which had been banned by the Soviet authorities, was flown and patriotic speeches were delivered. Out of nowhere the militia arrived. We fled in panic, running and jumping over fences. At the same time, other similar events were held without any interference. It was like walking on thin ice, slowly testing it carefully before taking another step.

Events began to speed up. In September 1987 the notion of a self-managing Estonia was introduced, and in April 1988 a massive opposition movement, *Rahvarinne* (the Popular Front) was organized by Edgar Savisaar and our professor, Marju Lauristin. In June 1988 semi-spontaneous "evening song festivals" took place on the Tallinn Song Festival Field. These were gatherings in which spontaneous speeches were made and both professional and amateur musicians performed. There was no specific schedule or plan, people came just to sing together and to enjoy the special emotional atmosphere of that summer. The largest festival had over 100,000 participants. This chain of events, now known as the Singing Revolution, culminated on September 11, 1988, with an event called the Estonian Song, where the leaders of the Popular Front made speeches and the people sang patriotic songs. A quarter of a million people participated, demanding the restoration of Estonian independence.[1]

A circle of my close friends and I participated in the song festivals. Undoubtedly, these events were sublime and people were elated. However, for young people, the entertaining side of these events was equally important. That summer I took an interest in mass movement and mobilization. Later, when I had an opportunity to visit foreign libraries, I studied the literature on mass movements, though it did not become my main field of research.

Despite the fact that Professor Marju Lauristin had entered actively into politics, the atmosphere in the Department of Journalism was more reflective than euphoric, more critical and analytic than elated. Differences between radical and moderate approaches to politics were clearly noticeable within the department. Most of the students who were interested in politics held radical views, while Lauristin, one of the leaders of the Popular Front, was in favor of a more moderate approach. Discussions arising from different political views were very interesting and educating. In the midst of the Singing Revolution, public discussions and spontaneous debates broke out during lectures.

Although the start of our studies coincided with momentous changes in Estonian society, my interest, like that of my peers, in participating in the events gradually faded away. Naturally, I was excited when in 1990 the Supreme Soviet of the Estonian Soviet Socialist Republic proclaimed the restoration of the Republic of Estonia, and I enthusiastically took part in the referendum on Estonia's independence. However, this was not paramount any more. The world was opening up quickly and we were eager to use our energy in many other spheres.

I tried to take advantage of the period when borders were opened and travelling aboard by Aeroflot flights was fairly cheap. The savings of my family and financial help from my relatives enabled me to travel quite a bit. Since the Soviet economic system had not yet completely collapsed, at the end of the 1980s foreign currency was being sold at an artificial exchange rate, not at its market price. This meant that the Soviet rouble was strongly overvalued in relation to the US dollar, and it was very cheap to travel for Soviet roubles. Naturally, many people took advantage of this opportunity, and the lines in front of the doors of embassies and travel agencies were enormous.

I became quite an expert in lining up for visas at the different embassies, which were mainly located in Moscow, and for flight tickets. I came to admire the ability of Russians to arrange a line and organize the crowd. Even though there were no ticket machines for lining up, there was no pushing or elbowing. The line was organized on paper. In a Russian line, somebody is always the chief who "maintains the records." Check-in times were set when everyone's name would be read out loud. If you were present and answered "yes," then your place in the line was preserved. If you missed the check-in, or were late, your name was crossed off. The chiefs changed as the line advanced. Newcomers sometimes tried to protest, but eventually they had to accept the system. As a result, it was possible to sit on a bench in a park and study, or to walk around.

While in Moscow, I stayed with a friend of my father's. He was a professor of philosophy, and our conversations at the dinner table were very amusing and interesting. A passport from the USSR was my travel document. I obtained visas to different countries by getting invitations from different people (i.e., relatives, organizers of conferences, etc.).

The difference in cultural backgrounds, and the experience of living in different societies, became most obvious to me when I visited my relatives who lived abroad. In 1987 I visited my paternal grandparents in Sweden. In 1989, the second wife of my maternal grandfather in Australia, and, in 1990, my great-uncle in Canada. In all of these places I met many Estonians who had emigrated out of fear of the Stalin regime. Since these were mainly elderly people, and I was a young person from the Soviet Union who was familiar with those aspects of Estonian culture and history which had not been touched upon or distorted in a Soviet school, I tried to keep a low profile during these conversations. Actually, I was more afraid of the differences in our values and viewpoints than in the differences in cultural background or those between generations.

While travelling, I grasped at the opportunity to study the development of Estonian communities abroad. In Australia I analysed a local Estonian language newspaper, and interviewed second- and third-generation Estonians living there. The majority of them were assimilated. On the basis of my research, I prepared several articles and wrote a term paper. This boosted my interest in ethno-cultural identity, acculturation processes, and issues related to multiple identities. The experience significantly broadened my perception of the world. Within the Estonian independence movement, nationality was considered primordial. A nationality was seen as something constant, something one inherits, even if it was suppressed such as by the Soviet regime. My spontaneous research opened a totally new world. How was ethnic identity maintained, reconstructed, and how may it change?

My first study trips to international conferences for students of journalism—Finland in 1988, and France in 1989—were exhilarating experiences for me. In order to be able to attend those conferences a competition was organized in the department. Participants were chosen on the basis of their performance and level of independent research work. I was surprised that, except for financial aid from the organizers of the conferences (i.e., free accommodation and some pocket money), the attitude toward students from the collapsing Soviet Union was no different from that toward students from other countries.

In fact, students from Western countries seemed to take it for granted that my tacit knowledge and cultural practices were the same as or similar to their own. These students were well aware of the political upheavals in the Soviet Union. However, it did not occur to them that a given political system might have an impact on a person's conception of the world. I figured that this was partly caused by their specialization. As future journalists, they were primarily focused on facts, events, and stories, and not the underlying structures behind them. This only strengthened my desire to become an analyst who could explain and interpret cultural and social processes.

I visited Rome and Vienna with my mother when she attended international conferences on biochemistry. These trips gave me a general idea of what occurred at international conferences, from modern presentation techniques to get-together parties. However, I was mainly a tourist in these cities and did a lot of sightseeing. These trips ignited my continuing passion for travelling. I prefer travelling alone to organized tours. The first trip I took by myself was to the United Kingdom. In order to get a visa, my Canadian great-uncle asked his friends in England to send me and my husband invitations.

My husband and I were hitchhiking in England when the failed August *coup d'état* against Mikhail Gorbachev took place in Moscow on August 20, 1991. That same day, the Supreme Soviet of the Republic of Estonia declared Estonian independence. Independent nationhood was restored and the country sought to re-establish diplomatic relations with the other nations of the world. Being in England, we had no idea to what kind of a country we would be returning. I tried to find out about the situation in the USSR and Estonia from the drivers who gave us a lift, but nobody seemed to know much.

Eventually, we returned safely to Estonia via Moscow. Estonia immediately began to build up a civil society and was striving to become a free market economy. Because of its liberalist policy, it soon became the star pupil of the World Bank. Since that time I have had many interesting opportunities to realize my ambitions and to participate in policy-making at grass-roots level. For example, through the Integration of Non-Estonian-Youth Project, I participated in the creation of the Estonian integration program. The initiators of the project, Marju Lauristin and Mati Heidmets, played an important role in devising the integration program that was approved by the government of the Republic of Estonia, in 1997.

Academic atmosphere in Tartu in the late 1980s and early 1990s

The curriculum for the Department of Journalism was created by following the best practices from other universities as much as possible. Since the department was a part of the Faculty of Philology, a lot of attention was paid to the humanities, i.e., literary theory, Russian literature, Estonian literature, and world literature were a part of the curriculum. I am happy that the foundation I obtained there enabled me to perceive the possibilities of the humanitarian approach in social research and analysis.

During the first years of my studies there was no escaping the so-called "red subjects." These included the history of the Communist Party of the Soviet Union, Marxist-Leninist philosophy, political economy, etc. Fortunately, as I advanced in my studies the curriculum was supplemented by more interesting and modern courses, such as fundamentals of economy, current public affairs, environmental protection, history of social philosophy, and a special course on global issues. We also had courses on the psychology of reading, methods of sociological research, social psychology, and the theory of public opinion.

The fourth year consisted of subjects like journalistic genres, stylistics, and the history of Soviet journalism. My interest in social studies and society in general, and the realization that I wanted to be a social analyst, became even stronger in 1989 and 1990 during my visits abroad. The Department of Journalism had a strong tradition of readership surveys, and my course paper for the second year was a descriptive analysis of readers of two Russian language cultural journals published in Estonia, *Tallinn* and *Raduga.* In practice, the survey embraced the whole Russian-speaking community in Estonia, their lifestyle, etc.[2]

By the end of the third year of study I had developed a desire to gain an in-depth insight into the cultures and the relations between the different ethnicities. Professor Peeter Vihalemm prepared an individualized program for me, including the exams I had to sit, that was registered in the Faculty. It included cultural anthropology directed by Jaan Kaplinski, ethnic sociology directed by Klara Hallik, ethnic psychology by Peeter Tulviste, the history of sociology by Vihalemm, sociolinguistics by Tiit Hennoste, and cultural theory directed by Aili Aarelaid. Virtually none of these subjects was taught officially and my studies were based mainly on independent work and reading. Each instructor with whom I worked would provide me with a list of books and articles to be studied. For example, information about cultural anthropology came from copies of articles. The instructors also lent me books in English from their home libraries—for example, Max Weber's *The Protestant Ethics and Spirit of Capitalism*, as well as the works of Ruth Benedict, Margaret Mead, Claude Lévi-Strauss, and others.

The network of home libraries had a significant role in the academic life of Tartu. People knew who had which books at home. Books were brought from trips abroad, and as these trips were rare people also asked their friends and relatives to send books. There were no problems with sending classical literature, and books were often copied. Contacts with colleagues from Moscow and Leningrad were also helpful. There were various seminars and collaborative projects. For example, in 1965, Professor Vladimir Yadov, who had been Peeter Vihalemm's supervisor, worked in England for about six months, and later travelled to Western countries quite often.

A significant amount of literature, in Russian, was available in the university library. In the 1960s many good books had been translated into Russian. Some of the surveys in Russian were quite good. For example, a survey of the history of Western sociology by Igor Kon introduced various theories from Auguste Comte and Émile Durkheim to the different approaches of the 1970s, in a rather systematic and ideologically unbiased manner.[3] Books on ethnopsychology by Kon and Sergei Korolyov gave insight into attitudes about ethnicity and ethnic stereotypes, and studies of ethnic character.[4] They made reference to Ruth Benedict, Harold Inkeles, Margaret Mead, Harry Triandis, Clyde Kluckhohn, and others. They also described several methodological techniques, including direct observation, interviewing, twenty statement tests (TST), Rorschach tests, and analysis of folklore. I was most influenced by and interested in the phenomenological and constructivist approaches, including hermeneutics, symbolic interactionism, and ethnomethodology. Works of several Western authors in these areas also had been translated into Russian.[5]

My exams and assessments were in the form of essays and discussions, and my grades were entered into an academic report attached to the diploma. My earlier interest in the Russian language community in Estonia grew. Each year I was required to conduct a survey and write a course paper. Inspired by a Finnish survey on ethnic prejudice, I conducted a similar one, in 1989, in Russian and Estonian schools. I prepared a questionnaire in Estonian and Russian for pupils in the Estonian-language and Russian-language schools. The questionnaire was completed by more than 560 pupils from the schools of Tallinn, Tartu, Voru, Kohtla-Jarve, and Narva. Specialists from the Ministry of Education gave me a hand with the sampling and obtaining the necessary permissions.

When analysing the data, I compared the answers of Russian and Estonian pupils. Russians chose the option "don't know" more often, and also left open-ended questions unanswered more often. However, they wrote both negative and positive comments on the edges or at the end of the questionnaire. This gave me the idea to use a non-standardized interviewing technique which I carried out the following year when I conducted about 50 semi-structured interviews in Estonian and Russian schools. As a part of these interviews I asked the pupils to interpret cartoons with ethnic references, which had been published in the press. I conducted an analysis of ethnic prejudice through the respondents' reactions to ethnic humor.

In my diploma thesis, *Kooliopilaste etnilised hoiakud* (Ethnic prejudices among Estonian and Russian pupils), I tried to combine quantitative and qualitative data. The paper was rather empirical, as was noted by the reviewer, Oleve Must, assistant professor of social psychology. The main conceptual source I used was van Dijk's work on ethnic prejudice.[6] I attempted to analyse the structure of ethnic prejudice within the framework created by Teun van Dijk, and it seemed to work. However, I must admit that by the end of my Bachelor studies I was not able to combine theory and practical experience. The theories which I had studied were at one pole and my empirical experience at the other.

MA studies from 1991 to 1993: enthusiastic empiricism and hard work

Immediately after graduating *cum laude* in June 1991, with the hope of combining theory and practice, I began MA studies in the recently opened Department of Sociology at Tartu University.[7] While sociology had been taught at Tartu since the 1980s, the Department of Sociology was only formally established as a teaching unit in 1989. The head of the department was the former chairman of the Committee of the Communist Party of the university. In 1991, one's connection with the Communist Party was still vividly remembered. However, it did not affect our relationship. Since I and three young men were the first MA students, we did not have any systematic curriculum. We had various seminars, English for advanced students, and a course that was mainly based on a textbook written by Anthony Giddens.[8]

I also spent short periods at Swedish and Finnish universities. In 1992 I spent two weeks at the University of Lund, through a grant from the Nordic Council of Ministers. In 1993 I was at the University of Helsinki for four weeks, with a grant from the Tuglas Society. During these trips I read theory on acculturation, ethnic prejudice, and identity. I also improved my knowledge of qualitative research methods.[9]

At first I intended to continue exploring ethnic prejudice in my MA thesis. Inspired by the narrative analysis of van Dijk, during my last year of BA study I had already collected prejudiced narratives for my master's paper. However, in 1991 I felt that the social context required a change in the focus of my work. I wanted to record people's reflections and interpretations of the social changes since 1991, when Estonian society had entered the period of fast political and economic transformation. Thus I refocused my research on the strategies used by ethnic Russians in Estonia to adapt themselves to the changed situation. I successfully applied an Individual Research Support Scheme Grant offered through the Central European University and funded by the Soros Foundation.

It was not my ambition to create any models or to generalize the process, but rather to describe and understand it in concrete terms. I chose a qualitative approach, using in-depth interviews with Russian-speaking specialists, white-collar workers, secondary school students, and graduates. In the sample, I included different types of enterprises and schools, successful and not, from different districts. I also included seven registered unemployed workers that I found through the labor market board. The purpose was to get as wide a range of experiences and perspectives as possible.

With the support of the grant I was able to use up-to-date technology and form a small research team. My close friend and colleague, psychologist Jelena Jedomskihh, invited her friends Maie Kotsheulova and Dimitri Grozdhov to assist me in data collection. Jelena and I decided that ethnocultural background and Russian as a mother tongue were more important for our team members than excellence in interviewing skills. We encouraged them to engage in rather free discussions with respondents while keeping to the key topics. The study lasted from the spring of 1992 to the summer of 1993.

At the same time as my master studies, I worked for the Estonian Marketing and Opinion Research Company (EMOR Ltd). EMOR Ltd is a private company that was created with Estonian and Finnish capital and established by people who had experience in conducting public opinion polls. When I joined the company at the beginning of the 1990s they had just begun monitoring household income and expenditures for the National Office of Statistics, and doing media research. The media research was carried out by Baltic Media Facts, a subsidiary of EMOR Ltd, established with Finnish Gallup.

In the first half of the 1990s, EMOR Ltd became the largest research company in the Baltic countries. Unlike other research companies, many strategic investments were made at EMOR Ltd. For example, in computer-assisted telephone interviewing techniques, and later computer-assisted personal interviewing, as well as the purchase of various licenses for data processing programs.

The company developed quickly from a co-operative type of venture into a formally organized company with a specialized division of labor. Currently, it employs more than 50 people. Its employees have participated in the World Association of Marketing Professionals (ESOMAR) conferences and training programs, and studied at the Finnish Marketing Institute.

EMOR Ltd's clients have been both local and foreign companies who desired to invest in the Baltic region. Finnish Gallup built up a collaborative network in Latvia, Lithuania, Russia, and Ukraine. In developing co-operation with a Latvian and Lithuanian research company, an important role was played by Karin Niinas and Margo Veskimagi, the leaders of EMOR Ltd. When Taylor Nelson Sofres acquired Finnish Gallup, they also acquired EMOR Ltd. The analysts working at EMOR Ltd have MA degrees. They are specialists in various fields, including economy, the English language, and engineering. The company started to hire graduates of the Department of Sociology at the end of 1990s. At that time, more important than the skills of statistical analysis were the skills of communicating with clients, project management, and being aware of the developments of a particular field. Those who studied sociology were no more skilled in these areas than those from other fields.

In 1992, as a part-time research fellow of the company, I conducted a study on the use of languages in Estonian medical establishments. I used a combination of quantitative and qualitative methods.[10] In 1993, my relationship with EMOR Ltd strengthened and I started to work as the project manager for qualitative research. Among other things, I managed several projects for first- and third-sector organizations such as the Bank of Estonia, the Information Bureau of the Estonian Government, and Radio Free Europe. Karin Niinas, the manager of the company, endorsed the development of qualitative marketing research in the company. The working atmosphere and colleagues were open and friendly.

In the meantime, in the summer of 1992, I had given birth to my son, and our family was struggling to make ends meet. Working at EMOR Ltd alleviated those economically hard times. During the day, my son was in the care of a babysitter, and in the afternoons his father and I looked after him. Life was very busy. I was beginning to worry that I would not be able to finish my MA thesis by 1993. Since I had to report on the use of my grant, I was determined to make an effort and to finish it on time.

EMOR Ltd had its main headquarters in Tallinn, but also a branch office in Tartu, 260 kilometers away. Its focus groups and client meetings were held mainly in Tallinn. However, I had enough work in Tartu and thus didn't have to commute to Tallinn. I was allowed to use the computer for writing my paper. I spent every day, and a good part of the nights, in the office preparing reports for the company, and writing my master's thesis.

During my MA studies, my philosophical beliefs and preference for a school of thought started to form, mainly due to discussions with my father. He is a chemist and a scholar, and we had discussed the history of sociology on several occasions. It is not surprising that I began to think that social research and analysis were not the same as natural science. My personal feeling is that the term "science" refers first and foremost to natural sciences. I prefer to use the term "research," or "analysis," to refer to other activities. Therefore, I have never shared the viewpoint of those sociologists who are desperately trying to prove that sociology, notably that part of sociology which deals with quantitative analysis, is "real" science. To me, to approach society with a model based on the natural sciences is like looking for a lost key only in those areas illuminated by the beam of one's flashlight. I am interested in looking for the key, even if I have to step into the shadows beyond the safe pool of light.

I consider myself a representative of the phenomenological and constructivist approaches. Even though in many of my works I have, either directly or indirectly, tried to combine the quantitative and qualitative approaches, my most memorable discoveries as a researcher have come through qualitative fieldwork and analysis. Such an approach was clearly visible in my master's thesis which I finished in 1993. In it, I described two critical areas: the identity crisis and the main forms of (non-)adaptation: professional (non-)adaptation, civic (non-)adaptation and linguistic (non-)adaptation. I described different cases, such as attitudes towards the Estonian language and citizenship among the employed and unemployed. The theoretical part of the paper is rather modest. Its main value lies in the empirical data, as well as in its service as an exemplar of the qualitative approach to a post-Soviet Estonian sociology that up to that point had been limited to a mainly positivist paradigm.

In the summer of 1993 I was the first person in the re-established Republic of Estonia to receive a master's degree in sociology. Those who obtained their master's degree in sociology in the 1990s are working mainly as top specialists or officials in both the public and private sectors. Some continued their studies and have obtained a Ph.D. degree. Since a system of scholarships is virtually non-existent (a one-time state scholarship is only worth about US$650 per year), students must work to earn a living and their studies stretch beyond the typical four years required to complete the Ph.D.[11]

Those Ph.D. students who receive a research grant are in a better position since they are paid for their research work and articles, usually US$100–300 per month. Many students have read for their Ph.D. degree at foreign universities, especially in Finland. However, most students would prefer to be able to stay in Estonia rather than spend four years abroad. Such a long period away cuts one's links with domestic projects and it is difficult to find a position upon return.

In the middle of transitions: new challenges and contacts

After receiving a master's degree, I continued to work for EMOR Ltd. From 1994 to 1995 I was the deputy director of field market research. For a short period before taking a maternity leave, I served in the capacity of managing director, while Karin Niinas was busy developing the Baltic research division of the Finnish Gallup Group. After the birth of my daughter, in 1995, I resumed my career at EMOR Ltd as the development manager. I was responsible for the development of three partially intertwined fields, qualitative research techniques, marketing communication research, and value orientations research. I had good contacts with clients, and I believe that my training as a journalist was helpful in this regard.

The work at EMOR Ltd was interesting and offered me a good opportunity to develop my skills and knowledge. My superiors and colleagues appreciated my academic background, extensive reading, and skills at generalizing. I educated myself in the field of marketing by reading professional magazines and attending conferences. I also studied at the Finnish Marketing Institute.

In the autumn of 1994 I had started my Ph.D. studies in the Department of Journalism and Communication at the University of Tartu. I did not plan to quit work or to study abroad as I had a small son and wished to have another child. My choice of the Department of Journalism and Communications was affected by the fact that I and my colleagues had a collaborative international project in process (Balticom), the library in the department was relatively good, and its foreign contacts seemed promising. I also continued co-operation with the Department of Sociology, and in the spring of 1995 began to teach a course on qualitative research methods.

The reason why I decided to return to the university after only one year of working for EMOR Ltd was that I wanted to continue in the field which I had become interested in during my BA and MA studies: acculturation and assimilation of the Russian population in Estonia. The ongoing transformation of Estonian society was creating new issues. I also felt that the academic sphere suited me better, since I liked to analyze problems in-depth, and day-to-day project management typically did not allow for that. To avoid any monetary problems I continued to work at EMOR Ltd while carrying out my Ph.D. studies. Although the busy schedule and shortage of time caused stresses and strains, I was satisfied with my choice because it forced me to further improve my knowledge and skills.

I obtained a grant from the Finnish Vaino Tanner Foundation, which supports empirical research within the Ph.D. studies. It supported my studies from 1994 to 1996. It did not require studying or working in a Finnish institution, so I was able to continue my work and studies in Estonia. I used a part of the grant to participate in international conferences and to do some research at Finnish universities.

The focus of my Ph.D. research shifted towards language, value orientations, and identity as they related to the cultural integration of the Russian community in Estonia. I published a number of articles and made presentations on the integration of the Russian community, including economic coping and stratification. However, I became more and more interested in the communicative competence of Russians, the factors affecting the formation of such competence, and the prerequisites for the formation of cultural and civil identity in Estonian society. My interest was increased through participation in two research networks: the international Balticom project, and a local inter-university project "Integration of Non-Estonian Youth into Estonian Society."

I was a member of a Swedish–Estonian research team within the Balticom project from 1993 until 1997. The project was initiated by Karl Erik Rosengren from the University of Lund, Lennart Weibull from the University of Göteborg, and Marju Lauristin and Peeter Vihalemm from the University of Tartu. Their wish was to take advantage of the unique historical opportunity to conduct a quasi-experimental study to compare Estonia, Latvia, and Lithuania—three countries which had undergone dramatic changes—with the relatively stable society of Sweden. Between 1991 and 1997, the project was supported by various funds from the Swedish Royal Academy of Science, the Estonian Science Foundation, and the Open Estonia Foundation. A comparative survey explored respondents' interest in countries other than their own, political attitudes, and values. The data on values were collected by using a system developed by Milton Rokeach.[12] The members of the research team welcomed my interest in ethnic issues and encouraged me to analyse the ethnic aspect of the transition process.

In addition, since the person who was responsible for analysing values left for another job, and I had already analysed the values of Estonians and Russians, I also worked with Professor Lauristin on the part of the project that compared the values of Swedish, Latvian, Lithuanian, and Estonian people as well. In addition to the quantitative data that was collected, my Vaino Tanner Foundation scholarship enabled us to conduct 25 in-depth interviews. The interviews focused on people's perception of the change in values.

From 1995 to 1997 we started to prepare a book on the basis of the results of the project.[13] We had many interesting and educational discussions and seminars, both in Estonia and Sweden, and my analytic and conceptual skills improved significantly. I contributed three chapters to the book. Although the book was published in Estonia, it has enjoyed remarkable international attention. It has been referred to in more than 20 international journals, and has been used as a textbook in several universities in Sweden and Finland.

The Integration of Non-Estonian Youth into Estonian Society project was begun, in 1996, through the initiative of the minister of education and later rector of Tartu University, Professor Jaak Aaviksoo. The Ministry of Education financed its first stage, and later on, until 2001, it was financed by the Estonian Science Foundation. The team for the project was heterogeneous in nature. It included people of very different schools of thought, ages and interests, i.e. psychologists, social psychologists, education researchers, and sociologists. Participating in the project gave me a good experience in multi-subject analysis and a broad overview of the issues of the field. In 1998 and 1999 I worked as a researcher on this project. I was responsible for leading the research line of language behavior and identity, organizing a qualitative case study of Russian children in an Estonian language school, organizing two public conferences and three seminars for teachers, and overall co-ordination of the research network.

Two books, in Estonian, were published during the course of the project, in which I published seven chapters.[14] During my Ph.D. studies I also participated in several international conferences in Finland, Holland, and England, and spent short periods at foreign universities in order to improve my knowledge. In

1994 and 1995, with a grant from the Finnish Ministry of Education, I spent a total of four weeks at the University of Tampere. I studied different approaches to values, and general theories of ethnicity, community, and culture.[15] I also read the work on nations and nationalism by many different authors.[16]

In 1998, through a grant from the Open Estonia Foundation and the Transregional Center for Democratic Studies, I participated in the summer seminar "Nation, Identity, Community, Democracy, Continuity and Citizenship," in Krakow, Poland. There, I learned more about civil society, nations and nationalism. The seminar made me take interest in whether there is potential for the formation of a civic identity and common solidarity uniting Estonians and Estonian Russians in Estonia. It was also intriguing to observe the interaction and behavior of students from the USA and Soviet successor states. The students represented very different beliefs and approaches, such as essentialist and constructivist views, on the formation of nations. In 1998 and 1999 I was also a member of the media working group of a project sponsored by the Nordic Countries, "Support for the National Integration Program," and a member of the working group of media experts of the Integration Foundation.

Ph.D. thesis: a milestone in a journey

In 1999 I dedicated myself to writing and preparing to defend my Ph.D. thesis. According to the rules established at Tartu University, a candidate for a Ph.D. degree must publish a book, or at least three articles in internationally reviewed journals. So I decided to prepare my thesis as a collection of articles, united by an umbrella text, rather than in the form of a monograph.[17] I selected surveys which dealt with the question whether the Russophone population in Estonia would remain a relatively diffuse assemblage of individuals with some similar features and interests, or would it develop into a collective subject, an ethnic group characterized by a distinct group self-awareness and collective behavioral strategies in relation to the Estonian state and Estonians.

I found that the previous analyses had paid more attention to the relative deprivation and ambiguous political loyalty of Estonian Russians. Collective mobilization had been regarded as a possible response to their political exclusion. My conceptual starting point was that the collective self-concept could be formed when the members of a community shared certain symbols, and were united within a common meaningful space that would enable them to communicate their experiences and desires.

Based on the qualitative and quantitative studies, I found that the linguistic prescription of the political context and the established patterns of inter-group interaction made the Russophone population aware of the role of their common language of communication as a symbol of group exclusiveness. Citizenship and language laws amplified this process, causing the dilemma as to whether one should overcome one's linguistic distinction when competing with others on an individual basis, or use it as a common resource. I expect that the linguistic diversity between the two groups is likely to continue in the future; and it will probably continue to serve as a basis for the development of the collective self-consciousness of the Russophone population as an ethnically and culturally exclusive group.

I defended my dissertation in June 1999. The reviewer-discussants were Professor Vladimir Yadov from the Institute of Sociology of the Russian Academy of Sciences in Moscow, and Professor Mati Heidmets, a psychologist from the Faculty of Social Sciences of Tallinn Pedagogical University. Thus, there was an outside discussant and an inside discussant. The discussion was interesting and substantial, even if a little tense. It was in English, as the thesis was written in English and one of the opponents was from a foreign country. In a sense, it was symbolic, since some of my later research dealt with the influence of the English language on ethnic and language relations in Estonia.

Defense of the thesis was carried out in a Nordic manner: a short overview by me followed by a 2½ hour discussion. After a 15-minute introduction of the work by me, both opponents presented their opinions and asked questions. This took about an hour. Then the audience asked questions. Defending a thesis is a public event and everybody who is interested can participate. There were about 40 people listening to my presentation. My colleagues who have defended their theses in Norway and Finland have gone through the ordeal of four-hour discussions. Actually, I enjoyed the discussion very much, and also the fact that many questions were asked by the audience. As I learned later, the discussion was the main reason why I got the mark *cum laude*.

I had been working on the subject off and on for five years, and written many articles and working papers. Sometimes it seemed that the subject became indistinct. Now, a part of it was joined into the thesis and had been assessed by experts; this gave me the courage to move on. I saw my dissertation and the defence as one of the first milestones in a long journey, rather than the final statement of a research project. I felt that I had become a fully-fledged young researcher who was taken seriously by others.

I remember that after the discussion and congratulations I watched my four-year-old daughter run around the room. I had finished one of the articles in the thesis just before she was born. She was like a symbol of the four-year period, representing a completely different aspect of life, and I was happy that I had tried to do everything together, not building hierarchies of priorities.

A new century and new challenges

After 1999 I worked as a lecturer in the Department of Journalism and Communication at the University of Tartu. I submitted my *venia legendi* in June 2002, and was elected an associate professor. The *venia legendi* is a traditional 1½-hour lecture on a freely chosen subject which a candidate to the post of associate professor must give to the public. It should provide an overview of his/her teaching competence. However, it is a rather symbolic exercise.

I teach research methods in media and communication, marketing communication and marketing research, qualitative research methods and introduction to social research, using a small pilot study by students. I plan to continue with courses on collective identity with the focus on ethnicity and transformation.

I have continued to do research in the field of the formation of political and cultural identity, as well as the meaning of minority media in a multi-cultural society, regional and cultural orientations of media consumption, and the role of media in the integration of a minority groups and the formation of their identity.[18] My work in the inter-university research group continued also. We prepared a book on the project in English, and I was involved in preparing three sub-chapters.[19] The chapter dealing with identity is the most complete of them.

In 1999 and 2000 I was a member of the Minorities' Round Table of the President of the Republic, and participated in preparing several government documents and reviews, such as the chapter on mass media in the Report of the Government of Estonia and an Estonian national report about youth policy.[20] I was responsible for the media monitoring funded by the Integration Foundation.

International conferences inspire and provide an opportunity to meet people who hold the same views. I have participated in all ESA conferences since 1997. The ESA is valuable as it provides a broad overview of what researchers are dealing with. One can see both the best experts in the field and the average level and the frame of mind of researchers. Unfortunately, as of yet, no research network has formed in the ESA to study identity. However, there is an Estonian circle of researchers in the field of cultural studies, most being women in their thirties, and although I do not identify myself fully with the paradigm of cultural studies, we do communicate actively. This informal network includes researchers of sub-culture and the media. We have considered creating a website, but the idea has not been realized yet, mainly because of the lack of time.

Beginning in 2001, I supervised an MA student, Anu Masso. Anu successfully defended her MA thesis at the Tallinn Pedagogical University, and our collaboration continued with her Ph.D. studies. We have published several articles together.[21] In general, I like writing articles in collaboration with other scholars. It is more interesting, there are more discussions, and the work is more efficient. Also, my interest in an interdisciplinary approach to ethnic and identity issues has increased. I have also considered a secondary analysis of the interviews conducted at the beginning of 1990s, which reflect the mood and ways of thinking at that time.

In 2002 a new research network was formed in the Department of Journalism and Communication, focused on a funded project "Formation of the 21st Century Media Society in Estonia." The project is led by Professor Lauristin. We have discussed theories of transition and culture developed by Claus Offe, Michael Kennedy, and Piotr Sztompka, and the theories of late and postmodern society on the basis of the works of Manuel Castells and Zygmunt Bauman.

In January of 2004 I received a research grant from the Estonian Science Foundation for a four-year interdisciplinary project, "Changing Collective Identities in the Context of Estonia Moving into the Global Space." Earlier research shows that one cannot talk about the fragmentation of identities outside of late-modern societies. Estonia has rapidly entered the current of fragmented late-modernism (i.e., individualization and risk), bypassing the "classic" phase of civil society. In this context, collective identities are (re)created, both via inter-group identity creation, characteristic of the new global space, and by a reworking of the old narratives of identity. I assume that in the Estonian case, where the opening up of the cultural space to the global flow of information and the media market has been faster than in other post-Soviet societies, the cultural contradictions typical of the transformation period might be especially visible—that is, the simultaneity and conflicting nature of the paradigms of traditionalism, modernism and post-modernism. It is a new challenge for social researchers.

Several new lines of social research have developed as a result of the transformation and in response to new challenges and opportunities made possible by it. First, "classical" problems such as mobility, differentiation, family issues, environment, and regional studies have been able to take advantage of the large comparative international research networks stimulated by programs of the European Union. A relatively strong tradition of quantitative analysis already existed during the Soviet era, and this knowledge, experience, and tradition of teaching can be used nowadays. Second, a wide field of research into cultural practices and perceptions has opened up. In my opinion, since culture is a contextual phenomenon, the interdisciplinary case study approach is appropriate. A challenge for Estonian researchers, and a greater guarantee for success, lies in the co-operation between researchers of different fields and the ability to study Estonian cases from a broader perspective.

A third area of potential research is regional co-operation. Many issues of time and space in Estonia are similar to those in other (neighbouring) countries. For example, issues of the big and the small countries, relations between the center and the periphery, and the peculiarity of the post-Soviet transformation. Researchers should more boldly discuss what the message of Estonia as an original quasi-experimental model is, or what the case of Estonia adds to general knowledge.

I believe that social research and analysis have quite good foundations for development in Estonia. Undoubtedly, the Soviet system hindered the development of sociological thinking, allowing only the positivist approach to dominate, and forcing an ideological manner of interpretation upon researchers. It did not stimulate in-depth (micro) analysis. At the same time, the undermining impact of the Soviet ideological system on researchers and research activities was significantly weaker in Estonia than in other Soviet republics. The ultra-liberal reforms of economy, the academies, and the education system have created some insecurity among sociologists. Yet, the research community has found its objectives. The system of higher education is more or less organized. The system of grants is working, and research groups are plugged into international co-operation networks. Although there are some problems, I do not believe that the negative legacies from the past or the administrative hindrances of the present are stronger than the good will and enthusiasm of the members of the community.

Much depends on people themselves. In my opinion, the biggest challenges Estonian sociologists must meet are to become more reliable and competent in the eyes of Estonian society, to participate successfully in the new EU programs, and to shorten the period of studies in order to more quickly produce a new generation of researchers. In general, I am full of hope for the future of social research and analysis in Estonia.

Notes

1 A full overview of the restoration of independence is available at http://www.estonica.org/eng.

2 After the Soviet annexation, Estonia became an object of a colonial policy stimulating a mass migration. Thus, a sizeable (36 percent), but somewhat isolated Russian-speaking community developed in Estonia. The Russian-speaking community is concentrated in a number of cities and towns in the northern part of the country: Tallinn, Johvi, and Narva. During the Soviet time they enjoyed extraterritorial status, the right to use their own language, and to have their own Russian-language institutions throughout the country. This development, which took place without violence during Soviet rule and continued for the first decade of Estonian independence, has been called the "quiet separation." As a result, two language communities exist side by side in Estonia. For a more thorough discussion, see Marju Lauristan and Mati Heidmets, eds, *The Challenge of the Russian Minority* (Tartu: Tartu University Press, 2002).

3 Igor Kon, ed., *Istorija burzhuaznoi sotsiologii XIX-natshala XX vv* (Moscow: Nauka, 1979).

4 Igor Kon, ed., *K probleme natsionalnogo haraktera* (Moscow: Nauka, 1971); and Sergei Korolyov, ed., *Voprosо etnopsihologi v rabotah zarubeznih avtorov* (Moscow: Progress, 1984).

5 For example, Teun van Dijk, *Jazyk, poznanie, kommunikatsia* (Moscow: Progress, 1989).

6 Teun van Dijk, *Communicating Racism: Ethnic Prejudice in Thought and Talk* (Newbury Park: Sage, 1987).

7 In the former Soviet Union, undergraduate studies lasted for five years, and the diploma level was close to the Western MA level. Postgraduate studies followed, and the degree received was similar to the Western Ph.D. The Western system was adopted by Estonian universities at the end of the 1990s. As a result, in effect, everyone who obtained an MA degree in Estonia in the 1990s took a master's program twice. After graduating from a university at the undergraduate level they studied 2–4 more years to obtain a MA degree, and then went on to the Ph.D. This generation uses the following system of notation in their CVs: BA = five years of studies + university diploma, MA = 2–4 years of MA studies + MA thesis, Ph.D. = 4+ years of Ph.D. studies + dissertation.

8 Anthony Giddens, *Sociology* (Oxford: Polity Press, 1989).

9 In qualitative methodology I read Bruce Berg, *Qualitative Research Methods for the Social Sciences* (Boston: Allyn & Bacon, 1989); Steven Taylor and Robert Bogdan, *Introduction to Qualitative Research Methods: The Search for Meanings* (New York: John Wiley & Sons, 1984); and Michael Patton, *Qualitative Evaluation and Research Methods* (Newbury Park: Sage, 1990).

10 See Triin Vihalemm, "Keelesituatsioonist Eesti meditsiiniasutustes," *Eesti Arst* 5 and 6 (1992): 343–348, 419–423.

11 A program for improving Ph.D. studies in Estonia is being developed. Departments in which a Ph.D. thesis has been defended get a one-time bonus equal to thirty to

forty thousand dollars, at least at Tartu University. However, this bonus system has not yet been fully implemented.

12 Milton Rokeach, *The Nature of Human Values* (New York: Free Press, 1973).

13 Marju Lauristin, Peeter Vihalemm, Karl-Erik Rosengren, and Lennart Weibull, eds, *Return to the Western World: Cultural and Political Perspectives on the Estonian Post-Communist Transition* (Tartu: Tartu University Press, 1997).

14 Pritt Jarve, ed., *Vene noored Eestis* (Tallinn: Avita, 1997); Marju Lauristin, Silvi Vare, Tiia Pedastsaar, and Marje Pavelson, eds, *Mitmekultuuriline Eesti: väljakutse haridusele* (Tartu: University of Tartu and Vali Press Ltd, 1998).

15 Works I consulted included, Louis Alfred Kroeber and Clyde Kluckhohn, *Culture: A Critical Review of Concepts and Defiitions* (Cambridge: Museum, 1952); Frederik Barth, ed., *Ethnic Groups and Boundaries* (London: George Allen & Unwin, 1969); Rokeach, *The Nature of Human Values*; Roland Inglehart, *The Silent Revolution: Changing Values and Political Styles Among Western Publics* (Princeton: Princeton University, 1977); Edward Hall, *Beyond Culture* (Garden City: Anchor Books, 1981); Homi Bhabha, *Nation and Narration* (London: Routledge, 1990); Geert Hofstede, *Cultures and Organizations: Software of the Mind* (New York: McGraw Hill, 1991); and Shalom Schwartz, "Universals in the Content and Structure of Values: Theoretical Advances and Empirical Tests in 20 Countries," *Advances in Experimental Social Psychology* 25 (1992): 1–65.

16 Ernest Gellner, *Nations and Nationalism* (Oxford: Blackwell, 1983); Eric Hobsbawm, *The Invention of Tradition* (Cambridge: Cambridge University, 1983); John Hutchinson, *The Dynamics of Cultural Nationalism* (London: Allen & Unwin, 1987); Benedict Anderson, *Imagined Communities: Reflections on the Origin and Spread of Nationalism* (London and New York: Verso, 1991); John Hutchinson and Anthon Smith, eds, *Nationalism* (Oxford: Oxford University Press, 1994).

17 Triin Vihalemm, "Eesti kool kui vene laste voimalik sotsialiseerumiskeskkond," pp. 337–399 in *Mitmekultuuriline Eesti: väljakutse haridusele* , eds Marju Lauristin, Silvi Vare, Tiia Pedastsaar, and Marje Pavelson (Tartu: University of Tartu and Vali Press Ltd, 1998); "Estonian Language Competence, Performance and Beliefs about its Acquisition Among the Russian-speaking Habitants of Estonia, 1989–1997," *International Journal of Sociology of Language* 139 (1999): 69–85; "Group Identity Formation Processes Among Russian-Speaking Settlers of Estonia: A Linguistic Perspective," *Journal of Baltic Studies* 30, 1 (1999): 18–39; and Tiit Hennoste and Triin Vihalemm, "Vene noorte toimetulek spontaanses argivestluses eesti eakaaslastega: sissejuhatus probleemistikku," pp. 249–276 in *Mitmekultuuriline Eesti*.

18 See Trinn Vihalemm, "Local and Global Orientations of Media Consumption in Estonia 1993–1998," pp. 45–53 in *Estonian Human Development Report* (Tallinn: United Nations Development Project, 1999); "The Informative and Identity-building Significance of Media: The Case of Estonian Russophones," pp. 44–48 in *Integration of Estonian Society. Monitoring 2000*, eds Marju Lauristin and Raivo Vetik (Tallinn: Institute of International and Social Studies, 2000); "Mass Media," pp. 56–62 in *Integrating Estonia 1997–2000* (Tallin: Government of Estonia, 2000).

19 See Marju Lauristan and Mati Heidmets, eds, *The Challenge of the Russian Minority* (Tartu: Tartu University Press, 2002).

20 Triin Vilhalemm, "Youth Election Activity and Bases for Political Preferences," pp. 225–237 in *Review of National Youth Policy*. Estonian National Report (Tallinn: Ministry of Education, Council of Europe, 2000).

21 Triin Vihalemm and Anu Masso, "Identity Dynamics of Russian-Speakers of Estonia in the Transition Period," *Journal of Baltic Studies* 34, 1 (2003): 92–116; "Dinamika identitshnosti russkih v Estonii v period postsovetskih transformatsii," *Diaspory/Diasporas* 5, 2 (2003): 230–257; and "Transformation of Identities in Changing Sociopolitical Space: The Case of Estonian Russians," *Journal of Borderlands Studies* 17, 2 (2003): 35–52.

12 Autobiographies of transformation

Mike F. Keen and Janusz L. Mucha

All of the stories in this collection are "sociological autobiographies" in the Mertonian sense, i.e., the authors use the sociological perspective, and sociological categories of analysis to present their own biographies within the context of the history of their own times. As C. Wright Mills suggests to scholars who wish to exercise their sociological imaginations, they link history and structure to agency and their own lives. But what else could we have expected? From the autobiographies, we can learn a great deal about the growth and development of sociology as a scholarly discipline in Central and Eastern Europe, about the ways it was studied in various institutions of higher education, and about the various career paths of sociologists. We can also learn about the topics that were of interest to Central and Eastern European sociologists and the methods and theories they used. But we don't need to repeat this fascinating information here.

Our authors are women and men. As we might have predicted, there is more personal information in the narratives written by women. It seems that life for them is much broader than work. We know from the autobiographies (not to mention our external knowledge) that our male authors also have children. But here, in this volume, the children are actors in the stories of the women rather than the men. For the women, it is very important to be both mothers and scholars. We hardly see the men as fathers, even if they mention their children. No doubt this is in part a reflection of the influence of traditional gender roles that until recently have been relatively pervasive throughout the region, including within sociology. Maca Jogan appears to have been most sensitive to the particular position of women as a marginalized group. In fact, she is a genuine feminist pioneer of the late-career cohort. Our other female authors rather prefer to stress other issues. For example, the problem of marginalization in the sense of giving voice to a marginalized population (East Germans in unified Germany) is strongly present in the story written by Vera Sparschuh. In general, we would have preferred to have learned more about the personal lives of our authors than they have been willing to reveal to us.

Naturally, there are a lot of discontinuities and turning points in the narratives of our authors. However, we could say that, due to the professional rather than personal character of their stories, these are very often collective turning points and discontinuities. As one might expect, one of them is the 1989/90 fall of Communism in Central and Eastern Europe (in each individual country the particular date was slightly different). Interestingly, all of our authors clearly profited from this systemic transformation; but those for whom it was more of an immediate and existential issue i.e., the late- and mid-career cohorts are also quite critical of its unexpected consequences. These negative consequences are also visible in the field of social relations i.e., post-Communist marginalization of large social collectivities. They can also be seen in the field of empirical social research i.e., budget cuts and decreased funding of academic research. In sociology, this has led to the imposition of a concentration on preparing and writing of policy papers and commercial market research reports, in place of more traditional and longer-term sociological research. This particular turn of events of the 1980s/90s has been a major discontinuity for our two older cohorts, though even a couple of our younger authors express a desire for a more "academic" environment.

The late-career cohort

The late-career authors were born before World War II (for example, Wladyslaw Kwasniewicz), or during it. Kwasniewicz mentions his participation in the war and the Polish underground Home Army, and the poverty that the war caused his family. The war had a particular impact on his life due to its geopolitical consequences—that is, it transferred Poland into the Soviet sphere of interest. It also delayed his educational process. For Maca Jogan, the trauma of the war is very significant from the point of view of her immediate family history, but she does not have any personal recollections of it. Valery Mansurov and Ladislav Machacek do not even mention the war as an influence on their life histories, or the histories of their families and countries.

Our late-career cohort, all members of the first post-World War II generation, was strongly affected by Communism having been indoctrinated by the apologetic and bureaucratic version of Marxism. Three of our authors mention their membership in the Communist Party. Kwasniewicz, who during the war had belonged to the anti-Communist underground army, and later was strongly dissatisfied with socialism in Poland, eventually joined the Party. He devotes a lot of thought to this turning point in his personal as well as public life because he feels that he needs to justify this step, which also brought on a personal crisis in his life in the form of his divorce. He notes that even after many years, people whom he respected felt that what he had done was wrong. He observes that before the end of 1981, and the imposition of the post-"Solidarity" martial law in Poland, no more than 60 percent of academic sociologists in Poland (as compared to 80 percent of academic philosophers) belonged to the Party. In other words, about 40 percent managed to work in academic sociology without joining the Party. He also gives us also an interesting analysis of the different attitudes of academics who were and who were not Communist Party members.

After joining the Party himself, he became very active on the national level in the central Party commission dealing with sociology.

Mansurov joined the Communist Party nearly immediately after graduating from college. He says that it was a rare and honorable reward for him, because at that time intellectuals were not easily admitted into the Party in his home town. He spent nearly his whole professional life working for, or strongly collaborating with, the Komsomol or the Communist Party apparatus. This was the way sociology functioned in the Soviet Union.

Machacek comes from a Communist family. He does not even mention how and why he joined the Party. It seems that it was very natural for him, given the family history and the general social climate in Czechoslovakia. He tells us about the purges of 1968 and afterwards, about his firing from the Party, and the rather significant consequences it had for the rest of his professional life. Only Jogan does not mention the Party (League of Communists of Yugoslavia) as a factor important in her own life.

These autobiographies present interesting insights into the post-World War II role of the Communist parties in academia in general, and in sociology in particular. We learn about the critical attitudes some sociologists had towards the Party and the system, as well as the tensions between the scholars who had strong institutional ties with the Communist Party and the Party's apparatus. Sociology has always been a politicized enterprise and this is quite clear in the accounts of these authors as well.

We are also given interesting insights into Eastern, as opposed to critical or humanistic Western, Marxism. According to the stereotypical view, Marxism-Leninism was the standard intellectual equipment of sociologists in Central and Eastern Europe. They were either strictly forced to study and implement it, or at least deeply socialized to do so. Yet our autobiographies suggest a more nuanced reality. Kwasniewicz started his career as a student of sociology by translating a textbook written by Pitirim Sorokin, and early on came to the conclusion that there was and should be room for various points of view in social science. He was strongly influenced by Kazimierz Dobrowolski, a sociologist and economic historian of moderately Marxist persuasion who for a long time refused to accept Marxism-Leninism as a scientific theory. Dobrowolski sympathized with those Polish sociologists who tried to avoid discussions of the relationship between sociology and historical materialism, and in this way avoided confrontation with dogmatic Marxism-Leninism. Kwasniewicz himself, in his sociological work, also was not engaged in theoretical issues. This is what probably allowed him to avoid the problems posed by orthodox Marxism.

Though he does not discuss it, Mansurov most probably had to study Soviet Marxism when in college. We learn from him that he was criticizing Western sociology from a Marxist stance in the 1960s, though we do not know his particular argument. Later, he mentions quite a few times the Soviet discussions of the "Marxist" and "bourgeois" currents within Soviet sociology. In his own work he has been using Western methodology, but it seems that, at least until the collapse of the Soviet Union, he never gave up the Marxist label.

Machacek does not even mention Marxism. However, for Jogan it is quite important. When likely forced to study it, she did not want to limit herself to a second-hand acquaintance, but studied the original works of the classics. She gives us her own analysis of the apologetic versus critical elements of the Marxist approach in Yugoslav society. She analyzes Marxism as a theory opposed to "bourgeois sociology." But, she does not present herself as a follower of Marxism in the intellectual or institutional sense.

During the interwar period in Eastern and Central Europe, sociology was only fully institutionalized in Poland. Even there, however, it disappeared during the Stalinist period after World War II and only reemerged in the mid-1950s. Only after the war and following the Stalinist period did sociology begin to be institutionalized throughout the region, and then, as noted above, under severe limitation by the Party and state, and in conflict and competition with historical materialism and scientific Communism. We could say that postwar institutional sociology was growing at the same time as were careers of our late-career cohort. What made them become sociologists?

In the case of Kwasniewicz we have a turning point when, at the age of 19, he was an instructor at a scout camp and an older person (probably in his thirties) gave a talk in which he said that the building of the foundations of a democratic system required the use of the findings of sociology. This talk transformed Kwasniewicz's perspective on the choice of a subject for his future university studies. Kwasniewicz's turning point, however, had prior roots. On the one hand, his father had been talking with great respect about sociology, and on the other hand he himself realized that sociology encompassed the kind of problems in which he had taken a special interest. So he enrolled in the sociology program, along with a second major in ethnology, at Jagiellonian University in Cracow. He graduated, eventually got a university job, and, despite the problems caused by Stalinism, became a professional sociologist.

Mansurov's road to sociology was not so simple, because sociology, as a major, did not exist in the Soviet universities, and particularly in his provincial colleges. He originally chose as his career to be a teacher of Western languages. At the same time, being an activist in the Komsomol, he participated in many courses, where he learned about sociology. He also did some interviewing and surveys for the Komsomol, without even initially knowing how they were connected with empirical sociology. Eventually he became more and more interested in social research and got accepted into postgraduate studies in the department of philosophy at Moscow State University, but with a concentration in sociology, which institutionally was only just emerging at that time. He joined the Soviet Sociological Association as one of its first members. Institutional Soviet sociology was growing before his eyes.

Machacek enrolled in the double program of philosophy and history at Comenius University in Bratislava. He met an instructor who suggested he write some sociologically oriented essays. It was both fashionable and politically risky. Still, he succeeded in publishing an early review essay in the field of sociology when he was a student, and then in publishing a part of his MA thesis.

This landed him a good job in the social research section of the Institute of Philosophy of the Slovak Academy of Sciences. The Institute of Sociology was only just about to be created. Institutionalized sociology was growing with Machacek.

Jogan's story of becoming a sociologist is even simpler. When she graduated from high school she had to decide what major to choose. To some extent by chance, she entered the newly opened MA program in sociology at the University of Ljubljana. She liked it and she stayed there until retirement.

We have not learned a lot about the intellectual influences that the work of various scholars exerted on the professional careers of our authors. Kwasniewicz is extremely loyal to his professor Kazimierz Dobrowolski, who was his role model as a teacher and as a scholar. He devotes a lot of attention and space to Dobrowolski's social, political, and sociological views. Kwasniewicz was also influenced by Sorokin's panoramic view of sociological theory, and by Peter Blau and Otis Duncan's book on American occupational structure.

Mansurov mentions his teacher in the Ph.D. program, Galina Andreeva, and her book on American empirical methodology in sociology. He also refers to Yuri Levada and his book on the role of sociology in the modern world, and to Boris Grushin's research program within the field of the sociology of public opinion. He does not seem to have had an individual mentor.

The same can be said about Machacek. A large number of his university teachers were important for his education. In addition, he calls our attention to Alojz Chura and Juraj Cecetka, two scholars of the interwar period who were specialists in the field of youth studies. He also mentions the contemporary classic of Polish sociology, Jan Szczepanski and his Warsaw team studying education problems. Perhaps Szczepanski's book on higher education could be considered the single most important book mentioned by Machacek.

Jogan is completely silent about the influences on her way of thinking and of doing sociology. Moreover, in a somewhat different context she says she was always lonely in her academic life. Perhaps her loneliness had also this diachronic dimension—she had no mentor, no role models. The fact that she was a woman in what was still a largely male-dominated field may also have contributed to this sense of intellectual isolation.

This situation among our late-career authors is not unexpected. As we know, sociology had been earlier institutionalized only in Poland. Dobrowolski had a very strong personality. For the first decades after the war he was a highly recognized scholar in the fields of sociology, ethnology, and history. There was probably nobody who could serve as a mentor to future sociologists in Moscow, Bratislava or Ljubljana during the years our late-career authors studied at their universities.

The authors of our late-career autobiographies were, in principle, concentrated on their professional activity (research, teaching, organization of academic life in their institutions). However, to some of them, being scholars meant doing something else as well. Their activity outside of the university was strongly connected with sociology. Kwasniewicz was a member of the Executive

Board of the Polish Sociological Association and a member of the Editorial Board of the quarterly *Studia Socjologiczne*, a member of the Commission on Science and Education at the Central Committee of the Communist Party, chairman of the Committee on Sociological Sciences of the Polish Academy of Sciences, and a member of the Steering Committee of the European Sociological Association.

Mansurov was initially very active in the Komsomol, which brought him to sociology in the first place. Eventually, in the 1990s, he became president of the Russian Society of Sociologists. Machacek was a head of the youth section of the Slovak Sociological Society and has been the editor of the quarterly *Sociologia*. Jogan was writing and publishing poetry and short stories in which she reacted to current events. She also participated in TV debates and in radio programs in the fields of her professional competence, and offered some family consulting. She was an active member of the Slovene Sociological Association and a member of the Steering Committee, and later of the Executive Board of the European Sociological Association.

In the introductory chapter we briefly discussed the theoretical issues of activity and agency, turning points, deep changes and significant discontinuities in the life course, broken lines of life, and life trajectories. We would like to come back to this problematic. It is very important to bear in mind that not every change in the life course can be called a turning point; not all situations of being helpless or even betrayed start a new trajectory in the Straussian sense. Moreover, our autobiographies are relatively short, and the personal, intimate life is hardly their subject. However, the slogan "the personal is political" does seem to get a full embodiment in some autobiographies. We find here several collective turning points, collective discontinuities, and collective trajectories.

Let us return now to the late-career authors. It seems very interesting to us that only Kwasniewicz's story is the narrative of a person who is self-consciously proud of the fact that he has been an active participant of history on the scene of Polish sociology. Our other late-career authors had similar, even pioneering, influence on the state of art of the discipline in their countries. They have been very active and they are aware of this fact. But only Kwasniewicz stresses the fact that he has accomplished something important. For instance, his membership in the Communist Party gave him a chance to influence various significant processes taking place at his university. The chairmanship of the Department of Sociology enabled him to build a very strong institution. His membership on the Executive Board of the Polish Sociological Association and on the Editorial Board of the quarterly *Studia Socjologiczne* helped him to influence various aspects of Polish sociology. Even retirement was not a turning point or discontinuity for him, as he continued to be very active, to the extent his health allowed him.

In our late-career autobiographies, we can find a number of collective turning points. The first is the end of World War II, though actually only very important for Kwasniewicz and his early colleagues, students of sociology in Cracow. A very important collective turning point that Machacek experienced was August 1968 in Czechoslovakia. It soon led to the trajectory of the "normalization processes," i.e. the de-Stalinization of the country. For Kwasniewicz, a collective trajectory began with the imposition of socialism in Poland after World War II. A somewhat more limited collective trajectory that he experienced with his fellow members of the faculty was the take-over and control of the chair of Sociology at Jagiellonian University by the Communist Party apparatus. Mansurov recalls censorship and the sense of the losing of control over his intellectual production, as well as the sense of his professional dependence on non-liberal political decision-makers. Jogan recalls the witnessing of the process of brutal decomposition of the Yugoslav Federation.

There are not very many examples of individual turning points among our late-career authors, such as the scout camp where Kwasniewicz decided, in 1947, to study sociology, or his reading of Sorokin's textbook. Mansurov's telephone call from Moscow, inviting him to work in the Academy of Sciences of the Soviet Union, and the betrayal of Jogan by the head of her department when she graduated from the university are two others.

The mid-career cohort

Our mid-career authors have been professionally active, though not necessarily within the realm of sociology as such, during the whole post-socialist period. They were also active during a part of the socialist era, but cannot remember World War II, and even the Stalinist epoch. They were born in the 1950s. Sociology was soon to be institutionalized in Central and Eastern Europe, though, as we already know, in different ways and to a different extent in each country.

Peter Robert graduated with a BA from the foreign trade department in 1974, and only much later with a MA in sociology. Between 1980 and the end of socialism, he worked in the Institute for Social Sciences at the Hungarian Communist Party, without being a Party member. He says that he was never fully involved in the political activities of his Institute, and that he was never discriminated against as a scholar. Most probably, out of the whole socialist system, this positive situation was possible only in Hungary. Karel Turza had been a member of the League of Communists of Yugoslavia, and even worked for its Central Committee's science department; but his comrades never did trust him very much. Vera Sparschuh does not even mention any involvement in any Communist affairs.

For Robert, Marxism-Leninism is not an issue at all; but it is one for Sparschuh. She had to study Marxist theory and Lenin's writings in detail when she was a student in Leningrad. Later, when she worked in East Germany as a sociologist, she participated in research projects in which she was obliged to contribute to the Marxist encyclopedia of sociology, to the history of Marxist sociological thinking in Germany, and to the analysis of the Marxist heritage in German intellectual history. Marxist analysis was never important in the later sociological work of Robert, but the broadly understood Marxist heritage of

German social thought remained significant for Sparschuh. Turza writes with enthusiasm about critical Marxism in the academic circles of Yugoslavia in the 1970s, and contrasts it with the bureaucratic "stay-in-power oriented" version of official Marxism and Communism which dominated the country. Marx, especially the early writings, was one of the sociological classics which most influenced Turza.

Why did they all become sociologists? There was still not a very smooth and simple road to the discipline. Robert's first wife worked in the Institute of Sociology of the Hungarian Academy of Sciences, so he was familiar with the subject. His first job was at the Hungarian Radio, interviewing people for the Institute of Mass Communication. He became more and more interested, not only in the interviewing but also in the analysis and interpretation of data. Later, he found a job as sociologist, but only under the condition that he enrolled in the graduate program in sociology. He graduated in 1984, with a MA, and received his Ph.D. in 1986.

Sparschuh began her university studies in Berlin in journalism, even though in practice her interests were sociological, though at first she did not know it. Soon, she went to Leningrad to study philosophy. There she took a mandatory course in sociology. Her teacher was Vladimir Yadov, a very famous scholar. He became her mentor. When she returned to East Berlin after graduation, she found a job at Humboldt University as a teaching and research assistant in the sociology department. She chose contemporary French sociology as the topic of her Ph.D. dissertation, which she defended in 1984.

In the Yugoslav educational system, social sciences were one of the important high school subjects. Thanks to a teacher of social sciences, Turza became interested in sociology, which seemed to him an enlightening discipline. Even against father's wishes, he took the entrance exams, passed them, and was accepted to the Department of Sociology of Belgrade University. He graduated with a BA, and only much later returned to the university to complete his graduate education.

Robert, in his work in the field of social stratification, was influenced by many different scholars. We could divide them into three groups. First are Hungarian scholars working in the field of stratification and mobility, with Tamas Kolosi, Rudolf Andorka, Zsuzsa Ferge, Ferenc Gazso, and others. Second are American sociologists, beginning with Peter M. Blau and Otis D. Duncan, and later Robert M. Hauser and David L. Featherman. Third would be still-younger Dutch scholars Harry Ganzenboom, Ruud Luijkx, and Paul de Graaf, with whom Robert has collaborated and written articles.

Surprisingly, Sparschuh was influenced first and foremost by Russian sociologists. The first was Yadov, whom she describes as a "Mertonian." The second was Igor S. Kon, who introduced her to the history of sociology. In the German classic humanities, she had enormous respect for Immanuel Kant, though we do not know if and how he influenced her own writing. Karl Mannheim's work was a subject of her analysis, and she also used his concept of "generation" in her non-historical studies.

Turza was influenced by a large number of scholars. He mentions classic social theorists such as Karl Marx and Herbert Spencer, philosophers Wilhelm Dilthey, Heinrich Rickert Jean-Paul Sartre, and Wilhelm Windelbandt, psychoanalysts Sigmund Freud and Erich Fromm, leaders of the Frankfurt School Theodor Adorno, Max Horkheimer, Herbert Marcuse, and Jürgen Habermas, and American sociologist C. Wright Mills. He also refers to Zygmunt Baumann, Ulrich Beck, and Anthony Giddens. When Turza was the editor of a publishing house in Belgrade, he met a number of Yugoslavian intellectuals who later had a great impact on his thinking. Zarana Papic was the most important of them. When he returned to the graduate school of Belgrade University, another group of scholars were his mentors. Finally, we should mention Seymour Mandelbaum, from the University of Pennsylvania, who helped him when he was studying for his doctorate.

Interestingly, it seems that our mid-career authors have been largely focused on their work, though Sparschuh also on her family. Robert had been writing and publishing short stories when he was very young, but later stopped. He has been involved in the activities of the International Sociological Association, but almost exclusively in their research committees and conferences. He did serve, with pride, for eight years on the board of Research Committee 28. Sparschuh does not mention any association and non-academic and non-family activities. An academic sociological career started for Turza quite late, although he had published earlier sociological articles and books. He did not limit his activity to work and family, though. He was an activist and even president of the Yugoslav Sociological Association.

It seems to us that the systemic transition in Central and Eastern Europe was not the collective turning point it represented for our late-career cohort. Robert spent most of the transition years abroad, and what he personally experienced was smooth and gradual. Sparschuh calls the fall of the Berlin Wall an "incredible biographical event," but we cannot be sure if it is of a positive or negative character from her point of view. She presents a balance of both positive and negative consequences. The "transition" itself was not very important for Karel Turza. Wars in Yugoslavia were much more significant in his narrative. It seems to us that they still exert a powerful influence on his personal and sociological outlook.

In addition to a few strictly personal crises, we learn about some interesting professional individual turning points in the autobiographies of our mid-career authors. Robert recalls a conference of ISA's RC 28 in Budapest, in 1984, where he presented a paper that was later published and attracted a lot attention. He began to collaborate with some Dutch participants at the conference, was invited to the Netherlands, and the co-operation proved to be very successful and long-lasting, continuing until this day.

For Sparschuh, 1973 was a turning-point year because she decided to study in the Soviet Union, with many positive, personal, and professional consequences. In 1996, when she was particularly productive as a scholar, she became unemployed, another turning point for her. Fortunately, in the same year, she received a good habilitation grant. In 2003, when she was only 48, she became a freelance *privatdozentin*, a highly qualified "private scholar" for whom there was no other more traditional and formal position within the German research and higher education system.

Turza experienced some personal turning points which had nothing to do with the wars in the 1990s. He mentions three such moments. One was being drafted into the army, at the turn of the 1980s. For him, as an individualistically and liberally oriented young man, it was a horrible, bureaucratic, and collectivistic institution. The second moment was his release from the army, from which he needed several months to recover. The third was the unexpected offer from the Marxist Center to become its secretary for scholarly affairs.

The early-career cohort

The three women who make up our early-career cohort were born between 1967 and 1977. Two of them had some contacts with the old economic, political, and cultural system through their high schools, and at the beginning of their university studies. However, the youngest represents a completely new generation of Central and Eastern European scholars, without any first-hand experience of socialism. Even she, however, cannot be considered a typical young European scholar without any geopolitical adjectives. All of our early-career authors took advantage of special programs and grants created and limited to the graduate students coming from the post-socialist part of the world.

Although it is theoretically possible that two of these women could have joined the Communist Party, or at least the Komsomol, neither of them mentions this. To the contrary, they present themselves as persons hostile to the old system, and under the influence of the opposition forces or at least of the *perestroika* and *glasnost* of Mikhail Gorbachev. Marxism is another story. Natalia Pohorila describes in an interesting way how she had, at the beginning of her studies in the Department of Sociology of Kiev State University, to take the courses in historical materialism. She recalls how, during *perestroika*, Vladimir Lenin was first presented as misled by his comrades, then presented as wrong in his own ideas. Later, even Marx was considered wrong. When Pohorila left Ukraine for Poland, neither Marxism nor Leninism was an issue for her.

Triin Vihalemm, from Estonia, recalls that at the beginning of her studies at Tartu State University she had to take the so-called "red subjects": history of the Communist Party of the Soviet Union, Marxist and Leninist philosophy, etc. Later, she does not even mention Marxism and Leninism. Petya Slavova, the youngest author, who was born ten years after the other two, did not have to study Marx's ideas, but she took an optional course in his sociological thought at Sofia University. By the end she was very glad that she had studied original texts of Marx and of some of his important followers. For her, Marx had neither political nor ideological meaning nor consequences, but held considerable intellectual interest.

Why did they become sociologists? As in many of the other cases, there was a lot of a chance, and no clear decision made in high school. However, Pohorila did take the entrance exams at Kiev State University directly to the Department of Sociology, even if she knew little about the discipline. Vihalemm's road was more complicated. She started her university studies in the Department of Journalism at the Faculty of Philology of Tartu University. This department had a relatively strong tradition of social surveys and analysis. She was writing term papers that were of a strongly sociological character. Her family connections with professors of sociology helped her in building a sociologically oriented individual curriculum. With her BA in journalism, she started her MA studies in the recently opened Department of Sociology of Tartu University. In 1993 she was the first person in the re-established Republic of Estonia to receive a master's degree in sociology. She defended her Ph.D. dissertation in 1999, and Vladimir Yadov was one of her reviewers. Slavova originally wanted to study law, but she did not receive a high enough score in the entrance exam to Sofia University. She was offered sociology as a second choice. She accepted it just for one year, but she liked the discipline so much that she stayed. Currently, she is finishing her Ph.D. in sociology.

All three authors of the youngest cohort traveled, participated in many conferences, and studied abroad. They have had a lot of domestic and international intellectual contacts. However, only Pohorila gave us many names of scholars who influenced her sociological thinking. While she was still in Kiev, she was impressed by books written by Poles Stanislaw Ossowski and Wlodzimierz Wesolowski, but also by her mentor, with whom she worked on her thesis, Alexander Vinogradov. Later, she studied in Poland at the international schools. There she met a large number of impressive sociological personalities, but Henryk Domanski, Kazimierz M. Slomczynski, and Krzysztof Zagorski were particularly significant for the shaping of her way of thinking about sociology.

Vihalemm recalls first and foremost two professors of the Department of Journalism, Marju Lauristin and Peeter Vihalemm (her uncle), who have been her mentors from the very beginning of her undergraduate studies. Slavova, the youngest author, who studied in three countries, was strongly influenced by an urban sociologist from France, Florent Champy. Though she has not personally met him, she has read his books and papers and corresponded with him.

Interestingly, our youngest generation of sociologists has not been very active in the institutional sense. Both Pohorila and Vihalemm were active as students during the last years of *perestroika* and first years of the systemic transformation of the Soviet Union, but they do not inform us about any organized political or social activity beyond the university or academia afterwards. We also do not learn anything about their participation in any professional sociological associations. However, this could be as much an artefact of their relatively early-career positions as anything else.

Although these three women are young, we can already discover in their lives as sociologists a small number of interesting turning points. The fact that they have traveled a lot and studied in several places has contributed to some extent to this situation. Pohorila and Vihalemm have also experienced the collective turning points of their respective nations, i.e., the re-establishment of the sovereignty of their countries.

It might seem to the casual Western observer that Poland and the Soviet Union belonged to the same economic and political system until 1989, and that at the beginning of the 1990s the differences between them could not have been all that big. This was not the case for Pohorila, who traveled from Kiev in Ukraine to study at the Central European University (CEU) in Warsaw. The CEU was an international, Western-style academic institution with English as the language of instruction. In addition, in Warsaw, Pohorila had to communicate in Polish, the language she partly knew from having read Polish sociological literature in Kiev. The beginning of her studies in Warsaw was a true turning point for her, with very significant consequences for her whole academic life. The second turning point came when she returned to Kiev. With her education, research experience, and skills, having presented at many scholarly conferences throughout Europe and published papers in international periodicals and in various academic books, she was considered to be overqualified and eventually lost all her academic jobs.

Interestingly, Vihalemm's autobiography does not reveal any turning points. Hers seems to be a smooth, continuous professional life. Contrary to that, Slavova, our youngest author, has had a more dramatic life. First, she had to take a decision what to do when she was not accepted by the law department at Sofia University. Eventually, she decided to go for sociology, and this choice was the beginning of a promising career. Second, when she graduated she became unemployed. Fortunately, this trauma did not last very long. Third, she was accepted to a one-year social science program in Bucharest, Romania, and she did not like it. And, fourth, she was accepted to the social science program in Brussels, Belgium, and as a result will write a dissertation on a topic she likes, based on the materials she collected in Brussels and thanks to the collaboration with scholars she met abroad. So we can say that her turning points were of both positive and negative character.

Conclusion

We originally began our investigation of the recent history of Central and Eastern European sociology with the year 1956, because in this year, after the Stalinist system was gone, sociology started to return to the academic life of many countries in the region. The first two volumes present the intellectual and institutional history of sociology in individual countries as they existed on the political map of that part of Europe in the 1990s and the beginning of the 2000s. In this volume, our sociological witnesses have told us the stories of individual people, people belonging to three different generations, including scholars who were building institutional sociology in their countries and scholars who later simply studied in departments of sociology at their universities. Thanks to their stories we learn about their individual lives, about the social, political and cultural history of Central and Eastern Europe after World War II, and about sociology in this region as well as about sociology as such.

In closing, from our perspective, the men and women of this volume, of our previous work, and all those who have struggled to keep the sociological imagination alive in the region, are heroes. Not the flamboyant heroism of the current culture of celebrity that appears to be flooding the region, as it already has its Western counterpart, but rather that of the quiet courage of ordinary women and men who determinedly go about their daily lives in what have arguably been extraordinary circumstances. As participants, they have witnessed the intersection of history and biography in Central and Eastern Europe. As sociologists, they have tried, and continue to try, to connect the two so that they and their fellow citizens may better understand these circumstances.

Bibliography

Abel, Theodore. 2001. *The Columbia Circle of Scholars: Selections from the Journal (1930–1957)*, ed. Elzbieta Halas. Frankfurt/Main: Peter Lang.

Adorno, Theodor W., Else Frenklel-Brunswick, Daniel J. Levinson, and R. Nevitt Sanford. 1950. *The Authoritarian Personality*. New York: Harper & Row.

Alexander, Jeffrey C. 1986. Science, Sense, and Sensibility. *Theory and Society* 15(3): 443–463.

Anderson, Benedict. 1991. *Imagined Communities: Reflections on the Origin and Spread of Nationalism*. London and New York: Verso.

Andorka, Rudolf and Krzysztof Zagorski. 1980. *Socio-occupational Mobility in Hungary and Poland*. Budapest: Hungarian Central Statistical Office.

Andorka, Rudolf and Tamas Kolosi, eds. 1984. *Stratification and Inequality: Hungarian Sociological Studies I*. Budapest: Institute of Social Sciences.

Andreeva, Galina. 1965. *Sovremennaya Amerikanskay Burguaznaya Empiricheskaya Sotsiologia*. Moscow: Misl.

—— 1966. *Burguaznaya Sotsiologia v Poiskah Teorii*. Moscow: Znanie.

Arum, Richard and Walter Müller, eds. 2004. *The Reemergence of Self-employment: A Comparative Study of Self-employment Dynamics and Social Inequality*. Princeton: Princeton University.

Barbakova, Klara and Valery Mansurov. 1981. *Molodaya Inteligentsia v Razvitom Sotsialisticheskom Obshestve*. Moscow: Nauka.

Barth, Frederik, ed. 1969. *Ethnic Groups and Boundaries*. London: George Allen & Unwin.

Beck, Ulrich and Elisabeth Beck-Gernscheim. 1996. Individualization and "Precarious Freedom:" Perspectives and Controversies of a Subject-Oriented Sociology, pp. 23–48 in *Detraditionalization*, eds Paul Heelas, Scott Lash, and Paul Morris. Cambridge: Blackwell Publishers.

Berdahl, Daphne, Matti Bunzl, and Martha Lampland. 2000. *Altering States: Ethnographies of Transition in Eastern Europe and the Former Soviet Union*. Ann Arbor: University of Michigan.

Berg, Bruce. 1989. *Qualitative Research Methods for the Social Sciences*. Boston: Allyn & Bacon.

Berger, Bennett M., ed. 1990. *Authors of Their Own Lives: Intellectual Autobiographies by Twenty American Sociologists*. Berkeley: University of California.

Berger, Peter L. 1963. *Invitation to Sociology*. New York: Anchor.

Bernsdorf, Wilhelm and Horst Knospe. 1980. *Internationales Soziologenlexikon*. Stuttgart: Enke Verlag.

Bertaux, Daniel, ed. 1981. *Biography and Society: The Life History Approach in the Social Sciences*. Beverly Hills: Sage.

Bertaux, Daniel and Martin Kohli. 1984. The Life Story Approach. *Annual Review of Sociology* 10: 215–237.

Bhabha, Homi. 1990. *Nation and Narration*. London: Routledge.

Bienkowski, Wieslaw and Wladyslaw Kwasniewicz, eds. 1994. *Kazimierz Dobrowolski—czlowiek i uczony. Praca zbiorowa w stulecie urodzin* Krakow: Jagiellonian Press.

Bjorklund, Diane. 1998. *Interpreting the Self: Two Hundred Years of American Autobiography*. Chicago: University of Chicago.

Blossfeld, Hans-Peter, Eric Klijzing, Melinda Mills, and Karin Kurz, eds. 2005. *Globalization Uncertainty and Youth in the Society*. London: Routledge.

Breckner, Roswitha, Devorah Kalekin-Fishman, and Ingrid Miethe, eds. 2000. *Biographies and the Division of Europe: Experience, Action, and Change on the Eastern Side.'* Opladen: Leske + Budrich Verlag.

Breen, Richard, ed. 2004. *Social Mobility in Europe*. Oxford: Oxford University Press.

Brown, James F. 2001. *The Grooves of Change: Eastern Europe at the Turn of the Millennium*. Durham: Duke University.

Bulmer, Martin. 1984. *The Chicago School of Sociology: Institutionalization, Diversity, and the Rise of Sociological Research*. Chicago: University of Chicago.

Burawoy, Michael and Katherine Verdery. 1999. *Ethnographies of Change in the Postsocialist World*. New York: Rowman & Littlefield.

Cecetka, Juraj. 1965. *Medzil'udske vzt'ahy a rovesnicke skupiny*. Bratislava: SPN.

—— 1965. *Sociologia v pedagogike*. Bratislava: SPN.

Chalasiński, Józef. 1981. The Life Records of the Young Generation of Polish Peasants as a Manifestation of Contemporary Culture, pp. 119–132 in *Biography and Society: The Life History Approach in the Social Sciences*, eds Daniel Bertaux. Beverly Hills: Sage.

Chamberlayne, Prue, Joanna Bornat, and Tom Wengraf, eds. 2000. *The Turn to Biographical Methods in Social Sciences: Comparative Issues and Examples*. London: Routledge.

Champy, Florent. 1998. *Les architects et la commande publique*. Paris: PUF.

—— 2001. *Sociologie de l'architecture*. Paris: La Decourverte.

Charmaz, Kathy. 1991. Turning Points and Fictional Identities, pp. 71–86 in *Social Organization and Social Process: Essays in Honor of Anselm Strauss*, ed. David R. Maines. New York: Aldine de Gruyter.

Chernykh, Alla, Sinaida I. Golenkova, Vera Sparschuh, Helmut Steiner, Jan Wielgosh, Rose-Luise Winkler, and Sergej V. Zakharov, eds. 1987. *Portrats russischer und sowjetischer Soziologen*. Sonderheft: Akademie der Wissenschaften der DDR.

—— 1990. *Portraits of Russian and Soviet Sociologists*. Moscow: USSR Academy of Sciences.

Chura, Alojz. 1970. Sexualita mladeze, pp. 39–52 in *Sociologia mladeze '70*. Bratislava: Smena.

Cole, Sally. 1992. Anthropological Lives: The Reflexive Tradition in a Social Science, pp. 113–129 in *Essays in Life Writing: From Genre to Critical Practice*, ed. Marlene Kadar. Toronto: University of Toronto.

Coser, Lewis A. 1984. Georg Simmels vernachlaessigter Beitrag zur Soziologie der Frau, pp. 80–90 in *Georg Simmel und die Moderne*, eds Heinz-Jürgen Dahme and Otthien Rammstedt. Frankfurt am Main: Suhrkamp.

Dahrendorf, Ralf. 1957. *Soziale Klassen und Klassenkonfkt in der industriellen Gesellschaft* . Stuttgart: Ferdinand Enke Verlag.

Denzin, Norman K. 1989. *Interpretive Biography*. Newbury Park: Sage.

—— 1989. *Interpretive Interactionism*. Newbury Park: Sage.

Durkheim, Émile. 1991. O *razdelenii truda. Metod sotsiologii*. Moscow: Nauka.

Elder, Glen. 1981. History and the Life Course, pp. 77–118 in *Biography and Society: The Life History Approach in the Social Sciences*, ed. Daniel Bertaux. Beverly Hills: Sage.

Elias, Norbert. 1994. *Reflctions on a Lifetime* . Translated by Edmund Jephcott. Cambridge, Mass.: Polity Press.

Evans, Mary. 1993. Reading Lives: How the Personal Might Be Social. *Sociology* 27(1): 5–13.

Faris, Robert E.L. 1967. *Chicago Sociology 1920–1932*. Chicago: University of Chicago Press.

Feyerabend, Paul. 1995. *Killing Time: The Autobiography of Paul Feyerabend*. Chicago: University of Chicago Press.

Fleming, Donald and Bernard Bailyn. 1969. *The Intellectual Migration: Europe and America, 1930–60*. Cambridge, Mass.: Belknap Press.

Friedrichs, Jürgen, Vera Sparschuh, and Iris Wrede. 1993. *Sozialwissenschaftliche Dissertationen und Habilitationen in der DDR, 1951–1991: Eine Dokumentation*. Berlin: de Gruyter Verlag.

Friedrichs, Robert W. 1970. *A Sociology of Sociology*. New York: Free Press.

Ganzeboom, Harry B.G., Paul M. De Graaf, and Peter Robert. 1990. Reproduction Theory on Socialist Ground: Intergenerational Transmission of Inequalities in Hungary, pp. 79–104 in *Research in Social Stratifiation and Mobility* , Volume 9, ed. Arne L. Kalleberg. Greenwich: JAI Press.

Ganzeboom, Harry B.G., Ruud Luijkx, and Peter Robert. 1989. *Trends in Intergenerational Occupational Mobility in Hungary Between 1930 and 1989*. Working Paper Series 58. Tilburg: Tilburg University, Department of Sociology.

Gardner, Hall, Elinore Schaffer, and Oleg Kobzeff. 2000. *Central and Southeastern Europe in Transition: Perspectives on Success and Failure Since 1989*. Westport: Praeger.

Gellner, Ernest. 1983. *Nations and Nationalism*. Oxford: Blackwell.

Giddens, Anthony. 1984. *The Constitution of Society: Outline of the Theory of Structuration*. Los Angeles: University of California.

—— 1989. *Sociology*. Oxford: Polity Press.

—— 2001. *Sociology*. Cambridge: Polity Press.

Goetting, Ann. 1995. Introduction. Fictions of the Self, pp. 3–19 in *Individual Voices, Collective Visions: Fifty Years of Women in Sociology*, eds Ann Goetting and Sarah Fenstermaker. Philadelphia: Temple University Press.

Goetting, Ann and Sarah Fenstermaker, eds. 1995. *Individual Voices, Collective Visions: Fifty Years of Women in Sociology*. Philadelphia: Temple University.

Gottshalk, Louis, Clyde Kluckhohn, and Robert Engell. 1945. *The Use of Personal Documents in History, Anthropology, and Sociology*. New York: Social Science Research Council.

Gouldner, Alvin W. 1962. Anti-Minotaur: The Myth of a Value-Free Sociology. *Social Problems* 9: 199–213.

—— 1970. *The Coming Crisis of Western Sociology*. New York: Basic Books.

—— 1973. *For Sociology: Renewal and Critique in Sociology Today*. Harmondsworth: Penguin Books.

Gusdorf, Georges. [1956] 1980. Conditions and Limits of Autobiography, trans. James Olney, pp. 28–48 in *Autobiography: Essays Theoretical and Critical*, ed. James Olney. Princeton: Princeton University.

Haerpfer, Christian W. 2002. *Democracy and Enlargement in Post-Communist Europe: The*

Democratisations of the General Public in Fifteen Central and Eastern European Countries, 1991–1998. London: Routledge.

Hall, Edward. 1981. *Beyond Culture*. Garden City, N.Y.: Anchor Books.

Haller, Max, Tamas Kolosi, and Peter Robert. 1990. Social Mobility in Austria, Czechoslovakia, and Hungary: An Investigation of the Effects of Industrialization, Socialist Revolution, and National Uniqueness, pp. 153–192 in *Class Structure in Europe: New Findings from East–West Comparisons of Social Structure and Mobility*, ed. Max Haller. Armonk: M.E. Sharpe.

Halmos, Paul. 1970. *The Sociology of Sociology*. Keele: University of Keele.

Harrison, Barbara and E. Stina Lyon. 1993. A Note on Ethical Issues in the Use of Autobiography in Sociological Research. *Sociology* 27(1): 101–109.

Hegel, Georg Wilhelm Friedrich. 1964. *Osnovne crte fozofe prava* . Sarajevo: Veselin Maslesa.

Helling, Ingeborg K. 1988. The Life History Method: A Survey and a Discussion with Norman K. Denzin. *Studies in Symbolic Interaction* 9: 211–243.

Hennoste, Tiit and Triin Vihalemm. 1998. Vene noorte toimetulek spontaanses argivestluses eesti eakaaslastega: sissejuhatus probleemistikku, pp. 249–276 in *Mitmekultuuriline Eesti: valjakutse haridusele*, eds Marju Lauristin, Silvi Vare, Tiia Pedastsaar, and Marje Pavelson. Tartu: Vali Press Ltd.

Hobsbawm, Eric. 1983. *The Invention of Tradition*. Cambridge: Cambridge University Press.

Hofstede, Geert. 1991. *Cultures and Organizations: Software of the Mind*. New York: McGraw Hill Book Company.

Homans, George P. 1984. *Coming to My Senses: The Autobiography of a Sociologist*. New Brunswick: Transactions.

Horowitz, Irving Louis. 1983. *C. Wright Mills: An American Utopian*. New York: Free Press.

—— ed. 1969. *Sociological Images: A Collective Portrait*. Beverly Hills: Sage.

Hutchinson, John. 1987. *The Dynamics of Cultural Nationalism*. London: Allen & Unwin.

Hutchinson, John and Anthon Smith, eds. 1994. *Nationalism*. Oxford: Oxford University Press.

Inglehart, Roland. 1977. *The Silent Revolution: Changing Values and Political Styles Among Western Publics*. Princeton: Princeton University Press.

Janez, Pavel II. 1989. *Apostolsko pismo o dostojanstvu zene*. Ljubljana: Cerkveni dokumenti 40.

Jarve, Pritt, ed. 1997. *Vene noored Eestis*. Tallinn: Avita.

Jogan, Maca. 1972. *Kategorija razreda v socioloski teoriji*. Ljubljana: FSPN.

—— 1978. *Sociologija reda. Kriticen oris funkcionalizma in konfktne teorije* . Maribor: Obzorja.

—— 1986. *Zenska, cerkev in druzina*. Ljubljana: Delavska enotnost.

—— 1990. *Druzbena konstrukcija hierarhije med spoloma*. Ljubljana: Fakulteta za sociologijo, politicne vede in novinarstvo.

—— 1992. Erinnerungsfragmente, pp. 364–374 in *BRD ade! Vierzig Jahre in Rueckansichten von Sozial- und Kulturwissenschaftlern*, eds Otthein Rammstedt and Gert Schmidt. Frankfurt am Main: Suhrkamp.

—— 1992. Sociological Theoretical Heritage and the Construction of Women's Social Reality, pp. 123–132 in *Emerging Sociology: An International Perspective*, eds Joseph Langer. Sydney: Avebury.

—— 1994. Modern Slovenian Sociology, pp. 125–130 in *Eastern Europe in*

Transformation: The Impact on Sociology, eds Mike F. Keen and Janusz L. Mucha. Westport: Greenwood Press.

—— 1995. Redomestication of Women and Democratization in Postsocialist Slovenia, pp. 229–236 in *Family, Women and Employment in Central-Eastern Europe*, ed. Barbara Lobodzinska. Westport: Greenwood Press.

—— 1995. *Sodobne smeri v socioloski teoriji*. Ljubljana: Fakulteta za druzbene vede.

—— 2001. *Seksizem v vsakdanjem zivljenju*. Ljubljana: Fakulteta za druzbene vede.

—— ed. 2000. *Tranzicija in (ne)enakost med spoloma*. Ljubljana: Univerza v Ljubljani, Slovensko sociolosko drustvo.

Jurovsky, Anton. 1965. *Kulturny vyvin mladeze*. Bratislava: SPN.

Kaase, Max, Vera Sparschuh, and Agnieszka Wenninger, eds. 2002. *Three Social Science Disciplines in Central and Eastern Europe: Handbook on Economics, Political Science and Sociology, 1989–2001*. Budapest/Berlin: IZ Sozialwissenschaften.

Kadar, Marlene, ed. 1992. *Essays on Life Writings from Genre to Critical Practice*. Toronto: University of Toronto.

Keen, Mike F. and Janusz L. Mucha, eds. 1994. *Eastern Europe in Transformation: The Impact on Sociology*, Westport, Conn.: Greenwood.

—— 2001. History in the Making: Sociology and the Transformation of Eastern and Central Europe, pp. 40–52 in *Mirrors and Windows. Essays in the History of Sociology*, eds Janusz Mucha, Dirk Kaesler, and Wlodzimierz Winclawski. Torun: Nicolaus Copernicus University Press.

—— eds. 2003. *Sociology in Central and Eastern Europe: Transformation at the Dawn of a New Millennium*. Westport, Conn. and London: Praeger.

—— 2004. Sociology in Central and Eastern Europe in the 1990s: A Decade of Reconstruction. *European Societies* 6(2): 123–147.

Kon, Igor S. 1968. *Der Positivismus in der Soziologie. Geschichtlicher Abriß*. Berlin: Akademie Verlag.

—— ed. 1971. *K probleme natsionalnogo haraktera*. Moscow: Nauka.

—— ed. 1979. *Istorija burzhuaznoi sotsiologii XIX-natshala XX vv*. Moscow: Nauka.

Konapasek, Zdenek, ed. 2000. *Our Lives as Database. Doing a Sociology of Ourselves. Czech Social Transition in Autobiographical Research Dialogues*, trans. Andrew Hawker. Praha: Karolinum.

Korolyov, Sergei, ed. 1984. *Voproso etnopsihologi v rabotah zarubeznih avtorov*. Moscow: Progress.

Kroeber, Louis Alfred and Clyde Kluckhohn. 1952. *Culture: A Critical Review of Concepts and Defiitions* . Cambridge: The Museum.

Kwasniewicz Wladyslaw. 1968. *Przemiany spoleczne mlodzieży akademickiej Uniwersytetu Jagiellonskiego w dwudziestoleciu Polski Ludowej*. Krakow: Zeszyty Naukowe UJ, Prace Historyczne.

—— 1970. *Wiejska spolecznosc rzemieslnicza w procesie przemian: Studium socjologiczne wsi Swiatniki Gorne pow. Krakowskiego*. Warszawa i Krakow: Prace Komisji Socjologicznej Oddzialu PAN w Krakowie.

—— 1983. Makrostrukturalne aspekty kryzysu lat osiemdziesiatych. *Studia Socjologiczne* 4: 31–51.

—— 1985. Problems of Polish Applied Sociology. *The Polish Sociological Bulletin* 1–4: 59–72.

—— 1988. Moim zdaniem. *Zycie Warszawy*, No. 281, 3–4 grudnia, p. 1.

—— 1991. Sociological Dilemmas of the Intelligentsia: The Case of Poland. *The Polish Sociological Bulletin* 3: 169–193.

—— 1993. Between the Universal and the Native: The Case of Polish Sociology, pp. 165–187 in *Sociology in Europe: In Search of Identity*, eds Brigitta Nedelmann and Piotr Sztompka. New York: de Gruyter.

—— 1994. Dialectics of Systemic Constraint and Academic Freedom: Polish Sociology under Socialist Regime, pp. 24–38 in *Eastern Europe in Transformation: The Impact on Sociology*, eds Mike F. Keen and Janusz L. Mucha. Westport: Greenwood.

—— 2000. Procesy zywiolowe, pp. 209–215 in *Encyklopedia socjologii*, Vol. 3. Warszawa: Oficyna Naukowa.

—— 2003. Between a Post-feudal and Post-industrial Model: Polish Society in the 20th Century. *Polish Sociological Review* 4, 144: 387–397.

Kwasniewicz, Wladyslaw *et al.*, eds. 1996, 1999, 2000, 2003. *Encyklopedia socjologii*, Vols 1–4. Warszawa: Oficyna Naukowa.

Ladonyi, Janos and Ivan Szelenyi. 2002. *Poverty and Social Structure in Transition Society*. New Haven: Yale University.

Laslett, Barbara. 1991. Biography as Historical Sociology: The Case of William Fielding Ogburn. *Theory and Society* 20(4): 511–538.

Laslett, Barbara and Barrie Thorne, eds 1997. *Feminist Sociology: Life Histories of a Movement*. New Brunswick, N.J.: Rutgers University Press.

Lauristin, Marju and Mati Heidmets, eds 2002. *The Challenge of the Russian Minority*. Tartu: Tartu University Press.

Lauristin, Marju, Silvi Vare, Tiia Pedastsaar, and Marje Pavelson, eds 1998. *Mitmekultuuriline Eesti: valjakutse haridusele*. Tartu: University of Tartu and Vali Press Ltd.

Lauristin, Marju, Peeter Vihalemm, Karl-Erik Rosengren, and Lennart Weibull, eds 1997. *Return to the Western World: Cultural and Political Perspectives on the Estonian Post-Communist Transition*. Tartu: Tartu University Press.

Lemert, Charles C. 1986. Whole Life Social Theory. *Theory and Society* 15(3): 431–442.

Leonski, Jacek and Teresa Rzepa, eds. 1996. *Historia nauki polskiej w autobiografch, tom III. Historia socjologii polskiej i nauk prawnych, częć*. Szczecin: Osrodek Badan Biograficznych, Uniwersytet Szczecinski.

Levada, Yury. 1969. *Lektsii po Sotsiologii*. Moscow: Institute Sotsiologicheskih issledovani AN SSSR.

Lilly, Graham C. 1987. *An Introduction to the Law of Evidence*, 2nd edition. St Paul, Minn.: West Publishing.

Lohr, Karin, Raj Kollmorgen, Dagmar Simon, and Vera Sparschuh. 1997. Ohne Netz und doppelten Boden: Lage und Zukunftsaussichten freier sozialwissenschaftlicher Institute und Vereine in den neuen Bundesländern, pp. 165–192 in *Soziologie und Soziologen im bergang. Beitrge zur Transformation der außruniversitäen sozialwissenschaftlichen Forschung in Ostdeutschland*. Opladen: Leske + Budrich Verlag.

Machacek, Ladislav. 1969. K funkcii skoly v akulturacnom procese. *Sociologia* 2–3: 182–195.

—— 1969. Situacia sociologie mladeze a vychovy na Slovensku, pp. 7–10 in *Sociologia mladeze '69: Situacia soziologie mladeze a vychovy ha Slovensku*. Bratislava: Smena.

—— 1970. Rozhovor s profesorom Janom Szczepanskim, in *Sociologia mladeze '70*. Bratislava: Smena.

—— 1996. *Obcianska participacia a mladez*. Bratislava: Sociologicky ustav SAV.

—— 2002. *Kapitoly zo sociologie mladeze*. Trnava: UCM.

—— 2003. *Participacia, obcianstvo, demokracia*. Trnava: UCM.

MacIver, Robert M. 1968. *As a Tale That Is Told: The Autobiography of R.M. MacIver*. Chicago: University of Chicago Press.

McKee, James. 1970. Some Observations on the Self-Consciousness of Sociologists, pp. 98–113 in *The Sociology of Sociology: Analysis and Criticism of the Thought, Research, and Ethical Folkways of Sociology and Its Practitioners*, eds Larry T. Reynolds and Janice M. Reynolds. New York: David McKay.

Magocsi, Paul R. 1996. *The History of Ukraine*. Toronto: University of Toronto.

Malinowski, Bronislaw. 1967. *A Diary in the Strict Sense of the Term*. London: Routledge & Kegan Paul.

Malinowski, Bronislaw and Elsie Masson. 1995. *The Story of a Marriage: The Letters of Bronislaw Malinowski and Elsie Masson*, Vols 1 and 2, ed. Helena Wayne. London: Routledge.

Merton, Robert K. 1988. Some Thoughts on the Concept of Sociological Biography, pp. 17–21 in *Sociological Lives*, ed. Matilda White Riley. Newbury Park: Sage.

—— 1959. Social *Theory and Social Structure*. Glencoe, Ill.: Free Press.

Merton, Robert K. and Matilda White Riley, eds. 1980. *Sociological Traditions from Generation to Generation: Glimpses of the American Experience*. Norwood, N.J.: Ablex.

Meurer, Barbel. 1974. *Mensch und Kapitalismus bei Max Weber*. Berlin: Duncker & Humblot.

Milic, Vojin. 1986. *Sociologija saznanja*. Sarajevo: Veselin Maslesa.

—— 1995. *Sociologija nauke*. Nove Sad: Novom Sadu I LDI.

Mills, C. Wright. 1959. *The Sociological Imagination*. London and New York: Oxford University Press.

—— 1964. *Socioloska imaginacija*. Beograd: Savremena skola.

Nisbet, Robert. 1979. Conservativism, pp. 80–117 in *A History of Sociological Analysis*, eds Tom Bottomore and Robert Nisbet. London: Heinemann.

Okely, Judith. 1992. Anthropology and Autobiography: Participatory Experience and Embodied Knowledge, pp. 1–28 in *Anthropology and Autobiography*, eds Judith Okely and Helen Callaway. London: Routledge.

Okely, Judith and Helen Callaway. 1992. *Anthropology and Autobiography*. London: Routledge.

Olney, James. 1972. *Metaphors of Self: The Meaning of Autobiography*. Princeton: Princeton University.

—— ed. 1980. *Autobiography: Essays Theoretical and Critical*, edited by James Olney. Princeton: Princeton University.

Ondrejkovic, Peter. 1998. *Uvod do sociologie vychovy*. Bratislava: Veda.

Ossowski, Stanislaw. 1966. *Dziela*, Vol. II: *Wiez spoleczna i dziedzictwo krwi*. Warszawa: Panstwowe Wydawnictwo Naukowe.

Parsons, Talcott. 1956. *Family, Socialization and Interaction Process*. London: Routledge & Kegan Paul.

Pasiak, Jan and Ladislav Machacek. 1994. Sociology in Slovakia: Fiction or Reality, pp. 89–99 in *Eastern Europe in Transformation: The Impact on Sociology*, eds Mike F. Keen and Janusz L. Mucha. Westport: Greenwood Press.

Patton, Michael. 1990. *Qualitative Evaluation and Research Methods*. Newbury Park: Sage.

Petersen, Roger D. 2001. *Resistance and Rebellion: Lessons from Eastern Europe*. Cambridge: Cambridge University Press.

Platt, Jennifer. 1998. *A History of Sociological Research Methods in America 1920–1960*. Cambridge: Cambridge University Press.

Plummer, Ken. 1983. *Documents of Life: An Introduction to the Problems and Literature of a Humanistic Method*. London: Allen & Unwin.

Pohorila, Natalia. 1999. Guest Editor's Introduction. *International Journal of Sociology* 29(3): 3–13.

—— 1999. Structure or Culture?: Cross-National Analysis of Market Values' Determination in Europe, pp. 45–62 in *European Value System*, ed. Jadwiga Koralewicz. Warsaw: Collegium Civitas and ISP PAN.

—— 2002. Depression as Psychological Consequence of Material Status Inconsistency: The Case of Poland and Ukraine. *Naukovi Zapysky. Sotsiologichni nauky* 20: 34–39.

—— 2002. Khto ne holosuvav na vyborach i chomu. *Politychnyi portret Ukrainy* 25: 83–93.

— 2002. Regional Split in Ukraine: The Case of Political Culture, pp. 57–69 in *Magisterium: politychni studii. Vypusk desiat*, eds Serhii Riabov and Olga Klimenko. Kiev: National University Kiev-Mohyla Academy.

— 2003. Dovira do dejakych politychnych ta publichnych instytutsi u porivnialnimu konteksti. *Sotsiologia: teoria, metody, marketing* 3: 144–156.

—— 2003. *Pershy raz v seredni klas* (http://dialogs.org.ua).

— 2003. Podzial regionalny na Ukrainie: problem kultury politycznej, pp. 527–548 in *Transgranicznosc w perspektywie socjologicznej*, ed. Maria Zielinska. Zielona Gora: Lubuskie Towarzystwo Naukowe.

—— 2003. Sociology in Ukraine, 1990–2000: A Decade of Firsts, pp. 175–186 in *Sociology in Central and Eastern Europe: Transformation at the Dawn of a New Millennium*, eds Mike F. Keen and Janusz L. Mucha. Westport: Praeger.

—— 2003. *U tini patrona* (http://dialogs.org.ua).

— 2003. *Ukraintsi-bidni?!* (http://dialogs.org.ua).

Pohorila, Natalia and Gennadi Korzhov. 2001. Social Identification in the Society of Crisis: A Case of Cross-Border Traders in Ukraine. *Naukovi Zapysky* 19: 58–64.

Pohorila, Natalia and Olexandr Shtokvish. 1995. Filosofs' ta sotsiologichni problemy burikratii. *Politologichna dumka* 1: 53–59.

Pohorila, Natalia and Kazimierz Slomczynski. 2000. Individual Income Gains and Losses in Ukraine, 1993–1996: A Test of the Human Capital and Mental Adjustment Hypothesis. *International Journal of Sociology* 29(4): 54–76.

Pohorila Natalia and Volodymyr Volovych. 1995. Sotsiologichni problemy vyvchennia sotsial'noi stratyfikatsii. *Buleten natsionalnoho Universytetu imeni T.H. Shevchenka* 1: 14–19.

Raushenbush, Winifred. 1979. *Robert E. Park. Biography of a Sociologist*. With a Foreword and an Epilogue by Everett C. Hughes. Durham, N.C.: Duke University Press.

Reynolds, Larry T. and Janice M. Reynolds, eds. 1970. *The Sociology of Sociology: Analysis and Criticism of the Thought, Research, and Ethical Folkways of Sociology and Its Practitioners*. New York: David McKay.

Riemann, Gerhard and Fritz Schutze. 1991. Trajectory As a Basic Theoretical Concept for Analyzing Suffering and Disorderly Social Processes, pp. 333–357 in *Social Organization and Social Process: Essays in Honor of Anselm Strauss*, ed. David R. Maines. New York: Aldine de Gruyter.

Riley, Matilda White, ed. 1988. *Sociological Lives*. Newbury Park: Sage.

—— 1988. Notes on the Influence of Sociological Lives, pp. 23–40 in *Sociological Lives*, ed. Matilda White Riley. Newbury Park: Sage.

Robert, Peter. 1984. A Multidimensional Approach to Social Mobility, pp. 223–244 in *Stratification and Inequality: Hungarian Sociological Studies I*, eds Rudolf Andorka and Tamas Kolosi. Budapest: Institute of Social Sciences.

—— 1984. A tarsadalmi mobilitas tobbdimenzios megkozelitese. *Statisztikai Szemle* 62(12): 1225–1240.

—— 1986. Tarsadalmi mobilitas-Statusmobilitatas. *Sociologia* 14(1–2): 111–142.

—— 1987. Mobilitas es reprodukcios folyamatok a magyar tarasdalomban. *Valosag* 30(10): 37–47.

—— 1998. *Tarsadalmi mobilitas: hagyomanyos es uj megkowelitesek Szoveggyujtemeny*. Budapest: Uj Mandatum.

—— 2000. *Tarsadalmi mobilitas a tenyek es velemenyek tukreben*. Budapest: ARTT-Szazadvego.

Robert, Peter and Hans-Peter Blossfeld. 1995. Hungary, pp. 211–226 in *The New Role of Women: Family Formation in Modern Societies*, ed. Hans-Peter Blossfeld. Boulder: Westview Press.

Robert, Peter and Erzsebet Bukodi. 2004. Changes in Intergenerational Class Mobility in Hungary: 1973–2000, pp. 287–314 in *Social Mobility in Europe*, eds Richard Breen and Ruud Luijkx. Oxford: Oxford University Press.

—— 2004. Winners or Losers?: Entry and Exit into Self-Employment in Hungary: 1980s and 1990s, pp. 245–276 in *Self-employment Dynamics in Advanced Economies*, eds Richard Arum and Walter Müller. Cambridge: Cambridge University Press.

Robert, Peter, Erzsebet Bukodi, and Ruud Luijkx. 2001. Employment Patterns in Hungarian Couples, pp. 307–331 in *Careers of Couples in Contemporary Society: From Male Breadwinner to Dual Earner Families*, eds Hans-Peter Blossfeld and Sonja Drobnic. Oxford: Oxford University Press.

Rokeach, Milton, 1973. *The Nature of Human Values*. New York: Free Press.

Roknic, Aleksandar. 2004. Neprekinuta represija. *DANAS PRAVO Plus* (September 10).

Rose, Nikolas. 1996. Authority and the Genealogy of Subjectivity, pp. 294–327 in *Detraditionalization*, eds Paul Heelas, Scott Lash, and Paul Morris. Cambridge: Blackwell Publishers.

Rosko, Robert. 2000. *Slovensko na konci tisicrocia*. Bratislava: Veda.

Rustin, Michael. 2000. Reflections on the Biographical Turn in Social Science, pp. 34–52 in *The Turn to Biographical Methods in Social Sciences: Comparative Issues and Examples*, eds Prue Chamberlayne, Joanna Bornat, and Tom Wengraf. London: Routledge.

Schubert, Ladislav. 1967. *Problemy s kriminalitou mladeze*. Bratislava: SAV.

Schutze, Fritz. 1992. Pressure and Guilt: War Experiences of a Young German Soldier and their Biographical Implications (Part I). *International Sociology* 7(2): 187–208.

—— 1992. Pressure and Guilt: War Experiences of a Young German Soldier and their Biographical Implications (Part 2). *International Sociology* 7(3): 347–367.

Schulz, Robert. 2000. Interview mit Robert Schutz: "Das war eine andere Generation...," pp. 35–54 in *Soziologie und Sozialismus. Die Gruenderereneration derr DDR-Soziologie*, eds Vera Sparschuh and Ute Koch. Opladen: Leske + Budrich Verlag.

Schutz, Alfred. 1975. *On Phenomenology and Social Relations*, ed. Helmut R. Wagner. Chicago: University of Chicago.

Schwartz, Shalom. 1992. Universals in the Content and Structure of Values: Theoretical Advances and Empirical Tests in 20 Countries. *Advances in Experimental Social Psychology* 25: 1–65.

Science and Society Program Committee. 2003. *Orientations for the Work Programme 2004*. Brussels: European Commission Research Directorate.

Simkus, Albert and Peter Robert. 1995–96. Attitudes Toward Inequality: Cross-National Comparisons and Class Divisions in Hungary. *International Journal of Sociology* (25)4: 85–102.

Simon, Dagmar and Vera Sparschuh. 1994. East German Sociology: Between the Production of Weltanschauung, Ideological Adaptation, and Empirical Research, pp. 101–112 in *Eastern Europe in Transformation: The Impact on Sociology*, eds Mike F. Keen and Janusz L. Mucha. Westport.: Greenwood.

—— 2001. *Der Nachlaßder DDR-Soziologiebloßs Archivmaterial oder soziologisches Forschungsfeld?* Discussion Paper P-92-001. Berlin: für Sozialforschung.

Slavova, Petya. 2002. L'architecture bulgare en transformation: quelques aspects organisationnels. *La nouvelle alternative* 17(3): 39–50.

Sloboda, Marcel. 1969. Niektore aspekty delikvencie ako spolocenskeho problemu, pp. 91–99 in *Sociologia mladeze* '69. Bratislava: Smena.

Slomczynski, Kazimierz and Wlodzimierz Wesolowski. 1973. *Struktura i ruchliwosc spoleczna*. Wroclaw: Ossolineum.

Soeffner, Hans-Georg. 1991. Trajectory as Intended Fragment: The Critique of Empirical Reason According to Anselm Strauss, pp. 359–371 in *Social Organization and Social Process: Essays in Honor of Anselm Strauss*, ed. David R. Maines. New York: Aldine de Gruyter.

Sorokin, Pitirim. 1947. *Teorie socjologiczne XIX i XX w*, trans. Wladyslaw Kwasniewicz. Krakowie: Kolo Socjologiczne i Etnologiczne Studentow UJ.

—— 1963. *A Long Journey: The Autobiography of Pitirim A. Sorokin*. New Haven: College and University Press.

—— 1992. *Chelovek. Cyvilizacia. Obschestvo*. Moscow: Politizdat.

Sparschuh, Vera. 2000. The Biographies of the Biographers. Some Remarks on the History of the Social Sciences in GDR, pp. 303–314 in *Biographies and the Division of Europe: Experience, Action, and Change on the Eastern Side*,' eds Roswitha Breckner, Devorah Kalekin-Fishman, and Ingrid Miethe. Opladen: Leske + Budrich Verlag.

Sparschuh, Vera and Ute Koch, eds. 1997. *Sozialismus und Soziologie. Die Grüdergeneration der DDR-Soziologie. Versuch einer Konturierung*. Opladen: Leske + Budrich Verlag.

Spencer, Herbert. 1969. *The Study of Sociology*. Ann Arbor: University of Michigan Press.

Stanley, Liz. 1993. On Auto/Biography in Sociology. *Sociology* 27(1): 41–52.

Stanley, Liz and David Morgan, eds. 1993. Special Issue: Biography and Autobiography in Sociology. *Sociology* 27(1).

Strauss, Anselm L. 1959. *Mirrors and Masks. The Search for Identity*. Glencoe, Ill.: Free Press.

Strauss, Anselm L. and Barney Glaser. 1970. *Anguish: The Case Study of a Dying Trajectory*. Mill Valley, Calif.: Sociology Press.

Strong, John W , ed. 1999. *McCormick on Evidence*, 5th edition. St Paul, Minn.: West Group.

Suchy, Juraj. 2003. *Generacny problem ako spolocny problem generacii*. Bratislava: Slovak Sociological Association Youth Section.

Szczepański, Jan. 1981. The Use of Autobiographies in Historical Social Psychology, pp. 225–234 in *Biography and Society: The Life History Approach in the Social Sciences*, ed. Daniel Bertaux. Beverly Hills: Sage.

Taylor, Steven and Robert Bogdan. 1984. *Introduction to Qualitative Research Methods: The Search for Meanings*. New York: John Wiley & Sons.

Thomas, W.I. and Florian Znaniecki. 1918–1920. *The Polish Peasant in Europe and America*. Boston: Richard Badger.

Turza, Karel. 1979. Kritika gradjanskog oblika porodice, pp. 372–375 in *Marksizam i savremeno drustvo*, ed. Jovica Trkulja. Beograd: Savremena administracija.

—— 1986. Trivijalizacija krize. *Treci Program Radio Beograda No. 70*. Beograd: Radio Beograda.

—— 1998. *Luis Mamford, Jedna kritika modernosti*. Beograd: Zavod za udzbenike i nastavna sredstva.

—— 2003. Da li su modernost i drustvo sinonimi? *Treci Program Radio Beograda No. 117–118*. Beograd: Radio Beograda.

—— 2003. On Modernity in General and On the Main Obstacles to Modernity in Serbia in the 20th Century—and Afterwards. *Sociologija* 45(2): 117–140.

van Dijk, Teun. 1987. *Communicating Racism: Ethnic Prejudice in Thought and Talk*. Newbury Park: Sage.

—— 1989. *Jazyk, poznanie, kommunikatsia*. Moscow: Progress.

—— 1996. *Cemu jos sociologija?* Beograd: Gutenbergora galksija.

—— 1996. *Modernost na biciklu*. Beograd: Akademia nova.

Vihalemm, Triin. 1992. Keelesituatsioonist Eesti meditsiiniasutustes, *Eesti Arst* 5: 343–348 and 6: 419–423.

—— 1998. Eesti keele oskus ja selle kasutamine vene noorte toimetuleku tegurina ning nende enesemääratluse kujundajana, pp. 225–248 in *Mitmekultuuriline Eesti: vljakutse haridusele*, eds Marju Lauristin, Silvi Vare, Tiia Pedastsaar, and Marje Pavelson. Tartu: University of Tartu and Vali Press Ltd.

—— 1998. Eesti kool kni vene laste viomalik sotsialiseerumiskeskkond, pp. 337–399 in *Mitmekultuuriline Eesti: vljakutse haridusele* , eds Marju Lauristin, Silvi Vare, Tiia Pedastsaar, and Marje Pavelson. Tartu: University of Tartu and Vali Press Ltd.

—— 1999. Estonian Language Competence, Performance and Beliefs About its Acquisition Among the Russian-speaking Habitants of Estonia 1989–1997. *International Journal of Sociology of Language* 139 (special issue): 69–85.

—— 1999. Group Identity Formation Processes Among Russian-Speaking Settlers of Estonia: A Linguistic Perspective. *Journal of Baltic Studies* 30(1): 18–39.

—— 1999. Local and Global Orientations of Media Consumption in Estonia 1993–1998, pp. 45–53 in *Estonian Human Development Report*. Tallinn: UNDP.

—— 2000. Mass Media, pp. 56–62 in *Integrating Estonia 1997–2000*. Tallinn: Government of Estonia.

—— 2000. The Informative and Identity-building Significance of Media: The Case of Estonian Russophones, pp. 44–48 in *Integration of Estonian Society. Monitoring 2000*, eds Marju Lauristin and Raivo Vetik. Tallinn: Institute of International and Social Studies.

—— 2000. Youth Election Activity and Bases for Political Preferences, pp. 225–237 in *Review of National Youth Policy*. Estonian National Report. Tallinn: Ministry of Education, Council of Europe.

Vihalemm, Triin and Anu Masso 2003. Identity Dynamics of Russian-Speakers of Estonia in the Transition Period. *Journal of Baltic Studies* 34(1): 92–116.

—— 2003. Dinamika identitshnosti russkih v Estonii v period postsovetskih transformatsii. *Diaspory/Diasporas* 5(2): 230–257.

—— 2003. Transformation of Identities in Changing Socio-political Space: The Case of Estonian Russians. *Journal of Borderlands Studies* 17(2): 35–52.

Vilhar, Albin. 1991. *Latinski citati*. Beograd: Matica srpska.

Vooglaid, Ulo. 1995. Noukogude Eesti sotsioloogia algus ja lopp: intervjuu Sirje Kiinile. *Looming* 1: 115–122.

Waltz, Jon R. 1983. *Introduction to Criminal Evidence*. Chicago: Nelson-Hall.

Waltz, Jon R. and Park, Roger C. 2004. *Evidence: Cases and Materials*. New York: Foundation Press.

Weber, Marianne. 1988. *Max Weber: A Biography*, trans. and ed. Harry Zohn. New Brunswick: Transaction Books.

Weber, Max. 1990. *Izbrannye proizviedienia*, ed. Yu Davydov. Moscow: Progress.

White, William Foote. 1994. *Participant Observer: An Autobiography*. Ithaca, N.Y.: ILR Press.

Willie, Charles Vert. 1988. Commentary on *Sociological Lives*, pp. 163–176 in *Sociological Lives*, ed. Matilda White Riley. Newbury Park: Sage.

Yadov, Vladimir. 1987. *Sotsiologicheskie issledovania: metodologia, programma, metody*. Moscow: Nauka.

Young, Michael W. 2004. *Malinowski: Odyssey of an Anthropologist*. New Haven and London: Yale University Press.

Zagorski, Krzysztof. 2000. Wstep: Opinia publiczna w okresie przemian ustrojowych, pp. 7–24 in *Nowa rzeczywistosc. Oceny i opinie 1988–1998*, ed. Michal Strzeszewski. Warszawa: Centrum Badania Opinii Spolecznej.

Zussman, Robert. 1996. Autobiographical Occasions. *Contemporary Sociology* 25(2), March: 143–148.

Index

Academic Association of Fighting Youth (AZWM), Poland 50
Academic Association of Polish Youth (ZAMP) 52
academic standards 144
Academy of Foreign Trade, Hungary 126–7
Academy of Sciences of the GDR 164–6, 167, 169
Academy of Sciences of the Soviet Union 93–5; Institute of Social Research 95–7, 98, 99, 100–3
Academy of Sciences, Hungary 138
age cohorts 11
Agence Universitaire de la Francophonie 153–4
Alexander, Jeffrey C. 6, 8, 13
All-Polish School of Marxism-Leninism 52
All-Union Center for the Study of Public Opinion, Russia 99–100, 101
Alliance College, Pennsylvania 48
American Bourgeois Empirical Society 88
Andorka, Rudolf 131, 132, 133–4, 135, 139, 141
Andreeva, Galina 88, 90, 91
Anthropus 40
Apolistic Letter on Dignity of Woman: Mulieris Dignitatem 33, 34
Arum, Richard 143
autobiography, as sociological witness 8–16

Bailyn, Bernard 5
Bauman, Zygmunt 115, 175
Beck-Gernsheim, Elisabeth 175
Beck, Ulrich 174–5
Berger, Bennett M. 7, 13, 16
Berlin Free University 170, 171
Berlin Wall, fall of 1–2
Berliner Journal füSoziologie 169
Berliner Verlag 161
Bertaux, Daniel 11
biography: intersection with sociology 5–8; *see also* autobiography
Bjorklund, Diane 10
Blossfeld, Hans-Peter 139, 143
Bohnsak, Ralf 170
Bokros-package, Hungary 140
Bornal, Joanna 9
Bourgeois Sociology in the Search for Theory 88
Breen, Richard 143
British Sociological Association 7
Bukharin, Nikolai 165

Castle 162
Catholic Church 33–4, 43, 44
Cecetka, Professor Juraj 73–4, 75
Center for European and Regional Youth Studies 82
Center for Express and Applied Research, Academy of Sciences of the Soviet Union 102–3
Center for the Study of Public Opinion, Soviet Academy of Sciences 99
Central European University (CEU) 109–11, 200
Central Statistical Office, Hungary 131, 132, 135, 144
Centrum Badania Opinii Spolecznej (CBOS), Warsaw 119
Cepelia 48, 54
Chamberlayne, Prue 9
Champy, Florent 156
Charmaz, Kathy 12
Chicago School of Sociology 5
Christie, Nils 123, 124

Chura, Alojz 73–4
Cicero 174
civil society research 80
Class and Class Conflct in Industrial Society 29
Collegium Budapest 171
Columbia University 48, 54
Communism 212–13, 217, 220–1
Communist Manifesto 180–1
Communist Manifesto for Beginners 183
Communist Party of the Soviet Union (CPSU) 86, 92, 93–4, 95, 97–9, 100, 106
Communist Party of Ukraine 93
Communist Party, Czechoslovakia 77, 79, 82
Communist Party, Estonia 199
Communist Party, Hungary 127–8, 129
Communist Party, Yugoslavia 179–87
Comte, Auguste 163, 198
conference life 112–15
conflict theory 29, 30
Coser, Lewis 30

Dahrendorf, Ralf 29, 30, 186
de Gaulle, General Charles 51
de Graaf, Paul 136
de Waele, Jean Michel 156
Decade for Women 36
democratic sociology 137–44
Denzin, Norman 10–11, 14
deStalinization 2–3
Deutsche Gesellschaft für Soziologie 169
Dnepropetrovsk University, Ukraine 105
Dobrowolski, Kazimierz 49, 50, 51–3, 54, 55–6, 57, 59, 60, 213, 215
Dohnke, Dieter 164
Domanski, Henryk 110
Dronkers, Jaap 143
Druzboslovne razprave 40, 43–4
dualism 25
Durkheim, Émile 106, 178, 198

early-career cohort 220–2
East German scientists, discrimination 168–9
Elder, Glen 11
emigration, Ukraine 123
empiricism 199–202
Encyclopedia of Sociology 65, 66
Engels, Friedrich 26, 180–1
Eotvos Lorand (ELTE) University, Hungary 129, 132, 139–41, 142
epiphanies *see* turning points

Estonian Marketing and Opinion Research Company (EMOR) Ltd 200–1, 202–3
Estonian Science Foundation 204, 207
Europe at the Margins 113
European Commission, Research Directorate 21
European Conferences of Feminist Research 40
European Consortium of Sociological Research 141
European Sociological Association (ESA) 40, 48, 207
European Union: Helsinki Group Women in Science 39; research programs 208
European University Institute 139, 143

Fenstermaker, Sarah 9
Ferge, Zsuzsa 132
Finnish Marketing Institute 203
Firsov, Boris 98
First Congress of Deputies of the USSR 101
Fleming, Donald 5
freedom to travel 24
French Cultural Institute, Sofia 153, 154
Friedrich Ebert Stiftung 134
Friedrichs, Jürgen 167
Fulbright fellowships 136
functionalism 25, 29–31

Ganzeboom, Harry 136
gender inequality 32–40
genetic-integral method 56
German Research Society 170
German Sociological Association 169
Giddens, Anthony 175, 187–8, 199
Glaessner, Gerd-Joachim 168, 169
Glaser, Barney 13
glasnost 2, 99–104
Goetting, Ann 9, 13
Goldthorpe, John 113, 135, 143
Golovakha, Evgeniy 120
Golubovic, Zagorka 180, 185
Gorbachev, Mikhail 2, 99, 106, 107, 163, 197
Gouldner, Alvin 21, 44
Graduate School for Social Research (GSSR), Warsaw 111–12, 113–14, 115–18
Grinnell College, Iowa 166
Grushin, Boris 88, 91, 95, 99, 100
Gusdorf, Georges 8, 13

Haller, Max 136

Hanse-Wissenschafts-Kolleg, Germany 143
Hauser, Bob 136
Hegel, Georg Wilhelm Friedrich 163, 174, 177
Heidmets, Mati 197, 206
Higher Certifying Commission, Ukraine 122
Hirszowicz, Maria 116
historicism 55, 174–5
Hitler, Adolf 21, 44
Homans, George Caspar 6, 8
Homo Sociologicus 186
Horizont 161
Horowitz, Irving Louis 5, 16
Hotel Russia 94–5
Humboldt University, Berlin 164, 168–70
Hungarian Academy of Sciences 128, 131–2, 135
Hydroprojekt 62

identity transformation 12
Informational Bulletin for Youth Research 76
Institut für Hohere Studien, Vienna 48
Institute for Social Sciences of the Workers' Socialist Party, Hungary 129–36, 137–9
Institute of Mass Communication, Hungarian Radio 127–8
Institute of Public Opinion, Soviet Union 88, 89, 95
Institute of Sociology, Soviet Academy of Sciences 100–3
INTAS 103
intellectual: freedom 3–4; influences 215, 218–19, 221
interdisciplinary co-operation 75
International Association for Mass Communication Research 38
International Classification of Occupations (ISCO) 108–9
International Institute of Sociology Conference, Krakow 114–15
International Journal of Sociology 118
International Research and Exchange Board (IREX) 48
International Social Survey Program (ISSP) 38, 136, 141
International Society for the Study of European Ideas 41
International Sociological Association (ISA) 76, 78–9, 92, 121, 190; Research Committee on Social Stratification 114, 133–5
International Women's Day 32, 35
international: contacts 24; life 112–15, 133–7; support 3; travel 195–7
Ivanov, Vilen 101
Izvestia 101

Jagiellonian University 48, 49–54, 56–9, 60, 62–3, 66
Janicka, Krystyna 112
Jaruzelski, General Wojciech 64
Jean Monet fellowships 143
Jedomskihh, Jelena 200
Jogan, Maca 21–45, 211, 212, 213, 214, 215, 216, 217

Kafka, Franz 162
Kant, Immanuel 163
Kapto, Alexandr 93
Karl Marx University, Hungary 132
Keen, Mike 120
Kharkov State University, Ukraine 105
Kiev International Institute of Sociology (KIIS) 108–9, 115, 117
Kiev State University (KSU) 105–8
Kohli, Martin 11
Kohn, Melvin 112, 115, 118
Kolosi, Tamas 129, 130, 131–2, 133–4, 135–6, 137, 138–9, 141, 143, 145
Komsomol, Soviet Union 86–8, 89, 91, 94, 95, 97, 98
Komsomolskaya Pravda 88–9, 95
Komsomolskoe Plemya 88
Kon, Igor S. 164, 198
Konopasek, Zdenek 10
Koordinierungs und Aufbauinitiative für die Forschung in den Neuen Bundesländern 167
Koralewicz, Jadwiga 111
Korolyov, Sergei 198
Korzeniewska, Katarzyna 116
Korzhov, Gennadi 117
Kossuth Kiado 130
Kruschchev, Nikita 95
Krygier, Martin 123
Kulturny zivot 72
Kuznika 50
Kwasniewicz, Wladyslaw 47–66, 212–13, 214, 215–16, 217

language 23, 41, 107, 110, 156
Laslett, Barbara 9–10
late-career cohort 212–17
Latour, Bruno 150
Lauristin, Marju 194, 195, 197, 204, 207

League of Communists of Serbia 184–5
League of Communists of Slovenia 37
League of Communists of Yugoslavia 24
Lenin for Beginners 183
Leningrad 162
Leningrad State University 98
Leninism 106–7, 213–14, 217–18
Leninist Young Communist League of the Soviet Union (LYCLSU) *see* Komsomol
Lepetit, Bernard 152
Levada, Yury 91, 99
Levinson, Alexandr 101
Levykin, Ivan 99
life lines 11
literary criticism 8

Mach, Bogdan 110
Machacek, Ladislav 70–83, 212, 213, 214–15, 216–17
McKee, James 6–7
Magocsi, Paul Robert 113
Malewska-Peyre, Hanna 111
Mandelbaum, Seymour 189
Mannheim, Karl 170
Mansurov, Valery 86–104, 212, 213, 214, 215, 216, 217
marginality 112
marginalized groups 9
Maribor, Slovenia 21
market research 4, 117
Marody, Mira 111
Marx for Beginners 183
Marxism 3, 52, 151, 165–6, 180–1, 213–14, 217–18
mass surveys 97–9, 100–1
Masso, Anu 207
Merton, Robert K. 7, 13, 14, 16
methodological pluralism 7
mid-career cohort 217–20
Miller, Robert 114
Mills, C. Wright 2, 211
Milosevic, Slobodan 42, 176, 177–9, 189, 190
Ministry of Education, Estonia 204
Ministry of Education, Finland 205
Ministry of Education, Hungary 140, 142
Ministry of Education, Science and Sport, Slovenia 39
Ministry of Higher Education, Soviet Union 100
Ministry of Science, Russia 103
Minorities' Round Table of the President of the Republic, Estonia 207
misogyny 39–40
Modernity on a Bicycle 188–9
Moscow State University 90–3, 94
motivational background 193–4
Mucha, Janusz 120
Müller, Walter 143
mythomania 177

National Library, Bulgaria 152
National Slovak Sociological Society 74
Nazis 21–2, 44, 48, 70
Netherlands Institute for Advanced Studies (NIAS) 142
New Economic Mechanism, Hungary 127
Niinas, Karin 201
Nowa Huta 52

"objective biography" 8
Offe, Claus 169
Olney, James 8–9
Open Estonia Foundation 204, 205
Osborn, Elizabeth 120–1
Ostdeutsche Gesellschaft für Soziologie 169
Ovchinikov, Alexandr 100
Oxford University 113

Papic, Zarana 184
Parsons, Talcott 25, 30, 31
Pecujlic, Miroslav 183
pedagogical sociology 73–4, 81–3
perestroika 2, 99–104
Ph.D. School for Social Sciences for Students from Central and Eastern Europe, Romania 155–7
"phosphate rock" war 194
Pilsudski, Jozef 51
Pohorila, Natalia 105–24, 220, 221, 222
Polish Academy of Sciences (PAN) 48, 65, 76, 109–11, 116, 121
Polish Peasant in Europe and America, The 5
Polish Socialist Party (PPS) 57–9
Polish Sociological Association 48, 59, 61, 65
Polish United Workers' Party (PZPR) 52, 57, 58–61, 62, 63–6
Polish Workers' Party (PPR) 50, 57, 58–9
Polish Youth Association (ZMP) 53
political: atmosphere, Estonia 194–7; controversies, Poland 51–2; parties, Poland 56–9
Polytechnic Institute, Kirov 91–2
post-Communist chaos 187–90
postal surveys 96
Praxis 179

professional activities 215–16, 219
prostitution 25–6, 38–9
public opinion polls 95–104

Rabochaya kniga sotsiologa 105–6
Radio Beograda 185, 186
Radionica SIC 183, 184
Raduga 198
Ragin, Charles 113
Rahvarinne (Popular Front), Estonia 194
rationing, Ukraine 109
resources 4, 130, 198
Riemann, Gerhard 13
Riga State University 98
Riley, Matilda White 7, 13, 16
Robert, Peter 126–46, 217, 218, 219
Robins, Kevin 113
Rokeach, Milton 204
Rose, Nikolas 174
Rosko, Robert 78, 79, 80
rumors, research on 94–5
Russian Academy of Sciences *see* Soviet Academy of Sciences
Russian Society of Sociologists *see* Soviet Sociological Association
Rustin, Michael 13

sabbaticals 142
Saganenko, Galina 98
Sakharov, Andrey 99, 102
Sarapata, Adam 6
Savisaar, Edgar 194
Schelsky, Helmut 170
Schulz, Robert 6
Schütze, Fritz 13
Science Informatics Center (TARKI), Hungary 135–6, 137, 138–9, 140, 141–2, 143, 144–5, 146
scientific Communism 3
Serbia, creation of 42
Shatrov, Michail 107
Shevchenko National University *see* Kiev State University
Simkus, Albert 136, 137
Simon, Dagmar 167
Slavova, Petya 148–59, 220, 221, 222
Slomczynski, Kazimierz M. 110, 112, 118, 120–1
Slovak Academy of Sciences (SAS) 72–81
Slovak Sociological Society 78–9
Slovenia, as independent state 41–4
Slovenian Public Opinion (SPO) 37–8
Slovenian Sociological Association (SSA) 40, 44
Slovensko bez dorastu 73
Smena 77
"social production of obscurity" 9
Social Science Information Centre (IZ) GDR 167, 171
Social Science Research Council, US 5
social: atmosphere 194–7; inequality 25, 30–31, 32; stratification 114, 133–5
socialism: nostalgia for 115, 145; studies under 129–32
Socialist Alliance of the Working People, Yugoslavia 24
Sociologia: Slovak Sociological Review 74, 76, 78, 81
sociological: beginners 88–93; witness 8–16
Sociologicky zbornik 74
Sociologija 40, 190
"sociologization" 3
Sociology 7
sociology: decision to study 49, 214–15, 218, 221; formal and information studies 129–32; institutionalization of 73–81; intersection with biography 5–8; period of *glasnost* and *perestroika* 99–104; Poland 52–4; of public opinion 95–7; recent history 2–5; as a social science 55–6; without society 32–3
Solidarity 63–5
Sorokin, Pitirim 50, 51, 106, 186, 213
Soros Foundation 200
Soviet Academy of Sciences 77, 100, 163
Soviet bloc, dismantling of 2–3
Soviet Sociological Association 88, 89, 95, 103
Soyuz–Apollo program 127
Sparschuh, Vera 6, 161–72, 211, 217–18, 219–20
special interest groups 145
Spencer, Herbert 30
Stalinism 52–4, 106–7, 163
Stasi system 162
State Archive, Sofia 152
State Teacher's Training Institute, Kirov 86, 88
Steiner, Helmut 165
Stratification and Inequality 133–4
Stratification Model Research Group 129–32
Strauss, Anselm 11–12, 13
Student 182
Studia Socjologiczne 61, 76
Suicide 106
Swedish Royal Academy of Science 204

Swiatniki Gorne, Cracow 54
systemic transformation 119
Szczepanski, Jan 76
Szechenyi fellowships 142
Szelenyi, Ivan 116, 136
Szociolológiai Szemle 135

Tallinn 198
Tallinn Song Festival Field 194–5
Tarkowska, Elzbieta 115, 116
Teorija in praksa 40
textbooks, lack of 50
Thorne, Barrie 9–10
Thünen Institute for Regional Development 172
Timar, Janos 132
Touraine, Alain 164
trajectory, concept of 13
Transregional Center for Democratic Studies 205
truth 14
turning points 10–12, 216–17, 219–20, 221–2
Turza, Karel 174–90, 217, 218, 219, 220

Ukranian Academy of Sciences 106, 115
Ukranian Institute for Social Research (UISR) 122–3
Union for Armed Struggle (ZWZ), Poland 47, 61
United Nations Educational, Scientific and Cultural Organization (UNESCO) 38, 39, 94
Université Libre de Bruxelles (ULB) 156–8
University of Belgrade 179–87, 189
University of Berkeley 102
University of Commenius, Bratislava 71–2, 74, 77, 78, 79, 81–2
University of Halle 161–2
University of Hamburg 48
University of Helsinki 200
University of Kassel 170, 171
University of Leipzig 161
University of Ljubljana 22–9, 31–2
University of Lodz 48
University of Lund 200, 204
University of Marxism-Leninism 92–3, 94
University of Minsk 25
University of Pennsylvania 189
University of Sofia 148–53, 158–9
University of St. Cyrillus and Methodius, Trnava 81–3
University of Tartu 6, 98, 193–4, 197–9, 203, 204, 205, 206–7
University of Wisconsin 136–7
University of Zielona Gora 115
urban sociology 152, 153
US developments in sociology 5, 6–7

Vaino Tanner Foundation 203, 204
Valosag 129, 135
van Dijk, Teun 199, 200
Vechernaya Moskva 101
Veskimagi, Margo 201
Vidici 183, 187
Vihalemm, Peeter 198
Vihalemm, Triin 193–209, 220, 221, 222
Viktiuk, Roman 108
Vinogradov, Alexander 108
'vocabularies of self' 10
Volan Transport Company, Hungary 128–9
Vooglaid, Ulo 6
Voprosi Filosophii 92
Vozimitel, Andrey 99

Wallace, Claire 117, 121
Waltz, Jon 14
Warsaw Pact 76–7
Warsaw Uprising 51
Weber, Max 106, 151
Wengraf, Tom 9
Whelan, Chris 113
Who Needs Sociology? 188
Wissenschaftler-Integrations-Programm (WIP) 167, 168, 169
Wissenschaftlicher Rat für Soziologische Forschung 169
Wnuk-Lipinski, Edmund 111
women: emancipation of 25–6; role in society 32, 33–40
Workers' University Society (TUR), Poland 57
World Association of Marketing Professionals (ESOMAR) 201
World Association of Public Opinion Researchers (WAPOR) 115, 121
World Barometer 99
World Conferences for Central and Eastern European Studies 43
World Congresses of Sociology 40, 92, 136
Wright Mills, C. 2, 211

Yadov, Vladimir 98, 100–1, 106, 163, 164, 198, 206
Yalta Agreement 51, 61

youth, research on 73–6, 80, 82
Yugoslav Association of Sociologists 29, 40, 42
Yugoslav Sociological Association (YSA) 189–90
Yugoslavia, decomposition of 41–3

Zaborowski, Wojtek 112
Zagorski, Krzysztof 111–12, 121, 123
Zaslavskaya, Tatyana 99
Zdanov University, St Petersburg 162–3
Zdravomyslov, Andrey 98
Zena 40
Znaniecki, Florian 5, 55
Zussman, Robert 8
Zygulski, Kazimierz 6